Lecture Notes in Artificial Intelligence   6619
Edited by R. Goebel, J. Siekmann, and W. Wahlster

Subseries of Lecture Notes in Computer Science

W0246098

Andrea Omicini   Sebastian Sardina
Wamberto Vasconcelos (Eds.)

Declarative Agent Languages and Technologies VIII

8th International Workshop, DALT 2010
Toronto, Canada, May 10, 2010
Revised, Selected and Invited Papers

 Springer

Series Editors

Randy Goebel, University of Alberta, Edmonton, Canada
Jörg Siekmann, University of Saarland, Saarbrücken, Germany
Wolfgang Wahlster, DFKI and University of Saarland, Saarbrücken, Germany

Volume Editors

Andrea Omicini
Università di Bologna
DEIS
via Venezia 52, 47521, Cesena, Italy
E-mail: andrea.omicini@unibo.it

Sebastian Sardina
RMIT University
School of Computer Science and Information Technology
Melbourne, VIC, 3001, Australia
E-mail: sebastian.sardina@rmit.edu.au

Wamberto Vasconcelos
University of Aberdeen
Department of Computing Science
Aberdeen, AB24 3UE, UK
E-mail: w.w.vasconcelos@abdn.ac.uk

ISSN 0302-9743   e-ISSN 1611-3349
ISBN 978-3-642-20714-3   ISBN 978-3-642-20715-0 (eBook)
DOI 10.1007/978-3-642-20715-0
Springer Heidelberg Dordrecht London New York

Library of Congress Control Number: 2011925656

CR Subject Classification (1998): I.2.11, C.2.4, D.2.4, D.2, D.3, F.3.1

LNCS Sublibrary: SL 7 – Artificial Intelligence

Typesetting: Camera-ready by author, data conversion by Scientific Publishing Services, Chennai, India

Printed on acid-free paper

Springer is part of Springer Science+Business Media (www.springer.com)

Preface

We are delighted to present you with the revised, selected and invited papers of the eighth edition of the International Workshop on Declarative Agent Languages and Technologies (DALT 2010), a well-established forum to foster discussion and sharing of experiences among researchers interested in declarative approaches and technologies for software agents and multi-agent systems.

DALT 2010 was held as a satellite workshop of the 9th International Joint Conference on Autonomous Agents and Multiagent Systems (AAMAS 2010), in Toronto, Canada, and it took place on May 10. Previous editions were held in 2003 in Melbourne, Australia; in 2004 in New York, USA; in 2005 in Utrecht, The Netherlands; in 2006 in Hakodate, Japan; in 2007 in Honolulu, USA; in 2008 in Estoril, Portugal; and in 2009 in Budapest, Hungary. All these past editions had their proceedings published in the *Lecture Notes in Artificial Intelligence* series as volumes 2990, 3476, 3904, 4327, 4897, 5397, and 5948, respectively.

Declarative approaches provide simpler and more natural means to connect theory with practical computing aspects. Algebras, logics and functions, to name a few, have been used as declarative formalisms, with which (together with their associated mechanisms) one can specify, verify, program and analyze computational systems. The well-understood mathematical underpinnings of declarative approaches provide clean, solid and natural means to bridge the gap between theory and practice, providing formalisms, tools and techniques to support the development of applications.

Declarative approaches offer useful abstractions to study computational phenomena, which are necessarily more compact than procedural accounts. Software agents and multi-agent systems have been pursued as means to realizing a new generation of very large-scale, distributed information systems. Declarative approaches to agent languages and technologies raise many fresh challenges with exciting prospects for agent programming, communication languages, reasoning and decision-making. The many challenges include, for instance, which formal foundations to use, how pragmatic concerns are addressed formally, how expressive approaches are, and so on.

DALT aims to make formal methods and declarative technologies and approaches available to and understood by a broader segment of the multi-agent research community. Another objective is to foster the application of theoretical results to the implementation of working systems. These issues are being addressed by DALT by providing a discussion forum to both (a) support the transfer of declarative paradigms and techniques to the broader community of agent researchers and practitioners; and (b) bring the issue of designing and verifying complex agent systems to the attention of researchers working on declarative languages and technologies. DALT has been of particular interest to multi-agent system researchers who are working in computational logic and formal methods in general. It has also been of great interest to researchers and practitioners applying these methods to particular applications such as service-oriented and grid computing. It has been of general interest to researchers interested in linking agent theory to concrete applications.

This volume contains 11 contributed articles selected by the Program Committee. The 2010 edition of the DALT workshop received 24 submissions, and these were reviewed by at least 3 reviewers, with 10 papers being accepted for presentation at the workshop. After the event, the authors of all accepted papers were invited to submit revised and extended versions of their papers, incorporating feedback and discussions from their presentations, and another round of reviews took place, leading to eight papers being accepted for inclusion in the present proceedings.

Fig. 1. Word Cloud for DALT 2010 Papers

We also invited authors of short papers presented at AAMAS 2010, and which addressed topics relevant to DALT, to submit extended versions of their papers. Figure 1 shows a "word cloud" with the 100 most frequently occurring terms found in the articles of this volume[1].

We would like to thank all authors for their contributions, the members of the Steering Committee for their valuable suggestions and support, and the members of the Program Committee for their excellent work during the reviewing phases. We would also like to thank Dave S. Robertson (School of Informatics, The University of Edinburgh, Edinburgh, UK), for his thought-provoking invited talk "Coordination as Practical Logic Programming."

December 2010

Andrea Omicini
Sebastian Sardina
Wamberto Vasconcelos

---

[1] The diagram was prepared using IBM's Word Cloud generator (http://www.alphaworks.ibm.com/tech/wordcloud) and the sizes of words reflect their frequency in the articles.

Organization

Organizing Committee

Andrea Omicini   Alma Mater Studiorum – Università di Bologna, Italy

Sebastian Sardina   RMIT University, Australia

Wamberto Vasconcelos   University of Aberdeen, UK

Steering Committee

Matteo Baldoni   Università di Torino, Italy

Andrea Omicini   Alma Mater Studiorum – Università di Bologna, Italy

M. Birna van Riemsdijk   Delft University of Technology, The Netherlands

Tran Cao Son   New Mexico State University, USA

Paolo Torroni   Alma Mater Studiorum – Università di Bologna, Italy

Pinar Yolum   Bogazici University, Turkey

Michael Winikoff   University of Otago, New Zealand

Program Committee

Thomas Ågotnes   University of Bergen, Norway

Marco Alberti   Universidade Nova de Lisboa, Portugal

Natasha Alechina   University of Nottingham, UK

Cristina Baroglio   Università di Torino, Italy

Rafael Bordini   Federal University of Rio Grande do Sul, Brazil

Jan Broersen   University of Utrecht, The Netherlands

Federico Chesani   Alma Mater Studiorum – Università di Bologna, Italy

Amit Chopra   Università di Trento, Italy

James Harland   RMIT University, Australia

Koen Hindriks   Delft University of Technology, The Netherlands

Shinichi Honiden   National Institute of Informatics, Japan

João Leite   New University of Lisbon, Portugal

Yves Lespérance   York University, Canada

Nicolas Maudet   LAMSADE, Univ. Paris-Dauphine, France

John-Jules Meyer   University of Utrecht, The Netherlands

Peter Novák   Czech Technical University, Czech Republic

Fabio Patrizi   Università "La Sapienza" di Roma, Italy

Enrico Pontelli   New Mexico State University, USA

Table of Contents

Operational Behaviour for Executing, Suspending, and Aborting Goals in BDI Agent Systems

John Thangarajah[1], James Harland[1], David Morley[2], and Neil Yorke-Smith[2,3]

[1] RMIT University, Melbourne, Australia
{johnt,james.harland}@rmit.edu.au
[2] SRI International, Menlo Park, USA
morley@AI.SRI.COM
[3] American University of Beirut, Lebanon
nysmith@aub.edu.lb

Abstract. Deliberation over and management of goals is a key aspect of an agent's architecture. We consider the various types of goals studied in the literature, including performance, achievement, and maintenance goals. Focusing on BDI agents, we develop a detailed description of goal states (such as whether goals have been suspended or not) and a comprehensive suite of operations that may be applied to goals (including dropping, aborting, suspending and resuming them). We show how to specify an operational semantics corresponding to this detailed description in an abstract agent language (CAN). The three key contributions of our generic framework for goal states and transitions are (1) to encompass both goals of accomplishment and rich goals of monitoring, (2) to provide the first specification of abort and suspend for all the common goal types, and (3) to account for plan execution as well as the dynamics of sub-goaling.

1 Introduction

Deliberation over what courses of action to pursue is fundamental to agent systems. Agents designed to work in dynamic environments, such as a rescue robot or an online travel agent, must be able to reason about what actions they should take, incorporating deliberation into their execution cycle so that decisions can be reviewed and corrective action taken with an appropriate focus and frequency.

In systems based on the well-known *Belief-Desire-Intention* (BDI) framework [17], most often a set of *goals* is ascribed to the agent, which is equipped with various techniques to deliberate over and manage this set. The centrality of reasoning over goals is seen in the techniques investigated in the literature, which include subgoaling and plan selection, detection and resolution of conflicts [29,23] or opportunities for cooperation [30], checking goal properties to specification [13,15], failure recovery and planning [22,21,24], and dropping, suspending and resuming [28], or aborting goals [27]. A variety of goals are described in the literature, including goals of *performance* of a task, *achievement* of a state, *querying* truth of a statement, *testing* veracity of beliefs, and *maintenance* of a condition [3,20].

An agent must manage a variety of goals, while incorporating pertinent sources of information into its decisions over them, such as (user) preferences, quality goals, motivational goals, and advice [13]. The complexity of agent goal management—which

A. Omicini, S. Sardina, and W. Vasconcelos (Eds.): DALT 2010, LNAI 6619, pp. 1–21, 2011.

stems from this combination of the variety of goals and the breadth of deliberation considerations—is furthered because each goal can be dropped, aborted, suspended, or resumed at arbitrary times. Note that while goals themselves are static (i.e., they are specified at design time, and do not change during execution), their behaviour is dynamic: a goal may undergo a variety of changes of state during its execution cycle [15]. This evolution may include its initial adoption by the agent, being actively pursued, being suspended and then later resumed, and eventually succeeding (or failing). (Maintenance goals have a subtle life-cycle: the goal is retained even when the desired property is true; it is possible that such goals are never dropped).

This paper analyzes the behaviour of the above types of goals, including the behaviour when goals are aborted or suspended. We consider the complete life-cycle of goals, from their initial adoption by the agent to the time when they are no longer of interest, and all stages in between, including being suspended and resumed.

Scenario. As a running example, consider a team of three robots—Alpha, Bravo and Charlie—that are searching for the survivors of an air crash. Each has a battery life of four hours, and has to return to its base to recharge within this time. The three robots search individually for survivors, but when one is found, each may call on the others for assistance to bring the survivor to the base.

Initially Alpha is told to search a particular area. After 30 minutes, Alpha finds a survivor with a broken leg. Alpha calls for help from Bravo, as it will require at least two robots to carry the survivor. Once Bravo arrives, both robots carry the survivor back to the base, and then both resume searching. A little later, Alpha receives a call for help from Bravo, who has found another survivor. It takes longer than expected for Alpha to get to the location. Before Alpha arrives, another message from Bravo is received, stating that the survivor has been transported back to the base and so Alpha's assistance is no longer required. Alpha resumes its search. Later it receives a call for help from Charlie, who has found a survivor. Once Charlie's survivor is safely back at the base, Alpha considers resuming its search, but as it has only 30 minutes of battery life left, and it predicts that it will take at least 15 minutes of travel time to get to where it needs to be, Alpha decides to recharge. Once this is done, Alpha resumes its search. Eventually it completes searching its given area, finding no more survivors, and returns to the base.

This example illustrates some of the complexity and richness of goal deliberation and management and the need for a comprehensive and principled approach. Alpha initially adopts the performance goal of searching its assigned area; this goal is suspended when a survivor is found, and later resumed. (We assume that each robot is given a similar area to search, and that Alpha's task is complete once it has searched this area.) In the interim times, Alpha adopts achievement goals (getting survivors to the base), which it may have to abort (when Alpha is too late to help Bravo). Alpha also has the important maintenance goal to monitor its power usage and recharge when appropriate.

Contribution. Our work extends previous efforts in two main directions. Our first area of innovation is to develop a rich and detailed specification of the appropriate operational behaviour when a goal is pursued, succeeded or failed, aborted, suspended, or resumed. We (1) include sophisticated maintenance goals, along the lines of Duff et al. [8], that encompass proactive behaviour (i.e., anticipating failure of a given condition) as well as reactive behaviour (i.e., waiting until the condition becomes false), and allow for different responses in each case. This contrasts over most work on maintenance goals, in which only the reactive behaviour is developed [20,15]. We (2) develop an appropriate set of states for goals (which generalizes the two states of suspended and active of van Riemsdijk et al. [20]), and a set of operations to move goals between these states. These operations are richer than previous works, by including suspending and resuming for all the common goal types, and the corresponding state transitions can be non-trivial. We provide a detailed specification and a nearly-complete formal semantics.

Our second area of innovation is to address execution of plans to achieve goals within our semantics. The spirit of our work is shared by Morandini et al. [15], who build on van Riemsdijk et al. [20] by providing operational semantics for non-leaf goals, i.e., semantics for subgoaling and goal achievement conditions. We (3) encompass the same dynamic execution behaviour, but further consider plans as well as goals. Thus we consider the execution cycle, not only the design phase like Morandini et al.

This paper elaborates our first and more brief report of a semantics for goal lifecycles at the DALT'10 workshop [26]; we gave a short overview in [25]. Our earlier works— that considered maintenance goals [8], or that established operations for aborting [27] and suspending and resuming [28] goals—did not treat the lifecycle of goals.

The paper is organized as follows. In Sect. 2 we discuss various types of goals. In Sect. 3 we specify goal management behaviours, particularly to support abort and suspend. In Sect. 4 we present our semantics and a worked example. In Sect. 5 we discuss related work, and in Sect. 6 we conclude.

2 Goal Types and Their Abstract States

We follow the syntax of goals given by Winikoff et al. [32], using the above robot rescue scenario as a running example. Goals have a specification with both declarative and procedural aspects. We take a goal G to have a *context* (or *pre-condition*) that is a necessary condition before the goal may be adopted, a *success condition S* that denotes when the goal may be considered to have succeeded, and a *failure condition F* that denotes when it may be considered to have failed. Any of these conditions may be empty. We take a plan P to have declarative success and failure conditions, and procedural success and failure methods that are invoked upon its success and failure respectively. A plan may have other dedicated methods attached, such as an abort clean-up method [27], and suspend and resume methods [28]. By *task* we mean an abstract action rather than a specific goal or plan.

Braubach et al. [3] are among those who survey the types of goals found in agent systems. The consensus in the literature agrees that perform, achieve, query, test, and maintain cover the widespread uses of goals [32,3,6,20]. We note that querying and testing goals can be reduced to achievement and performance goals, respectively [20].

perform(τ, S, F): *accomplish a task τ.* These goals, sometimes called *goals-to-do*, demand that a set of plans be identified to perform a task; they do not require a particular state of the world be achieved. A perform goal succeeds if one or more of its plans complete execution; it fails otherwise, such as if no plan is applicable or all applicable plans fail to execute. Hence, the success condition S will express that "one of the plans in the given set succeeds" to accomplish τ [32,20]. The perform goal also has a failure condition, F. If F is true at any point during execution, the goal terminates with failure, and execution of all plans is terminated. The association between the task τ, which is not more than an identifier, and the plans, is akin to the association between event type and plans in the agent programming language JACK [4].

Example: Search a particular area for survivors.

achieve(S, F): *reach a state S*. These goals, sometimes called *goals-to-be*, generate plans to achieve a state, S, and should not be dropped until the state is achieved or is found to be unachievable, signified by the condition F. An achieve goal differs from a perform goal in that it checks its success condition during plan execution and after a plan completes. If the success condition S is true (at any point during execution), the goal terminates successfully; if the failure condition F is true (at any point during execution), the goal terminates with failure. Otherwise, the goal returns to plan generation, even if the previous plan completed successfully.

An important difference between perform and achieve goals is their behaviour on multiple instances of the same goal. An agent that is given three identical instances of a perform goal will execute the goal three times (unless there is an unexpected plan failure). An agent that is given three identical instances of an achievement goal may achieve this goal between one and three times, depending on environmental conditions.

Example: Ensure a survivor gets to the base. Note that this is an achieve goal rather than a perform goal as it can only succeed when the survivor is at the base.

The goals we have considered so far are *goals of accomplishment*: they all directly result in activity. Maintenance goals, by contrast, are *goals of monitoring*, in that they may give rise to other goals when particular triggering conditions are met, but they do not themselves directly cause activity.

maintain(C, π, R, P, S, F): *keep a condition C true*. Maintenance goals monitor a *maintenance condition*, C, initiating a *recovery goal* (either R or P; see below) to restore the condition to true when it becomes false. Note that a recovery goal is initiated, not a plan. More precisely, as introduced by Duff et al. [8], we allow a maintain goal to be *reactive*, waiting until the maintenance condition is found to be false, $B \models \neg C$ (where B denotes the beliefs of the agent), and then acting to restore it by adopting a reactive recovery goal R; or to be *proactive*, waiting until the condition is *predicted* to become false, $B \models \pi(\neg C)$ (where π is some prediction mechanism, say using lookahead reasoning, e.g., [30,10]) and then acting to prevent it by adopting a proactive preventative goal P. Although not specified in prior work, we insist that R and P be achieve goals. The maintenance goal continues until either the success condition S or failure condition F become true.

Example: Ensure that Alpha is always adequately charged.

2.1 Abstract Goal States and Transitions

We now move towards a formal characterization of goal states and the transitions a goal undergoes between these states. Our focus is the life-cycle of each particular goal that

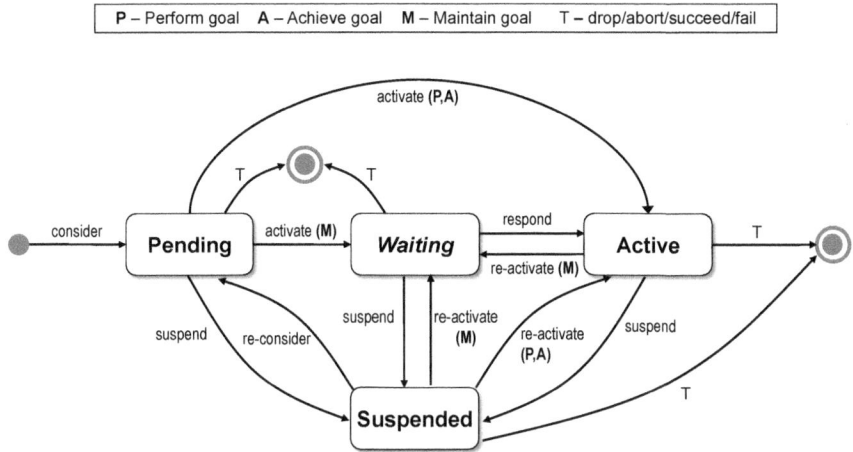

Fig. 1. Goal life-cycle composed of abstract states

the agent has. Hence, our perspective is that of an individual goal, rather than the overall agent per se. This means that we will not be concerned with issues such as the agent's overall deliberation, generation of goals (from Desires), or prioritization of goals. These relevant topics are outside the scope of this paper.

Our objective is to specify the life-cycle of goals and the mechanisms of the agent. The life-cycle we capture as four states, Pending, Waiting, Active, and Suspended, shown in Fig. 1, together with the initial state (left) and the terminal state (right). The transition from each state to the terminal state is shown. We combine the drop, abort, succeed, and fail transitions into a single transition, T, as shown.

The states can be arranged into a precedence order: Pending $\prec$ Waiting $\prec$ Active $\prec$ Suspended. Observe that, if a goal transitions from a state s to Suspended, it may not then next transition from Suspended to a state higher than s in the order. Some transitions are essentially controlled by conditions, while others depend on an explicit agent decision (or a combination of conditions and a decision), as will be made precise.

A new candidate goal may arise from a source external or internal to the agent's control cycle [16]. External to the control cycle, it may arise from obligations or commitments concerning other agents, or from the agent's own motivations. Internal to the control cycle, it may arise from subgoaling within an executing plan. Either way, a new candidate goal begins life in the Pending state if the agent has decided to consider the goal. In the next section we describe the goal control cycle in detail, including the mechanisms to perform the goal operations of interest.

3 Transitions between Goal States

The heart of our work is the effects that different operations an agent may apply to its goals of different types, in each of the four states introduced. We now describe in detail the life-cycle of a goal in each of the states. We call a *top-level command* a decision by the agent's deliberation to impose an operation upon a goal.

First, to any goal in any state, the *drop* operation implies that the goal and any goal-related actions are halted; the goal is discarded with no further action. The agent may choose to drop a goal if, for example, it believes the goal is accomplished, is no longer required, impossible, or if it inhibits a higher priority goal. Note that there are three essential cases here: the goal is dropped because it has succeeded, dropped because it has failed, or dropped because the agent has decided to drop it.

Pending State. Goals in the Pending state are inactive, awaiting the agent to deliberate over them and execute a particular operation. The *activate* operation on a perform or achieve goal transitions the goal to the Active state where the goal is pursued. By contrast, the *activate* operation on a maintain goal transitions the goal to the Waiting state.

The *suspend* operation takes a goal to the Suspended state. The *abort* operation simply drops the goal; no clean-up is required since no plans for the goal are in execution. If the success or failure condition become true in the Pending state, the goal is dropped. Note that although perform goals do not contain an explicit success condition (see Sect. 2), we make the distinction here for simplicity.

Waiting State. The Waiting state is shown with italics in Fig. 1 to emphasize that it exclusively applies to goals of monitoring: maintain goals that (actively) check for a triggering condition to be known. In this state, as in Pending, no plans are being executed. Goals transition into this state when they are (1) activated from Pending, (2) re-activated from Suspended, or (3) re-activated from Active when the subgoal succeeds, as described earlier. Should the maintenance condition be violated—or, in the proactive case, should it be predicted to be violated—then the goal transitions to the Active state with the *respond* operation. The *suspend* operation moves the goal to the Suspended state, whilst *abort* simply drops it since no plans are in execution. The goal may also be dropped if the success or failure condition becomes true.

Active State. Active goals are actively pursuing tasks: they may therefore have plan(s) associated. We must define how the agent manages the plan(s) in accordance with the operations it applies to the goal. Fig. 2 provides the internal details of the abstract Active state. Transitions with bold label denote top-level commands and other transitions occur when some condition is met. Sub-states of the active state that are shaded (e.g., aborting) are uninterruptable states where top-level commands cannot be applied.

Maintain goals enter the Active state from the Waiting state when the triggering condition is true, and move to a post subgoal sub-state. A maintain goal posts a recovery goal R if the maintenance condition was violated or a preventative goal P if the maintenance condition is predicted to be violated. Recovery and preventative goals are always achieve goals, and commence in the Pending state[1].

If the subgoal succeeds, then the parent maintain goal g transitions back to the Waiting state. If the subgoal fails, g is dropped. Should g be aborted or should its success or failure condition become true, then it transitions to the abort subgoal sub-state where the subgoal is aborted and then g is dropped. Should the goal g be suspended, the subgoal

---

[1] An argument can be made for commencing these goals in the Active state. However, commencing in the Pending state allows more flexibility, in that a trivial activation condition will see these goals immediately transition to the Active state, if that is desired.

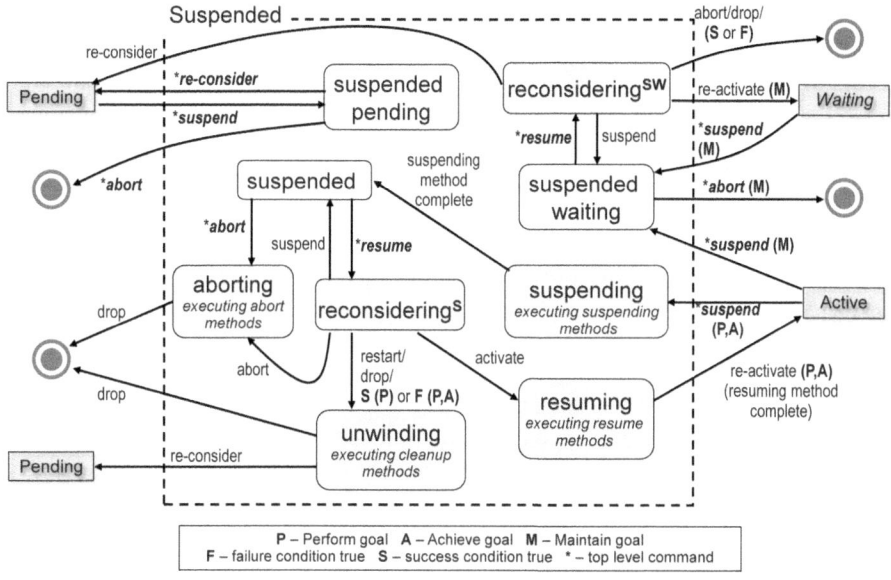

Fig. 2. Active state in detail

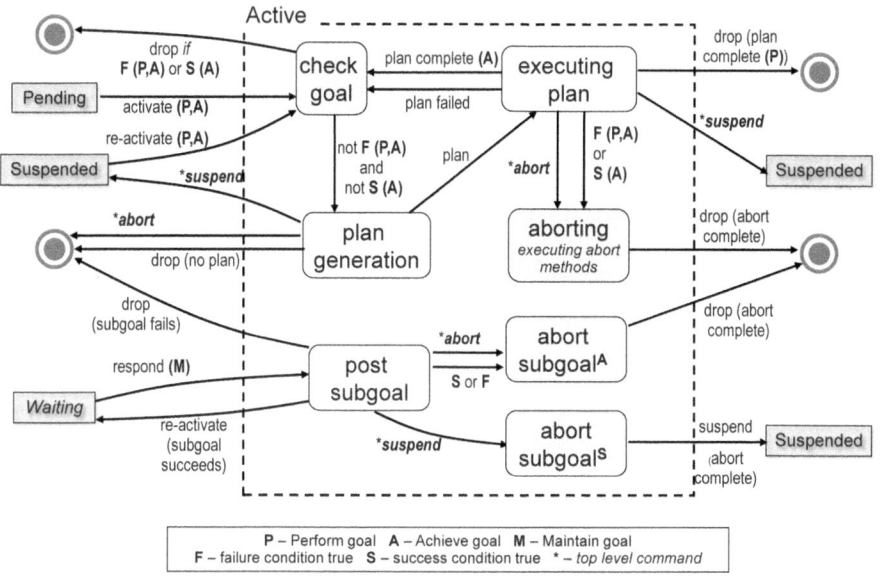

Fig. 3. Suspended state in detail

is aborted in the abort subgoal^S sub-state and then g moves to the suspended waiting sub-state of Suspended. Any generated plans are handled according to the mechanisms described in the literature [28].

Perform and achieve goals enter the Active state from the Pending state, or from the Suspended state when the re-activation condition becomes true. These goals are first examined in the check goal sub-state to determine if the success or failure condition is true; if either is true, the goal is dropped. Otherwise, a plan is generated to achieve the goal in the plan generation state. If no plan is found, the goal is dropped: this reflects the most common behaviour in BDI systems. A goal is also dropped if it is aborted in this sub-state since no plan is in execution. If a plan is found, then the goal transitions to the executing plan sub-state.

In the executing plan sub-state, if the plan fails then the goal moves back to the check goal state to retry the process of generating a new plan to achieve the goal.[1] If the plan completes for a perform goal, the goal succeeds and hence is dropped. If the plan completes for an achieve goal, however, the goal is checked for its success condition in the check goal state. If the success condition is not true then a new plan needs to be generated and executed to achieve it. While executing a plan in the executing plan sub-state, if the goal is aborted, or the success or failure condition become true, the goal transitions to the aborting sub-state where abort methods are executed [27]; the goal is dropped when they complete. If a goal is suspended in the executing plan sub-state it transitions to the Suspended state.

Suspended State. This state contains a goal of any type that is suspended, monitoring its reconsideration condition [28], awaiting possible resumption.

Goals of accomplishment may have one or more plans associated. We again must define how the agent manages the plan(s) in accordance with the operations it applies to the goal. Fig. 3 provides the internal details of the abstract Suspended state. Goals transition to this state when the *suspend* operation is applied to them. Goals arriving from the Pending state (top left) are held in a suspended pending sub-state and, when resumed, move back to the Pending state.

Maintain goals suspended from the Active state or the Waiting state are held in a suspended waiting sub-state. From this sub-state, a goal may be aborted, in which case it is simply dropped, or resumed. If resumed, a goal moves to a reconsidering sub-state where the agent deliberates over it and may either (re-)suspend the goal (back to suspended waiting sub-state), reconsider the goal (back to Pending state), re-activate it (back to Waiting), or simply abort or drop it. When a maintain is suspended, our semantics specifies that its subgoals be aborted.

Perform or achieve goals suspended from the Active state first require any suspend methods to be executed. This occurs in the suspending sub-state; then the goal moves to the suspended state. A goal may be aborted from this state, causing its abort method to be performed [27] in the aborting sub-state before it is dropped. If not aborted prior to resumption, a goal may be resumed when its *reconsideration condition* becomes true, or when the agent decides to resume it[2]. Upon resumption of the goal, the agent deliberates

---

[2] That is, *resume* is a top-level command. Hence, the reconsideration condition is a 'note' from the agent to itself to guide its deliberation over the suspended goal: a sufficient but not necessary condition for when the agent should next look at the goal.

over it in the reconsidering state. The agent may opt to (1) abort the goal (move to aborting sub-state), (2) (re)-suspend it (move to suspended sub-state), (3) re-activate the goal by performing resume methods [28] in the resuming sub-state before transitioning to the Active state, (4) *restart* the goal, or (5) drop the goal. To restart is to halt any suspended plans and re-consider the goal. Therefore, prior to restarting, any existing plans need to be terminated in the unwinding sub-state, before the goal transitions to the Pending state to be re-considered. Goals to be dropped follow a similar transition. Suspend and resume methods, like abort methods, are assumed not to fail [28].

4   Towards a Formal Semantics

In order to use Fig. 1 as a specification of a goal deliberation process, we need to determine what information is required for each goal, and how this information is used to make decisions about when the transitions of Fig. 1 should be applied. Ultimately, we wish to provide formal definitions of the transitions for each goal in an abstract, formal agent language such as CAN [32,22,21], utilizing the generic approach initiated by van Riemsdijk et al. [20], with some variations. Two of the key differences in our work (besides the choice of formal language)— which enable us to support the full variety of goal types and operations upon goals—are that we have four basic goal states (Pending, Waiting, Active and Suspended) rather than two, and that not all transitions are possible (for example, goals of accomplishment can never be in the Waiting state). This allows us to deal with suspended goals in a more detailed and realistic manner, as well as providing a more natural semantics for maintenance goals. Further, unlike Morandini et al. [15], our semantics deals with plans as well as goals. This means that we can incorporate subgoals into plans, allowing the agent designer a richer and more natural way to specify the system's behaviour.

   In order to specify the appropriate state transitions independently of any agent programming language, we will give an operational semantics for the goal transitions of Fig. 1 in CAN. This also means that we can study properties of the semantics at an appropriate level of abstraction. Using CAN as a basis means that the formal transitions are between agent configurations of the form $\langle B, \mathcal{G} \rangle$, where B is the agent's beliefs, and $\mathcal{G}$ is a set of goals that the agent is pursuing concurrently. Each element of $\mathcal{G}$ will contain more than just the goal itself; each $G \in \mathcal{G}$ is the *goal context* tuple $\langle \text{Id}, Goal, Rules, State, Plan \rangle$.

- Id is a unique identifier for each goal
- *Goal* is the goal content (as given in Sect. 2),
- *Rules* is a set of *condition-action* pairs of the form $\langle C, A \rangle$, where C is a condition and A is one of { activate, reactivate, reconsider, respond, suspend, drop, abort }
- *State* is one of { Pending, Waiting, Active, Suspended }
- *Plan* is the current plan (if any) being executed for this goal

The existence of unique identifiers ensures that goals can refer to each other. Recall that goals are fixed at design time and do not change during execution; hence *Goal* is fixed throughout execution. *Rules*, *State*, and *Plan* are dynamic and may change during execution. Note that our notation for G from this point on differs from the informal notational convenience used in Sect. 2.

Our deliberation process is specified by transitions between tuples of the form $\langle B, \mathcal{G} \rangle$. Our assumptions about this process are:

- *All goals are known at compile time, and are given unique identifiers.* This ensures that goals can explicitly refer to other goals, allowing the agent designer to specify transitions such as one goal being suspended when another specific goal is activated.
- *Any change in any goal's state has preference over any executing plans.* This means that execution can only take place when the set of goal contexts is stable, i.e., none of the transitions in Fig. 1 are currently able to take place. This is somewhat conservative, but it allows the agent designer the freedom to specify whatever interaction between goals is desired (such as making all achieve goals inactive whenever any maintenance goal becomes active), knowing that any change in any goal's status will result in the status of all goals being reconsidered. This, in turn, may result in a corresponding change in what is being executed.
- *Plans are not necessarily known in advance, but may be generated online.* This means that we do not assume that the agent *necessarily* has a plan library (although this is a perfectly valid option), and so we cannot rely on plans to be of a particular form. This also means that we have to explicitly allow for plan generation in our formal definition; we leverage previous techniques [20].
- *No restriction is made on the number of goals that may be active at once.* It may be desirable to allow that there should be at most one active goal at any time, or perhaps that there should be at most one goal active when any maintenance goal is active (but allow any number of concurrent achievement goals to be active otherwise). Hence we need to be able to provide the agent designer with mechanisms to enforce restrictions like these if desired, but not to build them into the CAN rules. Accordingly we will have a standard pattern for goal transition rules, which can be tailored by the designer to suit the particular application.
- *Goals of any type may be used as sub-goals in plans.* This means that a plan may contain a goal as a step, at which point the goal is executed, with the only difference being that success and failure are treated in the same way as success and failure for actions. In particular, if the subgoal fails (or is aborted), then this is treated as a plan failure, i.e., we search for an alternative plan.

4.1   Introduction to CAN Rules

Formalization of the semantics hinges on the appropriate definition of *Rules* for each goal. These definitions follow the same general principles, but can be tailored for individual goals. It is also helpful to use CAN's expressiveness to alter *Rules* dynamically, such as adding reconsideration conditions to suspended goals.

Our approach is the following. Given an action A that takes goal G from state S_1 to S_2, we ensure that there is a rule $\langle C, A \rangle \in Rules$ such that whenever $B \models c$ for some $c \in C$, we update the agent configuration from $\langle B, \{ \langle \text{Id}, G, R, S_1, P_1 \rangle \} \cup \mathcal{G} \rangle$ to $\langle B, \{ \langle \text{Id}, G, R, S_2, P_2 \rangle \} \cup \mathcal{G} \rangle$, unless A is either drop or abort, in which cases the new agent configuration is $\langle B, \mathcal{G} \rangle$.

A goal G changing state from S_1 to S_2 via action A (which is neither drop nor abort) is modelled by the following rule:

$$\frac{\langle C, A \rangle \in R_1 \quad c \in C \quad B \models c}{\langle B, \{\langle \mathrm{Id}, G, R_1, S_1, P_1 \rangle\} \cup \mathcal{G} \rangle \to \langle B, \{\langle \mathrm{Id}, G, R_2, S_2, P_2 \rangle\} \cup \mathcal{G} \rangle} \qquad (1)$$

The drop and abort actions are similarly modelled by the rule

$$\frac{\langle C, \mathsf{drop/abort} \rangle \in R_1 \quad c \in C \quad B \models c}{\langle B, \{\langle \mathrm{Id}, G, R_1, S_1, P_1 \rangle\} \cup \mathcal{G} \rangle \to \langle B, \mathcal{G} \rangle.} \qquad (2)$$

Note that for actions other than drop or abort, it is possible to change $G.Rules$, i.e., in Eq. (2), R_2 may be different from R_1. This is particularly important for reconsideration conditions.

In some cases, the agent wants a condition C to be evaluated 'autonomously', i.e., without any further deliberation. In other cases, the agent wants an explicit condition. Thus, we require that all conditions contain a formula of the form $reconsider(\mathrm{Id})$, so that a reconsideration condition $Cond$ is specified as $Cond \wedge reconsider(\mathrm{Id})$. This means that for the goal to change state, not only must $Cond$ hold, we must also have that the agent has explicitly decided to resume the goal by adding $reconsider(\mathrm{Id})$ to its beliefs. This mechanism also allows us to provide for the possibility that the agent may decide to drop, abort, or suspend any goal at any time: it can do so by adding $drop(\mathrm{Id})$ (resp. $abort(\mathrm{Id})$, $suspend(\mathrm{Id})$) to its beliefs.

As noted in Sect. 2, it is also common to include an activation condition of the form $\langle \{Cond \wedge \mathsf{activate}(\mathrm{Id})\}, \mathsf{activate} \rangle\}$, so that the goal can only be activated when both $Cond$ is true and the agent has decided to activate the goal. As a result, we will denote as $standard(\mathrm{Id}, Succ, Cond)$ the set of rules:

$$\{\langle \{Succ, \mathsf{drop}(\mathrm{Id})\}, \mathsf{drop} \rangle, \langle \{\mathsf{abort}(\mathrm{Id})\}, \mathsf{abort} \rangle,$$
$$\langle \{\mathsf{suspend}(\mathrm{Id})\}, \mathsf{suspend} \rangle, \langle \{Cond \wedge \mathsf{activate}(\mathrm{Id})\}, \mathsf{activate} \rangle\}$$

We now consider how to create parametrized rules within this framework for perform, achieve, and maintain goals.

perform(τ, S, F): We commence with $Rules$ as $standard(\mathrm{Id}, \{S, F\}, Cond)$, For a goal with identifier Id. We do not initially include any rules for the actions reconsider or reactivate; these are added to $Rules$ when the goal is suspended.

For the suspend action, we need to add reconsideration conditions to $Rules$. When suspending a goal in the Pending state, the first of the following rules is added by the transition; when suspending a goal in the Active state, both are added. This is because the reactivate action is not possible if the goal was in the Pending state when suspended.

$$\{\langle \{RC \wedge reconsider(\mathrm{Id})\}, \mathsf{reconsider} \rangle\}$$
$$\{\langle \{RC \wedge reactivate(\mathrm{Id})\}, \mathsf{reactivate} \rangle\}$$

In these rules, RC is the reconsideration condition, which is determined by the agent. The reconsider and reactivate actions remove the condition-action pairs for both of themselves when either of these actions is performed. This allows different reconsideration conditions to be attached each time a suspension occurs.

achieve(S, F)**:** The high-level rules for this goal type are the same as for a perform goal, i.e., $standard(\text{Id}, \{S, F\}, Cond)$. This reflects the fact that the transitions in Fig. 1 are the same for these goal types.

maintain$(C, \pi, Recover, Prevent, S, F)$**:** The two pertinent differences between monitoring versus accomplishment goals are that (1) there is now the extra state Waiting, in which the maintenance condition is being monitored, but no action is being taken yet, and (2) when the maintenance goal becomes active, it triggers the adoption of an extra achievement goal, with the intention that when this new goal is achieved, the violation of the maintenance condition (either actual or predicted) will be overcome. Hence, the respond action, which is only available to maintenance goals, will result in not only the maintenance goal becoming active, but also the adoption of a new achievement goal.

The initial set of rules is the same as for perform goals above. The transitions for drop and abort are as above. The transition for activate now puts the goal into the Waiting state rather than the Active state, and adds the rule: $\langle \{\neg C, C \wedge \pi(\neg C)\}, \text{respond} \rangle$. Hence the respond rule is only present when the goal is in the Waiting state. The only significant difference to perform goals is the transition from Waiting to Active states, as follows:

$$\langle C, \text{respond} \rangle \in R_1 \quad c \in C \quad B \models c$$
$$\langle B, G \cup \{\langle \text{Id}_1, MG, R_1, \text{Waiting}, e \rangle\} \rangle \longrightarrow \langle B, G \cup \{\langle \text{Id}_1, MG, R_2, \text{Active}, AG \rangle\} \rangle$$

where MG is maintain$(C, \pi, Recover, Prevent, S, F)$;
$Recover$ is achieve(S_R, F_R); $Prevent$ is achieve(S_P, F_P); SG is achieve(S_A, F_A);
S_A is S_R and F_A is F_R if $\neg C$ is true and S_P and F_P otherwise;
R_1 is $standard(\text{Id}, \{F_A, S, F\}, true) \cup \langle S_A, \text{reactivate} \rangle\}$; and
R_2 is $standard(\text{Id}_2, \{S_A, F_A\}, \neg C \vee (C \wedge \pi(\neg C))) \cup$
$\quad\quad \{\langle \{drop(\text{Id}_1), suspend(\text{Id}_1), abort(\text{Id}_1)\}, \text{abort} \rangle\}$.

The idea is that the goal SG has been has been added (initially in the Pending state) to attempt re-establishment of the maintenance condition. If SG succeeds, we reactivate MG (i.e., MG returns to the Waiting state), due to the success condition S_A of SG being the only condition for the reactivate rule in R_1. If SG fails or is dropped or aborted, one option would be to drop MG; however, as SG is treated as a sub-goal here, we do not drop MG but return to the planning level, in case another plan for MG can be found. If not such plan can be found, MG will be dropped in any case. MG is dropped if either its success condition S or failure condition F becomes true.

The rules R_2 for SG specify it will be activated immediately (due to the activation condition incorporating the maintenance condition), and that it should be aborted if the agent decides to drop, abort or suspend MG (as reflected in the rules for drop in R_2). Note also that if SG is suspended, the maintenance goal remains in the Active state.

As in the above cases, the suspend transition attaches a reconsideration condition. A minor difference is that the reactivate action can result in either the Waiting state or the Active state, following the semantics of Fig. 1.

4.2   Designing CAN Rules

In Fig. 4 below we give formal CAN rules corresponding to the states and transitions of Fig. 1. The rules may be divided into three groups:

$$\frac{type(G) = \mathsf{Perform}, \mathsf{Achieve} \quad B,R \vdash \mathsf{activate}}{\langle B, G \cup g(id,G,R,\mathsf{P},\pi)\rangle \longrightarrow \langle B, \ldots \mathsf{A}, \pi\rangle} \, act(P,A) \qquad \frac{type(G) = \mathsf{Maintain} \quad B,R \vdash \mathsf{activate}}{\langle B, G \cup g(id,G,R,\mathsf{P},\pi)\rangle \longrightarrow \langle B, \ldots \mathsf{W}, \epsilon\rangle} \, act(M)$$

$$\frac{B,R_1 \vdash \mathsf{respond}}{\langle B, G \cup g(id,MG,R,\mathsf{W},\epsilon)\rangle \longrightarrow \langle B, \ldots \mathsf{A}, AG\rangle} \, respond$$

$$\frac{B,R \vdash A \quad A \in \{\mathsf{drop},\mathsf{abort}\} \quad State \in \{\mathsf{S},\mathsf{A},\mathsf{W}\}}{\langle B, G \cup g(id,G,R,State,\pi)\rangle \longrightarrow \langle B, G\rangle} \, drop/abort$$

$$\frac{B,R \vdash \mathsf{suspend} \quad State \in \{\mathsf{P},\mathsf{A},\mathsf{W}\}}{\langle B, G \cup g(id,G,R,State,\pi)\rangle \longrightarrow \langle B, \ldots \mathsf{R}^+, \mathsf{S}, \pi\rangle} \, suspend \qquad \frac{B,R \vdash \mathsf{reconsider}}{\langle B, G \cup g(id,G,R,\mathsf{S},\epsilon)\rangle \longrightarrow \langle B, \ldots \mathsf{R}^-, \mathsf{P}, \epsilon\rangle} \, recon$$

$$\frac{type(G) = \mathsf{Perform}, \mathsf{Achieve} \quad B,R \vdash \mathsf{reactivate}}{\langle B, G \cup g(id,G,R,\mathsf{A},\pi)\rangle \longrightarrow \langle B, \ldots \mathsf{R}^-, \mathsf{W}, \epsilon\rangle} \, react(P,A)$$

$$\frac{type(G) = \mathsf{Maintain} \quad B,R \vdash \mathsf{reactivate}}{\langle B, G \cup g(id,G,R,\mathsf{S},\pi)\rangle \longrightarrow \langle B, \ldots \mathsf{R}^-, \mathsf{W}, \epsilon\rangle} \, react(M)$$

$$\frac{stable \quad \Pi = mer(G,B,G \cup g(G,R,\mathsf{A},\epsilon)) \quad \Pi \neq \epsilon}{\langle B, G \cup g(G,R,\mathsf{A},\epsilon)\rangle \longrightarrow \langle B, \ldots \mathsf{A}, \Pi\rangle} \, plan$$

$$\frac{stable \quad \Pi = mer(G,B,G \cup g(G,R,\mathsf{A},\epsilon)) \quad \Pi = \epsilon}{\langle B, G \cup g(G,R,\mathsf{A},\epsilon)\rangle \longrightarrow \langle B, G\rangle} \, noplan$$

$$\frac{stable \quad \pi \neq \epsilon \quad \langle B, G \cup g(G,R,\mathsf{A},\pi)\rangle \longrightarrow \langle B', G \cup g(G,R,\mathsf{A},fail)\rangle}{\langle B, G \cup g(G,R,\mathsf{A},\pi)\rangle \longrightarrow \langle B', G \cup g(G,R,\mathsf{A},\epsilon)\rangle} \, fail$$

$$\frac{stable \quad \neg simple(P_1\|P_2,\_) \quad \langle B,P_1\rangle \longrightarrow \langle B',P'\rangle}{\langle B, P_1\|P_2\rangle \longrightarrow \langle B', P'\|P_2\rangle} \, \|_1 \qquad \frac{stable \quad \neg simple(P_1\|P_2,\_) \quad \langle B,P_2\rangle \longrightarrow \langle B',P'\rangle}{\langle B, P_1\|P_2\rangle \longrightarrow \langle B', P_1\|P'\rangle} \, \|_2$$

$$\frac{stable \quad \neg simple(P_1 \triangleright P_2,\_) \quad \langle B,P_1\rangle \longrightarrow \langle B',P'\rangle}{\langle B, P_1 \triangleright P_2\rangle \longrightarrow \langle B', P' \triangleright P_2\rangle} \, \triangleright_1$$

$$\frac{stable \quad \neg simple(P_1 \triangleright P_2,\_) \quad \langle B,P_1\rangle \longrightarrow \langle \_,fail\rangle \quad \langle B,P_2\rangle \longrightarrow \langle B',P'\rangle}{\langle B, P_1 \triangleright P_2\rangle \longrightarrow \langle B', P'\rangle} \, \triangleright_2$$

$$\frac{stable \quad \neg simple(P_1;P_2,\_) \quad \langle B,P_1\rangle \longrightarrow \langle B',P'\rangle}{\langle B, P_1;P_2\rangle \longrightarrow \langle B', P';P_2\rangle} \, ; \qquad \frac{stable \quad B \models pre(a)}{\langle B,a\rangle \longrightarrow \langle B',nil\rangle} \, act_1 \qquad \frac{stable \quad B \not\models pre(a)}{\langle B,a\rangle \longrightarrow \langle B,fail\rangle} \, act_2$$

$$\frac{stable \quad simple(P,P')}{\langle B,P\rangle \longrightarrow \langle B,P'\rangle} \, simple \qquad \frac{stable}{\langle B,nil\rangle \longrightarrow \langle B,\epsilon\rangle} \, nil$$

$$\frac{stable}{\langle B,+b\rangle \longrightarrow \langle B \cup \{b\},\epsilon\rangle} \, add \qquad \frac{stable}{\langle B,-b\rangle \longrightarrow \langle B\backslash\{b\},\epsilon\rangle} \, del$$

$$\frac{stable \quad B \models \phi}{\langle B,?\phi\rangle \longrightarrow \langle B,\epsilon\rangle} \, query_1 \qquad \frac{stable \quad B \not\models \phi}{\langle B,?\phi\rangle \longrightarrow \langle B,fail\rangle} \, query_2$$

$$\frac{stable \quad \psi_i : P_i \in \Delta \quad B \models \psi_i}{\langle B, < \Delta >\rangle \longrightarrow \langle B, P_i \triangleright < \Delta \backslash \{\psi_i : P_i\} >\rangle} \, select$$

$$\frac{stable \quad \Delta = \{\psi_i\theta : P_i\theta \,|\, e' : \psi_i \leftarrow P_i \in \Pi \wedge \theta = mgu(e,e')\}}{\langle B,!e\rangle \longrightarrow \langle B \cup \{e\}, < \Delta >\rangle} \, event$$

$$\frac{stable \quad B \models \phi \quad \langle B,P\rangle \longrightarrow \langle B',P'\rangle}{\langle B,\phi : P\rangle \longrightarrow \langle B',P'\rangle} \, wait_1 \qquad \frac{stable \quad B \not\models \phi}{\langle B,\phi : P\rangle \longrightarrow \langle B,\phi : P\rangle} \, wait_2$$

$$\frac{}{\langle B, G \cup g(P,G,R,\mathsf{A},G_2)\rangle \longrightarrow \langle B, G \cup g(P,G,R,\mathsf{A},SubGoalPlan) \cup g(C,G_2,R_3,\mathsf{Pending},\epsilon)\rangle} \, Goal$$

Fig. 4. One formulation of CAN rules for the goal life-cycle

MG is $maintain(C,\pi,Recover,Prevent,S,F)$; $Recover$ is $achieve(S_R,F_R)$;
$Prevent$ is $achieve(S_P,F_P)$; AG is $\langle Id_2, achieve(S_A,F_A), R_2, \mathsf{Pending}, e\rangle$;
S_A is S_R and F_A is F_R if $\neg C$ is true and S_P and F_P otherwise;
R_1 is $standard(Id_1,\{F_A,S,F\},true) \cup \{\langle\{S\},\mathsf{reactivate}\rangle\}$;
R_2 is $standard(Id_2,\{S_A,F_A\},\neg C \vee (C \wedge \pi(\neg C))) \cup \{\langle\{drop(Id_1),suspend(Id_1),abort(Id_1)\},\mathsf{abort}\rangle\}$
$SubGoalPlan$ is $S_c \vee F_c \vee drop(Child) \vee abort(Child) :?S_c$
R_3 is $standard(Child, S_c \vee F_c, true) \cup \{\langle\{drop(Parent),abort(Parent),suspend(Parent)\},\mathsf{abort}\rangle\}$

- Goal transition rules: *act(P,A), act(M), respond, drop/abort, suspend, recon, react(P,A), react(M)*
- Planning rules: $plan_1, plan_2, fail$
- Execution rules: the remaining rules

Table 1. Alpha's sequence of goal states. Ser is the perform goal $\mathsf{perform}(search, S, F)$, $Main$ is the maintenance goal $\mathsf{maintain}(MC, \pi, Charge, Charge, \bot, \bot)$, MC is the condition $current\_charge > return\_time$, $Charge$ is the achievement goal $\mathsf{achieve}(recharged, \bot)$, si is $search_i; \ldots search_{10}; return$, ri is a plan which returns the robot to sector i, R_1 is $standard(search, \{S, F\}, \top)^4$, R_2 is $standard(recharge, \{\mathsf{drop}(charge), \mathsf{abort}(charge)\}, \top) \cup \{\langle recharged, \mathsf{reactivate}\rangle\}$, R_3 is $R_2 \cup \{\langle\{\neg MC, MC \wedge \pi(\neg MC)\}, respond\rangle\}$, R_4 is $standard(save, \{at(survivor, base)\}\top)$, R_5 is $R_1 \cup \{at(base, survivor), reconsider\rangle\}$, R_6 is $standard(help, satisfied(Other), \top)$, R_7 is $standard(charge, recharged, \neg C \vee (C \wedge \pi(\neg C))) \cup \{\langle\{\mathsf{drop}(recharge), \mathsf{suspend}(recharge), \mathsf{abort}(recharge)\}, \mathsf{abort}\rangle\}$.

Stage	Perform goals	Achievement goals	Maintenance goals
1	$\langle search, Ser, R_1, \text{Pending}, search\rangle$	-	$\langle recharge, Main, R_2, \text{Pending}, e\rangle$
2	$\langle search, Ser, R_1, \text{Active}, search\rangle$	-	$\langle recharge, Main, R_3, \text{Waiting}, e\rangle$
3	$\langle search, Ser, R_1, \text{Active}, s2\rangle$	-	$\langle recharge, Main, R_3, \text{Waiting}, e\rangle$
4	$\langle search, Ser, R_5, \text{Suspended}, s2\rangle$	$\langle save, Sav, R_4, \text{Pending}, e\rangle$	$\langle recharge, Main, R_3, \text{Waiting}, e\rangle$
5	$\langle search, Ser, R_5, \text{Suspended}, s2\rangle$	$\langle save, Sav, R_4, \text{Active}, assist\rangle$	$\langle recharge, Main, R_3, \text{Waiting}, e\rangle$
6	$\langle search, Ser, R_5, \text{Suspended}, s2\rangle$	(dropped after success)	$\langle recharge, Main, R_3, \text{Waiting}, e\rangle$
7	$\langle search, Ser, R_1, \text{Pending}, s2\rangle$	-	$\langle recharge, Main, R_3, \text{Waiting}, e\rangle$
8	$\langle search, Ser, R_1, \text{Active}, r2; s2\rangle$	-	$\langle recharge, Main, R_3, \text{Waiting}, e\rangle$
9	$\langle search, Ser, R_1, \text{Active}, s5\rangle$	$\langle help, Help, R_6, \text{Pending}, e\rangle$	$\langle recharge, Main, R_3, \text{Waiting}, e\rangle$
10	$\langle search, Ser, R_5, \text{Suspended}, s5\rangle$	$\langle help, Help, R_6, \text{Active}, assist\rangle$	$\langle recharge, Main, R_3, \text{Waiting}, e\rangle$
11	$\langle search, Ser, R_5, \text{Suspended}, s5\rangle$	(aborted)	$\langle recharge, Main, R_3, \text{Waiting}, e\rangle$
12	$\langle search, Ser, R_1, \text{Active}, r5; s5\rangle$	-	$\langle recharge, Main, R_3, \text{Waiting}, e\rangle$
13	$\langle search, Ser, R_1, \text{Active}, s8\rangle$	$\langle help, Help, R_6, \text{Pending}, e\rangle$	$\langle recharge, Main, R_3, \text{Waiting}, e\rangle$
14	$\langle search, Ser, R_5, \text{Suspended}, s8\rangle$	$\langle help, Help, R_6, \text{Pending}, e\rangle$	$\langle recharge, Main, R_3, \text{Waiting}, e\rangle$
15	$\langle search, Ser, R_9, \text{Suspended}, s8\rangle$	$\langle help, Help, R_6, \text{Active}, assist\rangle$	$\langle recharge, Main, R_3, \text{Waiting}, e\rangle$
16	$\langle search, Ser, R_5, \text{Suspended}, s8\rangle$	(dropped after success)	$\langle recharge, Main, R_3, \text{Waiting}, e\rangle$
17	$\langle search, Ser, R_5, \text{Pending}, r8; s8\rangle$	-	$\langle recharge, Main, R_3, \text{Waiting}, e\rangle$
18	$\langle search, Ser, R_5, \text{Active}, r8; s8\rangle$	-	$\langle recharge, Main, R_3, \text{Waiting}, e\rangle$
19	$\langle search, Ser, R_5, \text{Suspended}, r8; s8\rangle$	$\langle charge, Charge, R_7, \text{Pending}, e\rangle$	$\langle recharge, Main, R_3, \text{Active}, e\rangle$
20	$\langle search, Ser, R_5, \text{Suspended}, r8; s8\rangle$	$\langle charge, Charge, R_7, \text{Active}, charge\rangle$	$\langle recharge, Main, R_3, \text{Active}, e\rangle$
21	$\langle search, Ser, R_5, \text{Suspended}, r8; s8\rangle$	(dropped after success)	$\langle recharge, Main, R_3, \text{Active}, e\rangle$
22	$\langle search, Ser, R_5, \text{Suspended}, r8; s8\rangle$	-	$\langle recharge, Main, R_3, \text{Waiting}, e\rangle$
23	$\langle search, Ser, R_1, \text{Active}, r8; s8\rangle$	-	$\langle recharge, Main, R_3, \text{Waiting}, e\rangle$
24	(dropped after success)	-	$\langle recharge, Main, R_2, \text{Waiting}, e\rangle$

We believe that this is the first time that these three aspects have been combined into the one semantics. The goal transition rules, derived from Fig. 1, are most directly comparable to previous works [20,15]; the planning rules are similar to those of the former. The execution rules are based on the standard CAN rules, with some extensions. In particular, the extensions include the wait construct (i.e., $\phi : P$ where P is not executed unless ϕ is true), and the rule *goal*, which deals with the case when goals (of any type) can occur in plans, and hence as sub-goals of another goal.

When a subogal is encountered, it is executed *synchronously*, i.e., the parent goal waits until the subgoal has completed before moving on. If the subgoal succeeds, the subgoal is dropped, and execution proceeds (just as in the case of any other successful step). If the subgoal fails, or is dropped (other than after it has succeeded) or aborted, then this is treated as a plan failure, i.e., that the step failed and that an alternative, if available, should be pursued. Hence the plan for the parent goal is to wait for one of the success or failure conditions to become true, or for the subgoal to be dropped or aborted, and then query whether the subgoal succeeded. The parent goal's step then succeeds only if the success condition of the subgoal is true (see rule *goal* below).

Note also that we use a 'traditional BDI' approach to plans, in that if the precondition of an action is true, then we assume that the action succeeds. In other words, the only way for an action to fail is for its precondition to be false. Hence in the rules act_1 and act_2 below, we first test the precondition ($pre(a)$); if this is true, then the action succeeds and the beliefs are updated appropriately. Otherwise the action fails. It is possible to allow for more sophisticated processing, such as *sensory actions*, for which it is possible to tell immediately after execution whether it has succeeded or not. Designing rules for such actions is outside the scope of this paper; for now, we note that this is not a limitation of CAN, but is purely a design decision.

To simplify some of the execution rules, we define $simple(P, P')$ to be true iff P is one of the cases below and P' is its simplification:

P	P'		P	P'
$nil\|\|Q$	Q		$fail\|\|Q$	$fail$
$Q\|\|nil$	Q		$Q\|\|fail$	$fail$
$nil; Q$	Q		$fail; Q$	$fail$
$Q; nil$	Q			
$nil \triangleright Q$	nil		$fail \triangleright Q$	Q

To further ease legibility and reduce redundancy, we introduce some shorthand notations. We abbreviate the states to P, W, A, and S with the obvious meanings. We often abbreviate $\langle B, G \cup g(id, Goal, R, \mathsf{P}, \pi) \rangle \longrightarrow \langle B, G \cup g(id, Goal, R, \mathsf{A}, \pi) \rangle$ to $\langle B, G \cup g(id, Goal, R, \mathsf{P}, \pi) \rangle \longrightarrow \langle B, \ldots \mathsf{A}, \pi) \rangle$.

We denote by R^+ the rules in R with the rules for reconsider and reactivate added. We denote by R^- the rules in R with the rules for reconsider and reactivate deleted. We abbreviate the rule

$$Condition$$
$$\langle B, G \cup g(Goal, R, \mathsf{Active}, P_1) \rangle \longrightarrow \langle B', G \cup g(Goal, R, \mathsf{Active}, P_2) \rangle$$

to $\langle B, P_1 \rangle \longrightarrow \langle B', P_2 \rangle$ when no ambiguity occurs. We denote by $B, R \vdash A$ the statement that $\exists \langle C, A \rangle \in R \; \exists c \in C$ such that $B \models c$.

We denote by $stable(B, G)$ that for all goals Goal in G we have that if B, Goal.Rule $\vdash$ action, then action is not applicable. Applicable actions are defined by Fig. 1; for example, the activate action is only applicable in the Pending state. This definition is needed to allow for the possibility that B, Goal.Rule $\vdash$ activate when Goal is already in the Active state, and so the action will have no effect. We will often abuse notation and write just $stable$ when the beliefs and goals are clear from the context. Note that the presence of $stable$ in the premise of the execution rules is the mechanism that guarantees that execution does not take place in preference to changes of goal state.

4.3   Worked Example

The sequence of goal transitions in the robot rescue scenario are given in Table 1. Alpha's initial goals include the perform goal perform($search, S, F$) where $search$ is a search plan for a region 10 units square, which Alpha searches one square at a time. We will assume that $search$ consists of the eleven steps $search_1; \ldots search_{10}; return$ where $search_i$ searches column i of the grid and $return$ makes Alpha return to the base. The success condition S is that each column has been searched and Alpha is at the base.

Alpha's initial goals also include the maintenance goal that it should always retain sufficient charge to return to the base. This means that it needs to estimate how long it will take it to return to the base from its current position, and if its remaining charge falls to this level, it should immediately suspend whatever it is doing and return to the base to recharge. Hence Alpha's initial goals include maintain($C, \pi, R, P, \perp, \perp$) where

C is the condition that $current\_charge > return\_time$, π is an appropriate prediction mechanism (such as estimating the time that will be taken by each of the currently adopted plans), and R and P are both the achievement goal of returning to the base, i.e., achieve(at_base, $\perp$).

Alpha will adopt appropriate achievement goals when assisting a survivor back to the base, and when responding to calls for help: achieve(at(Survivor, base), $\perp$) and achieve($satisfied$(Other), $\perp$) respectively. The success condition for the former is when the survivor is safely back at the base. The success condition for the latter is determined by the other agent; hence the goal only succeeds when Alpha believes the other agent is satisfied, i.e., when the other agent sends a message to Alpha notifying it that the goal has been achieved. The plans to achieve this goal will also be generated by the other agent. Activation of either of these goals will suspend the search goal.

Each of these achievement goals will be triggered by a rule in Alpha's plan library[5], so that we assume that Alpha contains in its library the following two rules:

$survivor\_found$: $\top$ →achieve(at(Survivor, base), $\perp$)
$request\_received$: $\top$ → achieve($satisfied$(Other), $\perp$)

Alpha's sequence of goal states is given in Table 1. As shown, its initial goals are the perform goal Ser to search and the maintain goal $Main$ concerned with its battery power. The following states correspond to an actual execution from the initial goals.

Alpha's first decisions are to activate both goals, so that the perform goal moves into the Active state, and the maintain goal moves into the Waiting state (stage 2). Alpha thus starts to execute its search pattern. Alpha successfully executes $search_1$ and is in the midst of sub-plan $search_2$ when the survivor is found (stage 3). The event survivor_found is raised, and the rule in Alpha's plan library is fired, resulting the goal Sav being added to Alpha's goals (stage 4). This triggers the suspension of the search goal. The reconsideration condition is when the survivor is safely at the base.

Alpha now activates the Sav goal. It plans to achieve at(Survivor, base) by calling Bravo for help, asking the survivor about any others nearby, waiting until Bravo arrives and together carrying the survivor to the base (stage 5). This plan is executed successfully; thus Sav is achieved, the goal is dropped, and Alpha resumes searching (stages 6–8). It is in sector 5 when Bravo's call for help is received (stage 9). Again, this event fires the appropriate rule in Alpha's plan library, and a $Help$ goal is added to Alpha's goal state. Alpha then suspends the search plan and adopts the goal of assisting Bravo (stage 10). The reconsideration condition is when the survivor is safely at the base.

While Alpha is still executing the action find(bravo), a message from Bravo arrives saying that the survivor is now safely at the base, and so Alpha aborts the plan to find Bravo and the $Help$ goal is dropped (stage 11). Alpha resumes its search, and then gets the call from Charlie when it is in sector 8. As before, it suspends searching (stages 13–15), and adopts a $Help$ goal. The reconsideration condition is when the survivor is safely at the base. Alpha finds Charlie, the survivor is brought to the base, and so the $Help$ goal is dropped (stage 16).

---

[5] Another possibility is to have these two goals intially in the Pending state and to use the $survivor\_found$ and $request\_received$ events as part of the activation condition for them; pursuing this possibility is part of our future work.

At this point, Alpha reconsiders Ser, and activates the searching goal, only to discover that resuming its search will soon violate the maintenance goal, as it has only 30 minutes of charge remaining. Hence the searching goal is re-suspended while Alpha recharges (stages 17–20). Once charging is finished, $Charge$ is dropped (stage 21), and $recharge$ goes back to the Waiting state (stage 22), which means that searching can be resumed (stage 23). As the perform goal Ser has now succeeded, it is dropped, and Alpha is now idle (stage 24).

4.4 Implementation

A prototype implementation of the full CAN rules for our semantics consists of around 700 lines of Prolog. It has been tested under Ciao and SWI-Prolog. This implementation, denoted *Orpheus*, continues to be developed, and is available from the authors at
`http://www.cs.rmit.edu.au/~jah/orpheus`

It should be noted that this implementation is intended as a proof-of-concept development of the CAN rules, and should not be seen as a surrogate for well-known agent implementations such as JACK [4], Jadex [16], or Jason [11,1]. Its purpose is to allow some simple experimentation with the rules of CAN and the consequences of changes in the early forms of the rules above.

5   Related Work

Goals play a central role in *cognitive* agent frameworks [20]: "mental attitudes representing preferred progressions of a particular (multi)agent system that the agent has chosen to put effort into bringing about." Winikoff et al. [32] argue for the importance of both declarative and procedural representations, and present the specification of goals with context, in-conditions, and effects.

A goal type has been defined as "a specific agent attitude towards goals" [6]. The different types of goals found in the literature and in implemented agent systems are surveyed by Braubach et al. [3]. While there is broad agreement about perform and achieve goals, less attention has been directed towards maintain goals. The reactive and proactive semantics for maintenance goals is explored by Duff et al. [8]. However, they do not consider aborting or suspending goals, and do not give formal rules for the behaviour of maintenance goals. Mechanisms for adopting and dropping goals, and generating plans for them, have been variously explored at both the semantic theoretical and implemented system levels; we do not cite here the extensive body of work. Thangarajah et al. formalized the mechanisms for the operations of aborting, suspending, and resuming goals [27,28]. However, those authors considered only achieve goals. We find that the literature lacks a state and transition specification for all classes of goals that accounts for the current mechanisms for aborting and suspending. Beyond our scope are recent examples of exploring goal failure and re-planning [21,24].

Bordini and Hübner et al. [1] provide a semantics for Jason's 'internal actions', including its mechanism for handling plan failure. Inasmuch as they act to modify internal state, these internal are akin to the internals of our abstract goal states, seen in Fig. 2 and 3.

Braubach et al. [3] build the Jadex agent system [16] on an explicit state-based manipulation of goals. Goals begin in a New state. When adopted, they move to the Option state (akin to our Pending), and from there to Active (akin to our own Active). A goal moves to the Suspended state if its in-condition ("context" [3]) becomes false: this is a different concept from our deliberation-directed suspension and resumption. The aim of Braubach et al. is to define a principled yet pragmatic foundation for the Jadex system; no attempt is made for a generic formalization with a uniform set of operations on goals at an abstract representational level. Braubach et al. [2] discuss *long-term* goals, which may be considered as an input for determining when a goal should be dropped, aborted or suspended; here we are concerned with the consequences of such decisions, rather than the reason that they are made.

van Riemsdijk et al. [18,19] provide semantics based on default logic, emphasizing that, while the set of an agent's goals need not be consistent, its set of intentions must be. This and similar work is complementary to ours, in that we do not consider the process by which the agent decides whether to adopt a goal and whether to adopt an intention (plan) from it [5]. The authors [6,7] expand their analysis of declarative goals to perform, achieve goals, and maintain goals, providing a logic-based operational semantics.

van Riemsdijk et al. [20] present a generic, abstract, type-neutral goal model consisting of suspend and active states. Their two states can be thought of as "not currently executing a plan" and "currently executing a plan", respectively. Their work, which like ours encompasses achieve, perform, query, and maintain goals, has overly simple accounting for maintenance goals and for aborting and suspending. Further, we argue that the states of non-execution and suspension should be distinguished, and that goals should be created into the Pending not Suspend state. Winikoff et al. [31] extend this work with new types of time-varying goals, such as 'achieve and maintain', sketching a semantics in Linear Temporal Logic.

Morandini et al. [15] use the generic goal model of van Riemsdijk et al. to reduce the semantic gap between design-time goal models and run-time agent implementations. Their operational semantics is focused on providing an account of the relationship between a goal and its subgoals, including success conditions which are not necessarily the same as those of the subgoals. Our work likewise encompasses dynamic achievement of a goal according to logical conditions, enabled by a subgoaling mechanism. Crucially, since we are concerned with execution, our semantics accounts for plans as well as goals. This means that our goal states contain finer distinctions, and in particular the sub-division of the Active and Suspended states. Our work is further distinguished by a richer range of operations that may be applied to a goal (e.g., a richer semantics for suspending a goal and its children; aborting as well as failing), and by the inclusion of proactive maintenance goals.

Khan and Lespérance [12] tackle goal dynamics for prioritized goals through a logical approach. Their focus is to ensure that active goals are consistent with each other and the agent's knowledge. Lorini et al. [14] study in detail the dynamics of goals and plans under changes to the agent's beliefs. Such works that enable an agent to reconsider its goals in the light of belief updates are complementary to our work, and beyond our scope here.

6   Conclusion and Further Work

Management of goals is central to intelligent agents in the BDI tradition. This paper provides mechanisms for goal management across the common goal types in the literature, including goals of maintenance. The three key contributions of our generic framework for goal states and transitions are (1) to encompass both goals of accomplishment and rich goals of monitoring, (2) to provide the first specification of abort and suspend for all the common goal types, and (3) to account for plan execution as well as the dynamics of sub-goaling. To the best of our knowledge, no existing framework for goal operation accounts all of these points.

By developing the formal operational semantics for our generic framework in the agent language CAN [21], we have not been tied to any particular agent implementation. However, besides disseminating the formal semantics, a first priority is to implement our framework as proof of concept. As mentioned at the end of Sect. 4, we have implemented the CAN rules described in this paper and will continue to experiment with the above scenario and various other examples.

This paper accounts for the life-cycle of each goal. We have not sought to address overall agent deliberation, plan deliberation, resource management, or plan scheduling. Thus far we have examined the same questions as Braubach et al. [3]; future work is to address the other questions they pose. Likewise, we have not considered failure handling and exceptions. Our work is complementary to works that consider generic or application-specific reasoning about goal interactions, such as [30,23], works that consider goal generation, such [5], and works that consider goal and plan selection, such as [9,14].

References

1. Bordini, R.H., Hübner, J.F.: Semantics for the Jason Variant of AgentSpeak (Plan Failure and some Internal Actions). In: Proceedings of the European Conference on Artificial Intelligence, Lisbon, Portugal, pp. 635–640 (August 2010)
2. Braubach, L., Pokahr, A.: Representing Long-Term and Interest BDI Goals. In: Braubach, L., Briot, J.-P., Thangarajah, J. (eds.) ProMAS 2009. LNCS, vol. 5919, pp. 201–218. Springer, Heidelberg (2010)
3. Braubach, L., Pokahr, A., Moldt, D., Lamersdorf, W.: Goal Representation for BDI Agent Systems. In: Bordini, R.H., Dastani, M.M., Dix, J., El Fallah Seghrouchni, A. (eds.) PROMAS 2004. LNCS (LNAI), vol. 3346, pp. 44–65. Springer, Heidelberg (2005)
4. Busetta, P., Rönnquist, R., Hodgson, A., Lucas, A.: JACK Intelligent Agents — Components for Intelligent Agents in Java. AgentLink News (2), 2–5 (1999)
5. da Costa Pereira, C., Tettamanzi, A.: Belief-Goal Relationships in Possibilistic Goal Generation. In: Proceedings of the European Conference on Artificial Intelligence, Lisbon, Portugal, pp. 641–646 (August 2010)
6. Dastani, M., van Riemsdijk, M.B., Meyer, J.J.C.: Goal Types in Agent Programming. In: Proceedings of the Fifth International Conference on Autonomous Agents and Mult-Agent Systems, Hakodate, Japan, pp. 1285–1287 (May 2006)
7. Dastani, M., van Riemsdijk, M.B., Meyer, J.J.C.: Goal Types in Agent Programming. In: Proceedings of the European Conference on Artificial Intelligence, Riva del Garda, Italy, pp. 220–224 (July 2006)

8. Duff, S., Harland, J., Thangarajah, J.: On Proactivity and Maintenance Goals. In: Proceedings of the Fifth International Conference on Autonomous Agents and Mult-Agent Systems, Hakodate, Japan, pp. 1033–1040 (May 2006)
9. Hindriks, K.V., van der Hoek, W., van Riemsdij, M.B.: Agent Programming with Temporally Extended Goals. In: Proceedings of the Eighth International Conference on Autonomous Agents and Mult-Agent Systems, Budapest, pp. 137–144 (May 2009)
10. Hindriks, K.V., van Riemsdijk, M.B.: Using Temporal Logic to Integrate Goals and Qualitative Preferences into Agent Programming. In: Baldoni, M., Son, T.C., van Riemsdijk, M.B., Winikoff, M. (eds.) DALT 2008. LNCS (LNAI), vol. 5397, pp. 215–232. Springer, Heidelberg (2009)
11. Hübner, J.F., Bordini, R.H., Wooldridge, M.: Programming declarative goals using plan patterns. In: Baldoni, M., Endriss, U. (eds.) DALT 2006. LNCS (LNAI), vol. 4327, pp. 123–140. Springer, Heidelberg (2006)
12. Khan, S.M., Lespérance, Y.: A Logical Framework for Prioritized Goal Change. In: Proceedings of the Ninth International Conference on Autonomous Agents and Mult-Agent Systems, Toronto, Canada, pp. 283–290 (May 2010)
13. van Lamsweerde, A.: Goal-oriented Requirements Engineering: A Guided Tour. In: Proceedings of the International Conferece on Requirements Engineering, Toronto, pp. 249–263 (August 2001)
14. Lorini, E., van Ditmarsch, H.P., Lima, T.D.: A Logical Model of Intention and Plan Dynamics. In: Proceedings of the European Conference on Artificial Intelligence, Lisbon, Portugal, pp. 1075–1076 (August 2010)
15. Morandini, M., Penserini, L., Perini, A.: Operational Semantics of Goal Models in Adaptive Agents. In: Proceedings of the Eighth International Conference on Autonomous Agents and Mult-Agent Systems, Budapest, pp. 129–136 (May 2009)
16. Pokahr, A., Braubach, L., Lamersdorf, W.: Jadex: A BDI Reasoning Engine. In: Bordini, R., Dastani, M., Dix, J., Seghrouchni, A.E.F. (eds.) Multi-Agent Programming, pp. 149–174. Springer, Heidelberg (September 2005)
17. Rao, A.S., Georgeff, M.P.: An Abstract Architecture for Rational Agents. In: Rich, C., Swartout, W., Nebel, B. (eds.) Proceedings of Third International Conference on Principles of Knowledge Representation and Reasoning, pp. 439–449. Morgan Kaufmann Publishers, San Francisco (1992)
18. van Riemsdijk, M.B., Dastani, M., Meyer, J.J.C.: Semantics of Declarative Goals in Agent Programming. In: Proceedings of the Fourth International Conference on Autonomous Agents and Mult-Agent Systems, Utrecht, The Netherlands, pp. 133–140 (July 2005)
19. van Riemsdijk, M.B., Dastani, M., Meyer, J.J.C.: Goals in Conflict: Semantic Foundations of Goals in Agent Programming. J. Autonomous Agents and Multi-Agent Systems 18(3), 471–500 (2009)
20. van Riemsdijk, M.B., Dastani, M., Winikoff, M.: Goals in Agent Systems: A Unifying Framework. In: Proceedings of the Seventh International Conference on Autonomous Agents and Mult-Agent Systems, Estoril, Portugal, pp. 713–720 (May 2008)
21. Sardiña, S., Padgham, L.: Goals in the Context of BDI Plan Failure and Planning. In: Proceedings of the Sixth International Conference on Autonomous Agents and Mult-Agent Systems, Hawai'i, USA, pp. 16–23 (May 2007)
22. Sardiña, S., de Silva, L., Padgham, L.: Hierarchical Planning in BDI Agent Programming Languages: A Formal Approach. In: Proceedings of the Fifth International Conference on Autonomous Agents and Mult-Agent Systems, Hakodate, Japan, pp. 1001–1008 (May 2006)
23. Shaw, P.H., Farwer, B., Bordini, R.H.: Theoretical and Experimental Results on the Goal-Plan Tree Problem. In: Proceedings of the Seventh International Conference on Autonomous Agents and Mult-Agent Systems, Estoril, Portugal, pp. 1379–1382 (May 2008)

24. de Silva, L., Sardina, S., Padgham, L.: First Principles Planning in BDI Systems. In: Proceedings of the Eighth International Conference on Autonomous Agents and Mult-Agent Systems, Budapest, pp. 1105–1112 (May 2009)
25. Thangarajah, J., Harland, J., Morley, D., Yorke-Smith, N.: On the Life-Cycle of BDI Agent Goals. In: Proceedings of the European Conference on Artificial Intelligence, Lisbon, Portugal, pp. 1031–1032 (August 2010)
26. Thangarajah, J., Harland, J., Morley, D., Yorke-Smith, N.: Operational Behaviour for Executing, Suspending and Aborting Goals in BDI Agent Systems. In: Omicini, A., Sardina, S., Vasconcelos, W. (eds.) DALT 2010. LNCS (LNAI), vol. 6619, pp. 1–21. Springer, Heidelberg (2011)
27. Thangarajah, J., Harland, J., Morley, D., Yorke-Smith, N.: Aborting Tasks in BDI Agents. In: Proceedings of the Sixth International Conference on Autonomous Agents and Mult-Agent Systems, Hawai'i, USA, pp. 8–15 (May 2007)
28. Thangarajah, J., Harland, J., Morley, D., Yorke-Smith, N.: Suspending and Resuming Tasks in BDI Agents. In: Proceedings of the Seventh International Conference on Autonomous Agents and Mult-Agent Systems, Estoril, Portugal, pp. 405–412 (May 2008)
29. Thangarajah, J., Padgham, L., Winikoff, M.: Detecting and Avoiding Interference between Goals in Intelligent Agents. In: Proceedings of the International Joint Conference on Artificial Intelligence, Acapulco, Mexico, pp. 721–726 (2003)
30. Thangarajah, J., Padgham, L., Winikoff, M.: Detecting and Exploiting Positive Goal Interaction in Intelligent Agents. In: Proc. of AAMAS 2003, Melbourne, Australia, pp. 401–408 (July 2003)
31. Winikoff, M., Dastani, M., van Riemsdijk, M.B.: A Unfied interaction-aware goal framework. In: Proceedings of the European Conference on Artificial Intelligence, pp. 1033–1034 (2010)
32. Winikoff, M., Padgham, L., Harland, J., Thangarajah, J.: Declarative and Procedural Goals in Intelligent Agent Systems. In: Proceedings of the International Conference on Knowledge Representation and Reasoning, Toulouse, France, pp. 470–481 (April 2002)

BDI Agents with Objectives and Preferences

Aniruddha Dasgupta and Aditya K. Ghose

Decision Systems Lab
School of Computer Science and Software Engineering
University of Wollongong,
Wollongong, NSW 2522, Australia
{ad844,aditya}@uow.edu.au

Abstract. For many applications there is the need to handle user preferences and customize agents according to the user's specific needs. It is convenient to let the user provide elaborate specification consisting of constraints, preferences and objectives. Then, let the agent system make decisions about its actions by taking into account changes in the surrounding environment as well as the user preferences that come in real-time. In this paper we describe an agent programming language where we incorporate constraints, objectives and preferences into the BDI framework. Our work especially focuses on the use of soft constraints in an agent environment where we give a quantitative dimension to this agent deliberation process by apply c-semiring based techniques to determine the preferred solution.

1 Introduction

In the *multi-agent systems* (MAS) community, software agents are conceived as autonomous computational entities situated in some environments which they can sense and act upon in a dynamic (reactive and/or proactive) way according to the environment's changes and their design objectives [25]. Each agent is given the mandate to achieve defined goals. To do this, it autonomously selects appropriate actions, depending on the prevailing conditions in the environment, based on its own capabilities and means until it succeeds, fails, needs decisions or new instructions or is stopped by its owner. Thus decision agents can be designed to provide interactive decision aids for end-users by eliciting their preferences and then recommending matching products.

BDI [18] agent-oriented systems are flexible and responsive to the environment, and well suited for complex applications with real-time reasoning and control requirements [20]. However, not much work has been done regarding the practical implementation of BDI languages that incorporate user preferences into the BDI framework.

In this paper, we develop a traditional BDI-style agent programming language that has built-in decision making strategies based on user preferences. These preferences could be modeled as either hard constraints (constraints that

A. Omicini, S. Sardina, and W. Vasconcelos (Eds.): DALT 2010, LNAI 6619, pp. 22–39, 2011.

must be satisfied with explicit objectives like maximise or minimize *cost*) or soft constraints (constraints that the user would *like* to satisfy). We call this language BAOP (BDI Agent with Objectives and Preferences). Our work focuses on practical means-ends reasoning which deals with what actions to perform and how to perform the actions. We implement BAOP by extending CASO [7] and incorporating a mechanism by which user preferences can be added into the system.

The contributions of this paper are fivefold. Firstly, a BDI language framework is developed where user preferences can be handled by the system. Secondly, techniques are described whereby a particular behavior can be selected according to the preferences. Thirdly, the language framework is modified whereby we parameterize basic actions. Fourthly, formal semantics of the language is described and fifthly, we describe a method by which preferences and objectives can be integrated.

The remainder of this article is organized as follows. Section 2 gives a brief background on related work on BDI languages and constraints, section 3 describes the syntax of the language section 4 gives an overview of its operational semantics. Experimental results and concluding remarks are provided in the last sections.

2 Background

2.1 BDI Languages

One of the most popular and successful framework for Agent technology is that of Rao and Georgeff [18], in which the notions of *Belief*, *Desire* and *Intention* are central, and hence are often referred to as BDI agents. Beliefs represent the agent's current knowledge about the world, including information about the current state of the environment inferred from perception devices and messages from other agents, as well as internal information. Desires represent a state which the agent is trying to achieve. Intentions are the chosen means to achieve the agent's desires, and are generally implemented as plans and post-conditions. As in general an agent may have multiple desires, an agent can have a number of intentions active at any one time. These intentions may be thought of as running concurrently, with one chosen intention active at any one time.

AgentSpeak(L) [17] is one of the most influential abstract languages based on the BDI architecture. It is an agent framework/language with explicit representations of beliefs and intentions for agents. AgentSpeak(L) is a programming language based on a restricted first-order language with events and actions. Due to its simplicity and elegance, AgentSpeak(L) can be easily extended. There have been several languages based on AgentSpeak(L) and Jason [3] is one of its well-know interpreters.

There are a number of other agent programming languages in the BDI tradition, such as 3APL [10], JACK [5], CASL, [22], Dribble [23] and CAN [24].

2.2   Hard and Soft Constraints

Hard constraints are those which we definitely want to be true. These might relate to the successful assembly of a mechanism. Soft constraint are those we would like to be true - but not at the expense of the others. These might say that a mechanism must follow a given path. There is not point in trying to match every point exactly if this can only be done by breaking the assembly of the links.

Soft constraints model quantitative preferences by generalizing the traditional formalism of hard constraints. In a soft constraint, each assignment to the variables of a constraint is annotated with a level of its desirability, and the desirability of a complete assignment is computed by a combination operator applied to the local preference values. By choosing a specific combination operator and an ordered set of levels of desirability, a specific class of soft constraints can be selected.

A soft constraint may be seen as a constraint where each instantiation of its variables has an associated value from a partially ordered set which can be interpreted as a set of preference values. Combining constraints will then have to take into account such additional values, and thus the formalism has also to provide suitable operations for *combination* (x) and *comparison* (+) of tuples of values and constraints. Semiring-based constraint satisfaction proposed by Bistarelli et.al [2] is a meta-approach for modelling problems with preferences. This framework uses a semiring structure, where the set of semiring specifies the preference associated to each tuple of values. The two semiring operations (+ and x) then model constraint projection and combination respectively.

In semiring-based constraint satisfaction, each tuple in the constraint is marked by a preference level expressing how good the tuple satisfies the constraint. The preference level is taken from a set A equipped with the c-semiring structure $(A,+,x,0,1)$. A is a set of preferences, + is a commutative, associative, idempotent $(a+a=a)$ binary operation on A with the unit element 0 $(0+a=a)$ and the absorbing element 1 $(1+a=1)$, x is a commutative, associative binary operation on A with the unit element 1 $(1xa=a)$ and the absorbing element 0 $(0xa=0)$ and x distributes over +.

The multiplication operation x is used to combine constraints. Let $vars(c)$ be a set of variables over which the constraint c is defined, δc be a mapping of all tuples over $vars(c)$ to A, i.e., $\delta c(V)$ is a preference of the tuple V in the constraint c, and let $U \downarrow Y$ be a projection of some tuple U to variables Y. Then we can describe a preference of some tuple V by combining preferences of this tuple (its projection) in all the constraints C:

$$p(V) = x_{c \in C} \delta c(V \downarrow vars(c))$$

To compare the preferences of tuples we need some ordering on A. This ordering can be defined using the additive operation + in the following way: $a \leq b \iff a + b = b$. If $a \leq b$ then we say that b is better than a. Note that the relation $\leq$ defines a partial ordering on A opposite to the total ordering used in the valued constraint satisfaction.

The *semiring-based constraint satisfaction problem* is defined formally by the c-semiring structure (A,+,x,0,1), the set of variables X, their domains D, and the set of constraints C described via δc. The task is to find an assignment V with the best preference $p(V)$.

2.3 Using Constraints in BDI Languages

Incorporating constraints into BDI languages can be be of great advantage to agent decision making. Some of the advantages of using constraints are:

- Constraints can capture qualitative and quantitative preferences and costs.
- Constraints offer a declarative representation that is easy to understand.
- Constraints are supported by a large set of algorithms, solvers, and tools.

In our earlier work in [6] and [7], we have shown that the concept of using constraints and explicit objectives in a high-level agent specification language like AgentSpeak(L) yields significant advantages in terms of both expressivity and efficiency. This technique applies constraint and objective directed solving on the context section of a BDI agent's plan specification in order to determine an application plan to fire. The new language is called CASO (Constraint AgentSpeak(L) with objectives). We have also defined efficient plan and intention selection techniques with the notion of parametric look-ahead. An implementation of CASO is also described in [7], which provides the user with the flexibility of adding explicit objectives and constraints to achieve final goals. CASO uses a modified version of the Jason interpreter, together with another open-source constraint solver ECLiPSe [1], thereby combining reactive agent programming with constraint solving techniques.

3 BAOP: A Reactive BDI Language

In this section we give an overview of our BDI based language BAOP and describe its syntax. BAOP is a programming language based on AgentSpeak and is implemented using Jason.

Informally, an agent program in BAOP consists of a set of beliefs β which includes a set of constraints, a set of objective functions Θ, a set of user preferences μ, a set of events E, a plan library P, a set of intentions I, an objective store OS and a preference store PS. There are three selection functions S_E, S_P, S_I to select an event, a plan and an intention respectively. There is also a look-ahead parameter n which determines how many steps the agent is going to look ahead before committing to a plan or intention.

Let us now explain each of terms mentioned in the above informal definition,

3.1 Belief Base (β)

β is a Constraint Logic Program(CLP)[13] and not a just a set of simple facts. As we will see later, such an approach which combines the flexibility of logic with the power of search to provide high-level constructs for solving computationally hard problems can help an agent to choose a plan or intention intelligently.

3.2   Set of Plans (P)

P is a repository which contains all the available pre-compiled plans for the agent to use. When a triggering event occurs, all the plans triggered by this event that can be executed in the current circumstances are retrieved. Below we define a BAOP plan.

Definition 1. *A BAOP plan p is of the form $t[\varepsilon]:b_1 \wedge b_2 \wedge \cdots \wedge b_n \wedge c_1 \wedge c_2 \wedge \cdots \wedge c_m \leftarrow sg_1, sg_2, \cdots, sg_k$ where t is the trigger; ε refers to the effect of the plan; each b_i refers to a belief; each c_i is an atomic constraint; each sg is either an atomic action or a subgoal.*

It should be noted that in the definition of the plan above, an *action* could have *parameters* whose values are instantiated when the agent actually executes the plan. Also, since CLP assumes Horn Clause, the *effets* can be Horn Clauses only as we use the effets together with β as we will see later.

3.3   Set of Objective Functions (Θ)

Θ represent objective functions like *maximize(exp)* or *minimize(exp)* where *exp* consists of global variables that are valid throughout the lifetime of the agent. Objectives represent quantitative measure of goals that the agent would like to achieve.

3.4   Set of User Preferences (μ)

μ is the set of preferences that the agent would like to achieve. Along with objectives, this is yet another natural way of representing softgoals. The preference is given using semiring values and is of the form $< \varepsilon, v_1 >$ which depicts a preference value v_1 for pursuing the plan. ε denotes the cumulative effect of plan (or plans).

3.5   Set of Events (E)

E is the set of events which could be external or internal. Agents talk to the external environment through events. The different types of external events which originate from perception of the agent's environment:

1. Addition and deletion of beliefs (with constraints).
2. Addition and deletion of achievement goals.
3. Addition and deletion of test goals.
4. Addition and deletion of objectives.
5. Addition and deletion of user preferences.

The first three types of events are triggering events (where the context of the plan is matched with relevant plans), while the last two are non-triggering.

Internal events are generated from the agent's own execution of a plan (i.e., as a subgoal in a plan generates an event of the type addition of an achievement goal). An internal event is accompanied with the intention which generated it (as the plan chosen for that event will be pushed on top of that intention).

3.6   Set of Intentions (I)

Intentions are particular courses of actions to which an agent has committed in order to handle certain events. I consists of a set of intentions where each intention is a stack of partially instantiated plans.

3.7   Objective Store(OS))

OS a consistent set of objective functions and is updated in case a new objective comes in as an event. Below we give the formal definition of what it means by augmenting the OS.

Definition 2. *Given an objective store OS and a new objective f, the result of augmenting OS with f, denoted by OS_f^*, is defined as $\gamma(MaxCons(OS \cup f))$ where γ is a choice function and $MaxCons(X)$ is the set of all $x \subseteq X$ such that x is consistent and there exists no x' such that $x \subset x' \subseteq X$ and x' is consistent.*

The new OS is now given by $\gamma(MaxCons(OS \cup \overline{O}) \cap OS)$ where γ is the choice function, and $\overline{O}$ is the negation of the objective O.

   Formally a *consistent objective store* is defined as below.

Definition 3. *Objectives O_1 and O_2 are inconsistent if and only if there exists a pair of solutions S_1 and S_2 such that S_1 is preferred over S_2 by O_1 and the reverse holds under O_2.*

3.8   Preference Store (PS)

PS a consistent set of user preferences and is updated in case a new preference comes in as an event. A PS is inconsistent if there exists at least two tuples whose conditions are logically equivalent but whose associated semiring values are different. The machinery we provide ensures such inconsistencies do not occur. The consistency of user preferences in the preference store is maintained by the following logic:

   When a new preference comes, it is compared to the set of preferences that are currently in the preference store. If the new user preference tuple is $< \varepsilon, v_1 >$ and if PS contains a tuple with ε_1' which is logically equivalent to ε_1 then replace the value of ε_1' with v_1 else insert the new tuple in PS.

3.9   Event Selection Function (S_E)

S_E selects an event and updates OS and μ in case it is an objective function and user preference respectively and in case it is a triggering event it passes it on to the interpreter which would unify it with the set of triggering events in the heads of plans.

3.10 Option Selection Function (S_O)

S_O selects a plan from P based on the current plan context, β, OS, PS and n. In order to understand the mechanism for selecting the best plan let us consider an example.

Let us consider we have two applicable plans - P1 and P2. In order to determine which plan to choose the agent generates the goal-plan tree for all possible paths. The parameter n creates the pseudo leafs and therefore we get distinct paths from root to these pseudo leafs. Figure 1 shows all the possible paths from root to pseudo leafs for the set of plans P1 to P10. The value of n is 2 which means the goal-plan tree is expanded up to 2 levels.

Multiple Effect Scenarios

Let us now consider any given path (say Path 1) in our earlier example. We follow [12] to discuss the issue of *multiple effect scenarios* in this context. The cummulative effect of this path is not merely a conjunction of the effects of Plan1, Plan3 and Plan5. The effects of each plan are accumulated into cumulative effect annotations in a context-sensitive manner, such that the cumulative effect annotations associated with any plan would describe the effects achieved by the execution of plans were it to execute up to that point. Since we are trying to find out what would be the final effect if we took Path 1 we use multiple effect scenarios as we cannot find the result deterministically. An *effect scenario* at a given point in a path is one consistent set of cumulative effects of a process if it were to execute up to that point. This is because we may arrive at a given point through multiple paths which cannot be predicted at design time and also activities in a path might *undo* the effects of activities earlier in the path.

Let $< P_i, P_j >$ be an ordered pair of plans connected via a sequence flow such that P_i precedes P_j , let ε_i be an effect scenario associated with ε_i and ε_j be the immediate effect annotation associated with P_j . Let $\varepsilon_i = c_{i1}, c_{i2}, \cdots, c_{im}$ and $e_j = c_{j1}, c_{j2}, \cdots, c_{jn}$. If $\varepsilon_i \bigcup \varepsilon_j$ is consistent, then the resulting cumulative effect, denoted by $acc(\varepsilon_i, \varepsilon_j)$, is $\varepsilon_i \bigcup \varepsilon_j$. Else, we define $\varepsilon_i' \subseteq \varepsilon_i$ such that $\varepsilon_i' \bigcup \varepsilon_i$ is consistent and there exists no ε_i'' such that $\varepsilon_i' \subset \varepsilon_i'' \subseteq \varepsilon_i$ and $\varepsilon_i'' \bigcup \varepsilon_j$ is consistent. We define $acc(\varepsilon_i, \varepsilon_j) = \varepsilon_i' \bigcup \varepsilon_j$. We note that $acc(\varepsilon_i, \varepsilon_j)$ is non-unique as there are multiple alternative sets that satisfy the requirements for ε_i. Thus the cumulative effect of the two plans consists of the effects of the second plan plus as many of the effects of the first plan as can be consistently included. We remove those clauses in the effect annotation of the first plan that contradict the effects of the second plan. The remaining clauses are undone, i.e., these effects are overridden by the second plan.

Now each of these effects may have semiring value associated with them and hence we have get the semiring value for the cumulative effects. If PS contains $(< \varepsilon_p, v_p >, < \varepsilon_q, v_q >)$ then the semiring value of $acc(\varepsilon_p, \varepsilon_q)$ would be $v_p \bigotimes v_q$ where $\bigotimes$ is the semiring combination operator. Since we have multiple effect scenarios, the user would have the option to select a particular scenario which can be pessimistic or optimistic. Thus from each of the paths, a particular effect scenario is chosen and we get a semiring value for the cumulative effect at each pseudo leaf.

Plan1: $+!t[\varepsilon_1] : BContext_1 \cup CContext_1 \leftarrow SG_1; SG_2.$
Plan2: $+!t[\varepsilon_2] : BContext_2 \cup CContext_2 \leftarrow SG_3; SG_4.$
Plan3: $+!SG_1[\varepsilon_3] : BContext_3 \cup CContext_3 \leftarrow a_1.$
Plan4: $+!SG_1[\varepsilon_4] : BContext_4 \cup CContext_4 \leftarrow a_2.$
Plan5: $+!SG_2[\varepsilon_5] : BContext_5 \cup CContext_5 \leftarrow a_3.$
Plan6: $+!SG_2[\varepsilon_6] : BContext_6 \cup CContext_6 \leftarrow a_4.$
Plan7: $+!SG_3[\varepsilon_7] : BContext_7 \cup CContext_7 \leftarrow a_5.$
Plan8: $+!SG_3[\varepsilon_8] : BContext_8 \cup CContext_8 \leftarrow a_6.$
Plan9: $+!SG_4[\varepsilon_9] : BContext_9 \cup CContext_9 \leftarrow a_7.$
Plan10: $+!SG_4[\varepsilon_10] : BContext_{10} \cup CContext_{10} \leftarrow a_8.$

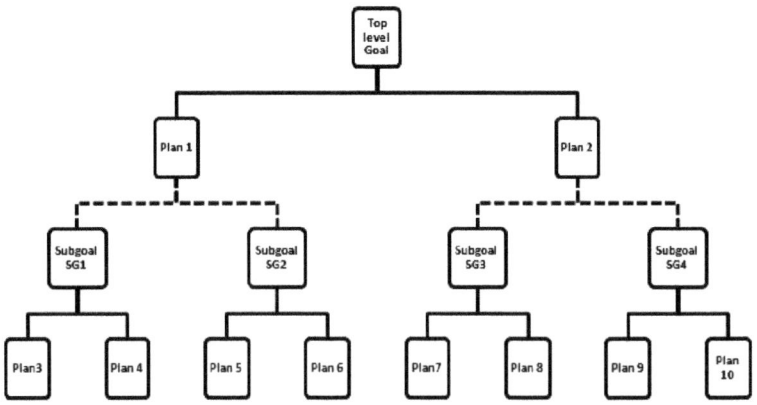

Broken line (- - -) refers to AND nodes and Solid line (——) refers to OR nodes.
$BContext_i$ is the conjunction of non-constraint predicates in the context of Plan$i$;
$CContext_i$ is the conjunction of constraint predicates in the context of pPan$i$;
SG_i is subgoal for Plan$i$;
a_i is an atomic action for Plan$i$;
ε_i is the effect of Plan$i$;

Path id	Possible Path
1	Plan1-Plan3-Plan5
2	Plan1-Plan4-Plan5
3	Plan1-Plan3-Plan6
4	Plan1-Plan4-Plan6
5	Plan2-Plan7-Plan9
6	Plan2-Plan8-Plan9
7	Plan2-Plan7-Plan10
8	Plan2-Plan8-Plan10

Fig. 1. Agent Plans and corresponding goal-plan tree

The next item to consider is the OS where we have the set of consistent objective functions that the agent wants to pursue. At each pseudo leaf of the goal plan tree we have

- β and context of all plans in the path.
- Semiring value for the effect scenarios.
- Objective function O.

There are several choices now. First, the CLP uses constraint satisfaction and optimization problem (CSOP) techniques to find the value of the objective function O for each pseudo leaf. CSOPs are mathematical problems where one must find states or objects that satisfy a number of constraints or criteria and also satisfy an objective function. Second, the semiring value v of cumulative effect could be considered for each of these leafs. The leaf to be considered would be the one which has both these values as the highest. It is a policy that the user can decide beforehand to give priority to either the objective or the semiring value as these values are nothing but natural means of representing softgoals that the agent would like to achieve. Next we choose the path which has the maximum value at the pseudo leaf based on the strategy chosen.

3.11   Intention Selection Function (S_I)

S_I function selects one of the agent's intentions, i.e., one of the independent stacks of partially instantiated plans within the set of intentions by applying techniques similar to that of S_O. Each intention stack is a choice for the agent. In order to determine right intention, the agent first considers the top element (i.e., a partially instantiated plan) of every intention stack. Each of these intentions for a goal plan tree and here also we solve the CSOP which consists of β, OS, PS and n. Like before, we have several choices and we can apply different strategy to choose a particular intention. However, one of the most notable difference with S_O is that we *instantiate the action parameters* (if any) with values obtained from solving the CSOP.

4   Differences with AgentSpeak(L)

Most of the syntax and semantics of BAOP are similar to that of AgentSpeak(L) and its interpreter Jason. However, the most notable additions are:

1. A constraint directed technique is incorporated into the computation strategy employed during the interpretation process.
2. Plan context consists of conjunction of predicates some of which could be constraint predicates (unlike Agentspeak(L)) which could be dealt with CLP machinery using specialized constraint solvers.
3. A look-ahead technique is now built into the system that helps the user to determine which particular plan or intention to select by setting the value of a look-ahead parameter.

4. An external event can be a triggering event as well as an addition or sub-traction of an *objective function* or a *user preference*.
5. Two new data structures are added - an *objective store* and a *preference store* to store the set of global objectives and preferences respectively.
6. Plans are now annotated with effects. Jason provides annotation facility where meta information of various kinds could be specified. We use this facility to specify effects of plans.
7. Unlike AgentSpeak(L), applicable plans are those relevant plans for which
   - there exists a substitution which, when composed with the relevant unifier and applied to the context, is a logical consequence of β *and*
   - the constraint predicates in the context of the plans are unified with β and dealt with the CLP machinery using specialized constraint solvers to determine if these are consistent.
8. The set of basic *actions* that the agent has to perform as part of an intention execution process may also contain parameters, the values of which may be set by the value of the constraint variables obtained from solving of a CSOP relevant to a given applicable plan. These values are instantiated during intention execution.

Items 1 to 3 and parts of items 4 and 5 above have been developed in CASO. In BAOP we extend CASO to incorporate the rest of the items.

5 BAOP Interpreter

The BAOP interpreter is depicted in Figure 2 which greatly facilitates the under-standing of the interpreter. It is very similar to the AgentSpeak(L) interpreter with the differences being mainly in handling of the seletion functions. The in-terpreter manages a set of events, a preference store, an objective store and a set of intentions with three selection functions which are described below. In the figure, sets (of beliefs, events, plans, preference store, objective store and intentions) are represented as rectangles, diamonds represent selection (of one element from a set) and circles represent some of the processing involved in the interpretation of BAOP programs. A CLP solver is plugged into the system which is responsible for generating the applicable plans as well as for the option and intention selection functions.

6 Representing Beliefs and Plans

Let us take a simple example where I have to buy orange juice and milk for tomorrow. I need to buy at least 4 lt. of milk(M) and 2 lt. of orange juice(OJ). Let the amount of money(A) I have is $50. The cost of milk is $2/lt. and orange juice is $4/lt. I cannot buy more than 10 lt. in total as there is no space in the fridge. How much of each should I buy and what should be the total cost(C) if I want to have the maximum amount of money left on me? The problem can

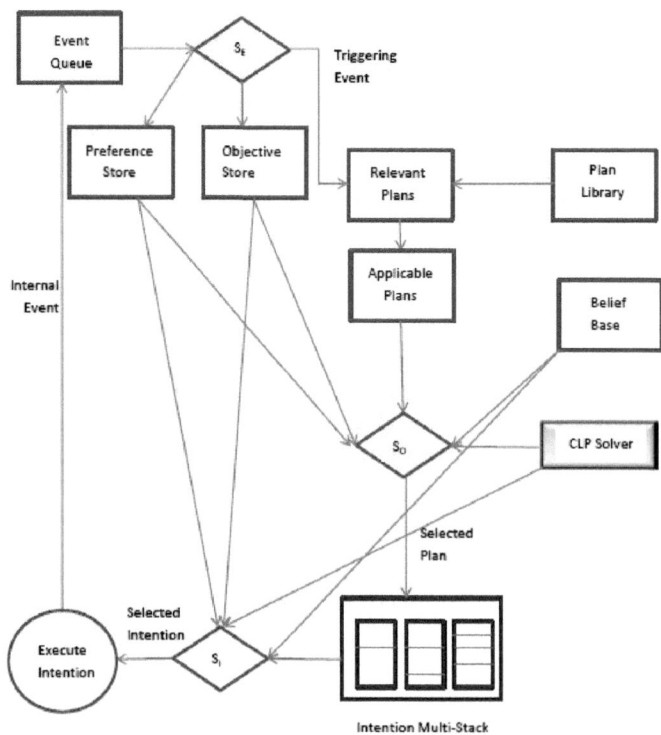

Fig. 2. BAOP execution cycle

easily be solved using constraint logic programming techniques. This problem can be formulated as follows:

```
A=50; y >= 2; x >= 4; x + y <= 10;
M>=4;  OJ>=2;  M + OJ <=10; C = 2*M-4*OJ;
maximize(A-C);
```

The above CSOP is fairly trivial and the result is M=4, OJ=2 and C=16. Hence the money left after buying these items is $34.

In the agent context, the above could be a belief base denoted by *moneyAvailable()*. Let us consider that I want to go either to a concert or go to a movie. Which one to choose may depend on a number of factors: the amount of money I have to buy ticket, the availability of the seats of my choice etc. As an example, for a concert I may want to choose front seats but for a movie I may want to choose back seats at the theater. In any case, if I want to go, I have to first book tickets over the phone. Also, let us assume that I have to buy milk and orange juice. All the above can be described using BAOP plans which would in turn have a series of subplans and basic actions. As an example, some of the plans (denoted by P1, P2 and P3) related to the concert or movie booking could be written as follows where *A* refers to the concert or movie and *V* refers to the venue:

```
***** Booking tickets related plans *****

P1::+concert (A,V) [BookedConcertTickets(V)] :
    likes(A) & moneyAvailable()>20 <- !book_tickets(A,V).

P2::+movie (A,V) [BookedMovieTickets(V)] :
    likes(A) & moneyAvailable()>30 <- !book_tickets(A,V)

P3::+!book_tickets(A, V)[called(V) & SeatsChosen(A,V)] :
    -busy(phone) <- call(V); !choose_seats(A,V).
...


***** Buying milk and orange juice related plans *****

P10::+!buy_MilkandJuice()[boughtMilkandJuice] :
    true <- get_milk(actionParam M); get_juice(actionParam OJ);
            pay_amount(actionParam C).
```

Note that *concert (A, V)* and *book_tickets(A, V)* are the triggering events; *likes(A)*, and *-busy(phone)* are contexts; *!book_tickets(A, V)* and *!choose_seats (A, V)* are subgoals; *call(V)* is a basic action and *BookedMovieTickets(V)*, *BookedConcertTickets*, *called(V)* and *shallChooseSeats(A, V)* are the various effects for plans related to booking tickets. *M*, *OJ* and *C* refer to the *action parameters* which we shall discuss shortly. The constraints are denoted by *moneyAvailable()>* 20 and *moneyAvailable()>* 30 which are part of the context.

The example above basically says that if I have more than \$20 on me and there is a movie playing at a venue and I like the movie then I will book the tickets over the phone and choose seats. Similarly for concert tickets I have to have \$30 on me and rest of the terms and conditions remain the same. It must be mentioned here that plans P1 and P2 are very similar - one refers to the process of booking concert tickets and the other one movie tickets. In normal circumstances, I would choose either of the two if all the conditions match - however I may have a preference of going to the concert today rather than to the movie. This preference is something that is not built into the plan but can be supplied by the user at any point in time to help make the decision. This can be done by giving quantitative values to the effects - say $< BookedMovieTickets(V), 0 >$ and $< BookedConcertTickets(V), 1 >$ to imply the fact that I prefer booking concert tickets to booking movie tickets.

For buying milk and orange juice we have plan P10. This plan has *true* in the context which means this will always be executed. Notice the parameters of the actions get_milk(), get_juice() and pay_amount(). The *actionParam M*, *OJ* and *C* simply state that I have to buy M lt. of milk, OJ lt. of orange juice and pay \$C.

7   BAOP: Operational Semantics

The operational semantics of BAOP is defined using Plotkin's Structural Operational Semantics [16]. We use a method similar to that shown in [15] which describes operational semantics of AgentSpeak(L). A BAOP *configuration C* is a tuple $C = \langle \beta, I, E, A, R, Ap, OS, PS, \iota, \epsilon, \rho, \alpha \rangle$ where

- β is a set of beliefs
- I is a set of intentions $\{i, i', \cdots\}$ and i is a stack of partially instantiated plans
- E is a set of events
  $\{(te, i), (oe), (sge), (te', i'), (oe'), (sge') \cdots\}$ where
  (1) *a triggering event pair* is denoted by (te, i) where *te* is the triggering event and the intention i has the plans associated with it;
  (2) *an objective event* is denoted by *oe* which adds or removes element from the objective store;
  (3) *a softgoal event* is denoted by *sge* which is a c-semiring structure with possible states and their corresponding values.
- A is a set of actions
  $\{(a_1, param_{1'}, \cdots), (a_2, param_{2'}, \cdots), \cdots\}$. Each action is a tuple $(a_i, param_{i'}, \cdots)$ where a_i is the basic action and $param_{i'}$, $param_{i''}$ etc. are the action parameters.
- R is a set of relevant plans.
- Ap is a set of applicable plans.
- OS is the objective store
- PS is the preference store
- Each configuration has 4 components denoted by ι, ϵ, ρ and α which keep record of a particular *intention, event,* an *U-preferred* plan (the selected plan with user preference) and a set of *action parameters* associated with actions of an U-preferred plan respectively that are being considered along the execution of a plan.

In order to present the semantic rules for BAOP we adopt the following notations:

- If C is a BAOP configuration, we write C_E to make reference to the component E of C. Similarly for other components of C.
- We write $C_\iota = \_$ (the underline symbol) to indicate that there is no intention being considered in the agent's execution. Similarly for C_ρ, C_ϵ and C_α.
- We write $i[p]$ to denote the intention that has plan p on its top.
- We write *beliefs* to denote the set of current beliefs together with the set of constraints.

The set of semantic rules related to Event, Plan and Intention selections are now given below.

Event Selection: S_E selects events from a set of Events E. The selected event is removed from E and is either assigned to the component ϵ of the configuration in case it is a triggering event or is added or removed to/from OS/PS if it is a objective/preference. The selected event is removed from E and is assigned to the ϵ component of the configuration. Below we give the three semantic rules governing this function.

$$SelEv_1 \quad \frac{S_E(C_E)=(te,i)}{C,beliefs\rightarrow C',beliefs} \quad C_\epsilon = \_, C_{AP} = C_R = \{\}$$
$$\text{where:} \quad C'_E = C_E - (te,i) \quad \text{and} \quad C'_\epsilon = (te,i)$$

$$SelEv_2 \quad \frac{S_E(C_E)=oe}{C,beliefs\rightarrow C',beliefs} \quad C_\epsilon = \_, C_{AP} = C_R = \{\}$$
$$\text{where:} \quad C'_E = C_E - oe, \quad C'_{OS} = C_{OS} + oe \quad \text{and} \quad C'_\epsilon = oe$$

$$SelEv_3 \quad \frac{S_E(C_E)=sge}{C,beliefs\rightarrow C',beliefs} \quad C_\epsilon = \_, C_{AP} = C_R = \{\}$$
$$\text{where:} \quad C'_E = C_E - sge, \quad C'_{PS} = C_{PS} + oe \quad \text{and} \quad C'_\epsilon = sge$$

Option Selection: S_O selects an U-preferred plan (p) from the set of applicable plans Ap. The plan selected is then assigned to the ρ of the configuration and the set of applicable plans is discarded. We also assume that there is a selection function S_{OS} which selects a consistent objective store (ConsOS) where the maximal set of objectives that are consistent are kept and the rest are discarded. The action parameters associated with the U-preferred plan are initialized by solving the relevant CSOP in case there are hard constraints and objectives.

$$SelOpr \quad \frac{S_O(C_{Ap})=p \quad S_{OS}(C_{OS})=ConsOS}{C,beliefs\rightarrow C',beliefs}, C_\alpha = \_, C_\epsilon \neq \_, C_{Ap} = \{\}$$
$$\text{where:} \quad C'_\rho = p, \quad C'_{OS} = ConsOS, \quad C'_\alpha \neq \{\} \quad \text{and} \quad C'_{Ap} = \{\}$$

Creating Intentions: Rule TrigEv says that if the event ϵ is external triggering event indicated by T in the intention associated to ϵ, a new intention is created and its single plan is the plan p annotated in the ρ component. If the event is internal, rule IntEv says that the plan in ρ should be put on top of the intention associated with the event. Either way, both the event and the plan can be discarded from the ϵ and ι components respectively.

$$TrigEv \quad \frac{}{C,beliefs\rightarrow C',beliefs} \quad C_\epsilon = (te,T), C_\rho = p$$
$$\text{where:} \quad C'_I = C_I \bigcup\{[p]\}, \quad C'_\epsilon = \_, \quad C'_\rho = \_$$
$$IntEv \quad \frac{}{C,beliefs\rightarrow C',beliefs} \quad C_\epsilon = (te,T), C_\rho = p$$
$$\text{where:} \quad C'_I = C_I \bigcup\{i[p]\}, \quad C'_\epsilon = \_, \quad C'_\rho = \_$$

Intention Selection: S_I selects an intention for processing.

$$SelInt \quad \frac{S_I(C_I)=i}{C,beliefs\rightarrow C',beliefs} \quad C_i = \_$$
$$\text{where:} \quad C'_i = i$$

8   Experiment and Results

We implemented BAOP by extending CASO and incorporating a mechanism by which user preferences can be added as soft constraints into the system. As mentioned earlier, BAOP has been developed using a modified version of Jason (Java based interpreter) and Eclipse (constraint solver). In order to evaluate our approach, we ran a series of experiments to test out the various scenarios described earlier pertaining to option selection using constraints, objectives and user preferences. The objective of our experiment was to find out if BAOP is capable of handling the different situations and choose the right plan and intention at every interpreter cycle.

We randomly generated several plans having a variety of AND-OR node structure. Each of these plans included, effects and the semiring values (user preferences) were set for each of the effects. We also defined partial order among the various effects The following table depicts the various experimental runs that we conducted on a Pentium Dual Core 2.4GHz CPU with depth of tree kept at 3. If the environment had inconsistencies between user preferences and objectives, the objectives were given higher precedence. Thus at each node both objective and user preferences were evaluated.

Plans	Possible Paths	CSOPs solved	time taken(millisec.)
10	8	8	100
20	15	0	78
30	22	14	134
40	34	20	146
50	40	25	178

The results indicate that the larger the number of CSOPs, the longer it takes to evaluate and get the right plan. If there are user preferences only and no CSOP, the time taken to find the selected plan was the least.

9   Related Work

Many of the other BDI languages have been extended to incorporate constraints and preferences to guide the agent to select the best possible plan.

In [8] a system that allows the user to express all these kinds of constraints and preferences is described by extending GOLOG [14]. The authors address the problem of combining non-Markovian qualitative preferences, expressed in first-order temporal logic, with quantitative decision-theoretic reward functions and hard symbolic constraints in agent programming. In another approach [21], prioritized goals have been integrated with the IndiGolog agent programming language.

In our approach the semiring specifications are richer than their specification of prioritized goals. Also, we combine both qualitative and quantitative constraints.

In [11] an approach has been made to extend GOAL (a language based on propositional logic) with temporal logic for the representation of goals and preferences for additional expressiveness. In this approach hard and soft constraints have been integrated into it as well as as achievement goals, maintenance goals, and temporally extended preferences. Here if an agent has the ability to lookahead a number of steps, it can also use its goals to avoid selecting those actions that prevent the realization of (some of) the agents goals. Effects of basic actions are taken into account which change the mental state of agents. The work is based on the fact that planners could be guided to select preferred plans.

One of the major differences with regards to our work is that the preferences and objectives are dynamic - they work like belief updates when the user his changes mind. Also, unlike other approaches, the hard constraints that we talk about here are objective functions in the current environment and not the agent goals.

In another approach [4], the authors describe a model where preferences and constraints over goals can be specified. They also mention an algorithm PREF-PLAN for solving the resulting constrained optimization problem. PDDL3 [9] is an action-centred language in the planning domain where strong and soft constraints on plan trajectories (possible actions in the plan and intermediate states reached by the plan), as well as strong and soft problem goals has been incorporated.

One of the differences between agent programming and planning is that in planning one compares complete plans against the available constraints, while in agent programming the constraints are into account continuously during execution. In this context, the above frameworks deal mainly with plan uncertainty whereas our approach has been to incorporate similar notions into BDI agent paradigm.

There are a number of frameworks which mix planning and BDI-style execution. Of particular interest is CANPLAN [19] which have built-in capacity for *lookahead*.

In contrast, our *lookahead* mechanism is domain independent and is built into the BDI architecture. Moreover, when to do a lookahead is dependent on the user and in a highly reactive system, full lookahead may not give the best possible outcome.

10   Conclusion

While there has been some work in guiding an agent to select the best plan based on preferences, our approach is different from the ones mentioned earlier. Unlike most other work, we assume that our agent environment is highly reactive in nature and therefore constraints, preferences and objectives could change at every point in time. We give the user the ability to change objectives and preferences thereby making this a highly flexible system. In this work, we developed our agent programming language BAOP to incorporate preference relations. The preference relation is modelled using c-semirings. We applied the techniques to help the agent make decisions on selecting a particular plan at any given point of time. We also defined the formal semantics of BAOP as well as described algorithm with lookahead techniques for selecting the best plan. Our experiments show that the reactive property of BAOP agents are still maintained even when decisions are taken to find the path to take in order to achieve a particular goal. We have not paid much attention to the constraint solving techniques to find the best algorithm so that we can develop good elicitation strategies that reduce the time to find out the preferred plan quickly.

The preferences mentioned in this paper depict the relationship preference among the set of activities that are part of each plan as well as the objective functions. This notion could be further extended in a multi-agent environment where each agent would have a set of preferences and there could be a global preference set that would try to achieve an overall system optimization across all agents. This is also particulary useful in agent negotiation where each agent tries to negotiate in order to achieve its own goal.

References

1. Apt, K.R., Wallace, M.: Constraint Logic Programming using Eclipse. Cambridge University Press, New York (2007)
2. Bistarelli, S., Montanari, U., Rossi, F.: Semiring-based constraint satisfaction and optimization. Journal of ACM 44, 201–236 (1997)
3. Bordini, R.H., Hübner, J.F., Wooldridge, M.: Programming Multi-Agent Systems in AgentSpeak using Jason. Wiley Series in Agent Technology. John Wiley & Sons, Chichester (2007)
4. Brafman, R.I., Chernyavsky, Y.: Planning with goal preferences and constraints. In: Biundo, S., Myers, K.L., Rajan, K. (eds.) Proceedings of the 15th International Conference on Automated Planning and Scheduling, pp. 182–191. AAAI, Menlo Park (2005)
5. Busetta, P., Ronnquist, R., Hodgson, A., Lucas, A.: JACK intelligent agents - components for intelligent agents in java. In: AgentLink News Letter, Agent Oriented Software Pty. Ltd. (January 1999)
6. Dasgupta, A., Ghose, A.K.: CASO: a framework for dealing with objectives in a constraint-based extension to AgentSpeak(L). In: Proceedings of the 29th Australasian Computer Science Conference, ACSC 2006, Darlinghurst, Australia, vol. 48, pp. 121–126. Australian Computer Society, Inc. (2006)
7. Dasgupta, A., Ghose, A.K.: Implementing reactive BDI agents with user-given constraints and objectives. Int. J. Agent-Oriented Software Engineering 4, 141–154 (2010)
8. Fritz, C., Mcilraith, S.A.: Decision-theoretic golog with qualitative preferences. In: Proceedings of the 10th International Conference on Principles of Knowledge Representation and Reasoning (KR), Lake District, UK, June 25, pp. 153–163 (2006)
9. Gerevini, A., Long, D.: Plan constraints and preferences in PDDL3. Technical report, Dipartimento di Elettronica per l'Automazione, Universit di Brescia (2005)
10. Hindriks, K.V., de Boer, F.S., der Hoek, W.V., Meyer, J.-J.C.: Agent programming in 3APL. In: Autonomous Agents and Multi-Agent Systems, Hingham, MA, USA, November 1999, vol. 2, pp. 357–401. Kluwer Academic Publishers, Dordrecht (1999)

11. Hindriks, K.V., Birna Riemsdijk, M.: Using temporal logic to integrate goals and qualitative preferences into agent programming. In: Baldoni, M., Son, T.C., Birna Riemsdijk, M., Winikoff, M. (eds.) DALT VI 2008. LNCS (LNAI), vol. 5397, pp. 215–232. Springer, Heidelberg (2009)
12. Hinge, K., Ghose, A.K., Koliadis, G.: Process seer: A tool for semantic effect annotation of business process models. In: Proceedings of 2009 IEEE International Enterprise Distributed Object Computing Conference (EDOC 2009), pp. 54–63 (2009)
13. Jaffar, J., Maher, M.: Constraint logic programming: A survey. Journal of Logic Programming, Special 10th Anniversary Issue (19/20) (May/July 1994)
14. Levesque, H.J., Reiter, R., Lespérance, Y., Lin, F., Scherl, R.B.: Golog: A logic programming language for dynamic domains. Journal of Logic Programmming 31(1-3), 59–83 (1997)
15. Moreira, I.F., Bordini, R.H.: An operational semantics for a BDI agent-oriented programming language. In: Proceedings of the Workshop on Logics for Agent-Based Systems (LABS 2002), Toulouse, France, pp. 45–59 (April 2002)
16. Plotkin, G.D.: A structural approach to operational semantics. Technical Report DAIMI FN-19, University of Aarhus (1981)
17. Rao, A.S.: Agentspeak(L): BDI agents speak out in a logical computable language. In: Perram, J., Van de Velde, W. (eds.) MAAMAW 1996. LNCS, vol. 1038, pp. 42–55. Springer, Heidelberg (1996)
18. Rao, A.S., Georgeff, M.P.: BDI agents: From theory to practice. In: Proceedings of the 1st International Conference on Multi-Agent Systems (ICMAS 1995), San Fransisco, USA, pp. 312–319 (1995)
19. Sardina, S., de Silva, L., Padgham, L.: Hierarchical planning in BDI agent programming languages: A formal approach. In: Proceedings of the Fifth International Joint Conference on Autonomous Agents and Multiagent Systems (AAMAS 2006), pp. 1001–1008. ACM Press, New York (2006)
20. Sardina, S., Padgham, L.: Goals in the context of BDI plan failure and planning. In: Proceedings of the 6th International Joint Conference on Autonomous Agents and Multiagent Systems (AAMAS 2007), pp. 1–8. ACM, New York (2007)
21. Sardina, S., Shapiro, S.: Rational action in agent programs with prioritized goals. In: Proceedings of the Second International Joint Conference on Autonomous Agents and Multiagent Systems (AAMAS 2003), pp. 417–424. University Press, New Haven (2003)
22. Shapiro, S., Lespérance, Y.: Modeling Multiagent Systems with CASL - A Feature Interaction Resolution Application. In: Castelfranchi, C., Lespérance, Y. (eds.) ATAL 2000. LNCS (LNAI), vol. 1986, pp. 244–259. Springer, Heidelberg (2001)
23. van Riemsdijk, B., van der Hoek, W., Meyer, J.-J.C.: Agent programming in dribble: from beliefs to goals using plans. In: Proceedings of the Second International Joint Conference on Autonomous Agents and Multiagent Systems (AAMAS 2003), pp. 393–400. ACM, New York (2003)
24. Winikoff, M., Padgham, L., Harland, J., Thangarajah, J.: Declarative & procedural goals in intelligent agent systems. In: Proceedings of the Eighth International Conference on Principles of Knowledge Representation and Reasoning (KR 2002), pp. 470–481 (2002)
25. Wooldridge, M., Jennings, N.R.: Intelligent agents: Theory and practice. Knowledge Engineering Review 10(2), 115–152 (1995)

Query-Driven Coordination of Multiple Answer Sets

Gauvain Bourgne and Katsumi Inoue

National Institute of Informatics,
2-1-2 Hitotsubashi, Tokyo, Japan
{bourgne,ki}@nii.ac.jp

Abstract. This article studies coordination protocols between logical agents to answer queries to different types of combined programs. More precisely, we consider a system of agents corresponding to different logic programs under the answer set semantics, and different kind of coordination semantics to combine them: generous coordination (gathering all the answer sets of all agents), rigorous coordination (selecting answer sets shared by all agents), composition (building consistent union of answer sets from each agent) and consensus (taking intersection of answer sets from each agent). Rather than explicitly building a coordination program, which would require to compute all answer sets of each agent, we propose to use coordination protocols that would only compute answer sets that are needed to answer a query to the coordination. In this paper, after presenting our context and the coordination semantics we are using, we define coordination protocols for answering queries on them, translating constraints on the coordination into local constraints. Some examples are then given to illustrate the expressiveness of these basic types of coordination when combined together and possible applications are discussed.

1   Introduction

In a multi-agent system, agents generally have different beliefs. Combining them to make decisions or to reach agreements is thus a main topic in this domain. Logic programming provides a formal language for representing knowledge and beliefs of an agent. Individual agents often have only incomplete information. To deal with this possible incompleteness of an agent's theory, a non-monotonic logic programming framework can be used. We consider here a multi-agent system in which each agent is associated with a logic program under the answer set semantics. Answer sets are sets of literals representing beliefs or intentions that can be built by a rational reasoner on the basis of a program [1]. An agent may have (conflicting) alternative sets of beliefs, which are given by multiple answer sets of its logic program. They represent different possible set of beliefs that are compatible with its knowledge.

Depending on the purpose of the agents, programs can be combined in different ways such as generous coordination (gathering the possible answer sets of any agent), rigorous coordination (seeking common answer sets among agents) [12], composition (combining answer sets from several agents in a consistent way) [10]

A. Omicini, S. Sardina, and W. Vasconcelos (Eds.): DALT 2010, LNAI 6619, pp. 40–59, 2011.

or consensus (seeking possible common beliefs of several agents) [11]. Our primary interest in this article is to present these coordination semantics and provide a family of protocols with which agents can derive combined answer sets. These basic operations provide a toolbox that can be used to produce more complex operations. As opposed to [12,10,11], we are not concerned with building a logic program to represent these combinations. Building such a program requires in most cases to compute all answer sets, whereas practically, an agent is only concerned with knowing if some belief is entailed by the combination, or getting a specific answer set. Moreover, in a dynamic system, programs may change over time. We thus adopt here a query-driven approach, allowing queries for entailment of some formula, or queries for answer sets satisfying some requirements. To specify what answer sets they are interested in, agents will use constraints to direct the selection of a proper answer. In our protocol, as we are concerned with efficiency and flexibility, we will only use (and thus compute) those answer sets that are needed to answer a given query. Note that not relying directly on the program also allows the agent to keep their internal reasoning private. However, abstracting away from the reasoning by using directly the resulting set of answer sets might result in slight loss of information when adding or retracting beliefs.

We will first, in Section 2, present the framework, introduce our four basic coordination semantics and extend them to groups of agents. Then, Section 3 describes the protocols themselves. Afterwards, we will illustrate in Section 4 some complex uses of these coordinations, before discussing the difference between our approach and compositional semantics based on the merging of programs in Section 5. At last, Section 6 will conclude.

2   Coordinating Answer Sets

2.1   Preliminaries

We first give a very succinct overview of the answer set semantics for a program defined over a set of literals Lit (see [8] for more details). An $extended\ disjunctive\ program$ (EDP) is a set of $rules$ of the form: $L_1; \cdots; L_l \leftarrow L_{l+1}, \ldots, L_m, not\ L_{m+1}, \ldots, not\ L_n$ $(n \geq m \geq l \geq 0)$ where each $L_i \in Lit$. For each rule r of the above form, $head(r)$, $body^+(r)$, $body^-(r)$, and $not\_body^-(r)$ denote the sets of (NAF-)literals $\{L_1, \ldots, L_l\}$, $\{L_{l+1}, \ldots, L_m\}$, $\{L_{m+1}, \ldots, L_n\}$, and $\{not\ L_{m+1}, \ldots, not\ L_n\}$, respectively. A program P with variables is semantically identified with its ground instantiation. The semantics of EDPs is given by the $answer\ set\ semantics$ [8]. A set $S \subseteq Lit$ $satisfies$ a rule r if $body^+(r) \subseteq S$ and $body^-(r) \cap S = \emptyset$ imply $head(r) \cap S \neq \emptyset$. S satisfies a ground program P if S satisfies every rule in P. Let P be a program such that $\forall r \in P, body^-(r) = \emptyset$. Then, a set $S \subset Lit$ is a (consistent) $answer\ set$ of P if S is a minimal set such that (i) S satisfies every rule from the ground instantiation of P, and (ii) S does not contain a pair of complementary literals L and $\neg L$. Next, let P be any EDP and $S \subseteq Lit$. For every rule r in the ground instantiation of P, the rule $r^S : head(r) \leftarrow body^+(r)$ is included in the $reduct$ P^S if $body^-(r) \cap S = \emptyset$. Then, S is an $answer\ set$ of P if S is an answer set of P^S.

In the following, we consider a system of n agents sharing a common *concern language* denoted by $\mathcal{C}$. Each of them has a logic program P accounting for its beliefs over $\mathcal{C}$ (ie $Lit = \mathcal{C}$). Its belief sets would then be the *answer sets* of P (see [8]). As programs may evolve, an agent might not maintain an explicit list of these answer sets, and compute them only if needed. An agent a_i's answer sets will be represented by $\mathcal{AS}(a_i) = \{B_1, \ldots, B_m\}$, where each $B_j \subseteq \mathcal{C}$ is a set of literals. If a literal L is not present in B_j (and neither is its negation), it means that the agent has no opinion over the truth value of L wrt B_j. It can thus accept to consider the opinion of other agents about it. A formula that is satisfied in every answer sets (resp. in at least one answer set) of an agent will be said to be *skeptically* (resp. *credulously*) entailed by it.

2.2   Beliefs Coordination Semantics

We define four kinds of agent's belief coordinations, using semantics for program combination in answer set programming: generous and rigorous coordination [12], composition [10], and consensus [11].

Definition 1. *Let a_1 and a_2 be two agents, associated with programs P_1 and P_2 defining their beliefs over a common concern language $\mathcal{C}$, and let $\mathcal{AS}(a_1)$ and $\mathcal{AS}(a_2)$ be the answer sets of repectively P_1 and P_2.*

The generous coordination *of a_1 and a_2 is $\mathcal{AS}(a_1) \oplus \mathcal{AS}(a_2) = \mathcal{AS}(a_1) \cup \mathcal{AS}(a_2)$.*

Their rigorous coordination *is $\mathcal{AS}(a_1) \otimes \mathcal{AS}(a_2) = \mathcal{AS}(a_1) \cap \mathcal{AS}(a_2)$.*

Their composition *is $\mathcal{AS}(a_1) \odot \mathcal{AS}(a_2) = \{S \cup T \mid S \in \mathcal{AS}(a_1), T \in \mathcal{AS}(a_2), S \cup T \text{ is consistent}\}$.*

Their consensus *is $\mathcal{AS}(a_1) \oslash \mathcal{AS}(a_2) = \{S \cap T \mid S \in \mathcal{AS}(a_1), T \in \mathcal{AS}(a_2)\}$.*

We shall use the term *combination* to refer to the set of answer sets resulting from any one of these coordination semantics. In order to preserve incomparability of answer sets, we define $\mathcal{AS}(a_1) \bigcirc^{\leq} \mathcal{AS}(a_2)$ and $\mathcal{AS}(a_1) \bigcirc^{\geq} \mathcal{AS}(a_2)$, the *minimal* and *maximal combinations* of a_1 and a_2, as being respectively $min(\mathcal{AS}(a_1) \bigcirc \mathcal{AS}(a_2))$ and $max(\mathcal{AS}(a_1) \bigcirc \mathcal{AS}(a_2))$ where $\bigcirc \in \{\oplus, \odot, \oslash\}^1$, $min(X) = \{S \in X \mid \forall T \in X, T \not\subset S\}$ and $max(X) = \{S \in X \mid \forall T \in X, T \not\supset S\}$.

Two agents adopting *generous coordination* between themselves retain all their answer sets, but admit the introduction of additional answer sets of the other agent, though they might have to restrict (in case of minimal generous coordination) or expand (in case of maximal generous coordination) some of their answer sets to preserve incomparability. We shall generally favor maximal generous coordination, as it is more informative. By contrast, adopting *rigorous coordination* forces each agent to give up some answer sets, but the result remains within the original answer sets for each agent. *Compositional semantics* is defined as the collection of sets which are obtained by combining answer sets of the original programs. It means that an agent using composition with another will complete each of its answer sets with beliefs from the other agent that are

---

consistent with it. It will have to drop those of its answer sets that are not consistent with any of the answer sets of the other agent. Finally, a *consensus* intuitively represents an agreement, that is, a set of beliefs which are included in both an answer set of a_1 and an answer set of a_2. When using *minimal consensus*, we get a set of answer sets such that at least one of them is included in any intersection of answer sets from each agent. It means that even if both agents chose to arbitrarily favor one of their answer sets, they would still agree on one of the answer sets of the minimal consensus. By contrast, *maximal consensus* gives the maximal agreements that can be attained if each agent favors some specific answer sets. It represents a kind of compromise, as the agent can reach agreement on more belief if they agree to retain only those of their answer sets that are most compatible with one another.

Example 1. To illustrate these combinations, we give here a simple example. Agents have answer sets representing combination of ice cream flavours that they like, with negated flavours indicating flavours that should not be added to the combination according to their tastes. With $\mathcal{AS}(a_0) = \{\{Vanilla, Chocolate, Strawberry\}, \{Chocolate, Mint\}, \{Chocolate, Orange, \neg Mint\}\}$ and $\mathcal{AS}(a_1) = \{\{Chocolate, Mint\}, \{Chocolate, Orange, \neg Mint, \neg Strawberry\}\}$, we get (representing each flavour by its first letter):

$\mathcal{AS}(a_0) \oplus^{\leq} \mathcal{AS}(a_1) = \{\{V, C, S\}, \{C, M\}, \{C, O, \neg M\}\}$,
$\mathcal{AS}(a_0) \oplus^{\geq} \mathcal{AS}(a_1) = \{\{V, C, S\}, \{C, M\}, \{C, O, \neg M, \neg S\}\}$,
$\mathcal{AS}(a_0) \otimes \mathcal{AS}(a_1) = \{\{C, M\}\}$, $\mathcal{AS}(a_0) \odot^{\leq} \mathcal{AS}(a_1) = \{\{C, M\}, \{C, O, \neg M, \neg S\}\}$,
$\mathcal{AS}(a_0) \odot^{\geq} \mathcal{AS}(a_1) = \{\{V, C, S, M\}, \{C, O, \neg M, \neg S\}\}$,
$\mathcal{AS}(a_0) \oslash^{\leq} \mathcal{AS}(a_1) = \{\{C\}\}$, $\mathcal{AS}(a_0) \oslash^{\geq} \mathcal{AS}(a_1) = \{\{C, M\}, \{C, O, \neg M\}\}$.

Generous coordination lists all combined flavours liked by one of the agents (with eventual restriction or expansion). It allows one to know all possible flavours mixing that are liked by at least one agent of the pair. *Rigorous coordination* indicates mixing that are liked by both agents (without modification). In our case, both agents agrees on the fact that chocolate and mint are a good match. *Composition* on the other hand, mix the answer set of the agents when it can be consistently done. Here, it means that it will provide some flavours mix that contains desired combination of flavours while avoiding to spoil one of these combinations with an unwanted flavour (specified by negative literals). Maximal composition yields larger sets, combining for example in our case vanilla-chocolate-strawberry from a_0 with chocolate-mint from a_1. At last, consensus will indicate which flavours are good basis to please everybody. *Minimal consensus* indicate the flavours (or combination of flavours) that can be found in any pair of mix from both agents. It represents flavours that would necessarily be present (or avoided) in any combination of flavours that is liked by both agents. In this case, having chocolate is a requirement to please both agents. *Maximal consensus* gives maximal combinations that could be used as a basis to please both agents. In our case, the agents agrees on the fact that chocolate can be used with mint, and that chocolate can be used with orange if no mint is added. It could for example be used to decide that those two combinations can be prepared for everyone, while each individual can afterward add other flavours if needed.

In some case, a combination might not give any answer sets. We shall say that the combination *succeeds* if it contains at least one answer set, and that it *fully succeeds* if it has at least one non-empty answer set. Full success means that the combination yields some non-empty result, which can be desirable if some decision has to be made on the basis of the combination.

Property 1. Let a_1 and a_2 be two agents with answer sets $\mathcal{AS}(a_1)$ and $\mathcal{AS}(a_2)$. Success and full success necessary and sufficient conditions for all type of combinations is given by the following table :

Combination	succeeds iff	fully succeeds iff
Min. generous coord.	$\exists i, \mathcal{AS}(a_i) \neq \emptyset$	it succeeds and $\forall i, \mathcal{AS}(a_i) \neq \{\emptyset\}$
Max. generous coord.	$\exists i, \mathcal{AS}(a_i) \neq \emptyset$	it succeeds and $\exists i, \mathcal{AS}(a_i) \neq \{\emptyset\}$
Rigorous coord.	$\exists U \subseteq \mathcal{C}, \forall i, U \in \mathcal{AS}(a_i)$	it succeeds and $\forall i, \mathcal{AS}(a_i) \neq \{\emptyset\}$
Min. or max. comp.	$\exists (U, V) \in \mathcal{AS}(a_1) \times \mathcal{AS}(a_2)$, U consistent with V	it succeeds and $\exists i, \mathcal{AS}(a_i) \neq \{\emptyset\}$
Min. consensus	$\forall i, \mathcal{AS}(a_i) \neq \emptyset$	$\exists (U, V) \in \mathcal{AS}(a_1) \times \mathcal{AS}(a_2)$, $U \cap V \neq \emptyset$
Max. consensus	$\forall i, \mathcal{AS}(a_i) \neq \emptyset$	$\forall (U, V) \in \mathcal{AS}(a_1) \times \mathcal{AS}(a_2)$, $U \cap V \neq \emptyset$

Proof. These properties are directly derived from the definitions of the combination, the incomparability of answer sets, and the fact that for any set of set X, $min(X \cup \{\emptyset\}) = \{\emptyset\}$.

Note that generous coordination is the only kind of combination that can succeed when one of the agents has no answer sets. Moreover, maximal generous coordination and (maximal or minimal) composition are the only combinations that can fully succeed when one of the agents has $\emptyset$ as an answer set. Finally, if none of the agents has $\emptyset$ as an answer set, consensus is the only combination that might succeed without fully succeeding.

2.3   Extension to n Agents

To extends these combination to groups of n agents, it is important to note that all these combinations are associative. In the following, we identify agents with their answer sets and denote any combination $\mathcal{AS}(a_1) \bigcirc \mathcal{AS}(a_2)$ by $a_1 \bigcirc a_2$.

Property 2. Generous coordination, rigorous coordination, composition and consensus are commutative and associative operations, meaning that, given agents a_1, a_2 and a_3, we have (with $\bigcirc \in \{\oplus^s, \otimes, \odot^s, \oslash^s\}$ and $s \in \{\geq . \leq\}$):

- $a_1 \bigcirc a_2 = a_2 \bigcirc a_1$.
- $(a_1 \bigcirc a_2) \bigcirc a_3 = a_1 \bigcirc (a_2 \bigcirc a_3)$. It will thus be denoted by $a_1 \bigcirc a_2 \bigcirc a_3$.

Proof. The commutativity and associativity of $\cap$ and $\cup$ directly give this result for most combinations. For composition, however, one should remind that if X is inconsistent, then $X \cup Y$ will also be inconsistent, and reciprocally, if X is consistent, any subset of X is also consistent. Thus, if we take an element of $a_1 \odot (a_2 \odot a_3)$, it is a consistent union of $U \cup P$ in resp. $\mathcal{AS}(a_1)$ and $\mathcal{AS}(a_2) \odot \mathcal{AS}(a_3)$, with $P = V \cup W$, $V \in \mathcal{AS}(a_2)$ and $W \in \mathcal{AS}(a_3)$. It can be interpreted as $U \cup (V \cup W) = U \cup V \cup W = (U \cup V) \cup W$. The consistency of $U \cup V \cup W$ ensures the consistency of $U \cup V$ which is thus an element of $a_1 \odot a_2$, so $U \cup V \cup W$ is in $(a_1 \odot a_2) \odot a_3$. Likewise, any element of $a_1 \odot (a_2 \odot a_3)$ can be interpreted as an element of $(a_1 \odot a_2) \odot a_3$.

For a group of agents $G = \{a_1, \ldots, a_n\}$, we can thus define :

$$\text{Generous Coordination:} \quad \bigoplus_{a_i \in G} a_i = a_1 \oplus \ldots \oplus a_n = \bigcup_{a_i \in G} \mathcal{AS}(a_i)$$

$$\text{Rigorous Coordination:} \quad \bigotimes_{a_i \in G} a_i = a_1 \otimes \ldots \otimes a_n = \bigcap_{a_i \in G} \mathcal{AS}(a_i)$$

$$\text{Composition:}$$

$$\bigodot_{a_i \in G} a_i = a_1 \odot \ldots \odot a_n = \{ \bigcup_{a_i \in G} U_i | U_i \in \mathcal{AS}(a_i) \text{ and } \bigcup_{a_i \in G} U_i \text{ is consistent}\}$$

$$\text{Consensus:} \quad \oslash_{a_i \in G} \, a_i = a_1 \oslash \ldots \oslash a_n = \{ \bigcap_{a_i \in G} U_i | U_i \in \mathcal{AS}(a_i)\}$$

Generous coordination collects the answer sets of each agents in the group, whereas *rigorous coordination* represents the answer sets that are common to all agents in the group. Then, *composition* of a group of agents represents answer sets that are built by consistently aggregating beliefs from answer sets of each agents in the group. For any answer set of the composition, each agent of the group has at least one answer set that is included in it (meaning that it supports at least a part of this answer set), and each belief in this answer set is included in at least one answer set of an agent (meaning that each belief of this answer set is supported by at least one agent). Finally, no matter which of the answer sets of each agent is taken, the whole group will agree on at least one of the answer sets of the *minimal consensus*. Moreover, by restricting their answer sets, the agents of the group can all agree on any answer set of the *maximal consensus* (and no superset of it).

Example 2. We briefly give examples of 3-agents combinations by adding another agent in the previous example. With $\mathcal{AS}(a_2) = \{\{Chocolate, Mint\}, \{Orange, Praline, \neg Mint\}\}$, we get :

$$\bigoplus_{i \in \{0,1,2\}}^{\leq} a_i = \{\{V, C, S\}, \{C, M\}, \{C, O, \neg M\}, \{O, P, \neg M\}\},$$

$$\bigoplus_{i \in \{0,1,2\}}^{\geq} a_i = \{\{V, C, S\}, \{C, M\}, \{C, O, \neg M, \neg S\}, \{O, P, \neg M\}\},$$

$$\bigotimes_{i \in \{0,1,2\}} a_i = \{\{C, M\}\}, \quad \bigodot_{i \in \{0,1,2\}}^{\leq} a_i = \{\{C, M\}, \{C, O, P, \neg M\}\},$$

$$\bigodot_{i \in \{0,1,2\}}^{\geq} a_i = \{\{V, C, S, M\}, \{C, O, P, \neg M\}\},$$

$$\oslash_{i \in \{0,1,2\}}^{\leq} a_i = \{\emptyset\}, \quad \oslash_{i \in \{0,1,2\}}^{\geq} a_i = \{\{C, M\}, \{O, \neg M\}\}.$$

2.4   Mixed Combinations

It is also possible to define more complex combination by combining these different semantics. We present here some of the more easily interpreted mixed uses of these combinations. In the following, we denote by $\mathcal{P}^p(G)$ the set $\{X \subseteq G | card(X) = p\}$. *General coordination* of degree p of group of agent G is then given by :

$$R_p(G) = \bigoplus_{X \in \mathcal{P}^p(G)} (\bigotimes_{a_i \in X} a_i)$$

It is equivalent to rigorous coordination when $p = card(G)$, and to generous coordination when $p = 1$. General coordination of degree p of a group of agent gives the set of all answer sets that are shared by at least p agents. We shall see later that it can be useful for defining a voting process.

By using respectively consensus (minimal or maximal) and composition instead of rigorous coordination in the previous definition, we can define respectively *partial consensus* of degree p (minimal of maximal) and *partial composition* of degree p for group of agents G. Partial maximal consensus $S_p^{\geq}(G)$ gives all possible maximal agreements between at least p agents of the groups, meaning that for every answer set B of the partial consensus, we can find at least p agents who have an answer set that contains B. Partial minimal consensus $S_p^{\leq}(G)$ is such that, even if each agent arbitrarily favors one of its answer sets, at least one of the answer sets of $S_p^{\leq}(G)$ is guaranteed to be included in the favored answer set of p agents. It gives the minimal sets of beliefs upon which at least p agents will agree. At last, partial composition $P_d(G)$ gives answer sets that can be consistent with at least p agents, each belief being supported by at least one agent.

As a last example of mixed coordination, we shall define *joint compromised consensus* of degree p as the composition of minimal consensus between p agents $(J_p = \bigodot_{X \in \mathcal{P}^p(G)}(\oslash_{i \in X}^{\leq} a_i))$. Then no matter what answer set might be favored by each individual agent, there is one answer set in J_p whose beliefs are each supported by at least p agents.

2.5   Conditional Combinations

When taking into account the opinion of other agents by using one of these combinations, one could impose some conditions about the resulting answer sets. Using conditional combinations adds a lot of expressive power to our mechanism, as the agents can then make specific queries. We shall represent these conditions by *constraints*, which will be used to ensure that some literals are present or absent from any answer set that satisfies them.

Definition 2 (Constraints). *Constraints will be defined as formulae on literals* $L \in \mathcal{C}$ *using unary operator* not *and binary operators* $\wedge$ *and* $\vee$.

Then we specify the *satisfaction* relation. Let $A \subseteq \mathcal{C}$ be a set of literals. Given a literal $L \in \mathcal{C}$, and constraints φ and ψ, A *satisfies* (or *respects*) the constraint

L iff $L \in A$. A satisfies *not* φ iff A does not satisfy φ. A satisfies $\varphi \wedge \psi$ (resp. $\varphi \vee \psi$) iff A satisfies both φ and ψ (resp. φ or ψ).

Let $S \subseteq \mathcal{C}$ be a set of literals. We shall denote by $\phi_\forall(S)$ the constraint $\bigwedge_{L \in S} L$. It is satisfied by a set of literals A iff $\forall L \in S$, $L \in A$, that is, iff $S \subseteq A$. Likewise, $\phi_\exists(S) = \bigvee_{L \in S} L$ will be satisfied by A iff $\exists L \in S$, $L \in A$, that is, iff $S \cap A \neq \emptyset$. Moreover, for any $S \subset \mathcal{C}$ and $A \subset \mathcal{C}$:

$$
\begin{array}{lll}
A \text{ satisfies } \phi_\supseteq(S) = \phi_\forall(S) & \text{iff } A \supseteq S \\
A \text{ satisfies } \phi_\subseteq(S) = not\ \phi_\exists(\mathcal{C} \setminus S) & \text{iff } A \subseteq S \\
A \text{ satisfies } \phi_\subset(S) = not\ \phi_\exists(\mathcal{C} \setminus S) \wedge not\ \phi_\forall(S) & \text{iff } A \subset S \\
A \text{ satisfies } \phi_\supset(S) = \phi_\exists(\mathcal{C} \setminus S) \wedge \phi_\forall(S) & \text{iff } A \supset S \\
A \text{ satisfies } \phi_=(S) = \phi_\forall(S) \wedge not\ \phi_\exists(\mathcal{C} \setminus S) & \text{iff } A = S
\end{array}
$$

Using these constraints, we can formally define conditional sets as follows.

Definition 3 (Conditional sets). *Given a set of literals $A \subseteq \mathcal{C}$, a constraint φ and two agents a_1 and a_2, A is a conditional answer set of a_1 (resp. a conditional combination of a_1 and a_2) with respects to φ iff A is an answer set of a_1 (resp. a combination of a_1 and a_2) that satisfies φ.*

2.6 Computing Conditional Answer Sets

As programs may evolve, an agent might not maintain an explicit list of these answer sets, and compute them only if needed. In order to get one or more answer sets satisfying a constraint φ, an agent will compute answer sets of the program $P \cup h_{IC}(\varphi)$, where $h_{IC}(\varphi)$ is a translation of φ in terms of *integrity constraints* (that is, rules with empty heads). We define (i) $h_{IC}(\top) = \emptyset$, $h_{IC}(\bot) = \{r_\emptyset\}^2$ and (ii) for any $L \in \mathcal{C}$, $h_{IC}(L) = \{\leftarrow not\ L\}$. Then, if φ and ψ are two constraints, (iii) $h_{IC}(not\ \varphi) = \{\leftarrow body^-(r), not\_body^+(r) | r \in h_{IC}(\varphi)\}$, where for any SC, $not\_S = \{not\ L | L \in S\}$; (iv) $h_{IC}(\varphi \wedge \psi) = h_{IC}(\varphi) \cup h_{IC}(\psi)$; (v) $h_{IC}(\varphi \vee \psi) = \{\leftarrow body(r_1), body(r_2) | r_1 \in h_{IC}(\varphi), r_2 \in h_{IC}(\psi)\}$.

Property 3. Let φ be a constraint, P a program, and $S \subseteq \mathcal{C}$ a set of literals. S is an answer set of P satisfying φ (that is, a conditional answer set of P wrt φ) iff S is an answer set of $P \cup h_{IC}(\varphi)$.

3 Protocols

In this section, we will describe how to answer queries concerning the combination of two sources or more. Given these answer sets (belonging to agents called *sources*), we want to build their (possibly conditional) combination. However, it is not always needed to build the full set of answer sets corresponding to that. From an agent's perspective, what is important is to determine if some beliefs are credulously or skeptically entailed for this combination, or to get an answer set satisfying some conditions. *Coordination protocols* will be given here

---

[2] where $body(r_\emptyset) = head(r_\emptyset) = \emptyset$. $r_\emptyset$ can also be defined as $p \leftarrow not\ p$ where $p \notin \mathcal{C}$. It is a rule that cannot be satisfied.

as specifications of the interactions between several agents, determining their choice of messages without detailing the internal processes of the agents to process them. We first describe the illocutions and the roles used in the protocols, before getting into the detail of their workings.

3.1   Illocutions

As said above, when considering a combination, an agent is usually concerned with knowing if some formula is credulously or skeptically entailed, or with getting answer sets satisfying some conditions. Such questions can be derived from one fundamental request, $askAS(typ, \varphi)$, which is the request for an answer set satisfying constraint φ. $typ \in \{F,C,N\}$ indicates if one just wants the first answer set (F), the current one (C) or the next one (N), which can be useful for incrementally enumerating solutions through multiple queries. Sometimes, however, it is enough to know if such an answer set exists. It can be asked using illocution $isCoherent(\varphi)$. Then, to answer such request, the illocutions $hasAS(S)$ and $noAS()$ will be used, to respectively reveal an answer set or express that there is no answer set satisfying the constraint. $hasAS()$ can also be used to answer positively to an $isCoherent$ request.

   Using these illocutions, an agent a_i can thus ask some source A if its answer sets credulously entailed a formula F with $isCoherent(F)$. If A has an answer set satisfying F, F is credulously entailed by A. Likewise skeptical entailment in F is checked with $isCoherent(not\ F)$. If A answers $noAS()$, none of its answer sets does not entail F. It means that either A does not have any answer sets, or that all answer sets of A entails F. In both cases, it follows that F is skeptically entailed by A (and reciprocally, if F is skeptically entailed by A, all its answer sets would entail F and A would answer $noAS()$ to the query $isCoherent(not\ F)$).

3.2   Roles in the Protocol

Four roles will intervene in the protocols presented. First one is the *querier* Q, that is, an agent making a request $askAS(typ, \varphi)$. It will only send its request and receive the final answer. Then, we have the two *sources* A and B[3]. The request concerns a combination of those two agents' answer sets. At last, there will be a *mediator* M, receiving the query from the querier, and communicating with the two sources in order to get an answer. A mediator for the combination $A \bigcirc B$ would be noted $M_{A \bigcirc B}$.

   It is important to note that even if the protocols are described as if these four roles were independent agents, it does not mean that four different agents have to be involved. These are just roles that can be undertaken by any agent having the required strategies (meaning they know what messages to produce and how to get the underlying information). As a matter of fact, in most cases, the querier and the mediator will be the same, and will be one of the sources (let us say that it is source A). In such a case, messages from M to A would in fact just be some internal processing as A and M would be the same agent.

---

[3] We consider only two sources here, but more can be used by chaining protocols.

Another interesting point to note is that the mediator will use the same illocutions to communicate with the sources that the querier uses to communicate with the mediator. The source for a specific request might then be a mediator for another combination, enabling more complex requests involving several combinations. If agent a_i is acting as a mediator $M_1 = M_{A \oslash B}$ for consensus of A and B, its answer sets as M_1 are virtually $\mathcal{AS}(M_1) = \mathcal{AS}(A) \oslash \mathcal{AS}(B)$. Then, an agent a_j that acting as mediator $M_2 = M_{M_1 \odot C}$ for composition of a_i and C would virtually have answer sets $\mathcal{AS}(M_2) = (\mathcal{AS}(A) \oslash \mathcal{AS}(B)) \odot \mathcal{AS}(C)$.

3.3   Basic Coordination Protocol

We define here protocols to get an answer set satisfying a constraint from a combination of two sources. They use a simple generate and check method, first generating a candidate answer set before checking its minimality (or maximality). Except for generous coordination, one answer set in the combination corresponds to one answer set in each of the sources, and can thus be written $U * V$ where U, V are answer sets of the first and second sources, and $*$ is a partial[4] binary operator on sets of literal. To get a candidate $U * V$ satisfying constraint φ, we need to get U and V from both sources such that $U * V$ exists and satisfies φ. Constraints on $U * V$ will be translated into constraints on U and V by *constraint (pre-)adjustment functions* f_*^1 and f_*^2.

Definition 4. *Let $*$ be a partial binary operator on sets of literals, and let f_*^1, f_*^2 be two functions (resp. from a constraint to a constraint and from a constraint and a set of literals to a constraint).*

f_*^1 is a constraint pre-adjustment function *for $*$ iff for any constraint φ, $f_*^1(\varphi)$ is a constraint such that for all $U \subseteq \mathcal{C}$, U satisfies $f_*^1(\varphi)$ iff there exists $V \subseteq \mathcal{C}$ such that $U * V$ exists and satisfies φ.*

f_*^2 is a constraint adjustment function *for $*$ iff for any $U \subseteq \mathcal{C}$ and for any constraint φ, $f_*^2(\varphi, U)$ is a constraint such that for all $V \subseteq \mathcal{C}$, V satisfies $f_*^2(\varphi, U)$ iff $U * V$ exists and satisfies φ.*

Figure 1 depicts the protocol by which a mediator M for $A \bigcirc B$ receiving a query $askAS(typ, \varphi)$ from querier Q can get a proper answer set $U * V \in \mathcal{AS}(A) \bigcirc \mathcal{AS}(B)$ to answer the query. Role concerned by a given state is given as superscript. This protocol can be parameterized to fit different semantics by defining $*$, f_*^1 and f_*^2. States 1 to 7 correspond to the generation step. It generates a candidate answer set $U * V$ respecting φ. Then states 8 to 15 check the minimality or maximality of the candidates by trying to generate a belief $U' * V'$ that is strictly included (or strictly includes) $U * V$. This step is parameterized by function g. We shall have $g = \phi_{\subset}$ if we are checking for minimality, or $g = \phi_{\supset}$ if checking for maximality. If we do not need to check minimality or maximality (e.g. rigorous coordination, simple consensus or composition), then the protocol can be modified by taking out the checking part. States 9,12,13,14,15 are removed, with all transitions connected to them, and states 8^M and 10^M are merged. We shall now see how to adapt this protocol for the different semantics.

---

[4] Meaning that it might not give any results if U and V do not satisfy some condition.

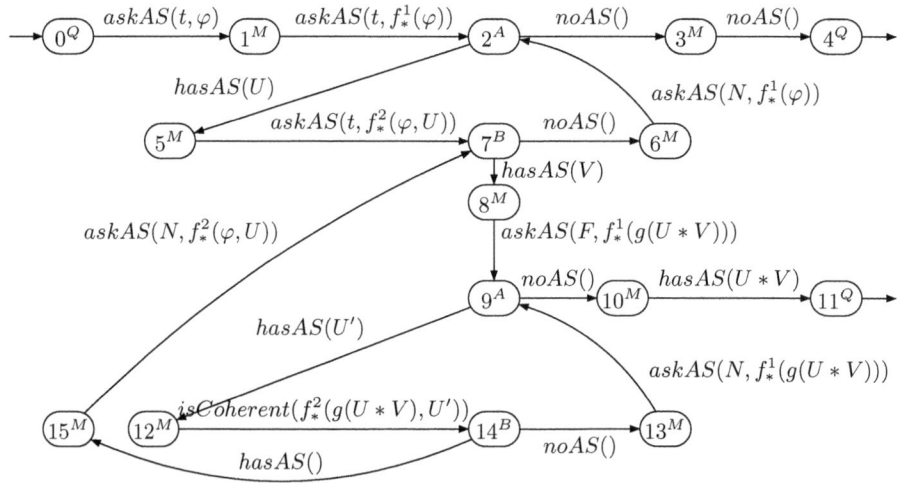

Fig. 1. General Generate and Check Protocol

Generous coordination. Figure 2 depicts a variant of the protocol for minimal/maximal generous coordination. Indeed, as an answer set resulting from generous coordination does not correspond to one answer set in each of the source, the generation cannot be done in the same manner. The principle is still the same. States 1 to 8 correspond to the generation part, and other states to the checking part. Generation part first asks an answer set from the first source, and only ask one to the second source if none is provided. The checking part relies on the fact that all answer sets in a given source are incomparable wrt to set inclusion between themselves. States 9 to 12 check the minimality (or maximality) of an answer set from the first source against answer sets of the second, and states 13 to 16 do it the other way around.

Rigorous coordination. An answer set in rigorous coordination corresponds to one answer set in each the sources, both being identical. Rigorous coordination of A and B could thus be defined as $\{U \lhd V \mid U \in \mathcal{AS}(A), V \in \mathcal{AS}(B), U \lhd V \text{ exists}\}$ where for any $U, V \subseteq \mathcal{C}, U \lhd V = U$ if $U = V$, and $U \lhd V$ does not exist otherwise. We can thus use the general protocol (in its variant without checking part) with $* = \lhd$. We then define the constraint adjustment functions for $\lhd$: $f_{\lhd}^1 = id$ and for any ψ and any U, $f_{\lhd}^2(\psi, U) = \psi \wedge \phi_=(U)$.

Property 4. $f_{\lhd}^1$ and $f_{\lhd}^2$ are respectively constraint pre-adjustment and constraint adjustment function for $\lhd$.

Proof. It is obvious from the definition of $\lhd$ that for any U, there is a V such that $U \lhd V$ satisfies ψ iff U satisfies $f_{\lhd}^1(\psi) = \psi$. Given U and ψ, for all $V, U \lhd V$ exists and satisfies ψ iff $V = U$ and U satisfies ψ, that is, iff $V = U$ and V satisfies ψ, which is true iff V satisfies $\phi_=(U)$ and ψ, that is $f_{\lhd}^2(\psi, U)$.

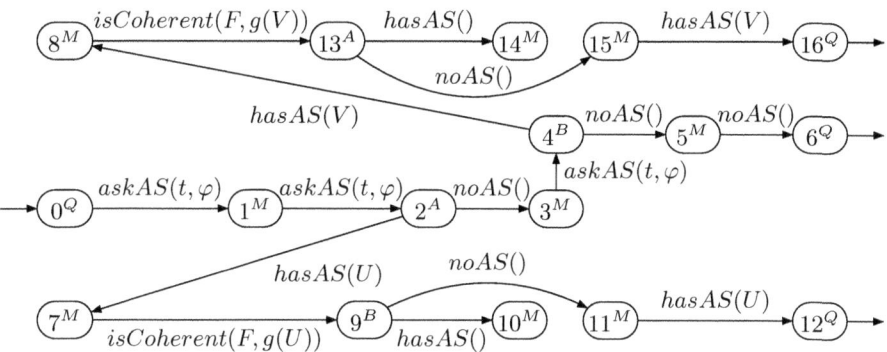

Fig. 2. Generous Coordination Protocol

Composition. For composition, we have $U * V = U \uplus V$, where $U \uplus V = U \cup V$ iff $U \cup V$ is consistent. We define $\phi_{Cons} = \bigwedge_{a \in I(\mathcal{C})} not\ \phi_\forall(\{a, \neg a\})$ where $I(\mathcal{C}) = \{a \in \mathcal{C} | \neg a \in \mathcal{C}\}$. Any set of literals $T \subseteq \mathcal{C}$ satisfying ϕ_{Cons} is consistent. Then, let $L \in \mathcal{C}$ be a literal, $S, T, U \subseteq \mathcal{C}$ be sets of literals, and φ, ψ be constraints. $f^1_\uplus$ is defined by:

(i) $f^1_\uplus(\phi_\forall(S) \wedge not\ \phi_\exists(T)) = \phi_{Cons} \wedge not\ \phi_\exists(\neg.S \cup T) \wedge \phi_\forall(S \cap (\neg.S \cup T));$
(ii) $f^1_\uplus(\varphi \vee \psi) = f^1_\uplus(\varphi) \vee f^1_\uplus(\psi).$

$f^2_\cup$ is defined by:

(i) $f^2_\cup(L, U) = \phi_{Cons} \wedge \phi_\forall(\{L\} \setminus U)$, meaning that $f^2_\cup(L, U) = \phi_\forall(\emptyset) = \top$ if $L \in U$ and $\phi_\forall(\{L\}) = L$ otherwise.
(ii) $f^2_\cup(not\ \varphi, U) = not\ f^2_\cup(\varphi, U),$
(iii) $f^2_\cup(\varphi \wedge \psi, U) = f^2_\cup(\varphi, U) \wedge f^1_\cup(\psi, U)$ and
(iv) $f^2_\cup(\varphi \vee \psi, U) = f^2_\cup(\varphi, U) \vee f^2_\cup(\psi, U).$

At last, $f^2_\uplus$ will be defined by $f^2_\uplus(\varphi, U) = f^2_\cup(\varphi, U) \wedge \phi_{Cons} \wedge not\ \exists(\neg.U)$ where $\neg.U = \{L \in U | \neg L \in \mathcal{C}\}.$

Property 5. $f^1_\uplus$ and $f^2_\uplus$ are respectively constraint pre-adjustment and constraint adjustment function for $\uplus$.

Proof. Given $\varphi = \phi_\forall(S) \wedge not\ \phi_\exists(T)$ and U, there is a V such that $U \uplus V$ exists and satisfies φ iff there is V such that $U \cup V$ consistent and $S \subseteq U \uplus V$ and $T \cap (U \uplus V) = \emptyset$, iff $U \cup S$ consistent and $T \cap U = T \cap S = \emptyset$, iff U and S are consistent, $U \cap \neg.S = U \cap T = T \cap S = \emptyset$, iff U satisfies $\phi_{Cons} \wedge not\ \exists(\neg.S \cup T)$ and $S \cap (\neg.S \cup T) = \emptyset$ [A]. If U satisfies $f^1(\varphi)$, then U satisfies $\phi_{Cons} \wedge not\ \exists(\neg.S \cup T)$ and $\phi_\forall(S \cap (\neg.S \cup T))$, thus we have $U \cap (\neg.S \cup T) = \emptyset$ which implies $U \cap (S \cap (\neg.S \cup T)) = \emptyset$. As $S \cap (\neg.S \cup T) \subseteq U$, we conclude $S \cap (\neg.S \cup T) = \emptyset$. Thus U satisfies $f^1(\varphi) \Rightarrow$ (A). If (A), then U satisfies $\phi_{Cons} \wedge not\ \exists(\neg.S \cup T)$, and $S \cap (\neg.S \cup T) = \emptyset$ implies $\phi_\forall(S \cap (\neg.S \cup T)) = \phi_\forall(\emptyset) = \top$ is also satisfied. Let φ is any constraint. We can formulate φ as a DNF $C_1 \vee \ldots \vee C_k$, where $C_i = \bigwedge_{L \in C_i^+} L \wedge \bigwedge_{L \in C_i^-} not\ L = \phi_\forall(C_i^+) \wedge not\ \phi_\exists(C_i^-)$. Then there is a V such that $U \uplus V$ exists and satisfies φ iff there is a V s. t. $U \uplus V$ satisfies C_1 or ... or C_k, iff U satisfies $f_\uplus^1(C_1)$ or ...or $f_\uplus^1(C_k)$, iff U satisfies $f_\uplus^1(\varphi)$. It proves that $f_\uplus^1$ is a constraint pre-adjustment function for $\uplus$.

Consensus. For consensus, we have $U * V = U \cap V$. Let $L \in \mathcal{C}$ be a literal, $U \subseteq \mathcal{C}$ a set of literal, and φ, ψ two constraints. We define $f_\cap^1$ by :

(i) $f_\cap^1(\bot) = \bot$;
(ii) $f_\cap^1(L) = L$ and $f_\cap^1(not\ L) = \top$;
(iii) $f_\cap^1(\varphi \wedge \psi) = f_\cap^1(\varphi) \wedge f_\cap^1(\psi)$ and $f_\cap^1(\varphi \vee \psi) = f_\cap^1(\varphi) \vee f_\cap^1(\psi)$.

Then, $f_\cap^2$ is defined by:

(i) $f_\cap^2(L, U) = \phi_\exists(\{L\} \cap U)$, meaning that $f_\cap^2(L, U) = \phi_\exists(\emptyset) = \bot$ if $L \notin U$ and $\phi_\exists(\{L\}) = L$ otherwise.;
(ii) $f_\cap^2(not\ \varphi, U) = not\ f_\cap^2(\varphi, U)$,
(iii) $f_\cap^2(\varphi \wedge \psi, U) = f_\cap^2(\varphi, U) \wedge f_\cap^2(\psi, U)$ and
(iv) $f_\cap^2(\varphi \vee \psi, U) = f_\cap^2(\varphi, U) \vee f_\cap^2(\psi, U)$.

Property 6. $f_\cap^1$ and $f_\cap^2$ are respectively constraint pre-adjustment and constraint adjustment function for $\cap$.

Example 3. We consider two agents a_0 and a_1 having resp. programs P_0 : { $(a \leftarrow not\ b)$, $(b \leftarrow not\ a)$, $(c; d \leftarrow)$ } and P_1 : { $(a; c \leftarrow)$, $(b \leftarrow not\ c)$, $(d \leftarrow)$}, and a query $askAS(F, a)$ for the maximal consensus.of P_0 and P_1. We give below the resulting interactions (with state number given as subscript).

$M_1 \rightarrow A_2$	$askAS(F, f_\cap^1(a) = a)$		$A_2 \rightarrow M_5$	$hasAS(\{c, a\})$
$M_5 \rightarrow B_7$	$askAS(F, f_\cap^2(a, \{c, a\}) = a)$		$B_7 \rightarrow M_8$	$hasAS(\{a, b, d\})$
$M_8 \rightarrow A_9$	$askAS(F, f_\cap^1(g(\{a\})) = (b \vee c \vee d) \wedge a)$		$A_9 \rightarrow M_{12}$	$hasAS(\{c, a\})$
$M_{12} \rightarrow B_{14}$	$isCoherent(f_\cap^2(g(\{a\}), \{c, a\}) = c \wedge a)$		$B_{14} \rightarrow M_{13}$	$noAS()$
$M_{13} \rightarrow A_9$	$askAS(N, f_\cap^1(g(\{a\})) = (b \vee c \vee d) \wedge a)$		$A_9 \rightarrow M_{12}$	$hasAS(\{a, d\})$
$M_{12} \rightarrow B_{14}$	$isCoherent(f_\cap^2(g(\{a\}), \{a, d\}) = a \wedge d)$		$B_{14} \rightarrow M_{15}$	$hasAS()$
$M_{15} \rightarrow B_7$	$hasAS(N, f_\cap^2(a, \{c, a\}) = a)$		$B_7 \rightarrow M_6$	$noAS()$
$M_6 \rightarrow A_2$	$askAS(N, f_\cap^1(a) = a)$		$A_2 \rightarrow M_5$	$hasAS(\{a, d\})$
$M_5 \rightarrow B_7$	$askAS(F, f_\cap^2(a, \{a, d\}) = a)$		$B_7 \rightarrow M_8$	$hasAS(\{a, b, d\})$
$M_8 \rightarrow A_9$	$askAS(F, f_\cap^1(g(\{a, d\})) = (b \vee c) \wedge a \wedge d)$		$A_9 \rightarrow M_{10}$	$noAS()$

In state 10, a_0 as M can then answer to the querier $hasAS(\{a, d\})$. Note that only 2 of the 4 answer sets of P_0 have been computed, and likewise, only one of the two answer sets of P_1 have been computed.

3.4   Group Protocol

As seen in 3.2, in order to make queries about combination involving more than two sources, or mixed combination such as those proposed in 2.3 and 2.4, we can chain basic protocols with mediator acting as sources, and thus get conditional combinations of group of agents. By having agents taking several roles, we can avoid unnecessary communications (who would then just become internal computations), and produce complex behaviors from our simple basic protocols.

Note that since the basic combinations are commutative and associative, there can be several ways to divide them in pairwise combinations. While any of the different ways to do it would produce the same result, some arrangement might be more efficient than other, as shown by the following example:

Example 4. We consider four agents a_1, a_2, a_3 and a_4, with $\mathcal{AS}(a_1) = \{\{p_1\}\}$, $\mathcal{AS}(a_2) = \{\{p_2\}\}$, $\mathcal{AS}(a_3) = \{\{p_3\}\}$ and $\mathcal{AS}(a_4) = \{\{\neg p_1\}\}$. If we want to compute their composition $a_1 \odot a_2 \odot a_3 \odot a_4$, there are several ways to do it. One way could be to compute it by $(a_1 \odot a_2) \odot (a_3 \odot a_4)$, having a mediator $M_{1,2}$ for $(a_1 \odot a_2)$, $M_{3,4}$ for $(a_3 \odot a_4)$ and combining them with a third mediator M_{all}. However, by doing so, we would first compute $\mathcal{AS}(a_1 \odot a_2) = \{\{p_1, p_2\}\}$ and match it with $\mathcal{AS}(a_3 \odot a_4) = \{\{p_3, \neg p_1\}\}$ to discover that the combination does not succeed. If we compute it by $(a_1 \odot a_4) \odot (a_3 \odot a_2)$, with mediators $M_{1,4}$ and $M_{3,2}$, then we see directly that $(a_1 \odot a_4)$ does not succeed, and we can stop there. Note that this choice impacts the order in which answer sets are computed (and as a result might affect the number of intermediate computations). However, with respect to the final results, it will only affect the order in which answers are given, and not the answers themselves. In our example, both ways conclude that the combination does not succeed, though the first one need more computation to discover it.

4   Applications

This section details some examples of systems of agents using these different kinds of coordination, before discussing other possible applications.

4.1   Voting

Using general coordination of degree p R_p, a voting process can easily by expressed using iterative applications of our protocols with increasing p. Let us consider a group G of n agents trying to choose the best answer sets for the group among their answer sets. $R_1(G)$ will give all possible candidate answer sets. Then, for $k \in \{2, n\}$, $R_k(G)$ gives the beliefs that are supported by k agents. When $R_k(G) = \emptyset$, it means that there is no answer set supported by k agents of more. R_{k-1} thus gives us the best possible candidates (the winners of the vote). We can find it by increasing k until $R_k(G) = \emptyset$ or $i = n$, and returning afterwards $R_{k-1}(G)$ (or $R_n(G)$ if it is not empty). We can also stop increasing k when $card(R_k(G)) = 1$ if we do not need to know the number of votes. Note that we can keep mediators (memorizing the answer sets they computed) from one step to the others to avoid repeating computations that have already been done. In some case, if the options (represented by answer sets) upon which the agent are deciding can be restricted or mixed, it might be better to use partial maximal consensus or partial composition of degree p with the same strategy.

Example 5. We consider 6 agents $a_1, \ldots, a_6$ voting for different exclusive options a, b, c, d, e, f. Each of them can vote for several options. We have : $AS(a_1) = \{\{a\}.\{b\}\}$, $AS(a_2) = \{\{a\}.\{c\}, \{d\}\}$, $AS(a_3) = \{\{c\}.\{e\}\}$, $AS(a_4) = \{\{b\}\}$, $AS(a_5) = \{\{b\}.\{c\}, \{d\}\}$, $AS(a_6) = \{\{a\}.\{c\}\}$.

Then $R_1(G) = \{\{a\}.\{b\}, \{c\}.\{d\}, \{e\}\}$, $R_2(G) = \{\{a\}.\{b\}, \{c\}.\{d\}\}$, $R_3(G) = \{\{a\}.\{b\}, \{c\}\}$, and finally $R_4(G) = \{\{c\}\}$. The option that would satisfy the more agents is thus c in this case.

4.2   Preference Management

We consider two friends, Ann and Bruce, who want to share some pizza. There are two different sellers, represented by the following logic programs:

Seller 1 (S_1)
$Tomato; Cream \leftarrow$
$Olive; Ham; Regular \leftarrow$
$\neg Tomato \leftarrow not\, Tomato$
$\neg Cream \leftarrow not\, Cream$
$\neg Olive \leftarrow not\, Olive$
$\neg Ham \leftarrow not\, Ham$
$\neg Mushroom \leftarrow$

$AS(S_1) = \{$
$\{T, R, \neg C, \neg O, \neg H, \neg M\},$
$\{T, \neg C, \neg O, H, \neg M\},$
$\{T, \neg C, O, \neg H, \neg M\},$
$\{C, R, \neg T, \neg O, \neg H, \neg M\},$
$\{C, \neg T, \neg O, H, \neg M\},$
$\{C, \neg T, O, \neg H, \neg M\}\}.$

Seller 2 (S_2)
$Tomato \leftarrow P_1$
$Ham \leftarrow P_1$
$Mushroom \leftarrow P_1$
$Tomato \leftarrow P_2$
$Ham \leftarrow P_2$
$Olive \leftarrow P_2$
$Cream \leftarrow P_3$
$Mushroom \leftarrow P_3$
$\neg Tomato \leftarrow not\, Tomato$
$\neg Cream \leftarrow not\, Cream$
$\neg Olive \leftarrow not\, Olive$
$\neg Mushroom \leftarrow not\, Mushroom$
$\neg Ham \leftarrow not\, Ham$

$AS(S_2) = \{\{P_1, T, \neg C, \neg O, H, M\},$
$\{P_2, T, \neg C, O, H, \neg M\}, \{P_3, \neg T, C,$
$\neg O, \neg H, M\}\}$

Now we consider the preferences of Ann and Bruce:

Ann (R_A)
$\neg Mushroom \leftarrow$
$Ham \leftarrow Cream$
$Tomato; Cream \leftarrow$

Bruce (R_B)
$\neg Olive \leftarrow$
$Ham; Mushroom \leftarrow$

To consider every possible pizzas from one of these seller, we can use generous coordination and create agent $S_{all} = M_{S_1 \oplus S_2}$. So if Ann wants the lists of all pizza, she could send $askAS(F, \top)$ then $askAS(N, \top)$ to S_{all} until she gets full lists. But in fact, Ann is only interested in pizza appropriate for her taste. To get them, she can ask for an answer set of the composition of its program with the sellers S_{all}, acting herself as querier, source, and mediator $C_A = M_{R_A \odot S_{all}}$ (choices of Ann). Here, $AS(C_A) = \{\{T, R, \neg C, \neg O, \neg H, \neg M\}, \{T, \neg C, \neg O, H, \neg M\}, \{T, \neg C, O, \neg H, \neg M\}, \{C, \neg T, \neg O, H, \neg M\}, \{P_2, T, \neg C, O, H, \neg M\}\}$. Then again, she wants to choose a common pizza with Bruce, and thus need to know if there are some common choices between them. Rigorous coordination will give us this. Answer set of $M_{AB} = M_{C_A \otimes C_B}$ are pizzas appropriate for both Ann and Bruce. Ann could act as querier, mediator M_{AB}, and source C_A whereas Bruce would act as source C_B (triggering in turn protocol with S_{all} to derive answer sets C_B). Here, $\mathcal{AS}(M_{AB}) = \{\{T, \neg C, \neg O, H, \neg M\}, \{P_2, T, \neg C, O, H, \neg M\}\}$. Bruce and Ann agree to have either a tomato and ham pizza from the first seller, or the pizza P_2 (tomato, ham, olive) from seller 2.

This example shows that creating multiple mediator agent enables us to answer request to complicate combinations. Indeed, we have $M_{AB} \equiv C_A \otimes C_B \equiv (R_A \odot S_{all}) \otimes (R_B \odot S_{all}) \equiv (R_A \odot (S_1 \oplus S_2)) \otimes (R_B \odot (S_1 \oplus S_2))$. It illustrates how different kinds of coordinations can be used together to produce complex useful requests.

4.3   Individual Plans with Consensus

We consider another situation. Amber and Barry, a couple, are thinking about buying a new car (C) and traveling this year. They can travel in summer (S), winter (W) or both. Amber can decide to spend or not all her vacation (V) this year. If not, she cannot go to one of the trip. She would prefer to go in winter, but if she does not then she wants to go in summer (so that she travels at least once). If she is going to a trip, she wants to buy a new car. Then, Barry would like to buy a new car and have a trip in winter and summer, but he cannot afford it. Therefore he must either take a loan (L) or forsake one of its plans. However, he is set on having a trip in winter. Their respected logical programs are:

Amber (A) :
$\neg S; \neg W \leftarrow \neg V$
$S \leftarrow \neg W$
$W \leftarrow not \ \neg W$
$V; \neg V \leftarrow$
$C \leftarrow S$
$C \leftarrow W$

Barry (B) :
$L; \neg S; \neg W; \neg C \leftarrow$
$S \leftarrow not \ \neg S$
$W \leftarrow not \ \neg W$
$C \leftarrow not \ \neg C$
$\leftarrow not \ W$

$\mathcal{AS}(A) = \{\{S, \neg W, C, \neg V\}, \{W, C, V\}, \{\neg S, W, C, \neg V\}\}$ and $\mathcal{AS}(B) = \{\{S, W, C, L\}, \{\neg S, W, C\}, \{S, W, \neg C\}\}$.

As buying a new car for the couple, or going to a trip together are a priori joint actions, Amber and Barry should consult each other to decide what to do. Most likely, they want to maximize the plans they do together. Maximal agreements are given by maximal consensus semantics (mediator role $M_+ = M_{A \oslash \geq B}$, taken by one of them). $\mathcal{AS}(M_+) = \{\{S, C\}, \{\neg S, W, C\}\}$. These consensus can only be reached for some choice of Amber and Barry. Selecting individual set of plans that respects the agreement can be done by composing the individual program with the maximal consensus. Amber could act as a mediator for $A_+ = M_{A \odot M_+}$ and get 4 plans that would be compatible with one of the possible agreements.

We give below a methodology for parallel plan selection with consensus :

0. Initialize counters : $p_M = p_A = p_B =$'F'.
1. Get a maximal consensus : $C_1 = askAS(p_M, \emptyset)_{M_+}$.
2a. Get matching plan of A: $P_1^A = askAS($'F'$, req\forall C_1)_{A_+}$. If no answer is given, try next consensus ($p_M =$'N', go to 1).
2b. Get matching plan of B: $P_1^B = askAS($'F'$, req\forall C_1)_{B_+}$. If no answer is given, try next plan of A ($p_A =$'N', $p_B =$'F', go to 2a).
3. Check resulting plan (P_1^A, P_1^B). If not ok, try next plan ($p_B =$'N', go to 2b).

Using this method with our example, we first get $C_1 = \{S, C\}$ at step 1, then $P_1^A = \{S, \neg W, C, \neg V\}$ and $P_1^B = \{S, W, C, L\}$ at step 2a and 2b. The first set of plan given by this method in our example is thus $(\{S, \neg W, C, \neg V\}, \{S, W, C, L\})$. Here, Barry wants to have a trip in winter whereas Amber does not agree with it. If Barry can go by himself in winter, then this solution is acceptable. If not, the second set of plan obtained would be $(\{S, W, C, V\}, \{S, W, C, L\})$. In this case, with partial plan of Amber being completed by consensus, we get a larger consensus.

4.4   Other Applications

We just presented some examples dealing with qualitatively different kinds of programs. In the pizza selection example, the logic programs of seller agent gave possible options. Other agents had their preferences specified by logic programs. In the second example, however, the logic programs represented requirement for some goals, and the answer sets were sets of goals that could be accomplished together. Depending on what is represented by a logic program (preference, goals, desires, facts), other applications can be proposed. For example, if agents have alternative beliefs about a system and its evolution, one could use these protocols in problem solving or diagnosis application. With logic programs representing action and fluents [9], multi-agent planning is natural (see [14,13]).

5   Discussion

There has been a number of study of *compositional semantics* of logic programs (see [3] for a survey). A semantic is compositional if the meaning of a program can be obtained from the meaning of its components. The union of programs is the simplest and most studied composition between programs, but the semantics of logic program is not compositional with respect to the union of programs even for definite logic programs. As compositionality and non-monotonicity are viewed as orthogonal issues [3], studies for compositional semantics of nonmonotonic logic programs mainly concern with the issue of devising a compositional semantics that can accomodate (restricted) nonmonotonicity, or imposing syntactic conditions on programs to be compositional (e.g. [4]). In this respect, our approach is different from those previous studies, as we are not merging a set of components, but rather defining some semantics that combine answer sets from the original programs. Though we gave a number of examples, one may wonder how well such combinations of answer sets reflect the meaning of original programs. For instance, given two programs $P_1 = \{\neg p \leftarrow not\, p\}$ and $P_2 = \{p \leftarrow\}$, one would consider the meaning of program composition as the answer set $\{p\}$ of $P_1 \cup P_2$. By contrast, composition and rigorous coordination do not succeed, consensus has a single empty answer set $\{\emptyset\}$ and generous coordination yields $\{\{p\}, \{\neg p\}\}$. To justify our position, consider the following situation (adopted from [11]): the agent P_1 does not believe the existence of an alien unless its existence is proved, while P_2 believes the existence of aliens with no doubt. This situation is encoded by the above programs. Then what conclusion should be drawn after combining these conflicting belief of agents? If one simply merges beliefs by program union, one would conclude that the group believes in the existence of alien (single answer set $\{p\}$), whereas our semantics describes that the two agents do not have a common belief (no rigorous coordination) and cannot even accomodate each other's belief (no composition), They cannot agree even on some partial belief (consensus is $\{\emptyset\}$), and generous coordination gives us all their individual beliefs ($\{p\}$ and $\{\neg p\}$). We believe that one can thus get a more accurate and unbiased description of the beliefs of the group this way. Indeed, in multi-agent environments, different agents have different levels of beliefs, A cautious agent might have beliefs in a default form, while an optimistic agent might have knowledge in a definite form. In this circumstance, it appears careless to simply merge knowledge from different information sources. Our approach retains beliefs of each agents and give them the same priority when combining them. In this sense, our combination are intended to provide synthesis and description of the beliefs of a group to coordinate agents, rather than to synthesize a program by its components. This means that the agents are unwilling to take other agents' beliefs as a basis for their own reasoning. A rule $a \leftarrow body$ in an agent program thus has a local interpretation: if the agent internally believes $body$ (*i.e* if it can prove the positive body and cannot prove the NAF literals), then it should also believe a. External beliefs that might be obtained from the other agents are not used for reasoning.

Since, for the reason discussed above, we focus on the answer sets rather than the explicit rules of the programs, our approach differ substantially from other works on combining ASP programs such as [4] and [5]. A more closely related notable work in the answer set paradigm, however, is [7], in which agents negotiate to augment the intersection of two answer sets as long as consistency is preserved, providing an interesting step between consensus and composition. Besides, knowledge base merging has extensively studied similar problems, though, with the exception of some works on flocks such as [2], it focuses on situations in which each agent has only one belief set. It can however provides useful leads for other kinds of coordinations.

6 Conclusion

This paper has presented protocols for simple kinds of belief coordination, instantiated in term of ASP. They are intended for cooperative agents. Based on sharing beliefs to find some common ground, they do not rely on the theory used for producing those belief. As long as the agents are able to translate their knowledge into sets of answer sets on a common concern $\mathcal{C}$, they can use these protocols, so it can be useful for coordinating heterogenous agents. Contrarily to some coordination or negotiation protocols such as [6], this work is not goal-driven. It describes how to inquire about shared or compromised answer sets with a minimum of queries, without modifying the agents' own beliefs. How the agents use the information they get from these coordinations is up to them. Our examples motivate some possible uses of these informations.

Future works should also take into account preference relations over answer sets of the sources, in order to derive from it a preference relation on the combination's answer sets, and ensure that the protocols produce first the preferred combinations. In order to ensure a better efficiency of the protocols, it would also be interesting to investigate some ways to direct the progressive building of answer sets in individual answer set solvers by introducing temporary integrity constraints that could direct their production while leaving the option to lift the constraints and backtrack to recover ignored answer set. It would be especially useful in a situation where a sequence of different queries have to be answered. At last, interesting uses of these semantics in applications should be further investigated to identify possible refinement of them, and develop goal-driven coordination protocols based on such combined beliefs.

References

1. Baral, C., Gelfond, M.: Logic programming and knowledge representation. Journal of Logic Programming 19, 73–148 (1994)
2. Bochman, A.: Two representations for iterative non-prioritized change. In: Benferhat, S., Giunchiglia, E. (eds.) Proceedings of the 9th International Workshop on Non-Monotonic Reasoning (NMR 2002), Toulouse, France, April 19-21, pp. 135–141 (2002)
3. Brogi, A.: On the semantics of logic program composition. In: Bruynooghe, M., Lau, K.-K. (eds.) Program Development in Computational Logic. LNCS, vol. 3049, pp. 115–151. Springer, Heidelberg (2004)
4. Brogi, A., Contiero, S., Turini, F.: Programming by combining general logic programs. Journal of Logic and Computation 9(1), 7–24 (1999)
5. Buccafurri, F., Gottlob, G.: Multiagent compromises, joint fixpoints, and stable models. In: Kakas, A.C., Sadri, F. (eds.) Computational Logic: Logic Programming and Beyond. LNCS (LNAI), vol. 2407, pp. 561–585. Springer, Heidelberg (2002)
6. Ciampolini, A., Lamma, E., Mello, P., Toni, F., Torroni, P.: Cooperation and competition in ALIAS: A logic framework for agents that negotiate. Annals of Mathematics and Artificial Intelligence 37(1-2), 65–91 (2003)
7. Foo, N., Meyer, T., Zhang, Y., Zhang, D.: Negotiating logic programs. In: Proceedings of the 6th Workshop on Nonmonotonic Reasoning, Action and Change (NRAC 2005), Edinburgh, August 1, pp. 561–585. Springer, Heidelberg (2005)

8. Gelfond, M., Lifschitz, V.: Classical negation in logic programs and disjunctive databases. New Generation Computing 9(3/4), 365–385 (1991)
9. Hopton, L., Cliffe, O., De Vos, M., Padget, J.A.: AQL: A query language for action domains modelled using answer set programming. In: Erdem, E., Lin, F., Schaub, T. (eds.) LPNMR 2009. LNCS, vol. 5753, pp. 437–443. Springer, Heidelberg (2009)
10. Sakama, C., Inoue, K.: Combining answer sets of nonmonotonic logic programs. In: Toni, F., Torroni, P. (eds.) CLIMA VI 2005. LNCS (LNAI), vol. 3900, pp. 320–339. Springer, Heidelberg (2006)
11. Sakama, C., Inoue, K.: Constructing consensus logic programs. In: Puebla, G. (ed.) LOPSTR 2006. LNCS, vol. 4407, pp. 26–42. Springer, Heidelberg (2007)
12. Sakama, C., Inoue, K.: Coordination in answer set programming. ACM Transaction on Computational Logic 9(2), 1–30 (2008)
13. Son, T.C., Pontelli, E., Sakama, C.: Logic programming for multiagent planning with negotiation. In: Hill, P.M., Warren, D.S. (eds.) ICLP 2009. LNCS, vol. 5649, pp. 99–114. Springer, Heidelberg (2009)
14. Son, T.C., Sakama, C.: Reasoning and planning with cooperative actions for multiagents using answer set programming. In: Baldoni, M., Bentahar, J., van Riemsdijk, M.B., Lloyd, J. (eds.) DALT 2009. LNCS, vol. 5948, pp. 208–227. Springer, Heidelberg (2010)

Commitment-Based Protocols with Behavioral Rules and Correctness Properties of MAS

Matteo Baldoni, Cristina Baroglio, and Elisa Marengo

Dipartimento di Informatica — Università degli Studi di Torino
c.so Svizzera 185, I-10149 Torino, Italy
{baldoni,baroglio,emarengo}@di.unito.it

Abstract. Commitment-based interaction protocols are a flexible way of representing the interaction of a set of agents, that is well-known and widely accepted by the research community. Normally these protocols consist of sets of actions with a shared meaning. From the point of view of an agent, however, the meaning of an action is completed by the context in which it is used: the context shapes the behavior of the agent in that the agent decides which actions to take depending on it. Indeed, since the seminal work of Searle (supported by other authors), two components of interaction protocols have been identified, constitutive rules and regulative rules, which altogether define the meaning of the interaction. Commitment-based protocols usually do not account for the latter. In this work we introduce a representation that explicitly includes regulative rules as constraints on commitments and, in the light of the work by Singh and Chopra [38], report the *first steps* in the analysis of the advantages brought by such introduction.

1 Introduction

The term "interaction protocol" refers to a pattern of behavior that allows a set of agents to become a multi-agent system when engaging in the expected interactions with one another. Protocols can be seen as public artifacts [38], ruling the interaction of agents playing the various roles. A role specification is just a formal definition of what is lawful for its player to do or to expect at any possible state of the interaction. This specification is given independently from the player that will enact the role.

Considering protocols as *models of the desired interaction* allows one to devise the verification of many properties and guarantee them before any interaction takes place. For instance, it is possible to check if the roles of a protocol are interoperable, i.e. if they allow any interaction to take place. An agent which accepts to conform to a protocol, whose roles are proved interoperable, is ideally guaranteed that its interaction with any other agents, playing the other roles foreseen by the same protocol, will succeed [2,31,10]. This is surely an advantage [4] w.r.t. checking directly the interoperability and the properties of interaction of a set of agents: in this latter case, the verification of properties can only be done after the composition is made, against the system as a whole; thanks to

A. Omicini, S. Sardina, and W. Vasconcelos (Eds.): DALT 2010, LNAI 6619, pp. 60–77, 2011.
© Springer-Verlag Berlin Heidelberg 2011

protocols, instead, the verification of the interoperability can be *distributed* in time and among the various agents that could take on the roles. A candidate role player could autonomously check its conformance to the model by comparing its behavior to the role that it means to play. To do this the agent does not need to have the implementations of the other roles. This modularity of the verification meets the requirements given by interaction protocol engineering.

Interaction protocols can be specified in different ways. Some representations, like proposals based on Petri nets, finite state machines or on Pi calculus have an algorithmic (procedural) nature that is suitable to capture the desired interaction flows. Singh and colleagues criticize the use of this kind of specification as being too rigid [16,36,44,43]: agents cannot, for instance, take advantage of opportunities that arise along the interaction and that are not explicitly included in their procedure. These authors propose the more flexible *commitment-based protocols*. A commitment can be seen as a literal which can hold in the social state of the system. It represents the fact that a debtor commits to a creditor to bring about some condition. All the agents that interact according to a commitment-based protocol share the semantics of a set of actions, which affect the social state by creating new commitments, canceling commitments, and so forth. The greatest advantages of the commitment-based protocols, w.r.t. other approaches to interaction, are that they *do not over-constrain* the behavior of the agents by imposing an ordering on the execution of the shared actions, and that by giving a shared meaning to the social actions, they allow working on actual knowledge of what happened (or what is likely to happen), rather than on beliefs about each others' mental state.

The only constraint that commitment-based protocols include, to specify that an interaction is successful, is that all commitments are discharged. The *research question* that we face in this work is whether the specification of patterns of interaction as part of a protocol compromises the autonomy of agents or whether it is an instrument that gives additional meaning to actions, a meaning that we lose when we remove all constraints. As Searle observes [33] in many contexts it is necessary to regulate antecedently existing forms of behavior. For example, a purchase protocol may state that the payment must occur first in order for the shipment to proceed. The fact that the payment must occur first is not motivated by the need of making the shipping action executable: shipping is executable if the purchased item is available. Rather, it is a superimposed pattern. Commitment-based protocols, however, do not allow the expression of such patterns. Sometimes authors fill this gap by enriching actions with preconditions to their (non-) executability [41,17], in this way they rule the order of action execution.

In our view, an interaction protocol must not only specify the agreed meaning of actions but it must express also an agreement on the way the agents will behave and use the protocol actions. This should be done in a way that does not compromise the autonomy of agents, which would be free to decide how to act and to take advantage of opportunities, that arise along the interaction, taking also the risk of being misunderstood when they get out of the boundaries given by the protocol. After an agreement we can shake hands twice, if we are happy to do so, but shaking hands before the agreement is not understandable in the context of that protocol.

In this paper, we take on the commitment-based interaction protocol model proposed in [6,5]. The main characteristic of this model is a decoupled representation of the constitutive and the regulative specifications of the protocol, which are both based on commitments. While the *constitutive* specification defines the meaning of actions based on their effects on the social state, the *regulative* specification is a set of behavioral rules, given in terms of constraints among commitments, which regulate the evolution of the social state independently from the executed actions. To the best of our knowledge, this decoupling, postulated since the seminal work of Searle [33,12], was not implemented in commitment-based interaction protocols before [6,5]. Then we survey the properties hoped for interaction protocols in [38] and report some initial considerations about how the introduction of the regulative specification not only does not compromise the advantages, given by the commitment-based approach, in their verification but it also allows the verification of such properties in a finer and modular way because the specification of protocols meets the specification of agents.

2   Commitment-Based Protocols

Commitment protocols [36,43,44] are interaction patterns given in terms of commitments, involving a set of predefined roles. Commitments are directed from a debtor to a creditor. The notation $C(x, y, r, p)$ denotes that the agent playing the role x commits to an agent playing the role y to bring about the condition p when the condition r holds. All commitments are conditional. An unconditional commitment is merely a special case where r equals *true*. Whenever this is the case, we use the short notation $C(x, y, p)$. Agents share a social state that contains commitments and other literals that are relevant to their interaction. Every agent can affect the social state by executing actions, whose definition is given in terms of modifications to the social state (e.g. adding a new commitment, releasing another agent from some commitment, satisfying a commitment, etc.). So a commitment protocol is made of a *set of actions*, involving the foreseen roles and whose semantics is agreed upon by all of the participants [43,44,15].

On the other hand, agents show a *behavior*, which is not captured by the action definitions but that rather involves a decision process (a procedure, a goal-driven plan [40], etc.) aimed at selecting the action to execute [42,32]. An autonomous agent situated in an environment *decides* which actions to perform depending on the particular situation it is facing.

Since protocols are intended to rule the interaction of agents, the expectation is that they show the same structure of agents. Indeed, Searle [33] and later other authors, e.g. [12,9,18], have pointed out the need for a distinction between the *regulative* and the *constitutive* specifications of an interaction protocol. The constitutive specification gives the semantics of actions, while the regulative one rules the *flow of execution*. The regulative specification, encoding the behavioral rules, however, is not explicitly represented in commitment-based approaches like [18,15,38,41,24,43], where only actions are represented.

An actual identification, not only in agents but also *in the protocol definition itself*, of two separated components (the constitutive specification and the regulative specification) we argue would bring many advantages in the construction of multi-agent systems. The *decoupling* of the two parts would allow an *easier re-use* of actions in different contexts, an *easier customization* on the protocol, an *easier composition* of protocols. As a consequence, multi-agent systems would gain greater *openness, interoperability*, and *modularity* of design. In particular, interoperability would be better supported because it would be possible to verify it w.r.t. specific aspects (e.g. interoperability at the level of actions [18,15,19] or at the level of regulation rules). Protocols would be more open in the sense that their modularity would allow designers to easily adapt them to different contexts. Moreover, it would be possible to check properties that concern a single agent, willing to play a role of the protocol, *against the protocol and independently from which other agents will play the other roles*. In other words, if an agent in a system is substituted by another agent, it would not be necessary to recheck the whole system from scratch, because certain verifications can be distributed.

In the literature it is possible to find approaches that include in the protocol representation some regulative specification. For instance [37], where *before* relations are applied to events to define rules of behavior, like [26], where preferences about alternative behaviors are specified, like [1], where temporal constraints among the times at which events occur are specified, or like [23], where interaction diagrams are introduced inside protocols to rule the use of actions.

Unfortunately, even when behavioral rules are explicitly represented in some way, the decoupling between the regulative and the constitutive specification is not sufficiently supported yet, see [6,5] for details. Our proposal, which is described hereafter, explicitly accounts for decoupled constitutive and regulative specifications of interaction protocols. In this light and by assuming a similar abstraction for agents, we re-read the correctness properties for multi-agent systems, discussed in [38].

3   Design of Commitment-Based Protocols

In this section we propose a representation of commitment-based protocols which encompasses a *constitutive* specification, defining the meaning of actions for all the agents in the system, and a *regulative* specification, constraining the possible evolutions of the social state (see Fig. 3). Instead, for what concerns players, we account both for the player's own actions and for its behavioral rules.

Definition 1 (Interaction protocol). *An interaction protocol* P *is a tuple* $\langle R, F, A, C \rangle$, *where R is a set of roles, F is a set of literals (including commitments) that can occur in the social state, A is a set of actions, and C is a set of constraints.*

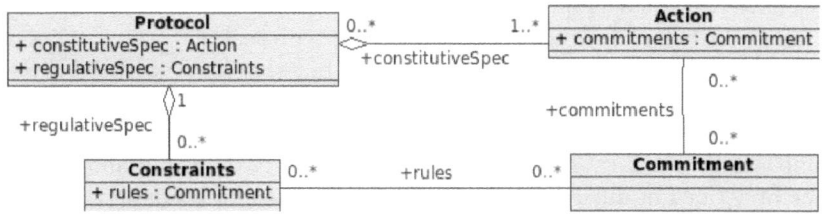

Fig. 1. Decoupling between constitutive (actions) and regulative (constraints) specifications

In words, the set of social actions A, defined on F and on R, forms the *constitutive specification* of the protocol, while the set of constraints C, defined on F and on R too, forms the *regulative specification* of the protocol.

Each role is identified by a unique label. Since both the constitutive and the regulative specifications are given also in terms of the roles involved in the actions or in the social commitments, it is possible to keep for each role, the set of the actions it can perform as well as the set of commitments it may be involved in as the interaction is carried on.

F is a set of positive and negative literals, where each literal can be a commitment or some other proposition which contributes to the social state (they are the conditions that are brought about). The set F represents the domain model and defines the vocabulary used by all agents (through roles) to communicate in the context of the protocol. Currently F is a flat set but this representation can easily be structured by integrating an ontology layer into the domain model.

Constitutive Specification. It defines the meaning of actions in the very same way as it is done in [15], i.e. in terms of how it affects the social state by adding or removing literals or by performing operations on the commitments, see [35,44]. For instance, the action *priceRequest* of the Net Bill protocol (which is used as an example below) is given in this way:

$$priceRequest(c, m, goods) \textbf{ means } \text{CREATE}(C(c, m, purchase(goods)))$$

i.e. its effect is to add to the social state a commitment $C(c, m, purchase(goods))$ by which the customer (role c) commits to a merchant (role m) to buy some goods. As we will see, the protocol includes also the action *rejectQuote*:

$$rejectQuote(c, m, goods, price) \textbf{ means }$$
$$rejectedQuote(goods, price) \land \text{DELETE}(C(c, m, purchase(goods)))$$

by which the customer rejects the quote received from the merchant. In this case, it deletes its commitment to buy. Commitment deletion is one of the basic operations on commitments, see [36].

An agent willing to play a role in a protocol, must understand the meaning of the social actions that are associated to the role at issue. In order to play the role, the agent must accept the meaning given to the social actions, which will be the same for all agents.

Regulative Specification. For the *regulative specification* C of an interaction protocol we propose a declarative, *constraint-based representation*. Due to the declarative nature of the specification, *any* evolution that respects the relations involving the specified literals (including commitments) is allowed. Notice that constraints *do not* specify *which* actions should bring conditions about. This allows the decoupling between the constitutive and the regulative specifications, see also [6,5], Fig. 1 and the discussion in the Conclusions. The regulative specification follows the grammar:

$C \rightarrow (Disj \ op \ Disj)^*$
$Disj \rightarrow Conj \lor Disj \mid Conj$
$Conj \rightarrow literal \land Conj \mid literal$

C, see Def. 1, is a set of constraints of the form $A \ op \ B$, where A and B are formulas of literals in disjunctive normal form and op is one of the operators in Table 1; *literal* can be either a commitment or a fact. Such constraints rule the evolution of the social state by imposing specific patterns on how states can progress. In order to specify constraints it is necessary to define a proper language. One possible language, that we originally introduced in [6,5], is 2CL (the acronym stands for "Constraints among Commitments Language"), whose operators are summarized in Table 1.

Table 1. 2CL operators and their semantics in LTL

Relation	Positive	LTL meaning	Negative	LTL meaning
Correlation	$a \bullet\!\!- b$	$\Diamond a \supset \Diamond b$	$a \not\bullet b$	$\Diamond a \supset \neg\Diamond b$
Co-existence	$a \bullet\!\!-\!\!\bullet b$	$a \bullet\!\!- b \land b \bullet\!\!- a$	$a \not\bullet\!\!\bullet b$	$a \not\bullet b \land b \not\bullet a$
Response	$a \bullet\!\!\!-\!\!\!\rightarrow b$	$\Box(a \supset \Diamond b)$	$a \not\bullet\!\!\!\rightarrow b$	$\Box(a \supset \neg\Diamond b)$
Before	$a \longrightarrow\!\!\!\bullet b$	$\neg b \mathsf{U} a$	$a \not\longrightarrow\!\!\!\bullet b$	$\neg a \mathsf{U} b$
Cause	$a \bullet\!\!\!-\!\!\!-\!\!\!\rightarrow\!\!\!\bullet b$	$a \bullet\!\!\!-\!\!\!\rightarrow b \land a \longrightarrow\!\!\!\bullet b$	$a \not\bullet\!\!\!-\!\!\!\rightarrow\!\!\!\bullet b$	$a \not\bullet\!\!\!\rightarrow b \land a \not\longrightarrow\!\!\!\bullet b$
Premise	$a \gg\!\!- b$	$\Box(\bigcirc b \supset a)$	$a \gg\!\!\not\!\!- b$	$\Box(\bigcirc b \supset \neg a)$
Immediate response	$a \longrightarrow\!\!\!\!\!\triangleright b$	$\Box(a \supset \bigcirc b)$	$a \not\longrightarrow\!\!\!\!\!\triangleright b$	$\Box(a \supset \bigcirc\neg b)$

The names of the operators and the graphical format, used in Section 3.2, are inspired by ConDec [30]. In order to allow the application of reasoning techniques, e.g. to check if the on-going interaction is respecting the protocol, to build sequences of actions that respect the protocol, or to verify properties of the system, it is necessary to give the operators a semantics that can be reasoned about. To this aim, in this work we use *linear temporal logic* (LTL, [21]), which includes temporal operators such as next-time ($\bigcirc$), eventually ($\Diamond$), always ($\Box$), weak until (U). Let us describe the various operators. For simplicity the descriptions are given on single literals rather than on formulas.

Correlation: this operator captures the fact that in an execution where a occurs, also b occurs but there is no temporal relation between the two. Its negation means that if a occurs in some execution, b must not occur.

Co-existence: the mutual correlation between a and b. Its negation captures the mutual exclusion of a and b. Notice that in LTL the semantics of negated co-existence is equivalent to the semantics of negated correlation.

Response: this is a temporal relation, stating that if a occurs b must hold at least once afterwards (or in the same state). It does not matter if b already held before a. The negation states that if a holds, b cannot hold in the same state or after.

Before: this a temporal relation, stating that b cannot hold until a becomes true. Afterwards, it is not necessary that b becomes true. The negation of $a \twoheadrightarrow\bullet\, b$ is equivalent to $b \twoheadrightarrow\bullet\, a$.

Cause: this operator states that if a occurs, after b must occur at least once and b cannot occur before a. The negation states that if a occurs, b cannot follow it and if b occurs, a is not allowed to occur before.

Premise: is a stronger temporal relation concerning *subsequent* states, stating that a must hold in all the states immediately preceding one state in which b holds. The negation states that a must never hold in a state that immediately precedes one where b holds.

Immediate Response: it concerns *subsequent* states, stating that b must occur in all the states immediately following a state where a occurs. The negation states that b does not have to hold in the states immediately following a state where b holds.

Notice that the negated operators semantics (column 5) not always corresponds to the negation of the semantics of the positive operator (column 3). This is due to the intention of capturing the intuitive meaning of negations. We show this need by means of a couple of examples. For what concerns correlation, the negation of the formula in column 3 is $\Diamond a \wedge \neg\Diamond b$ is too strong because it says that a must hold sooner or later while b cannot hold. What we mean by negated coexistence, instead, that *if a becomes true* then b must not occur in the execution. For completeness, the semantics of negated correlation is not equivalent to the semantics of $a \bullet\!\!- \neg b$. For what concerns immediate response, by negating the semantics in column 3 we obtain $\Diamond(\bigcirc b \wedge \neg a)$ which says that b occurs in some state and a does not occur in the previous state. Instead, the intended meaning of the negation is that a does not have to hold in the states that precede those in which b holds (but b not necessarily have to hold). Analogous considerations can be drawn for the other operators. The choice of sticking to the intuitive semantics of the operators is done to give the user only seven basic operators. Had we defined the negated operators semantics by negating the semantics of the positive operators, we would have given the user fourteen different operators.

3.1   Violation of Constraints and of Commitments

So, an interaction protocol includes a set of constraints, whose aim is to guarantee that all the interacting agents will achieve the expected results. This happens because by agreeing on the constraints they agree on the behavior they all will carry on. In this setting, does the violation of a constraint have the same nature of the violation of a commitment? According to Castelfranchi [11] and Singh [35], commitments have a *normative* nature: an agent can freely decide if and when committing to do something but when it does it is obliged to fulfill the commitment. In particular, suppose a merchant has a nested commitment like this to rule a sequencing in commitments:

$$C(m, c, C(c, m, purchase(goods)), C(m, c, sold(goods, price)))$$

Here the merchant commits to take the commitment $C(m, c, sold(goods, price))$ if the customer commits to $C(c, m, purchase(goods))$. The problem is that, since the merchant is free to decide whether or not taking the outer commitment, the customer has *no guarantee* that its decision to buy the goods will be followed by the merchant's commitment to sell because there is no guarantee that the external commitment will be taken by the merchant. If, instead, we use one of our constraints, like this one:

$$C(c, m, purchase(goods)) \longmapsto C(m, c, sold(goods, price))$$

by which the commitment of the customer c to buy some goods $C(c, m, purchase(goods))$ imposes that the merchant m will sell the goods at some price $C(m, c, sold(goods, price))$, the customer has the social *expectation* that the merchant will take the commitment to sell the goods if it decides to buy. Since this expectation is due to a rule of the protocol, we can interpret it as a *right* of the customer. The customer knows this before starting the interaction due to the fact that the protocol is public, and can use this information to decide whether to use the protocol. Also the merchant knows this before starting the interaction, therefore, it knows to which expectations on its own behavior it commits to. It is possible to speak about rights, however, only if constraints have a normative nature. The violation of a constraint, as well as the violation of a commitment, pushes the agent out of the protocol. By sticking to the constraints the agents "waive" part of their autonomy, exactly as they "waive" part of their autonomy when they take commitments, and they do this because it is deemed advantageous w.r.t. interacting without rules.

3.2   An Example: The Net Bill Protocol

The Net Bill Protocol [20] has the aim of satisfying the regulative necessities of the purchase of *electronic information goods* (simply goods, in the following) over a network. In this section we represent the part of the Net Bill Protocol that rules the interactions of a customer (or consumer) c, wishing to buy some information, and a merchant m. Intuitively, (1) the customer requests the price of certain goods to the merchant, (2) the merchant answers by quoting the goods, (3) the customer can either accept or reject the quote, (4) if the customer accepts, it is sent the requested information goods in an encrypted form, (5) the customer pays the merchant, (6) the merchant sends the key for the decryption and the receipt of the payment to the customer. The constitutive specification of the protocol defines the meaning of actions in terms of the changes they make on the social state:

(a) $priceRequest(c, m, goods)$ **means** CREATE($C(c, m, purchase(goods))$)
(b) $priceQuote(m, c, goods, price)$ **means** CREATE($C(m, c, sold(goods, price))$)∧
     CREATE($C(m, c, sentEnc(goods))$)
(c) $acceptQuote(c, m, goods, price)$ **means** CREATE($C(c, m, paid(goods, price))$)
(d) $rejectQuote(c, m, goods, price)$ **means** $rejectedQuote(goods, price)$∧
     DELETE($C(c, m, purchase(goods))$)
(e) $order(c, m, goods)$ **means** $purchase(goods)$
(f) $goodsDelivery(m, c, goods, price, key, receipt)$ **means**
     $sold(goods, price) \land sentEnc(goods)$∧
     CREATE($C(m, c, sent(key))$) ∧ CREATE($C(m, c, sent(receipt))$)
(g) $pay(c, m, goods, price)$ **means** $paid(goods, price)$
(h) $sendKey(m, c, key)$ **means** $sent(key)$
(i) $sendReceipt(m, c, receipt)$ **means** $sent(receipt)$

The action $priceRequest$ states the resolution (expressed by the commitment $C(c, m, purchase(goods))$) to buy certain goods from a merchant. This does not necessarily mean that the purchase will occur because the offer of the merchant can be rejected by the customer. By $priceQuote$ the merchant commits to sell the requested goods at a certain price and to send them in an encrypted form. The acceptance of a quotation produces the commitment $C(c, m, paid(goods, price))$. Instead, rejecting the quote causes the deletion of the commitment to buy; the literal $rejectedQuote$ is also asserted. $order$ asserts the fact $purchase(goods)$ and thus causes the discharge of the commitment to buy. $goodsDelivery$ asserts that the goods have been sold at a certain price, it causes the discharge of the corresponding commitment to sell, it records that the encrypted goods have been sent, and records the commitment of the merchant to send the key as well as the receipt. The meaning of the other actions is simple and we do not describe it.

The regulative specification of the Net Bill protocol is given by these constraints (also shown in graphical format in Fig. 2):

c1: $C(c, m, purchase(goods)) \bullet\!\!-\!\!\twoheadrightarrow C(m, c, sold(goods, price))$∧
     $C(m, c, sentEnc(goods))$
c2: $C(m, c, sold(goods, price)) \land C(m, c, sentEnc(goods)) \longrightarrow\!\!\bullet$
     $rejectedQuote(goods, price)$ XOR
     $(C(c, m, paid(goods, price)) \land purchase(goods))$
c3: $C(c, m, paid(goods, price)) \land purchase(goods) \bullet\!\!-\!\!\twoheadrightarrow C(m, c, sent(key))$∧
     $C(m, c, sent(receipt)) \land sold(goods, price) \land sentEnc(goods)$
c4: $C(m, c, sent(key)) \land C(m, c, sent(receipt)) \land sold(goods, price)$∧
     $sentEnc(goods) \bullet\!\!-\!\!\twoheadrightarrow paid(goods, price)$
c5: $paid(goods, price) \bullet\!\!-\!\!\twoheadrightarrow sent(key)$
c6: $sent(key) \bullet\!\!-\!\!\twoheadrightarrow sent(receipt)$

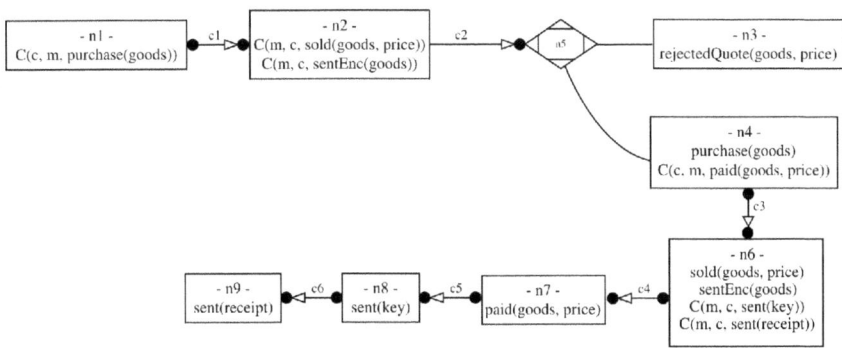

Fig. 2. Regulative specification of the Net Bill: boxes represent conjunctions of literals, circles represent conjunctions of boxes, diamonds represent the XOR of boxes

When a customer commits to buy some goods ($C(c, m, purchase(goods))$), the merchant will commit to sell the goods at a certain price and to send the encrypted information. This is specified as a *cause* (•→•, constraint $c1$) relation. In Fig. 2 a rectangle containing many literals (e.g. $n2$) represents a conjunction. These two literals must hold *before* (constraint $c2$) the XOR relation between the literal $rejectedquote(goods, price)$, which asserts that the quotation has been rejected, and the conjunction between the acceptance of the offer (literal $purchase(goods)$) and the commitment of the customer to pay the agreed price (node $n4$). Notice that the customer is not obliged to reject or accept the quotation (and commit to pay), but once the merchant observes these two literals in the social state it takes them as a guarantee that the customer will actually buy the information: so, the order of the execution of actions *order* and *goodsDelivery* is ruled indirectly. So, *afterwards* (constraint $c3$) it will send the encrypted information (node $n6$), confirm the price ($sold(goods, price)$), commit to send the key to decrypt the information and after (and only after) the customer has to pay (node $n7$). This condition *causes* (constraint $c5$) the dispatch of the key (node $n8$) and of the receipt (node $n9$).

Remark 1. Commenting the Net Bill, Chopra and Singh [16] criticize the use of finite state machines (FSM) because they lack flexibility: the strict encoding of a request followed by an offer does not allow the merchant to take the initiative by advertising an attractive deal. To avoid this limit they adopt commitment protocols, whose only constraint is that all commitments are discharged. In other terms, they remove the specification of any sequence. Even though we agree that FSM are too rigid, in our opinion the aim of the Net Bill is to guarantee that the client will have an quotation when it requests it. By removing all sequencing relations flexibility is obtained at the cost of losing such guarantee. By substituting the *cause relation* (•→•) in $c1$ with a *response relation* (•→), we obtain the desired flexible representation by the constraint $C(c, m, purchase(goods))$ •→ $C(m, c, sold(goods, price)) \land C(m, c, sentEnc(goods))$, both allowing to start from an offer and keeping the guarantee that the customer receives the expected quotations when performing a request.

4 Correctness Properties of MAS

In Section 2 we assumed that *agents* are made of two components: a set of actions and a set of behavioral rules. Actions, see Fig. 3, are the basic building blocks of the agent's behavior. We do not make any assumption on how agents' actions are represented. They can have (or have no) preconditions to their execution, effects, or conditional effects on the agent's mental state. Their implementation is local to the agent. In this work, following [15,38], we abstract away from the implementation details and represent the agents' actions as they are represented inside the interaction protocols. The same is done for the behavioral rules. In particular, we use the language 2CL, obtaining a representation that is homogeneous with the representation of the regulative specification of interaction protocols. This language is sufficiently expressive to abstractly represent any kind of behavior, as done for business processes by proposals like [30,27,28].

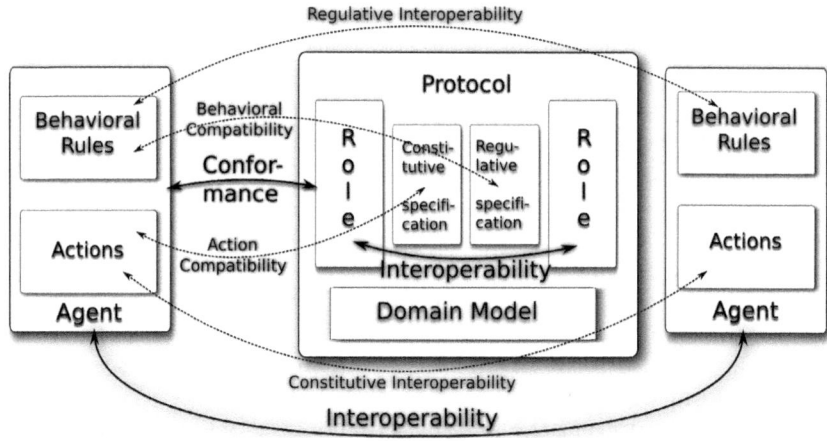

Fig. 3. Interoperability and conformance properties

Considering protocols as *models of the desired interaction* allows one to devise the verification of many properties of the interaction, before any interaction takes place. In order to compare this proposal to [38], in the following we discuss the properties of *interoperability* among agents/roles, and the *conformance* of agents to roles. We end the section with some considerations on the *refinement* property.

4.1 Agent Interoperability and Protocol Interoperability

Intuitively, a set of agents/roles is interoperable when it is stuck-free, i.e., when whatever point of interaction may be reached the system will not be blocked [4]; in other words, when the agents jointly meet the expectations they place on each other [38]. Singh and Chopra [38] consider interoperability as a conjunction of *liveness*, *safety* and *alignment*. *Liveness* means that the system will progress, i.e. it never happens that an agent waits for a message never sent by another agent. More generally, we say that liveness means that it never happens that an agent *waits for an action* that another agent is expected to execute, and that has never been performed. *Safety* means that an agent must be ready to handle messages that it receives. In other words, it is necessary to ensure that messages are sent in the order receivers wait for them. More generally, we say that agents must be *ready to re-act by performing an action* whenever this is expected by some other agent in the system.

Singh and Chopra propose to model liveness and safety by using *potential causality* of sends and receives of messages. The two properties are characterized by the compatibility among causal orders of sends and receives [25]. However, one of the key points of commitment protocols is that they allow ruling not only sends and receives but any social action whose meaning is agreed upon. For instance, the agents may agree upon the action *receiving goods* and *paying goods*, and the order expected by one of the two, say the customer, could be that goods will be paid only after reception. How to extend the notion of causality to the more general case? It would be necessary to express in some way the causal relations expected by the role players because they are not so obvious as with messages. Moreover, causality may be just one possible relation concerning the ordering of actions (other relations could be useful as shown in the Net Bill example). Even more importantly, agents rather than observing each other's *actions*, observe the *social state*, so it is more advisable that such relations concern the *evolution of the social state*. The regulative specification, being aimed at expressing constraints on the evolution of the social state, should indeed express such properties. We represent it by means of the language 2CL described in Section 3. In the case it is necessary to verify the interoperability of a set of protocol roles (also called *operability* in [38]), we suppose the regulative specification given as part of the protocol. Instead, in the case one wants to verify the interoperability of a set of agents, it is necessary that agents disclose, at least in a partial way, their own behavioral rules (same assumption of [38]). This, of course, supposing that they are already aligned on the meaning of their actions.

Alignment means that whenever an agent concludes to be the creditor of a commitment the corresponding debtor concludes that it is the debtor of the same commitment. The verification of alignment [15,19] includes the verification of *constitutive interoperability* [18,38]. Agents are constitutively interoperable when they would agree about whatever commitments as might result from any messages they might exchange. Constitutive interoperability can be verified by reasoning on the *Actions* component of the involved agents, Fig. 3. Constitutive interoperability is included also in our proposal. In addition, since we foresee a decoupled representation of the regulative and of the constitutive specifications, it is possible to check also interoperability at the level of regulative specifications and to see if agents are, for instance, compatible at the level of actions but not at the level of behavior or the other way around. As a final observation, some alignment rules [15,19] could actually be constraints specified in the regulative rules.

4.2   Conformance and Substitutability

The limit of verifying properties at the level of groups of individual agents is that the verifications can be done only when all such agents have been identified. The verifications are to be repeated whenever the group changes, i.e. when one of the agents leaves the group or is substituted by a new one. Protocols allow overcoming this limit. Given a protocol whose roles show the desired properties (mainly interoperability), it is possible to check agents one by one against the corresponding roles to see if they can interpret the role preserving the protocol properties (*substitutability*). When the protocol property of interest is interoperability, the substitutability is guaranteed by the *conformance* relation.

In our setting, we can specify two levels of conformance: conformance at the level of actions (*constitutive conformance*), and conformance at the level of behavior (*regulative conformance*). Constitutive conformance aims at verifying that an agent can establish a *count-as* relation between its own actions and the social actions. The reason is that when agents have to interact with one another in the context of a protocol they must be capable of providing an implementation for each of the actions accounted for by the role they want to play. Notice that it is not required that agents have actions that *exactly* match with the social actions [45,7,15]. It is not even required to have a 1-1 relation, so an agent may implement a social action by means of a sequence of its own actions.

By regulative conformance we mean the fact that the behavioral rules of the agent are not in conflict with the regulative specification of the protocol. Since, in general, the agent's behavioral rules can restrict the behaviors allowed by the regulative specification, it is also necessary to check that these restrictions do not impose constraints on the other players. In other words, the player is allowed to restrict its own behavior but it should not limit the freedom of the other agents, when they behave as specified by the protocol. For instance, in the Net Bill protocol the customer can continue to ask for offers until it receives one that it likes. If an agent playing the role of merchant has a constraint saying that it can produce only one offer, then, that agent limits the freedom of any agent playing the role of customer, which has the right (according to the protocol) to ask for as many offers as it likes. In general, the behavioral rules of an agent do not have to offend the autonomy of choice the protocol gives to the other agents.

One last property that it is interesting to mention is *compliance*, which amounts to verifying that an *execution* of an agent respects the expectations of the others, in the context of a protocol, e.g. [13]. As a difference with [38], the presence of the regulative specification of the protocol allows verifying along the run if the agent violates the constraints given by the protocol, without waiting to arrive to the end to see if all commitments are discharged. To put it simply, violations can be intercepted earlier.

4.3   Protocol Generalizations/Refinements

In interaction protocol engineering, it is often desirable to specialize or to generalize protocols so as to deal with more specific or wider contexts, e.g. [3].

The modular nature of our proposal allows the introduction of two levels of generalization/refinement: at the constitutive level, i.e. at the level of actions as in [38] as well as at the regulative level. In this latter case, we exploit the declarative nature of 2CL by producing broader or stricter sets of constraints. The so obtained protocols can be organized in a taxonomy. As an example, one might wish the Net Bill to handle in a special way the case in which some goods are free: when this happens no payment is requested. The implementation can be obtained (Figure 4) as a generalization of the Net Bill (Figure 2) by enriching the constraints with a XOR that introduces a new branch for the free-goods case:

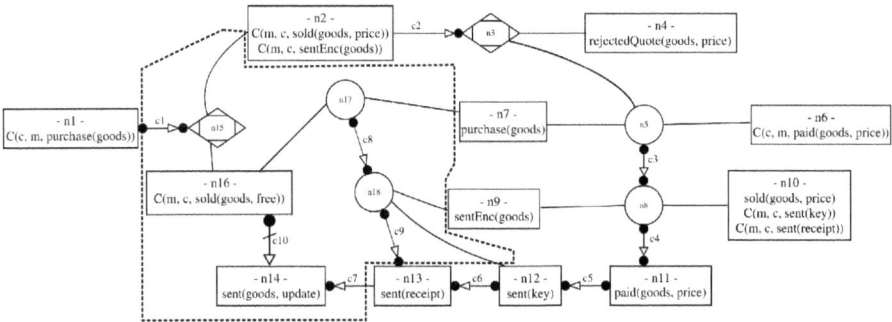

Fig. 4. Regulative specification of the generalized Net Bill: the dashed line highlights the constraints ruling the purchase of free goods. Boxes represent conjunctions of literals, circles represent conjunctions of boxes, diamonds represent the XOR of boxes

c1: $C(c, m, purchase(goods)) \bullet\!\!\!-\!\!\!\twoheadrightarrow C(m, c, sold(goods, free))$ XOR
     $(C(m, c, sold(goods, price)) \wedge C(m, c, sentEnc(goods)))$
c7: $sent(receipt) -\!\!\!\twoheadrightarrow sent(goods, update)$
c8: $C(m, c, sold(goods, free)) \wedge purchase(goods) \bullet\!\!\!-\!\!\!\twoheadrightarrow$
     $sentEnc(goods) \wedge sent(key)$
c9: $sentEnc(goods) \wedge sent(key) \bullet\!\!\!-\!\!\!\twoheadrightarrow sent(receipt)$
c10: $C(m, c, sold(goods, free)) \bullet\!\!\!-\!\!\!\not\twoheadrightarrow sent(goods, update)$

Constraint $c1$ was modified to explicitly tackle the free-goods case. Constraint $c8$ states that goods are sent together with the key if both the merchant has offered it for free and the customer has accepted to purchase it (literal *purchase(goods)*). The receipt is sent at the end ($c9$). Finally, ($c10$) if some information updates become available, the merchant does not send it if the customer bought the information for free.

5   Conclusion and Related Works

This work proposes a commitment-based approach to protocol definition, that is inspired by the work of Singh and colleagues [16,36,44,43,15,38], which introduces an explicit representation of both constitutive and regulative specifications in the spirit of [33,12]. Both specifications are given in a declarative way. The constitutive specification gives the meaning of the social actions, in terms of operations on the social state, as in [15]. The regulative specification is given as a set of constraints on the evolution of the social state expressed in 2CL. The semantics of 2CL is grounded on LTL. The proposed approach keeps the flexibility of commitment-based protocols, *indirectly* ruling the execution of the actions. The regulative specification is introduced because, in our opinion and we have tried to prove it in this analysis, the mere constitutive specification of actions is not sufficient, because agents have a behavior and this behavior makes them use actions according to specific patterns. By our proposal and by exploiting a declarative language, we have proved that it is possible to express interaction patterns without losing the flexibility of commitment-based protocols. We do this by putting constraints on the evolution of the social state and not on actions because, as shown in [6,5], this allows a greater modularity in the specification, with the advantages discussed in Section 2. In this paper, we have also shown that the introduction of a regulative specification does not compromise the proof of interoperability properties but rather it allows finer verifications.

Chopra and Singh [18] recognize the distinction between constitutive and regulative specifications in the definition of commitment-based protocols but focus their work on the constitutive component only, see [15,17,38]. When there is the need to constrain the behavior of agents, they use preconditions to the (non-)executability of the actions. This solution (which is adopted also by other works, like [24,43,44,15,41]) is characterized by a *strong localization* of the regulative specification; the constitutive and the regulative specifications are indistinguishable (being both inside the definition of actions) and actions become dependant on the protocol they are used in. This limits the openness of the system and in particular complicates the re-use of software (the agents' actions). A too tight relation to actions can be ascribed also to [37], although in this work it is possible to recognize the introduction of a regulative specification, based on the *before* relation. Such relations are, however, applied to events/actions. Fornara and Colombetti [22,23] recognize the need of a regulation of the flow of execution but adopted *interaction diagrams* in the definition of agent interaction protocols. Interaction diagrams force the ordering of action executions, loosing, in our opinion the flexibility aimed at by the adoption of commitments.

Outside the Agents research area, Pesic and van der Aalst [30] propose an approach that uses the declarative language ConDec for representing business processes (which, though not exactly interaction protocols, specify the expected behavior of a set of interacting parties by constraining the execution of their tasks). The nature of the specification is constitutive because it defines a behavior rather than regulating an antecedently existing reality. The constitutive specification is given at two levels: a level that specifies constraints, which builds upon a level that specifies the actions. In [27,14,28], the authors use this approach to specify interaction protocols and service choreographies. To this aim, they integrate ConDec with SCIFF thus giving a semantics to actions that is based on *expectations*. Even if one uses the above model not just to design processes but with a regulative intent, other problems emerge, due to the fact that constraints are defined over actions (events). This, in our opinion, clashes with the openness of MAS. With respect to [39], our proposal does not handle time explicitly so we cannot yet represent and handle timeouts and also compensation mechanisms. We plan to tackle these issues in future work.

Acknowledgements

The authors would like to thank the reviewers for the helpful comments. This research has partially been funded by "Regione Piemonte" through the project ICT4LAW.

References

1. Alberti, M., Daolio, D., Torroni, P., Gavanelli, M., Lamma, E., Mello, P.: Specification and Verification of Agent Interaction Protocols in a Logic-based System. In: Haddad, H., Omicini, A., Wainwright, R.L., Liebrock, L.M. (eds.) Proceedings of the 2004 ACM Symposium on Applied Computing (SAC), Nicosia, Cyprus, March 2004, pp. 72–78. ACM, New York (2004)
2. Alur, R., Henzinger, T.A., Kupferman, O., Vardi, M.Y.: Alternating Refinement Relations. In: Sangiorgi, D., de Simone, R. (eds.) CONCUR 1998. LNCS, vol. 1466, pp. 163–178. Springer, Heidelberg (1998)
3. Astefanoaei, L., de Boer, F.S.: Model-checking Agent Refinement. In: Padgham, et al [29], pp. 705–712
4. Baldoni, M., Baroglio, C., Chopra, A.K., Desai, N., Patti, V., Singh, M.P.: Choice, Interoperability, and Conformance in Interaction Protocols and Service Choreographies. In: Sierra, et al [34], pp. 843–850
5. Baldoni, M., Baroglio, C., Marengo, E.: Behavior-Oriented Commitment-based Protocols. In: Coelho, H., Studer, R., Wooldridge, M. (eds.) Proc. of 19th European Conference on Artificial Intelligence (ECAI 2010), Lisbon, Portugal, August 2010. Frontiers in Artificial Intelligence and Applications, vol. 215, pp. 137–142. IOS Press, Amsterdam (2010)
6. Baldoni, M., Baroglio, C., Marengo, E.: Constraints among Commitments: Regulative Specification of Interaction Protocols. In: Artikis, A., Bentahar, J., Chopra, A.K., Dignum, F. (eds.) Proc. of International Workshop on Agent Communication (AC 2010), held in conjuction with AAMAS 2010, Toronto, Canada, pp. 2–18 (May 2010)
7. Baldoni, M., Baroglio, C., Patti, V., Schifanella, C.: Conservative Re-use Ensuring Matches for Service Selection. In: Klugl, F., Padget, J. (eds.) Proc. of Sixth European Workshop on Multi-Agent Systems (EUMAS 2008), Bath, UK, Seneca Edizioni (December 2008)
8. Baldoni, M., Bentahar, J., van Riemsdijk, M.B., Lloyd, J. (eds.): DALT 2009. LNCS, vol. 5948. Springer, Heidelberg (2010)
9. Boella, G., van der Torre, L.W.N.: Regulative and Constitutive Norms in Normative Multiagent Systems. In: Dubois, D., Welty, C.A., Williams, M.-A. (eds.) Principles of Knowledge Representation and Reasoning: Proceedings of the Ninth International Conference (KR 2004), Whistler, Canada, June 2004, pp. 255–266. AAAI Press, Menlo Park (2004)

10. Bravetti, M., Zavattaro, G.: A Theory of Contracts for Strong Service Compliance. Mathematical Structures in Computer Science 19(3), 601–638 (2009)
11. Castelfranchi, C.: Commitments: From Individual Intentions to Groups and Organizations. In: Lesser, V.R., Gasser, L. (eds.) Proceedings of the First International Conference on Multiagent Systems (ICMAS), San Francisco, California, USA, June 1995, pp. 41–48. The MIT Press, Cambridge (1995)
12. Cherry, C.: Regulative Rules and Constitutive Rules. The Philosophical Quarterly 23(93), 301–315 (1973)
13. Chesani, F., Mello, P., Montali, M., Riguzzi, F., Sebastianis, M., Storari, S.: Checking compliance of execution traces to business rules. In: Ardagna, D., Mecella, M., Yang, J. (eds.) Business Process Management Workshops. LNBIP, vol. 17, pp. 134–145. Springer, Heidelberg (2009)
14. Chesani, F., Mello, P., Montali, M., Torroni, P.: Verifying A-Priori the Composition of Declarative Specified Services. In: Baldoni, M., Baroglio, C., Bentahar, J., Boella, G., Cossentino, M., Dastani, M., Dunin-Keplicz, B., Fortino, G., Gleizes, M.P., Leite, J., Mascardi, V., Padget, J.A., Pavón, J., Polleres, A., Fallah-Seghrouchni, A.E., Torroni, P., Verbrugge, R. (eds.) Proceedings of the Second Multi-Agent Logics, Languages, and Organisations Federated Workshops (MALLOW), Turin, Italy, September 2009. CEUR Workshop Proceedings, vol. 494. CEUR-WS.org (2009)
15. Chopra, A.K.: Commitment Alignment: Semantics, Patterns, and Decision Procedures for Distributed Computing. PhD thesis, North Carolina State University, Raleigh, NC (2009)
16. Chopra, A.K., Singh, M.P.: Nonmonotonic Commitment Machines. In: Dignum, F. (ed.) ACL 2003. LNCS (LNAI), vol. 2922, pp. 183–200. Springer, Heidelberg (2004)
17. Chopra, A.K., Singh, M.P.: Contextualizing Commitment Protocol. In: Nakashima, H., Wellman, M.P., Weiss, G., Stone, P. (eds.) 5th International Joint Conference on Autonomous Agents and Multiagent Systems (AAMAS 2006), Hakodate, Japan, May 2006, pp. 1345–1352. ACM, New York (2006)
18. Chopra, A.K., Singh, M.P.: Constitutive interoperability. In: Padgham, et al [29], pp. 797–804
19. Chopra, A.K., Singh, M.P.: Multiagent Commitment Alignment. In: Sierra, et al [34], pp. 937–944
20. Cox, B., Doug Tygar, J., Sirbu, M.: NetBill Security and Transaction Protocol. In: First USENIX Workshop on Electronic Commerce (WOEC 1995), pp. 77–88 (July 1995)
21. Allen Emerson, E.: Temporal and Modal Logic. In: van Leeuwen, J. (ed.) Handbook of Theoretical Computer Science. Formal Models and Sematics, vol. B, pp. 995–1072. North-Holland Pub. Co./MIT Press (1990)
22. Fornara, N.: Interaction and Communication among Autonomous Agents in Multiagent Systems. PhD thesis, Università della Svizzera italiana, Facoltà di Scienze della Comunicazione (December 2003)
23. Fornara, N., Colombetti, M.: A Commitment-Based Approach To Agent Communication. Applied Artificial Intelligence 18(9-10), 853–866 (2004)
24. Giordano, L., Martelli, A., Schwind, C.: Specifying and Verifying Interaction Protocols in a Temporal Action Logic. Journal of Applied Logic 5(2), 214–234 (2007)
25. Lamport, L.: Time, Clocks, and the Ordering of Events in a Distributed System. Communication of the ACM 21(7), 558–565 (1978)
26. Mallya, A.U., Singh, M.P.: Introducing Preferences into Commitment Protocols. In: Dignum, F., van Eijk, R.M., Flores, R.A. (eds.) AC 2005. LNCS (LNAI), vol. 3859, pp. 136–149. Springer, Heidelberg (2006)

27. Montali, M.: Specification and Verification of Declarative Open Interaction Models: a Logic-Based Approach. LNBIP, vol. 56. Springer, Heidelberg (2010)
28. Montali, M., Pesic, M., van der Aalst, W.M.P., Chesani, F., Mello, P., Storari, S.: Declarative Specification and Verification of Service Choreographiess. ACM Transactions on the Web (TWEB) 4(1) (2010)
29. Padgham, L., Parkes, D.C., Müller, J.P., Parsons, S. (eds.): 7th International Joint Conference on Autonomous Agents and Multiagent Systems (AAMAS 2008), Estoril, Portugal, May 12-16, vol. 2. IFAAMAS (2008)
30. Pesic, M., van der Aalst, W.M.P.: A Declarative Approach for Flexible Business Processes Management. In: Eder, J., Dustdar, S. (eds.) BPM Workshops 2006. LNCS, vol. 4103, pp. 169–180. Springer, Heidelberg (2006)
31. Rajamani, S.K., Rehof, J.: Conformance Checking for Models of Asynchronous Message Passing Software. In: Brinksma, E., Larsen, K.G. (eds.) CAV 2002. LNCS, vol. 2404, pp. 166–179. Springer, Heidelberg (2002)
32. Russell, S., Norvig, P.: Artificial Intelligence: A Modern Approach, 2nd edn. Series in Artificial Intelligence. Prentice-Hall, Englewood Cliffs (2003)
33. Searle, J.: Speech Acts. Cambridge University Press, Cambridge (1969)
34. Sierra, C., Castelfranchi, C., Decker, K.S., Sichman, J.S. (eds.): 8th International Joint Conference on Autonomous Agents and Multiagent Systems (AAMAS 2009), Budapest, Hungary, May 10-15, vol. 2. IFAAMAS (2009)
35. Singh, M.P.: An Ontology for Commitments in Multiagent Systems. Artificial Intelligence and Law 7(1), 97–113 (1999)
36. Singh, M.P.: A Social Semantics for Agent Communication Languages. In: Dignum, F., Greaves, M. (eds.) Issues in Agent Communication. LNCS, vol. 1916, pp. 31–45. Springer, Heidelberg (2000)
37. Singh, M.P.: Distributed Enactment of Multiagent Workflows: Temporal Logic for Web Service Composition. In: The Second International Joint Conference on Autonomous Agents & Multiagent Systems (AAMAS 2003), Melbourne, Victoria, Australia, July 2003, pp. 907–914. ACM, New York (2003)
38. Singh, M.P., Chopra, A.K.: Correctness Properties for Multiagent Systems. In: Baldoni, et al [8], pp. 192–207
39. Torroni, P., Chesani, F., Mello, P., Montali, M.: Social Commitments in Time: Satisfied or Compensated. In: Baldoni, et al [8], pp. 228–243
40. van Riemsdijk, M.B.: Cognitive Agent Programming, a Semantic Approach. PhD thesis, Dutch Research School for Information and Knowledge Systems, Utrecht University, the Netherlands (2006)
41. Winikoff, M., Liu, W., Harland, J.: Enhancing Commitment Machines. In: Leite, J.A., Omicini, A., Torroni, P., Yolum, P. (eds.) DALT 2004. LNCS (LNAI), vol. 3476, pp. 198–220. Springer, Heidelberg (2005)
42. Wooldridge, M.J.: An Introduction to MultiAgent Systems. John Wiley & Sons, Chichester (2002)
43. Yolum, P., Singh, M.P.: Commitment Machines. In: Meyer, J.-J.C., Tambe, M. (eds.) ATAL 2001. LNCS (LNAI), vol. 2333, pp. 235–247. Springer, Heidelberg (2002)
44. Yolum, P., Singh, M.P.: Designing and Executing Protocols using the Event Calculus. In: Proceedings of the Fifth International Conference on Autonomous Agents, pp. 27–28 (2001)
45. Zaremski, A.M., Wing, J.M.: Specification Matching of Software Components. ACM Transactions on Software Engineering and Methodology (TOSEM) 6(4), 333–369 (1997)

A Deduction System for Meaning Negotiation

Elisa Burato, Matteo Cristani, and Luca Viganò

Dipartimento di Informatica, Università di Verona, Italy
{elisa.burato,matteo.cristani,luca.vigano}@univr.it

Abstract. Meaning negotiation (MN) is the general process with which agents reach an agreement about the meaning of a set of terms. We give here a general model of MN for two agents, in which each agent discusses with the other one her viewpoint by exhibiting it in an actual set of constraints on the meaning of the negotiated terms. We call this presentation of individual viewpoints an angle. The two agents do not aim at forming a common viewpoint but, instead, at agreeing about an acceptable common angle. We formalize the process of reaching such an agreement by giving a deduction system that comprises of rules that are consistent and adequate for representing MN.

1 Introduction: Context and Contributions

A *negotiation* is a dialog (i.e., a conversation between two or more agents) intended to resolve disputes, to produce an agreement upon courses of action, to bargain for individual or collective advantage, or to craft outcomes to satisfy various interests. *Meaning negotiation* (MN) is the process that takes place when the involved agents have some knowledge (some data or information) to share but do not agree on what knowledge they share and how they reach an agreement about it. The knowledge of an agent represents her viewpoint and we call *angle* any partial representation of the viewpoint; hence, the knowledge of a negotiating agent is built by a single viewpoint and many angles. In this paper, we assume that angles are presented as *logical theories*, and in particular *propositional* ones. At the beginning of a MN process, agents are in disagreement, i.e., they have mutually inconsistent knowledge. By MN, they try to reach a common angle representing a shared acceptable knowledge, where the MN ends in positive way when the agents have a common knowledge, and it ends in a negative way otherwise: agents are in *agreement* when they have found a set of constraints on the meaning of the negotiated terms that is accepted by both agents (this new theory is named, here, a *common angle*); they are in *disagreement* when they are not in agreement.

MN has been considered, directly or indirectly, in a large number of works, ranging from works focusing on operations over ontologies (e.g., [8,10]), such as mapping, merging and alignment, to works dealing with contexts (e.g., [7]) or, more generally, to research in the field of knowledge representation (e.g., [5]). In particular, [6] considers the combination of agent communication and ontology alignment within a group of agents. Only a few works, however, have

A. Omicini, S. Sardina, and W. Vasconcelos (Eds.): DALT 2010, LNAI 6619, pp. 78–95, 2011.
© Springer-Verlag Berlin Heidelberg 2011

considered MN as a process; for instance, [12] deals with MN as an ontology mapping process through an argumentation framework, and [14,9,1,15,2] deal with negotiation issues from the point of view of game theory. A MN between two agents is similar to a *Bargaining Game* [11], i.e., the game in which two agents have to share, say, one dollar and do this by each making a proposal. If the sum of their demands is less than one, they share the dollar, otherwise they have to make a new demand. The Bargaining Game is built by two stages:

- *Demand stage*: agents make a proposal and if the proposals are compatible, the negotiation ends in positive way; otherwise the second stage begins.
- *War of attrition*: agents have incompatible viewpoints and perform new demands. If the demands are compatible, the process ends positively, otherwise they make new ones.

In the Bargaining Game, players have a *negotiation power* that represents how often an agent cedes during the negotiation and how much she resists about her current angle. The negotiation power of an agent is captured by a set of partially ordered angles of her viewpoint. The partial order among the angles allows an agent to choose the next proposal to perform, and to evaluate the acceptability of the received offers. Moreover, the set of partially ordered angles has a minimum that identifies the last offer an agent proposes in a negotiation. We say that each agent has a *stubborn* and many *flexible* angles that are respectively the limit proposal (i.e., the last offer) and the acceptable ones, where each flexible angle is consistent with the stubborn knowledge.

Example 1. As a running example, consider the definition of the term "vehicle". Alice (stubbornly) thinks that it always has two, three, four or six wheels; a handlebar or a steering wheel; a motor, or two or four bicycle pedals, or a tow bar. Moreover, Alice (flexibly) thinks that a "vehicle" may be defined only as a car, then having four wheels, a steering wheel, and a motor; or only as a bicycle, then having two wheels, a handlebar and two bicycle pedals. In other words, Alice has two acceptable ways to define a vehicle (i.e., a car or a bicycle as particular "vehicles") but she has only one general description of a "vehicle". □

The MN stages, shown in Fig. 1(a), are the following ones:

- *Init*: the first bidding agent makes a proposal;
- *Negotiate*: the agents propose their viewpoints in turns and evaluate whether they agree with the opponents;
- *Agreement*: all[1] the agents agree on a common viewpoint;
- *Disagreement*: the agents do not have a shared viewpoint.

The negotiation power of an agent is known only by herself, and when an agent makes a proposal, she includes stubborn and flexible knowledge in it. Conversely, when looking at the knowledge of the other agent, one is not able to say on what knowledge the other agent would be stubborn.

---

[1] [3] consider more than two negotiating agents and formalize a partial positive outcome, in which a degree of sharing denotes the minimum number of agreeing agents needed to consider the MN as positive.

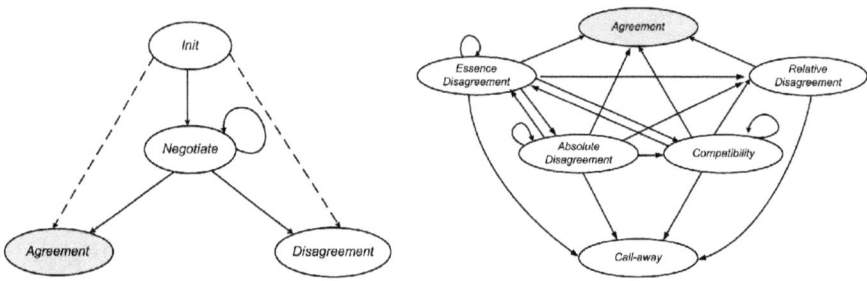

(a) Finite state diagram of the MN process

(b) Finite state diagram of each negotiating agent

Fig. 1. Finite state diagrams of the MN process (a) and of a negotiating agent (b)

The *first contribution* of this paper is the definition of a general model of MN in which the two agents have different viewpoints that are not completely compatible. In our model, the types of disagreement depend upon the relation among the proposal p and the stubborn and the flexible knowledge of the agent i who receives and evaluates p:

- *Call-away* occurs when p is a generalization[2] of the stubborn knowledge of i, thus it would correspond to dropping out some unquestionable knowledge.
- *Absolute disagreement* occurs when the stubborn knowledge of i is inconsistent with respect to p.
- *Essence disagreement* occurs when the flexible knowledge of i is inconsistent with respect to p.
- *Compatibility* occurs when p is consistent with the flexible knowledge of i but it is not a generalization or a restriction of i's viewpoint.
- *Relative disagreement* occurs when p is a generalization of the flexible knowledge of i.

The call-away situations arise when an agent does not accept all the necessary requests of the other one and thus exits the MN so that the MN ends negatively. In Fig. 1(b), we show the finite state diagram for each negotiating agent, where the disagreement node of Fig. 1(a) is expanded to the types of disagreement we consider here. In a MN process, all the states can be initial and final and the *agreement* state is the optimal final one.

This model accommodates within the same framework, for the first time, two different aspects of MN, not yet treated in an exhaustive manner and never joined in a single model: the relations among the negotiating agents, in terms of viewpoints, and the mechanism of MN by means of a game-theoretic approach.

---

[2] A theory A is a *generalization* of a theory B when the models of A are a superset of the models of B.

The *second contribution* of this paper is the formalization of a deduction system, which we call *MND*, to reason about the MN process. The two agents start the MN process with an initial proposal and concede to each other about the other's viewpoint until a common definition of the terms is obtained. Each agent has a limit in negotiation, since some of her knowledge is unquestionable and, thus, she will never concede about it. Consequently, if no agreement is reached in the first phase of the MN in which the agent is willing to concede, the MN proceeds but the agent becomes firm and she keeps on proposing her last feasible proposal, that is her unquestionable knowledge. If this situation is symmetric, the disagreement condition becomes perpetual and the two agents keep on proposing the same incompatible definitions for the terms under negotiation. The system controls the procedure in what condition is reached. When the agreement condition is reached, the two agents agree about a common definition of the terms and the system ends the MN with positive outcome; when the agents reach a perpetual disagreement condition, the system ends the MN by stating that the agreement cannot be reached.

This is the first formalization of a logical model of MN that hosts a dialogue framework and an agreement relational system together, as said before. This has been the major issue that encouraged us to develop such a system, where an investigation about MN can be carried out by considering all aspects of the process within one single formalism. We envision applications in which humans interact with software agents to reach agreement about the meaning of terms.

MND allows us to express the fact that agents communicate to each other not only the proposals, but also the disagreement conditions they have reached so far. The process is governed by a set of rules that manage the provisional disagreement condition the agents have reached. We first provide rules for deriving streams of dialog between two agents who discuss about the meaning of a set of terms, and then define a deduction system based upon these rules that derives a stream of dialog that ends with an agreement/disagreement condition.

We show that *MND* is consistent and adequate to represent the MN of two agents. Moreover, MN is decidable over theories with finite signature under the assumption of agents who are competitive (in a sense to be defined precisely below). We proceed by formalizing the knowledge and the language of negotiating agents (§ 2), and the language and rules of the MN process (§ 3). Then, in § 4, we draw conclusions and discuss future work. Due to lack of space, discussions and proofs have been shortened or omitted; further details can be found in [4].

2 A Formalization of Negotiating Agents

We consider here a general MN process, so we abstract away from the particular terms whose meaning the agents are negotiating. We formalize first the knowledge (§ 2.1) and then the language (§ 2.2) of negotiating agents.

2.1 The Knowledge of Negotiating Agents

When agents give the definition of a concept, they:

- give the necessary properties (properties about which the agent is stubborn — for short *stubborn properties*) and the characterizing ones (properties about which the agent is flexible — for short *flexible properties*);
- give the properties that necessarily have not to hold and the ones that plausibly (flexibly) have not to hold; and
- give the *relevant formulas*, which assert what has not to (stubbornly), or may not (flexibly), be used in the definition.

The notion of relevance of a formula is interesting at this stage of the definition, but instead of introducing a novel operator, we simply consider a formula as not relevant to an agent if she does not assert it. When i *asserts* a formula φ, she has a way to evaluate it: she thinks φ as positive or negative. If i does not assert φ then either i does not know φ, i.e., she is not able to evaluate it or i does not think φ is relevant in defining the negotiated meaning.

The necessary and the characterizing properties of a concept definition are closely related to *EGG/YOLK* objects, introduced by [13] to represent class membership based on typicality of the members: the egg is the set of the class members and the yolk is the set of the *typical* ones. (The EGG/YOLK model is a spatial metaphor for the concept of fuzzy set.) For instance, the class of "employees" of a company A may be defined as "the set of people that receive money from the company in exchange for carrying out the instructions of a person who is an employee of that company", thus excluding, e.g., the head of the company (who has no boss), and the typical employee would include regular workers like secretaries and foremen. Another company B might have a different definition, e.g., including the head of the company, resulting in a mismatch. Nevertheless, if both companies provide some typical examples of "employees" it is possible that all of A's typical employees fit B's definition, and all of B's typical employees fit A's definition: $YOLK_B \leq EGG_A$ and $YOLK_A \leq EGG_B$, in the terminology of [13].

Differently than in the original model, concept definitions are here restricted by stubborn properties to the largest acceptable set of models, hence represented by the egg, whilst the yolk is employed to denote the most restricted knowledge, i.e., the one on which the agents are flexible and about which they may cede.

The stubborn properties never change during the MN; thus, the egg is fixed at the beginning of the MN. Instead, the flexible part of the definition of a concept is the core of the proposal of a negotiating agent. Each proposal differs from the further ones in two possible ways: it may give a definition of the negotiated object that is more descriptive than the next ones, or the given definition specifies properties that the next ones do not and vice versa. In the former case, we say that the agent carries out a *weakening action*, in the latter the agent carries out a *changing theory action*. However, none of weakening or changing theory actions can be carried out with respect to a proposal if the proposal describes the necessary properties of the object in the MN. We say that in such a situation the agents always make a *stubbornness action* that is equivalent to *no more change*.

Table 1. Rules for making new proposals and the corresponding EGG/YOLKs. The dark gray yolk identifies $flex_i^{k+1}$ and the light gray one identifies $flex_i^k$.

$$\frac{flex_i^k \rightarrow flex_i^{k+1} \quad \neg(stub_i \leftrightarrow flex_i^k)}{flex_i^{k+1}} \ (W)$$

$$\frac{flex_i^k \quad \neg(stub_i \leftrightarrow flex_i^k) \quad \neg(flex_i^k \rightarrow flex_i^{k+1}) \quad \neg(flex_i^{k+1} \rightarrow flex_i^k)}{flex_i^{k+1}} \ (C)$$

$$\frac{\varphi \quad stub_i \leftrightarrow \varphi}{\varphi} \ (S)$$

2.2 The Language of Negotiating Agents

Each agent i is represented by her language $\mathcal{L}_i$, which is composed of two disjoint sublanguages: a *stubbornness* language containing the properties i deems as necessary in defining the negotiated meaning and a *flexible* language containing the properties i deems as not necessary in the MN.

Definition 1. *Let* Ag *be the set of the* negotiating agents. *The signature* Σ_i *of an agent* $i \in$ Ag *is the pair* $\langle \mathcal{P}_i, \alpha_i \rangle$ *where* $\mathcal{P}_i$ *is the set of the predicate symbols and* α_i *is the arity function for predicate symbols* $\alpha_i : \mathcal{P}_i \rightarrow \mathbb{N}$.
 The language $\mathcal{L}_i$ *of* $i \in$ Ag *comprises of* Σ_i*-formulas defined as follows:* (i) *if* $P \in \mathcal{P}_i$, $\alpha_i(P) = n$ *and* $t_1, \ldots, t_n$ *are terms then* $P(t_1, \ldots, t_n)$ *is a* Σ_i*-formula;* (ii) *if* φ *and* ψ *are* Σ_i*-formulas then so are* $\neg\varphi$, $\varphi \wedge \psi$, $\varphi \vee \psi$, *and* $\varphi \rightarrow \psi$.
 $\mathcal{L}_i = \mathcal{L}_{\mathcal{S}_i} \cup \mathcal{L}_{\mathcal{F}_i}$ *where the set* $\mathcal{L}_{\mathcal{S}_i}$ *of stubborn formulas is disjoint from the set* $\mathcal{L}_{\mathcal{F}_i}$ *of flexible formulas. We define* $stub_i = \bigwedge_{\varphi \in \mathcal{L}_{\mathcal{S}_i}} \varphi$ *and* $flex_i = \bigwedge_{\varphi \in \mathcal{L}_{\mathcal{F}_i}} \varphi$.

During a MN process, the viewpoint of each agent is presented in a specific *angle*. In other words, a viewpoint is a hierarchy of theories, related by the partial order relation of weakening, and an element of this hierarchy is an angle. Each agent presents angles in sequence during the MN. Thus we call *current angle formula* (CAF) the angle presented at the current stage of the MN. A flexible formula $flex_i^k$ expresses the kth *angle* asserted in the MN by the agent i and it changes during the process. We assume here that for each CAF $flex_i^k$ there is a stubborn formula in $\mathcal{L}_{\mathcal{S}_i}$ that is a generalization of it. In general, during a negotiation of the meaning of a term, the agents relax their viewpoint in order to meet the opponent's one, and they do this only if the relaxing formula is not too general. Then, for each assertion in the MN, the agents have a maximal generalization of it and this is a formula in the stubbornness set. For instance, if the object of the negotiation is the meaning of *pen*, an agent is flexible on the ink color of the object but not on the fact that the object contains ink; then, the *red ink* predicate is a flexible one and the *contains ink* predicate is a stubborn one.

 $flex_i^k$ changes during the MN by applying to it one of the rules for making new proposals given in Table 1: weakening (W), changing theory (C) or stubbornness (S)[3]. The EGG/YOLK representations show the collocation of the new proposal (in the stubbornness situation the new proposal is the same as the last one).

---

[3] Here and in the following, each rule simply has a set of premises above the inference line and a consequence below the inference line.

There are two ways for i to make a new proposal $flex_i^{k+1}$. The weakening rule (W) states that i can propose $flex_i^{k+1}$ if $flex_i^{k+1}$ is entailed by $flex_i^k$ (i.e., $flex_i^k \rightarrow flex_i^{k+1}$) and $flex_i^k$ is not the most general formula the agent can negotiate (corresponding to her stubbornness viewpoint, i.e., $flex_i^k \leftrightarrow stub_i$). Note that if i weakens, say, $flex_i^0$ to the new CAF $flex_i^1$, then i may be no more able to satisfy $flex_i^0$.

The rule (C) states that i can just change theory. Although we do not consider MN strategies in detail here, in general, an agent chooses whether to perform a weakening or a changing theory action by applying the corresponding rule, but there are situations in which one action is better than the other. For instance, when an agent checks the compatibility situation it seems better to weaken the theory so to try to entail the opponent's viewpoint, while in essence disagreement situations it seems better to change the theory so to try to meet the opponent's viewpoint.

If agent i is in stubbornness does she continue the MN or does she have to exit it? We assume that the agent exits the MN only if all the agents in the negotiation are stubborn. But an agent does not know the opponent's stubbornness viewpoint, so the exit condition is recognized only by the system. However, the stubborn agent always makes the same proposal during the MN, as expressed by the rule (S). If $flex_i^k \leftrightarrow stub_i$ then $flex_i^{k_1} = flex_i^{k_1+1}$ for all $k_1 > k$.

We introduce a set of Σ_i-structures as agents change angles during the MN process and these angles have to be satisfied in a different structure. We use a parameter k to denote the kth structure of the kth angle.

Definition 2. *Given a signature $\Sigma_i = \langle \mathcal{P}_i, \alpha_i \rangle$, a Σ_i-structure $\mathcal{A}_i$ is a pair $\langle \mathcal{D}_i, \mathcal{I}_i \rangle$ where the domain $\mathcal{D}_i$ is a finite non-empty set and the interpretation function $\mathcal{I}_i$ is such that $\mathcal{I}_i(P) \subseteq \mathcal{D}_i^n$ for all $P \in \mathcal{P}_i$ for which $\alpha(P) = n$.*

We define $\mathcal{S}_i = \{ \mathcal{A}_i^k \mid \mathcal{A}_i^k = \langle \mathcal{D}_i^k, \mathcal{I}_i^k \rangle \}$ where $\mathcal{D}_i^k \subseteq \mathcal{D}_i$ and, for all $(\mathcal{I}_i^k, \mathcal{I}_i^{k+1})$, if the $(k+1)^{\text{th}}$ rule that i applied is

- *(W), then $\mathcal{I}_i^k(P) \subseteq \mathcal{I}_i^{k+1}(P)$ for all $P \in \mathcal{P}_i$;*
- *(C), then $\mathcal{I}_i^k(P) \not\subseteq \mathcal{I}_i^{k+1}(P)$, $\mathcal{I}_i^k(P) \not\supseteq \mathcal{I}_i^{k+1}(P)$ and $\mathcal{I}_i^k(P) \neq \mathcal{I}_i^{k+1}(P)$, for all $P \in \mathcal{P}_i$;*
- *(S), then $\mathcal{I}_i^k(P) = \mathcal{I}_i^{k+1}(P)$, for all $P \in \mathcal{P}_i$.*

If φ and ψ are Σ_i-formulas then:

- *$\mathcal{A}_i^k \models P(t_1, \ldots, t_n)$ iff $(\mathcal{I}_i(t_1), \ldots, \mathcal{I}_i(t_n)) \in \mathcal{I}_i(P)$, where $P \in \mathcal{P}_i$ and $t_1, \ldots, t_n$ are terms;*
- *$\mathcal{A}_i^k \models \neg \varphi$ iff $\mathcal{A}_i^k \not\models \varphi$;*
- *$\mathcal{A}_i^k \models \varphi \wedge \psi$ iff $\mathcal{A}_i^k \models \varphi$ and $\mathcal{A}_i^k \models \psi$;*
- *$\mathcal{A}_i^k \models \varphi \vee \psi$ iff $\mathcal{A}_i^k \models \varphi$ or $\mathcal{A}_i^k \models \psi$;*
- *$\mathcal{A}_i^k \models \varphi \rightarrow \psi$ iff $\mathcal{A}_i^k \models \psi$ or $\mathcal{A}_i^k \models \neg \varphi$.*

Example 2. Suppose Alice defines "vehicle" as in Example 1. Then

$$stub_A = (has2wheels \vee has3wheels \vee has4wheels \vee has6wheels) \wedge (hasHandlebar \vee$$
$$hasSteeringWheel) \wedge (hasMotor \vee has2bicyclePedals \vee has4bicyclePedals \vee hasTowBar)$$

is the stubbornness part of Alice's knowledge whose interpretation is $\mathcal{I}(stub_A) = \{$bicycle, tandem, motorbike, scooter, truck, car, trailer, chariot$\}$. Let

$$flex_A^k = has4wheels \wedge hasSteeringWheel \wedge (hasMotor \vee has2bicyclePedals)$$

be the CAF of Alice that it is not equivalent to her stubbornness knowledge and its interpretation is $\mathcal{I}(flex_A^k) = \{\mathsf{car}, \mathsf{truck}\} \subset \mathcal{I}(stub_A)$. Suppose Alice changes her CAF by means of a weakening action (W); then:

$$flex_A^{k+1} = (has4wheels \vee has2wheels) \wedge (hasSteeringWheel \vee hasHandlebar) \wedge$$
$$(hasMotor \vee has2bicyclePedals)$$

The interpretation of $flex_A^{k+1}$ is $\mathcal{I}(flex_A^{k+1}) = \{\mathsf{motorbike}, \mathsf{scooter}, \mathsf{car}, \mathsf{truck}\} \subset \mathcal{I}(flex_A^k)$. Otherwise, suppose Alice changes her CAF by means of a changing theory action (C); then:

$$flex_A^{k+1} = has6wheels \wedge hasSteeringWheel \wedge (hasMotor \vee hasTowBar)$$

The interpretation of $flex_A^{k+1}$ is $\mathcal{I}(flex_A^{k+1}) = \{\mathsf{truck}, \mathsf{trailer}\}$ and $\mathcal{I}(flex_A^{k+1}) \not\subseteq \mathcal{I}(flex_A^k)$. □

3   The MN Process

In this section, we first formalize the MN process for two agents, and then formalize the language (§ 3.1) and the rules (§ 3.2) of the MN process. During the MN, agents make proposals and say if they are in agreement or not with respect to the proposals made by the opponent. Proposals are negotiation formulas like $j : \varphi$, where we assume that the opponent i is able to recognize the name label j in $j : \varphi$ and remove it in order to evaluate φ.

In general, negotiating agents may not share the same language but have different signatures. Hence, when i evaluates an assertion by j, she first has to *translate* the symbols occurring in it to symbols belonging to her signature. Such a translation depends, of course, on the particular terms that are being considered for the negotiation, so we assume abstractly that for each pair of agents (i, j) there is the *translation function* $\tau_{i,j} : \Sigma_j \to \Sigma_i$.

When j asserts φ (i.e., $j : \varphi$), i is not able to find which part of φ is in the stubbornness set of j as she only knows that $\varphi = stub_j \wedge \psi^k$ where $stub_j$ is the conjunction of all the formulas in $\mathcal{L}_{\mathcal{S}_j}$ and ψ^k is the kth flexible knowledge of j.

In the following, we describe the main conditions an agent has to test to evaluate the opponent's proposal and to identify the negotiation condition she is in. Suppose that j is the first proponent (bidding) agent and i is the agent evaluating j's proposal. Table 2 shows the EGG/YOLK representations in which i is identified by the plain line and j by the dashed line for each condition i tests; the numbering is that of [13]. Let φ be j's proposal; then, the main conditions i has to test are (as usual, consistency means the impossibility to derive $\bot$):

$(stub_i \to \tau_{i,j}(\varphi))$: are the agents in a *call-away* situation, i.e., is j's proposal a generalization of the stubbornness set of i? If it is the case, then the MN process ends negatively. The corresponding EGG/YOLK representation is shown in Table 2(a)

Table 2. EGG/YOLK representation of the opponent's offer (identified by dashed lines) from agent i's viewpoint (identified by plain lines)

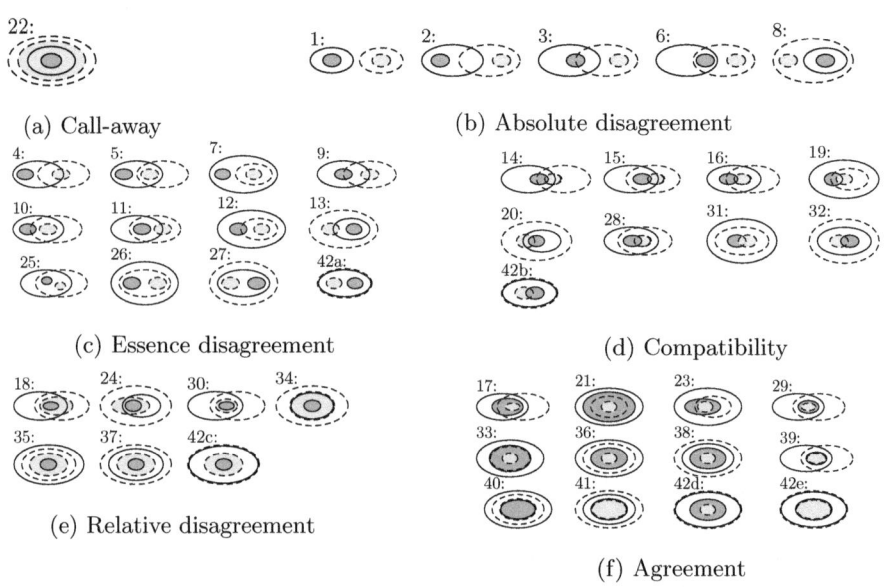

(a) Call-away

(b) Absolute disagreement

(c) Essence disagreement

(d) Compatibility

(e) Relative disagreement

(f) Agreement

$\neg(stub_i \wedge \tau_{i,j}(\varphi))$: is j's proposal consistent with respect to i's stubbornness set? If it is not, then the agents are in *absolute disagreement* (Table 2(b)).

$\neg(flex_i^k \wedge \tau_{i,j}(\varphi)) \wedge (stub_i \vee \tau_{i,j}(\varphi))$: i and j are not in absolute disagreement; is i's CAF consistent with respect to j's proposal? If it is not, then the agents are in *essence disagreement* (Table 2(c)).

$(flex_i^k \rightarrow \tau_{i,j}(\varphi)) \wedge \neg(\tau_{i,j}(\varphi) \rightarrow flex_i^k)$: i and j are not in essence nor in absolute disagreement; is j's proposal a generalization of i's CAF? If it is and if i's CAF is not equivalent to j's proposal, then the agents are in *relative disagreement* (Table 2(e)).

$(flex_i^k \vee \tau_{i,j}(\varphi)) \wedge \neg(flex_i^k \rightarrow \tau_{i,j}(\varphi)) \wedge \neg(\tau_{i,j}(\varphi) \rightarrow flex_i^k)$: i and j are not in absolute nor in relative disagreement; is i's CAF consistent with respect to j's proposal? If it is and if i's CAF is not a weakening of j's proposal, then the agents are in the *compatibility relation* (Table 2(d)).

$(flex_i^k \rightarrow \tau_{i,j}(\varphi))$: the proposal of j is a generalization of i's CAF. The agents are in *agreement* (Table 2(f)) when the received proposal is acceptable for i, i.e., when it is equivalent to her CAF or it is a generalization of her CAF. In the latter case, φ is an acceptable angle because, as said in § 2.2, for each $flex_i^k$ there is a stubborn formula in $\mathcal{L}_{S_i}$ that is a generalization of it. Thus, $flex_i^0 \rightarrow \tau_{i,j}(\varphi)$ and $flex_i^0 \rightarrow stub_i$ yield $\tau_{i,j}(\varphi) \rightarrow stub_i$. In fact, it is not possible that $stub_i \rightarrow \tau_{i,j}(\varphi)$ because this is the call-away condition.

After evaluating the received proposal, agents inform the opponent about the negotiation situation they think to be in. To this end, we extend the formulas in the agent language:

Definition 3. *If φ is a received proposal in the negotiation process, then it is a formula asserted by somebody as $j : \varphi$. We extend the language $\mathcal{L}_i$ with the formulas* $\mathbf{absDis}(j : \varphi)$, $\mathbf{essDis}(j : \varphi)$, $\mathbf{relDis}(j : \varphi)$, $\mathbf{comp}(j : \varphi)$, *and* $\mathbf{agree}(j : \varphi)$. *For* $\mathcal{A}_i^k = \langle \mathcal{D}_i^k, \mathcal{I}_i^k \rangle$ *a Σ_i-structure, the semantics of these additional formulas is:*

- $\mathcal{A}_i^k \models \mathbf{absDis}(j : \varphi)$ *iff* $\mathcal{A}_i^k \models \neg(stub_i \wedge \tau_{i,j}(\varphi))$;
- $\mathcal{A}_i^k \models \mathbf{essDis}(j : \varphi)$ *iff* $\mathcal{A}_i^k \models (stub_i \vee \tau_{i,j}(\varphi)) \wedge \neg(flex_i^k \wedge \tau_{i,j}(\varphi))$;
- $\mathcal{A}_i^k \models \mathbf{relDis}(j : \varphi)$ *iff* $\mathcal{A}_i^k \models (flex_i^k \rightarrow \tau_{i,j}(\varphi)) \wedge \neg(\tau_{i,j}(\varphi) \rightarrow flex_i^k)$;
- $\mathcal{A}_i^k \models \mathbf{comp}(j : \varphi)$ *iff* $\mathcal{A}_i^k \models (flex_i^k \vee \tau_{i,j}(\varphi)) \wedge \neg(flex_i^k \rightarrow \tau_{i,j}(\varphi)) \wedge \neg(\tau_{i,j}(\varphi) \rightarrow flex_i^k)$;
- $\mathcal{A}_i^k \models \mathbf{agree}(j : \varphi)$ *iff* $\mathcal{A}_i^k \models (flex_i^k \rightarrow \tau_{i,j}(\varphi))$.

We did not define a sentence $\mathbf{callAway}(j : \varphi)$ as the call-away condition interrupts the MN. Note also that in our system we restrict the evaluation of agent proposals to formulas in the basic agent language, so no assertion can be made by agents using extended (and nested) formulas like $\mathbf{agree}(\mathbf{comp}(j : \varphi))$. This restriction avoids nested MN processes.

3.1   MN Language

The MN language, $\mathcal{L}$, is built by the assertions of the agents during the MN, i.e., labeled formulas $i : \varphi$ meaning that agent $i \in$ Ag asserts the formula $\varphi \in \mathcal{L}_i$. Thus, $i : \varphi$ represents a proposal the agent i makes in the MN and typically represents her CAF.

Definition 4. *The signature of the MN language $\mathcal{L}$ is $\Sigma = \langle \mathcal{P}, \{\alpha_i\}_{i \in Ag} \rangle$ where $\mathcal{P} = \bigcup_{i \in Ag} \mathcal{P}_i$ and $\alpha_i : \mathcal{P}_i \rightarrow \mathbb{N}$ is the arity function for predicate symbols. Let φ be a $\mathcal{L}_i$ formula for some $i \in$ Ag; then $\mathcal{L}$ comprises of Σ-formulas defined as:*

- $i : \varphi$ *is a Σ-formula;*
- *if φ_1 and φ_2 are Σ-formulas then $\varphi_1 \cap \varphi_2$ is a Σ-formula.*

Let $\mathcal{N}^k = (\{\mathcal{A}_i^{k_i}\}_{i \in Ag, k_i \in \mathbb{N}}, \mathcal{F})$ be a Σ-structure where $\{\mathcal{A}_i^{k_i}\}_{i \in Ag, k_i \in \mathbb{N}}$ is the domain set and $\mathcal{F}$ is an evaluation function mapping name labels into Ag. Then:

- $\mathcal{N}^k \models i : \varphi$ *iff* $\mathcal{A}_{\mathcal{F}(i)}^{k'} \models \varphi$ *where* $k' = \lceil \frac{k}{2} \rceil$ *because the two agents make assertions in turns;*
- $\mathcal{N}^k \models \varphi_1 \cap \varphi_2$ *iff* $\mathcal{N}^k \models \varphi_1$ *and* $\mathcal{N}^k \models \varphi_2$.

3.2   MN Rules

We now give the transition rules the agents use to negotiate depending on the mutual negotiation position they test and on their flexibility; these rules are coupled with those in Table 1. There are different rules for the second proposing agent and the following ones. The transition rules represent the assertions an agent can make during the MN process and show the conditions to be satisfied

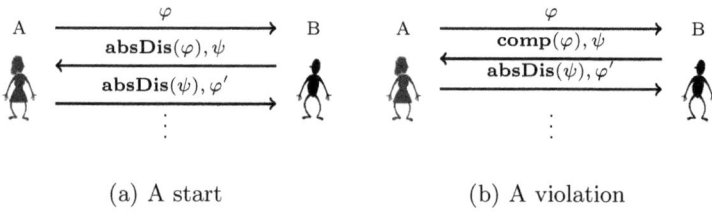

(a) A start   (b) A violation

Fig. 2. Two MN scenarios

Table 3. Rules for the second proposing agent

$$\frac{j:\varphi \quad \neg(stub_i \wedge \tau_{i,j}(\varphi))}{i:\mathbf{absDis}(j:\varphi) \cap i:flex_i^1} \; (AD) \qquad \frac{j:\varphi \quad \neg(flex_i^0 \wedge \tau_{i,j}(\varphi)) \wedge (stub_i \vee \tau_{i,j}(\varphi))}{i:\mathbf{essDis}(j:\varphi) \cap i:flex_i^1} \; (ED)$$

$$\frac{j:\varphi \quad \neg(flex_i^0 \rightarrow \tau_{i,j}(\varphi)) \vee (\tau_{i,j}(\varphi) \rightarrow flex_i^0)}{i:flex_i^0} \; (I) \qquad \frac{j:\varphi \quad (flex_i^0 \rightarrow \tau_{i,j}(\varphi))}{i:\mathbf{agree}(j:\varphi) \cap i:\tau_{i,j}(\varphi)} \; (Ag)$$

$$\frac{j:\varphi \quad (flex_i^0 \vee \tau_{i,j}(\varphi)) \wedge \neg(flex_i^0 \rightarrow \tau_{i,j}(\varphi)) \wedge \neg(\tau_{i,j}(\varphi) \rightarrow flex_i^0)}{i:\mathbf{comp}(j:\varphi) \cap i:flex_i^1} \; (Co)$$

in order to apply the rules. A precondition of the rules of the following proposing agent i is the evaluation of the opponent j about the last proposal of i to
emphasize that only a subset of the negotiation relations in Table 2 is reachable
from a negotiation position depending on the new CAF of agent i. Consider the
scenario in Fig. 2(a): Alice (A) makes the proposal φ and Bob (B) evaluates it
based upon two tests:

1. The relation between his CAF and φ. B's CAF may be in agreement $(\varphi \leftrightarrow flex_B^k)$ or not with φ and B recognizes it by testing the condition listed
   above.
2. His stubbornness condition, i.e., if his CAF is equivalent to $stub_B$ or not.
   Whenever B is stubborn, he performs the same counterproposal, otherwise
   he may relax his CAF by the (W) rule or change it by the (C) rule.

At the end of his evaluation, B replies to A with a counterproposal ψ. When
A evaluates ψ she has to consider the relation between her CAF and ψ, her
stubbornness condition $(stub_A \leftrightarrow flex_A^k)$ and B's evaluation. The evaluation of
the opponent agent helps agents in choosing the new proposal. The choice of the
action, weakening or changing theory, and of the next proposal depends on the
agent's attitude: a *collaborative agent* chooses the proposal that improves the
negotiation relation with the opponent, while a *competitive agent* chooses the
proposal that changes the least the relation with the opponent. For instance, if
B says to A that when A proposes φ they are in essence disagreement, and B
makes the proposal ψ, A will propose φ_1 or φ_2, both inferred from φ by applying
(W) or (C). When A is collaborative, she will propose φ_1 as she knows that they
will be in agreement. Conversely, A will propose φ_2, if A is competitive, as she

Table 4. Rules for the following proposing agents

$$\frac{j : \mathbf{absDis}(i : flex_i^k) \cap j : \psi \quad \neg(stub_i \wedge \tau_{i,j}(\psi))}{i : \mathbf{absDis}(j : \psi) \cap i : flex_i^{k+1}} \ (AD\text{-}AD)$$

$$\frac{j : \mathbf{absDis}(i : flex_i^k) \cap j : \psi \quad (stub_i \vee \tau_{i,j}(\psi)) \wedge \neg(flex_i^{k+1} \wedge \tau_{i,j}(\psi))}{i : \mathbf{essDis}(j : \psi) \cap i : flex_i^{k+1}} \ (AD\text{-}ED)$$

$$\frac{j : \mathbf{absDis}(i : flex_i^k) \cap j : \psi \quad (flex_i^{k+1} \vee \tau_{i,j}(\psi)) \wedge \neg(flex_i^{k+1} \to \tau_{i,j}(\psi)) \wedge \neg(\tau_{i,j}(\psi) \to flex_i^{k+1})}{i : \mathbf{comp}(j : \psi) \cap i : flex_i^{k+1}} \ (AD\text{-}Co)$$

$$\frac{j : \mathbf{absDis}(i : flex_i^k) \cap j : \psi \quad (flex_i^{k+1} \to \tau_{i,j}(\psi)) \wedge \neg(\tau_{i,j}(\psi) \to flex_i^{k+1})}{i : \mathbf{relDis}(j : \psi) \cap i : flex_i^{k+1}} \ (AD\text{-}RD)$$

$$\frac{j : \mathbf{absDis}(i : flex_i^k) \cap j : \psi \quad (flex_i^{k+1} \to \tau_{i,j}(\psi))}{i : \mathbf{agree}(j : \psi) \cap i : \tau_{i,j}(\psi)} \ (AD\text{-}Ag)$$

$$\frac{j : \mathbf{essDis}(i : flex_i^k) \cap j : \psi \quad \neg(stub_i \wedge \tau_{i,j}(\psi))}{i : \mathbf{absDis}(j : \psi) \cap i : flex_i^{k+1}} \ (ED\text{-}AD)$$

$$\frac{j : \mathbf{essDis}(i : flex_i^k) \cap j : \psi \quad (stub_i \vee \tau_{i,j}(\psi)) \wedge \neg(flex_i^{k+1} \wedge \tau_{i,j}(\psi))}{i : \mathbf{essDis}(j : \psi) \cap i : flex_i^{k+1}} \ (ED\text{-}ED)$$

$$\frac{j : \mathbf{essDis}(i : flex_i^k) \cap j : \psi \quad (flex_i^{k+1} \vee \tau_{i,j}(\psi)) \wedge \neg(flex_i^{k+1} \to \tau_{i,j}(\psi)) \wedge \neg(\tau_{i,j}(\psi) \to flex_i^{k+1})}{i : \mathbf{comp}(j : \psi) \cap i : flex_i^{k+1}} \ (ED\text{-}Co)$$

$$\frac{j : \mathbf{essDis}(i : flex_i^k) \cap j : \psi \quad (flex_i^{k+1} \to \tau_{i,j}(\psi)) \wedge \neg(\tau_{i,j}(\psi) \to flex_i^{k+1})}{i : \mathbf{relDis}(j : \psi) \cap i : flex_i^{k+1}} \ (ED\text{-}RD)$$

$$\frac{j : \mathbf{essDis}(i : flex_i^k) \cap j : \psi \quad (flex_i^{k+1} \to \tau_{i,j}(\psi))}{i : \mathbf{agree}(j : \psi) \cap i : \tau_{i,j}(\psi)} \ (ED\text{-}Ag)$$

$$\frac{j : \mathbf{comp}(i : flex_i^k) \cap j : \psi \quad (stub_i \vee \tau_{i,j}(\psi)) \wedge \neg(flex_i^{k+1} \wedge \tau_{i,j}(\psi))}{i : \mathbf{essDis}(j : \psi) \cap i : flex_i^{k+1}} \ (Co\text{-}ED)$$

$$\frac{j : \mathbf{comp}(i : flex_i^k) \cap j : \psi \quad (flex_i^{k+1} \vee \tau_{i,j}(\psi)) \wedge \neg(flex_i^{k+1} \to \tau_{i,j}(\psi)) \wedge \neg(\tau_{i,j}(\psi) \to flex_i^{k+1})}{i : \mathbf{comp}(j : \psi) \cap i : flex_i^{k+1}} \ (Co\text{-}Co)$$

$$\frac{j : \mathbf{comp}(i : flex_i^k) \cap j : \psi \quad (flex_i^{k+1} \to \tau_{i,j}(\psi)) \wedge \neg(\tau_{i,j}(\psi) \to flex_i^{k+1})}{i : \mathbf{relDis}(j : \psi) \cap i : flex_i^{k+1}} \ (Co\text{-}RD)$$

$$\frac{j : \mathbf{comp}(i : flex_i^k) \cap j : \psi \quad (flex_i^{k+1} \to \tau_{i,j}(\psi))}{i : \mathbf{agree}(j : \psi) \cap i : \tau_{i,j}(\psi)} \ (Co\text{-}Ag)$$

$$\frac{j : \mathbf{relDis}(i : \varphi) \cap j : \psi}{i : \mathbf{agree}(j : \psi) \cap i : \tau_{i,j}(\psi)} \ (RD\text{-}Ag)$$

Table 5. System transition rules

$$\frac{*(i,j) \quad i : \varphi \quad j : \mathbf{na}(i : \varphi) \quad j : \psi \quad stub_i \leftrightarrow \varphi \quad stub_j \leftrightarrow \psi}{Disagreement(i,j)} \ (D)$$

$$\frac{*(i,j) \quad i : \varphi \quad j : \mathbf{agree}(i : \varphi)}{Agreement(i,j)} \ (A) \qquad \frac{*(i,j) \quad i : \varphi \quad j : \mathbf{na}(i : \varphi) \quad j : \psi}{Negotiate(i,j)} \ (N)$$

knows that they will remain in essence disagreement. Suppose B says to A that when A proposes φ they are in relative disagreement ($\psi \to \varphi$) and B makes the proposal ψ, then A knows that they are in agreement when she proposes ψ.

To support the interaction sketched above, we define the system *MND* to consist of the standard introduction and elimination rules for the connectives of $\mathcal{L}_i$ and $\mathcal{L}$, and of two sets of rules: one set for the second proposing agent (Table 3) and another set for the following proposing agents (Table 4). For the sake of space, we omit the assumption of non call-away conditions in negotiation rules and explain only some of the rules by example.

Assume that A begins a MN by proposing $flex_A^0$ to B. B evaluates $\tau_{B,A}(flex_A^0)$ with respect to his initial angle $flex_B^0$ and suppose B thinks that $\tau_{B,A}(flex_A^0)$ is too strict, i.e., $\tau_{B,A}(flex_A^0) \rightarrow flex_B^0$. Thus, B cannot accept $\tau_{B,A}(flex_A^0)$ and re-initiates the MN by the rule (I) and proposes $flex_B^0$ by $B : flex_B^0$. Otherwise, suppose B thinks that $\tau_{B,A}(flex_A^0)$ is entailed by his initial angle $flex_B^0$ and that $\tau_{B,A}(flex_A^0)$ is not too general, i.e., it is not entailed by $stub_B$. In this case, B knows that A cannot accept $flex_B^0$ because it is too strict with respect to her viewpoint (explained in the beginning of § 3), thus B accepts $\tau_{B,A}(flex_A^0)$ by (Ag) because it satisfies the precondition $(flex_B^0 \rightarrow \tau_{B,A}(flex_A^0))$, and says $B : \mathbf{agree}(A : flex_A^0)$. This is the reason why there is no rule (RD) in Table 3 for the relative disagreement relation. Consider the case in which B thinks that the proposal of A, $flex_A^0$, is consistent to his initial angle $flex_B^0$ by (Co). B says to A that they are in the compatibility relation by $B : \mathbf{comp}(A : flex_A^0)$ and makes a new proposal $B : flex_B^1$ such that $flex_B^0 \rightarrow flex_B^1$ (rule (W)). Now A thinks that $\tau_{A,B}(flex_B^1)$ is an acceptable angle of her initial viewpoint, i.e. $flex_A^1 \leftrightarrow \tau_{A,B}(flex_B^1)$. Thus A agrees with B and says $A : \mathbf{agree}(B : flex_B^1)$ by $(Co\text{-}Ag)$. It may be the case that agents make proposals that become inconsistent with the received one. This inconsistency is tested by the bidding agent, because in MND agents choose the new proposal only with respect to their angles and not with respect to the opponent's one.

Consider now the scenario in Fig. 2(b). B evaluates A's proposal, tests the compatibility relation and makes a counterproposal. A evaluates it and finds they are inconsistent. In situations like this, agents make proposals that violate the MN relation among agents; we call such a proposal a *violation* and the rule causing it a *violation rule*. In Table 4, the violation rules are $(ED\text{-}AD)$ and $(ED\text{-}Co)$.

The MN develops by agents making proposals and asserting if they are in agreement or not. The entire process is controlled by a supervisor, an external viewpoint, which tests if the MN ends and if the outcome is positive or negative. Table 5 shows the transition rules for the system, which are a translation of the system transition graph in Fig. 1(a). We use $j : \mathbf{na}(i : \varphi)$ to say that agent j thinks she is not in agreement with $i : \varphi$ and $*(i, j)$ to say *whatever the system state is* different from the final ones (*Agreement* and *Disagreement*), i.e., whether the system is in *Init* or *Negotiate*[4]. The MN begins when agents make proposals in turns $(i : \varphi, j : \psi)$ and they are not in agreement $(j : \mathbf{na}(i : \varphi))$ by (N). The MN ends with a positive outcome (φ) when each agent agrees on a proposal $(j : \mathbf{agree}(i : \varphi))$, otherwise the MN ends with a negative outcome if there are

---

[4] An agent is *absolutely stubborn* when she only has unquestionable knowledge. If all the involved agents are absolutely stubborn then the finite state diagram is different from Fig. 1(a) because the state *Negotiate* does not exist and there are only the dashed edges. However, the formalization above works as well.

no more proposals to perform $(stub_i \leftrightarrow \varphi$ and $stub_j \leftrightarrow \psi)$ and agents do not agree on a common acceptable angle $(j : \mathbf{na}(i : \varphi))$.

Example 3. Suppose that the initial viewpoints of Alice and Bob are

$$flex_A^0 = has2wheels \wedge hasSteeringWheel \wedge (hasMotor \vee has2bicyclePedals)$$
$$flex_B^0 = has2wheels \wedge hasHandlebar \wedge has2bicyclePedals$$

and that Alice's stubbornness knowledge is as in Example 2, while Bob's stubbornness knowledge is

$$stub_B = (has2wheels \vee has3wheels \vee has4wheels) \wedge (hasHandlebar \vee hasSteeringWheel) \wedge$$
$$(hasMotor \vee has2bicyclePedals \vee has4bicyclePedals)$$

Alice is the first bidding agent and she proposes $flex_A^0$ to Bob, who receives the proposal and evaluates it. Bob tests that they are in compatibility because $(flex_B^0 \vee \tau_{B,A}(flex_A^0)) \wedge \neg(flex_B^0 \rightarrow \tau_{B,A}(flex_A^0)) \wedge \neg(\tau_{B,A}(flex_A^0) \rightarrow flex_B^0)$. Bob chooses the new CAF by a weakening action (W) in

$$flex_B^1 = (has2wheels \vee has4wheels) \wedge (hasHandlebar \vee hasSteeringWheel) \wedge has2bicyclePedals$$

Bob uses the (Co) rule and sends his CAF to Alice:

$$\frac{A : flex_A^0 \quad (flex_B^1 \vee \tau_{B,A}(flex_A^0)) \wedge \neg(flex_B^1 \rightarrow \tau_{B,A}(flex_A^0)) \wedge \neg(\tau_{B,A}(flex_A^0) \rightarrow flex_B^1)}{B : \mathbf{comp}(A : flex_A^0) \cap B : flex_B^1} \ (Co)$$

The system continues the MN by:

$$\frac{*(A, B) \quad A : flex_A^0 \quad B : \mathbf{comp}(A : flex_A^0) \quad B : flex_B^1}{Negotiate(A, B)} \ (N)$$

Alice receives $flex_B^1$ and she has to make a weakening or a changing theory action because Bob did not say they were in agreement nor in relative disagreement. Alice performs a changing theory action by the rule (C) and her CAF is

$$flex_A^1 = has2wheels \wedge (hasHandlebar \vee hasSteeringWheel) \wedge has2bicyclePedals$$

Alice thinks they are in relative disagreement since $(flex_A^1 \rightarrow \tau_{A,B}(flex_B^1)) \wedge \neg(\tau_{A,B}(flex_B^1) \rightarrow flex_A^1)$, and she uses the rule $(Co\text{-}RD)$ to inform Bob that they are in relative disagreement:

$$\frac{B : \mathbf{comp}(A : flex_A^0) \cap B : flex_B^1 \quad (flex_A^1 \rightarrow \tau_{A,B}(flex_B^1)) \wedge \neg(\tau_{A,B}(flex_B^1) \rightarrow flex_A^1)}{A : \mathbf{relDis}(B : flex_B^1) \cap A : flex_A^1} \ (Co\text{-}RD)$$

The system continues the MN by:

$$\frac{*(B, A) \quad B : flex_B^1 \quad A : \mathbf{relDis}(B : flex_B^1) \quad A : flex_A^1}{Negotiate(B, A)} \ (N)$$

Bob receives $flex_A^1$ and accepts it as Alice said they are in relative disagreement.

$$\frac{A : \mathbf{relDis}(B : flex_B^1) \cap A : flex_A^1}{B : \mathbf{agree}(A : flex_A^1) \cap B : \tau_{B,A}(flex_A^1)} \ (RD\text{-}Ag)$$

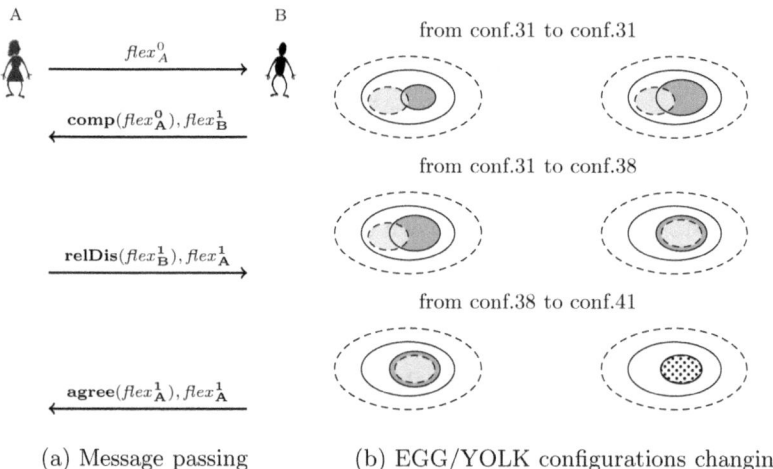

(a) Message passing   (b) EGG/YOLK configurations changing

Fig. 3. The MN scenario of Example 3: the message passing flow (a) and the changes of the EGG/YOLKs of the agents (b). Alice is identified by plain lines and Bob by dashed lines. White yolks represent the previous proposal of the agent and the dotted gray yolk is the positive outcome of the scenario.

The system closes the MN by:

$$\frac{*(A, B) \quad A : flex_A^1 \quad B : \mathbf{agree}(A : flex_A^1)}{Agreement(A, B)} \quad (A)$$

with a positive outcome, $flex_A^1$. Fig. 3 shows the message flow between Alice and Bob, and the changes of their EGG/YOLK configurations.   □

The classification of the agreement conditions given above is complete, in the sense that there is no other possible configuration of EGG/YOLKs, as shown in [13]. Based on the completeness of that analysis, we have the following results.

Theorem 1. *MND is consistent.*

Proof. Consider two agents represented in the *MND* system with sets $\mathcal{L}_{\mathcal{S}_1}$ and $\mathcal{L}_{\mathcal{S}_2}$ of stubbornness formulas and sets $\mathcal{L}_{\mathcal{F}_1}$ and $\mathcal{L}_{\mathcal{F}_2}$ of flexible formulas. To prove that *MND* is consistent, we show that if a Σ_i formula ξ is inferred using the *MND* rules, or, in other terms, is deduced as a theorem in the system, then ξ represents a proposal that is acceptable by both agents. In other words, we aim at proving that when the rules yield ξ then ξ generalizes both $\mathcal{L}_{\mathcal{F}_1}$ and $\mathcal{L}_{\mathcal{F}_2}$ and is generalized by both $\mathcal{L}_{\mathcal{S}_1}$ and $\mathcal{L}_{\mathcal{S}_2}$. To prove this, we need to show that:

(i) The rules for making new proposals yield a relation that is acceptable from the viewpoint of the agent who made the proposal before and infer a new proposal again still acceptable. In other terms, if an agent makes a proposal that is generalized by the set of stubbornness formulas $\mathcal{L}_{\mathcal{S}_i}$, and is a generalization of the set of flexible formulas $\mathcal{L}_{\mathcal{F}_i}$, for one agent, the rules infer a new proposal that is in the same relationships with $\mathcal{L}_{\mathcal{S}_i}$ and $\mathcal{L}_{\mathcal{F}_i}$.

(ii) The rules for the second proposing agent infer the relation between the agents at that step of the negotiation.

(iii) The rules for the following proposing agent do the same as the rules for the second proposing agent, taking into account that this step takes place after the step of the second proposing agent.

(iv) The system transition rules close the MN only when the proposal is acceptable by both agents, namely generalizes both $\mathcal{L}_{\mathcal{F}_i}$ and is generalized by both $\mathcal{L}_{\mathcal{S}_i}$ sets.

Let us now consider a formula ξ that is acceptable by the two agents, and let us consider the rules that produce transitions in the system. In particular, if ξ is inferred by means of one of the rules (AD), (ED), (I), (Co), (Ag) for the second proposing agent, or by means of one of the rules given in Fig. 4 for the following proposing agent, then the possible results of the step described above are given by the application of the system transition rules. Evidently, if ξ is inferred, then the rule (D) does not apply. If (N) applies, and one more inference is performed, then the rules (W), (C), (S) allow us to infer a different formula. Suppose now, by contradiction, that the new formula ξ is not acceptable by one of the agents (in the sense that either is not a generalization of her set of flexible formulas or it is not generalized by the set of stubbornness formulas. As a consequence, one agent has called herself away, as we stated above. This, however, is impossible, by construction of the rules for the second and following proposals. Conversely, if the transition rule (D) applies and, therefore, the agents have incompatible viewpoints, then ξ is not inferred through the system, because it is not a generalization of both flexible sets of formulas and generalizes by both stubbornness sets of formulas. Clearly, by means of the full set of rules, it is not possible to do so when the agents have compatible viewpoints.   □

It is not difficult to show that *MND* is adequate in representing MN, i.e. if an agreement is reachable between the agents then *MND* finds it, otherwise *MND* does not produce any result.

Theorem 2. *MND is adequate to represent the MN of two agents.*

For MN processes that are built on finite signature theories, we then have:

Corollary 1. *MN is decidable for theories with finite signature under the assumption of two competitive agents.*

4   Conclusions

As we remarked, the literature has dealt with many different issues of the negotiation of meaning, but what has been only partially treated is the description of the process of reaching agreement conditions. This was the focus of this paper, whose main results can be summarized in three points: *(i)* we defined the agreement conditions and classified the ways in which agents can be in disagreement; this refines the state-of-the-art, where the only distinguishable conditions are agreement and disagreement alone; *(ii)* we defined rules for deriving streams of dialog between two meaning negotiating agents; and *(iii)* we defined a deduction system, *MND*, based upon these rules, which derives a stream of dialog that ends with an agreement (or disagreement) condition.

Although these results are only a first step, we believe that they show the usefulness and strength of our approach. Much is still to be done, in particular investigating the formal properties of *MND*, such as soundness and completeness. The proofs of consistency and adequacy do not fix the relation to a given semantics, which is needed for a proof of soundness and a proof of completeness. Usually, a deduction system can be proved sound and complete against a standard interpretation of the language, which is difficult to circumscribe in our case, because of the presence of the relations between agents to be represented. A standard definition of the semantics for the *MND* systems is therefore needed in front of any further investigation of the soundness and completeness properties.

In this paper, we assumed that agents are truthful thus they never inform the opponents about something wrongly. Fraudulent agents may try to drive the MN in a way that is in some sense optimal for themselves. It would be interesting to study the optimality and minimality of the MN outcomes and the ways, legitimate or not, that the agents use to reach optimal outcomes. It would also be interesting to develop a decision making algorithm for those cases in which the system is decidable, in particular for finite signatures in addition to the case of competitive agents considered here. This would foster the automation both of the subjective decision process (i.e., the automation of the deduction system alone) and of the whole process per se (i.e., the definition of a procedure to establish the agreement terminal condition). We shall also clarify how the different choices that every agent makes with respect to the sequence of proposals affect the general strategies and results of the MN process.

The investigation we carried out can also be extended by studying the ways in which agents can be limited to specific strategies in choosing the next action. Jointly with the definition of an algorithm for negotiating a common angle, this study can also enlarge the boundary of decidable cases. In particular, agents using some specific strategies can apply the rules in a finite number of steps even if the signature is infinite.

Finally, we envisage two further extensions of our approach: (i) to more than two negotiating agents, where it is well-known from game theory (e.g., [3]) that such an extension is all but trivial; (ii) to applications in information security, e.g., investigating the relationships between the MN process and the management of authorization policies in security protocols and web services.

Acknowledgments. The work presented in this paper was partially supported by the FP7-ICT-2007-1 Project no. 216471, "AVANTSSAR: Automated Validation of Trust and Security of Service-oriented Architectures".

References

1. Ben-ameur, H., Chaib-draa, B., Kropf, P.: Multi-item auctions for automatic negotiation. Information and Software Technology 44(5), 291–301 (2002)
2. Burato, E., Cristani, M.: Contract clause negotiation by game theory. In: ICAIL 2007: Proceedings of the 11th International Conference on Artificial Intelligence and Law, Stanford Law School, Stanford, California, USA, pp. 71–80. ACM Press, New York (2007)
3. Burato, E., Cristani, M.: Learning as meaning negotiation: A model based on english auction. In: Håkansson, A., Nguyen, N.T., Hartung, R.L., Howlett, R.J., Jain, L.C. (eds.) KES-AMSTA 2009. LNCS, vol. 5559, pp. 60–69. Springer, Heidelberg (2009)
4. Burato, E., Cristani, M., Viganò, L.: Meaning negotiation as inference (2011), http://arxiv.org/abs/1101.4356
5. Davis, E.: Knowledge and communication: a first-order theory. Artificial Intelligence 166(1-2), 81–139 (2005)
6. Diggelen, J., Beun, R.J., Dignum, F., Eijk, R.M., Meyer, J.-J.: Combining normal communication with ontology alignment. In: Dignum, F., van Eijk, R., Flores, R. (eds.) AC 2005. LNCS (LNAI), vol. 3859, pp. 181–195. Springer, Heidelberg (2006)
7. Giunchiglia, F., Serafini, L.: Multilanguage hierarchical logics (or: how can we do without modal logics). Artificial Intelligence 65(1), 29–70 (1994)
8. Horrocks, I., Sattler, U.: Ontology reasoning in the SHOQ(D) description logic. In: Nebel, B. (ed.) Proceedings of the Seventeenth International Joint Conference on Artificial Intelligence, IJCAI 2001, Seattle, Washington, USA, August 4-10. Morgan Kaufmann, Los Altos (2001)
9. Jennings, N.R., Faratin, P., Lomuscio, A.R., Parsons, S., Wooldridge, M., Sierra, C.: Automated negotiation: Prospects methods and challenges. Group Decision and Negotiation 10(2), 199–215 (2001)
10. Kalfoglou, Y., Schorlemmer, M.: Ontology mapping: the state of the art. The Knowledge Engineering Review 18(1), 1–31 (2003)
11. Kambe, S.: Bargaining with imperfect commitment. Games and Economic Behavior 28(2), 217–237 (1995)
12. Laera, L., Blacoe, I., Tamma, V., Payne, T., Euzenat, J., Bench-Capon, T.: Argumentation over ontology correspondences in mas. In: Durfee, E.H., Yokoo, M., Huhns, M.N., Shehory, O. (eds.) 6th International Joint Conference on Autonomous Agents and Multiagent Systems (AAMAS 2007), Honolulu, Hawaii, USA, May 14-18, pp. 1–8. ACM Press, New York (2007)
13. Lehmann, F., Cohn, A.G.: The egg/yolk reliability hierarchy: semantic data integration using sorts with prototypes. In: Proceedings of the Third International Conference on Information and Knowledge Management (CIKM 1994), Gaithersburg, Maryland, November 29-December 2, pp. 272–279. ACM Press, New York (1994)
14. McBurney, P., Van Eijk, R., Parsons, S., Amgoud, L.: A dialogue-game protocol for agent purchase negotiations. Autonomous Agents and Multi-Agent Systems 7(3), 235–273 (2003)
15. Sadri, F., Toni, F., Torroni, P.: Dialogues for negotiation: Agent varieties and dialogue sequences. In: Meyer, J.-J., Tambe, M. (eds.) ATAL VIII 2001. LNCS (LNAI), vol. 2333, pp. 405–421. Springer, Heidelberg (2002)

Declarative Abstractions for Agent Based Hybrid Control Systems*

Louise A. Dennis[1], Michael Fisher[1], Nicholas K. Lincoln[2],
Alexei Lisitsa[1], and Sandor M. Veres[2]

[1] Department of Computer Science, University of Liverpool, UK
[2] School of Engineering, University of Southampton, UK
L.A.Dennis@liverpool.ac.uk

Abstract. Modern control systems are limited in their ability to react flexibly and autonomously to changing situations by the complexity inherent in analysing environments where many variables are present. We aim to use an agent approach to help alleviate this problem and are particularly interested in the control of satellite systems using BDI agent programming as pioneered by the PRS.

Such systems need to generate discrete abstractions from continuous data and then use these abstractions in rational decision making. This paper provides an architecture and interaction semantics for an abstraction engine to interact with a hybrid BDI-based control system.

1 Introduction

Modern control systems are limited in their ability to react flexibly and autonomously to changing situations. The complexity inherent in analysing environments where many continuous variables are present, and dynamically changing, has proved to be a challenge. In some situations one control system may need to be swapped for another. This, quite severe, behavioural change is very difficult to handle just within the control systems framework.

We approach the problem from the perspective of satellite control systems. Consider a single satellite attempting to maintain a geostationary orbit. Current systems maintain orbits using feedback controllers. These implicitly assume that any errors will be minor and easily corrected. In situations where more major errors occur, e.g., caused by thruster malfunction, it is desirable to change the controller or modify the hardware configuration. The complexity of the decision task has proved to be a challenge to the type of imperative programming approaches traditionally used within control systems programming.

There is a long standing tradition, pioneered by the PRS system [16], of using agent languages (and other logic programming approaches – e.g., [28]) to control and reason about such systems. We consider a satellite to be an *agent* which consists of a discrete (rational decision making) engine together with a continuous (calculation) engine. The rational engine uses the *Belief-Desire-Intention*

* Work funded by EPSRC grants EP/F037201/1 and EP/F037570/1.

A. Omicini, S. Sardina, and W. Vasconcelos (Eds.): DALT 2010, LNAI 6619, pp. 96–111, 2011.
© Springer-Verlag Berlin Heidelberg 2011

(BDI) theory of agency [21] to make decisions about appropriate controllers and hardware configurations for the satellite. It is assisted by the continuous engine which can perform predictive modelling and other continuous calculations.

In order for such an architecture to be clear and declarative it is necessary to generate discrete abstractions from continuous data. It is also necessary to translate discrete actions and queries back into continuous commands and queries. In order to do this we introduce an *Abstraction Engine* whose purpose is to manage communication between the continuous and discrete parts of the system in a semantically clear way. (See Figure 1, later).

This paper provides an architecture and interaction semantics which describe the way an Abstraction Engine interacts with a hybrid BDI-based control system. We present a case study and discuss its implications for the choice and design of declarative languages for hybrid control systems.

This paper is organised as follows. Section 2 provides some background material. Section 3 provides an architecture for a hybrid control system with explicit abstraction. Section 4 provides an operational semantics for interaction between the major components of such a system. Section 5 presents a prototype implementation of the architecture and semantics and Section 6 discusses a case study performed in this system. Section 7 draws some preliminary conclusions and discusses the further work motivated by the prototype and case study.

2 Background

2.1 Control Systems

Satellite systems are typically governed by feedback controllers. These continuously monitor input sensors and compare the values to a desired state. They then alter various aspects of the system accordingly, for instance by increasing or decreasing power or adjusting direction. Typically the actual controller is specified using differential equations and operates in a continuous fashion.

A *hybrid system* is one in which the desired controller is a function which not only has continuous regions but also distinct places of discontinuity between those regions, such as the moment when a bouncing ball changes direction on impact. In practical engineering contexts, such as satellites, it is frequently desirable to change feedback controllers at such points. Appropriate control mechanisms for such hybrid systems is a very active area of research [25; 7; 11].

2.2 BDI Agents

We view an agent as an *autonomous* computational entity making its own decisions about what activities to pursue. Often this involves having goals and communicating with other agents in order to accomplish these goals [29]. *Rational agents* make decisions in an explainable way and, since agents are autonomous, understanding *why* an agent chooses a particular course of action is vital.

We often describe each agent's *beliefs* and *goals* which in turn determine the agent's *intentions*. Such agents make decisions about what action to perform, given their current beliefs, goals and intentions. This approach has been popularised through the influential BDI (Belief-Desire-Intention) model of agency [21].

2.3   The Problem of Abstraction

Generating appropriate abstractions to mediate between continuous and discrete parts of a system is the key to any link between a control system and a reasoning system. Abstractions allow concepts to be translated from the quantitative data necessary to actually run the underlying system to the qualitative data needed for reasoning. For instance a control system may store precise location coordinates, represented as real numbers, while the reasoning system may only be interested in whether a satellite is within reasonable bounds of its desired position.

The use of appropriate abstractions is also important for verification techniques, such as model checking, for hybrid systems [1; 14; 24; 23] and potentially for declarative prediction and forward planning [18]. These require the continuous search space to be divided into a finite set of regions which can be examined.

Ideally the generation of such abstractions should itself be declarative. This would make clear say, that a decision to change a fuel line corresponds directly to the activation of certain valves within the satellite system.

3   Architecture

Our aim is to produce a hybrid system embedding existing technology for generating feedback controllers and configuring satellite systems within a decision making part based upon agent technologies and theories. The link is to be controlled by a semantically clear *abstraction layer*. At present we consider a single agent case and leave investigation of multi-agent scenarios to future work.

Figure 1 shows an architecture for our system. Real time control of the satellite is governed by a traditional feedback controller drawing its sensory input from the environment. This forms a *Physical Engine* (Π). This engine communicates with an agent architecture consisting of an *Abstraction Engine* (A) that filters and discretizes information. To do this A may a use a *Continuous Engine* (Ω) to make calculations involving the continuous information. Finally, the *Rational Engine* (R) contains a "Sense-Reason-Act" loop. Actions involve either calls to the Continuous Engine to calculate new controllers (for instance) or instructions to the change these controllers within the Physical Engine. These instructions are passed through the Abstraction Engine for reification.

In this way, R is a traditional BDI system dealing with discrete information, Π and Ω are traditional control systems, typically generated by MatLab/Simulink, while A provides the vital "glue" between all these parts.

4   Semantics of Interaction

We assume a hybrid control system consisting of a Physical Engine (Π), a Continuous Engine (Ω), an Abstraction Engine (A) and a Reasoning Engine (R).

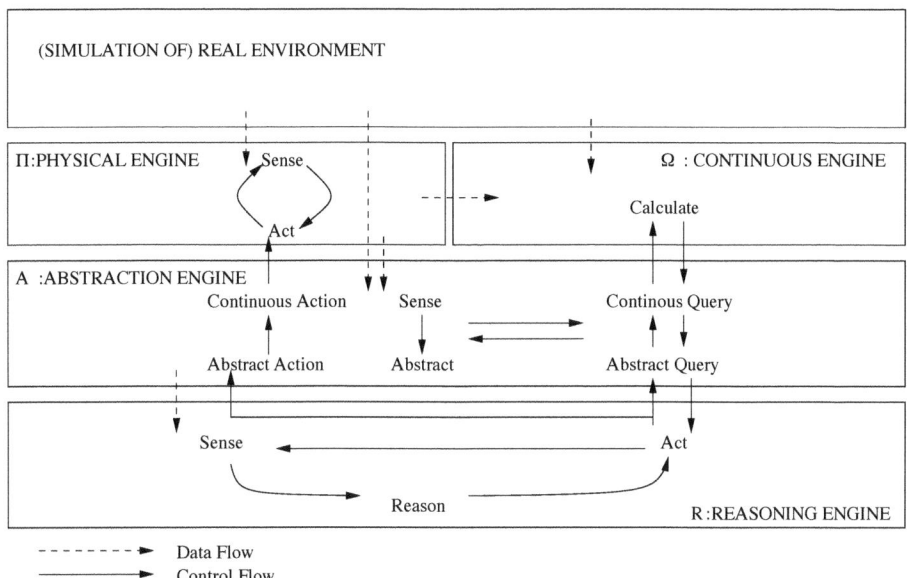

Fig. 1. Hybrid Agent Architecture

We present an operational semantics for the interaction of these engines. This semantics makes minimal assumptions about the internals of the engines, but nevertheless places certain constraints upon their operation and the way they interact with the external environment. This semantics is designed to allow a *declarative abstraction language* to be developed for the Abstraction Engine, A. An implementation of the architecture and the semantics is discussed in Section 5 and a case study using the implementation is discussed in Section 6. The implementation and case study influenced the development of the semantics and serve as additional motivation for the design of its components.

We assume the Abstraction Engine has access to four sets of data. These are Δ (description of the real world and Physical Engine), Σ (beliefs/abstractions shared with the Reasoning Engine), Γ (abstract actions the Reasoning Engine wishes the Physical Engine to take), Q (abstract queries the Reasoning Engine wishes to make of the Continuous Engine). Σ, Γ and Q are all assumed to be sets of ground atomic formulae. Therefore, we can represent the entire system as a tuple $\langle \Pi, \Omega, A, R, \Delta, \Sigma, \Gamma, Q \rangle$. For space reasons, in the semantics we will sometimes replace parts of this tuple with ellipsis (...) if they are unchanged by a transition.

4.1 Abstraction and Reification

We assume that the Abstraction Engine, A, contains processes of *abstraction* (*abs*) and *reification* (*rei*) and that these form the primary purpose of A. Indeed we use the reification process in the semantics via the transition $A \xrightarrow{rei(p)} A'$

which indicates any internal changes to the abstraction engine as it reifies some request p from the Rational Engine.

An example of *abs* would be the conversion, by the Abstraction Engine, of the current physical position of the satellite, represented as real-valued coordinates, to the belief that the satellite was within acceptable bounds of a desired position. Conversely, reification might involve converting a thruster change request (i.e., p above might be the predicate $change\_thruster(x)$), to a sequence of valve and switch activations, or adding additional information about the current real-valued position of the satellite to a request for the calculation of a new feedback controller to move the satellite along a path.

Implicitly we assume that *abs* represents a function from Δ to the shared beliefs Σ. Similarly we assume that reification takes Γ and Q and converts them into sequences of instructions for the Physical Engine or calls for calculations from the Continuous Engine.

4.2   Internal Transitions

We assume all four engines may take internal transitions which we represent as $\overset{?}{\rightarrow}$ to indicate some unknown internal state change. So, for instance,

$$\frac{\Pi \overset{?}{\rightarrow} \Pi'}{\langle \Pi, \Omega, A, R, \Delta, \Sigma, \Gamma, Q \rangle \xrightarrow{?_\Pi} \langle \Pi', \Omega, A, R, \Delta, \Sigma, \Gamma, Q \rangle} \tag{1}$$

represents an internal state change in the Physical Engine which leaves the rest of the system unaltered. Similar rules exist for the three other engines.

4.3   Perception

We assume that both the Abstraction Engine and Reasoning Engine incorporate a perception mechanism by which they can "read in" data represented as first-order predicates and represent this information internally as, for instance, beliefs. We write $A \xrightarrow{per(S)} A'$ as the process by which A reads in first-order data S. Similarly we write $R \xrightarrow{per(S)} R'$ for the Reasoning Engine's perception process. We represent this as a transition since the Reasoning Engine and Abstraction Engine will change state (e.g., adding beliefs and/or events) during perception.

We have data, Δ, that arrives from the Physical Engine. This data might not be represented in first-order form. We require a function $fof(\Delta)$ that transforms the language of Δ into appropriate ground atomic predicates (though these may represent real numbers).

Furthermore we assume that A keeps a log, L, of snapshots of the current state of the physical system, as represented by Δ. So A can be represented as (L, A_r) where A_r represents all of A's internal data structures apart from the log. We treat the log as a list with ':' as the **cons** function.

This allows us to define a semantics for perception as follows, (2) gives the semantics for perceiving Δ, while (3) and (4) give semantics for the abstraction and reasoning engine perceiving the shared beliefs. In (2) the incoming data is removed once it has been processed by the Abstraction Engine (although it is logged). This prevents the Abstraction Engine from processing such data several times.

$$A_r \xrightarrow{per(fof(\Delta))} A_r'$$
$$\langle \Pi, \Omega, (L, A_r), R, \Delta, \Sigma, \Gamma, Q \rangle \xrightarrow{per_A(\Delta)} \langle \Pi, \Omega, (fof(\Delta) : L, A_r'), R, \emptyset, \Sigma, \Gamma, Q \rangle \tag{2}$$

The Abstraction and Rational engines may also perceive the shared beliefs.

$$A \xrightarrow{per(\Sigma)} A'$$
$$\langle \Pi, \Omega, A, R, \Delta, \Sigma, \Gamma, Q \rangle \xrightarrow{per_A(\Sigma)} \langle \Pi, \Omega, A', R, \Delta, \Sigma, \Gamma, Q \rangle \tag{3}$$

$$R \xrightarrow{per(\Sigma)} R'$$
$$\langle \Pi, \Omega, A, R, \Delta, \Sigma, \Gamma, Q \rangle \xrightarrow{per_R(\Sigma)} \langle \Pi, \Omega, A, R', \Delta, \Sigma, \Gamma, Q \rangle \tag{4}$$

4.4   Operating on Shared Beliefs

Both the Abstraction Engine and Reasoning Engine can operate on the memory they share. We assume that both these engines can perform transitions $+_\Sigma b$ and $-_\Sigma b$ to add and remove shared beliefs where b is a ground first-order formula. Since we have not specified the internal transition systems of the Abstraction and Reasoning engines we can not be sure whether they undergo any internal change of state as a result of operating on the shared memory - e.g., removing the intention to make a changed to the shared memory. As such we not that their may be state change by specifying that they undergo a transition to a new state as well.

$$A \xrightarrow{+_\Sigma b} A'$$
$$\langle \Pi, \Omega, A, R, \Delta, \Sigma, \Gamma, Q \rangle \xrightarrow{+_{\Sigma, A} b} \langle \Pi, \Omega, A', R, \Delta, \Sigma \cup \{b\}, \Gamma, Q \rangle \tag{5}$$

$$A \xrightarrow{-_\Sigma b} A'$$
$$\langle \Pi, \Omega, A, R, \Delta, \Sigma, \Gamma, Q \rangle \xrightarrow{-_{\Sigma, A} b} \langle \Pi, \Omega, A', R, \Delta, \Sigma \setminus \{b\}, \Gamma, Q \rangle \tag{6}$$

$$R \xrightarrow{+_\Sigma b} R'$$
$$\langle \Pi, \Omega, A, R, \Delta, \Sigma, \Gamma, Q \rangle \xrightarrow{+_{\Sigma, R} b} \langle \Pi, \Omega, A, R', \Delta, \Sigma \cup \{b\}, \Gamma, Q \rangle \tag{7}$$

$$R \xrightarrow{-_\Sigma b} R'$$
$$\langle \Pi, \Omega, A, R, \Delta, \Sigma, \Gamma, Q \rangle \xrightarrow{-_{\Sigma, R} b} \langle \Pi, \Omega, A, R', \Delta, \Sigma \setminus \{b\}, \Gamma, Q \rangle \tag{8}$$

We do not specify here whether the individual components of the system can act in parallel or are forced to act in some sequential order. This means it is possible, in a parallel implementation, for both A and R to make transitions at the same time. This might mean that both rules (5) and (7) were applicable at once. In this situation an implementation would need to either select one at random, or have a preference order enforced.

Note that the abstraction process employed by the Abstraction Engine is intended to be one of transforming the predicates generated via $fof(\Delta)$ into a set of shared beliefs which are then added to Σ. One of our interests is in finding ways to present this transformation in as expressive and declarative a fashion as possible. We discuss this further in Sections 6 and 7.

4.5   Calculation

We allow the Abstraction Engine to transform the predicate representation of the calculation, p, into the input language of the Continuous Engine. This is similar to the inverse of the operation performed by fof and so we term it fof^{-1}. Usually this involves trivial changes (e.g., $set\_valve(x)$ becomes set_x_valve – translating between the parameterised form used by the Rational Engine and the non parameterised form used by the Physical and Continuous Engines).

When the Abstraction Engine requests a calculation from the Continuous Engine it could wait for an answer. However such an answer may take time to calculate and the Abstraction Engine may need to continue handling incoming data. Some agent languages (such as *Jason* [6]) allow intentions to be suspended while other parts of an agent may continue to run. We follow this approach and represent requesting and receiving the answer to a calculation via two rules. We indicate the process of requesting a calculation by $A \xrightarrow{calc(p,V)} A'(V)$, where we write $A'(V)$ to indicate that the state of the Abstraction Engine contains a free variable, V, that is awaiting instantiation. We represent the change in state of Ω when it is not performing a calculation to when it is via $\Omega \xrightarrow{calc} \Omega(fof^{-1}(p))$.

$$\frac{A \xrightarrow{calc(p,V)} A'(V) \qquad \Omega \xrightarrow{calc} \Omega(fof^{-1}(p))}{\langle \Pi, \Omega, A, R, \Delta, \Sigma, \Gamma, Q \rangle \xrightarrow{calc(p,V)} \langle \Pi, \Omega(fof^{-1}(p)), A'(V), \Delta, \Sigma, \Gamma, Q \rangle} \qquad (9)$$

When the Continuous Engine finishes its calculation it returns a value, t. The Continuous Engine's internal state is unchanged by performing the calculation. The Abstraction Engine then instantiates V to t where appropriate and may possibly make other changes to it's internal state so that $A(V)$ becomes $A'(t)$. The engines contain local state information and, query calculations could be specified further by providing detailed rules for their evaluation on the local beliefs/variables. However, we do not wish to overly constrain the internal semantics of the engines. The local variables/beliefs could be described in a number of alternate ways. The one we use here is sufficient for our purposes.

$$\frac{\Omega(fof^{-1}(p)) = t \qquad A(V) \xrightarrow{V=t} A'(t)}{\langle \Pi, \Omega, A(V), R, \Delta, \Sigma, \Gamma, Q \rangle \xrightarrow{V=t} \langle \Pi, \Omega, A'(t), R, \Delta, \Sigma, \Gamma, Q \rangle} \qquad (10)$$

When the Reasoning Engine, R, wishes to request a continuous calculation it places a request in the query set, Q, which A then reifies. We implicitly assume that the reification will include one or more calculation requests to the Continuous Engine but that the only change to the overall system state is to the internal state of A and, in particular, that the free variable V will be instantiated to t. We write reification as a transition $\langle \Pi, \Omega, A, R, \Delta, \Sigma, \Gamma, \rangle \xrightarrow{rei(q,V=t)} \langle \Pi, \Omega, A', R, \Delta, \Sigma, \Gamma, Q \rangle$.

$$\frac{(q,V) \in Q \qquad \langle \Pi, \Omega, A, R, \Delta, \Sigma, \Gamma, Q \rangle \xrightarrow{rei(q,V=t)} \langle \Pi, \Omega, A', R, \Delta, \Sigma, \Gamma, Q \rangle}{\langle \Pi, \Omega, A, R, \Delta, \Sigma, \Gamma, Q \rangle \xrightarrow{qcalc(q,V)} \langle \Pi, \Omega, A', R, \Delta, \Sigma, \Gamma, Q\{V/t\} \rangle} \tag{11}$$

As with the Abstraction Engine, we split the processes of requesting a calculation and receiving an answer in the Reasoning Engine:

$$\frac{R \xrightarrow{rcalc(q,V)} R'(V)}{\langle \Pi, \Omega, A, R, \Delta, \Sigma, \Gamma, Q \rangle \xrightarrow{rcalc(q,V)} \langle \Pi, \Omega, A, R'(V), \Delta, \Sigma, \Gamma, \{(q,V)\} \cup Q \rangle} \tag{12}$$

$$\frac{\langle \ldots, A, R(V), \ldots, Q \rangle \xrightarrow{rei(q,V=t)} \langle \ldots, A', R(V), \ldots, Q' \rangle \quad (q,t) \in Q' \quad R(V) \xrightarrow{V=t} R'(t)}{\langle \ldots, A, R(V), \ldots, Q \rangle \xrightarrow{V=t} \langle \Pi, \Omega, A', R'(t), \ldots, Q' \backslash \{(q,t)\} \rangle} \tag{13}$$

4.6   Performing Tasks

Finally, A can request that Π makes specific updates to its state.

$$\frac{A \xrightarrow{run(\gamma)} A' \qquad \Pi \xrightarrow{fof^{-1}(\gamma)} \Pi'}{\langle \Pi, \Omega, A, R, \Delta, \Sigma, \Gamma, Q \rangle \xrightarrow{run(\gamma)} \langle \Pi', \Omega, A', R, \Delta, \Sigma, \Gamma, Q \rangle} \tag{14}$$

R can request changes to Π, but A reifies these requests. The reification may involve several calls to $run(\gamma)$ and these are all amalgamated into one system transition: $\langle \Pi, \Omega, A, R, \Delta, \Sigma, \Gamma, Q \rangle \xrightarrow{rei(\gamma)} \langle \Pi', \Omega, A', R, \Delta, \Sigma, \Gamma, Q \rangle$.

$$\frac{R \xrightarrow{do(\gamma)} R'}{\langle \Pi, \Omega, A, R, \Delta, \Sigma, \Gamma, Q \rangle \xrightarrow{do_R(\gamma)} \langle \Pi, \Omega, A, R', \Delta, \Sigma, \{\gamma\} \cup \Gamma, Q \rangle} \tag{15}$$

$$\frac{\gamma \in \Gamma \qquad \langle \Pi, \Omega, A, R, \Delta, \Sigma, \Gamma, Q \rangle \xrightarrow{rei(\gamma)} \langle \Pi', \Omega, A', R, \Delta, \Sigma, \Gamma, Q \rangle}{\langle \Pi, \Omega, A, R, \Delta, \Sigma, \Gamma, Q \rangle \xrightarrow{do(\gamma)} \langle \Pi', \Omega, A', R, \Delta, \Sigma, \Gamma \backslash \{\gamma\}, Q \rangle} \tag{16}$$

5   Implementation

We have implemented a prototype system to explore the requirements for the Abstraction Engine. The simulated environment, Physical and Continuous Engines are all implemented in MatLab using the Simulink tool kit.

The Abstraction Engine and Reasoning Engine are both written in the JAVA-based Gwendolen agent programming language[1] as separate agents. Requests for calculations or actions from the Reasoning Engine are read into the Abstraction Engine as 'perform' goals Therefore the plans for handling these goals are equivalent to the function rei in the abstract semantics and execution of those plans is equivalent to the transition $A \xrightarrow{rei(p)} A'$. The Continuous Engine may, as a side effect of its calculations, place configuration files in the shared file system for use by the Physical Engine. Communication between the JAVA process and the two MatLab processes is via JAVA sockets and exists in a thin JAVA "Environment" layer between the Abstraction Engine and the MatLab parts of the system.

The Physical Engine is assumed to have direct access to a satellite's sensors. At present the information is transmitted to the Abstraction Engine in the form of a simple string tag (which relates to the way the data values flow around the Simulink model), followed by a number of arguments which are mostly real numbers. These tags and values are then converted to predicates by the Abstraction Engine. For instance the Physical Engine groups data by 'thruster' and tags them, for instance "xthruster1" (for the data from the first thruster in the X direction) followed by values for the *current, voltage* and *fuel pressure* in the thruster (say C, V and P). It is more natural, in the Abstraction Engine, to represent this data as a predicate $thruster(x, 1, C, V, P)$ than as the predicate $xthruster1(C, V, P)$. At the moment the JAVA environment handles the necessary conversion which is equivalent to the *fof* function from the semantics.

The JAVA environment also handles all four data sets, Δ, Σ, Γ and Q and sends predicates to the relevant agents at appropriate moments. Γ and Q are treated as messages with performatives indicating the type of goal they should be transformed into by the Abstraction Engine.

When the Abstraction Engine requests calculations from the Continuous Engine it requests that an M-file (MatLab function) is executed. It sends the Continuous Agent the name of the M-file followed by any arguments the M-file requires. Gwendolen allows intentions to be suspended until some event occurs. We use this explicitly in both engines to force the agent to wait until it perceives the result of calculation. In particular this allows the Abstraction Engine to continue processing new information even while waiting for a result. Once the M-file has been executed the Continuous Engine of the agent returns the resulting data to the Abstraction Engine. (We are exploring whether the Continuous Engine should also sense data from the system model to assist its calculations).

Both the Physical Engine and Continuous Engine need to work with the Abstraction Engine to produce abstractions for the Reasoning Engine. To make the

---

[1] The choice of language was dictated entirely by convenience. One of the purposes of this case study is to explore the desirable features of a BDI-based control language.

meanings of abstractions clear, concise and easy to remember for the programmer of the agent system, a high-level notation called *system English* (sEnglish, [22; 26; 27]), is used to generate the MatLab `M-files` used by the Continuous Engine and parts of the Physical Engine. sEnglish also provides a natural link between a predicate style formulation and the underlying MatLab code.

Finally, at present the Abstraction Engine only keeps the most recent snapshot of Δ and discards older information rather than keeping it as a log.

6 Case Study: Geostationary Orbit

A geostationary orbit (a GEO orbit) is characterized as an equatorial orbit (zero inclination), with near zero eccentricity and an orbital period equal to one sidereal day. A satellite maintaining such an orbit will remain at a fixed longitude at zero degrees latitude. Thus, with respect to an Earth based observer, the satellite will remain in a fixed overhead position. Numerous benefits follow from the use of geostationary orbits, the principal one of these being highlighted originally in [3]: three geostationary satellites stationed equidistantly are capable of providing worldwide telecommunications coverage.

While telecommunications is an obvious application area for such orbits, observation satellites and other applications also make heavy use of them. Consequently the geostationary orbit represents prime real-estate for satellite platforms. GEO locations are hotly contested and their allocation is politicized. This makes it important that such locations are used optimally and that satellites do not stray far from their assigned position.

Once placed in a GEO orbit at a specified longitude, *station keeping procedures* are used to ensure that the correct location is retained. Such station keeping procedures are required because the disturbances caused by solar radiation pressure (SRP), luni-solar perturbations and Earth triaxiality naturally cause an object to move from an orbit location in which it has been placed. These disturbances result in changes to the nominal orbit which must be corrected for. A standard feedback controller is able to handle these tasks.

6.1 Scenario

We implemented a Simulink model of a satellite in geostationary orbit. A MatLab function (an `M-file` written in sEnglish) was created to calculate whether a given set of coordinates were within an acceptable distance of the satellite's desired orbital position (comp_distance). A second function (plan_approach_to_centre), based on [19], was also written to produce an optimal path back to its desired orbital position (for use if the satellite strayed out of bounds – e.g., because of fuel venting from a ruptured line). These functions were made available to the agent's Continuous Engine.

Controls were made available in the Physical Engine which could send a particular named *activation plan* to the feedback controller (set_control), switch thrusters on and off (set_x1_main, set_x2_main, set_y1_main, etc.), control the valves that determined which fuel line was being utilised (set_x1_valves, etc.) and change the thruster being used in any direction (set_x_bank, etc.).

The satellite was given thrusters in three directions (X, Y and Z) each of which contained two fuel lines. This enabled the agent to switch fuel line in the event of a rupture (detectable by a drop in fuel pressure). We also provided up to five redundant thrusters, allowing the agent to switch to a redundant thruster if both fuel lines were broken.

6.2   The Abstraction Engine

The Abstraction Engine code in the case of one redundant thruster is shown in code fragment 6.1. We use a standard BDI syntax: $+b$ indicates the addition of a belief; $!g$ indicates a perform goal, g, and $+!g$ the commitment to the goal. A plan $e : \{g\} \leftarrow b$ consists of a trigger event, e, a guard, g, which must be true before the plan can be executed and a body b which is executed when the plan is selected.

Gwendolen allows plan execution to be suspended while waiting for some belief to become true. This is indicated by the syntax $*b$ which means "wait until b is believed". This is used in conjunction with 'calculate' to allow the engine to continuing producing abstractions from incoming data while calculation occurs. The new belief is then immediately removed so that further calls to 'calculate' suspend as desired. Ideally, a language would handle this more cleanly without the awkward "call-suspend-clean-up" sequence.

Abstraction and Reification. Ideally we would like to be able to clearly derive the functions *abs* and *rei* from the Abstraction Engine code.

In the above the *abs* process is represented by plans triggered by belief acquisition. For instance the code in lines $30-32$ represents an abstraction from the predicate $thruster(X, N, C, V, P)$, where C, V and P are real numbers, to the predicate $broken(X)$. However, it is harder to see how the acquisition of location data (line 1) generates abstractions about "proximity to centre".

The reification of the abstract query "plan_approach_to_centre(P)" (line 20), converts it to a call with real number arguments (the current location) and then causes the intention to wait for the result of the call. Similarly the code in lines $42-49$ shows the reification of the predicate, $change\_bank(T)$, into a sequence of commands to set the bank and turn the relevant thrusters off or on, but this is obscured by housekeeping to manage the system's beliefs.

An area of further work is to find or develop a language for the Abstraction Engine that expresses these two functions in a clearer way.

6.3   The Reasoning Engine

The reasoning engine code is shown in fragment 6.2. We use the same syntax as we did for the Abstraction Engine. Here the actions, 'perform' and 'query', request that the Abstraction Engine adopt a goal.

Code fragment 6.1 Geostationary Orbit:Abstraction Engine

```
+location(L1, L2, L3, L4, L5, L6) : {B bound_info(V1)} ←            1
        calculate (comp_distance(L1, L2, L3, L4, L5, L6), Val),      2
        ∗result (comp_distance(L1, L2, L3, L4, L5, L6), Val),         3
        −result(comp_distance(L1, L2, L3, L4, L5, L6), Val),         4
        +bound_info(Val);                                            5
                                                                     6
+bound_info(in) : {B proximity_to_centre(out)} ←                     7
        −bound_info(out),                                            8
        −ₛproximity_to_centre(out), +ₛproximity_to_centre(in);       9
                                                                     10
+bound_info(out) : {B proximity_to_centre(in)} ←                     11
        −bound_info(in),                                             12
        −ₛproximity_to_centre(in), +ₛproximity_to_centre(out);       13
                                                                     14
+!maintain_path : {B proximity_to_centre(in)} ← run(set_control (maintain));   15
+!execute(P)    : {B proximity_to_centre(out)} ← run(set_control (P));         16
                                                                     17
+!plan_approach_to_centre(P) : {B location (L1, L2, L3, L4, L5, L6)} ←   18
        calculate (plan_approach_to_centre(L1, L2, L3, L4, L5, L6), P),   19
        ∗result (plan_approach_to_centre(L1, L2, L3, L4, L5, L6), P),      20
        −result(plan_approach_to_centre(L1, L2, L3, L4, L5, L6), P),       21
        +ₛplan_approach_to_center(P);                                22
                                                                     23
−broken(X) :                                                         24
    {B thruster_bank_line (X, N, L), B thruster(X, N, C, V, P), P1 < 1} ←   25
        +ₛ(broken(X));                                               26
                                                                     27
+thruster(X, N, C, V, P):                                            28
    { ˜B broken(X), B thruster_bank_line (X, N, L), P1 < 1} ←        29
        +ₛbroken(X);                                                 30
+thruster(X, N, C, V, P):                                            31
    {B broken(X), B thruster_bank_line (X, N, L), 1 < P1} ←          32
        −ₛbroken(X).                                                 33
                                                                     34
+!change_fuel_line (T, 1) : {B thruster_bank_line (T, B, 1)} ←       35
        run(set_valves (T, B, off, off, on, on)),                    36
        −ₛthruster_bank_line(T, B, 1),                               37
        +ₛthruster_bank_line(T, B, 2),                               38
        −ₛbroken(T);                                                 39
+!change_bank(T) : {B thruster_bank_line (T, B, L)} ←                40
        B1 is B + 1;                                                 41
        run(set_bank(T, B1)),                                        42
        run(set_main(T, B, off)),                                    43
        run(set_main(T, B1, on)),                                    44
        −ₛthruster_bank_line(T, B, L),                               45
        +ₛthruster_bank_line(T, B1, 1),                              46
        −ₛbroken(T);                                                 47
```

Code fragment 6.2 Geostationary Orbit: Reasoning Engine

```
+proximity_to_centre(out) : {⊤} ← −proximity_to_centre(in),          1
    +!get_to_centre ;                                                2
+proximity_to_centre(in) : {⊤} ← −proximity_to_centre(out),          3
    perform(maintain_path);                                          4
                                                                     5
+!get_to_centre   : {B proximity_to_centre(out)} ←                   6
    query(plan_approach_to_centre(P)), *plan_approach_to_centre(P),  7
    perform(execute(P)),                                             8
    −Σplan_approach_to_centre(P);                                    9
                                                                    10
+broken(X): {B thruster_bank_line(X, N, 1)} ←                       11
    perform(change_fuel_line(X, N));                                12
+broken(X): {B thruster_bank_line(X, N, 2)} ←                       13
    perform(change_bank(X, N));                                     14
```

The architecture lets us represent the high-level decision making aspects of the program in terms of the beliefs and goals of the agent and the events it observes. So, for instance, when the Abstraction Engine observes that the thruster line pressure has dropped below 1, it asserts a shared belief that the thruster is broken. When the Reasoning Engine observes that the thruster is broken, it then either changes fuel line, or thruster bank. This is communicated to the Abstraction Engine which then sets the appropriate valves and switches.

7   Conclusions

This paper has explored creating declarative abstractions to assist the communication between the continuous and discrete parts of a hybrid control system.

We believe that it is desirable to provide a clear separation between abstraction and reasoning processes in hybrid autonomous control systems. We believe this is beneficial not only for the clarity of the code, but also for use in applications such as forward planning and model checking.

We have created a formal semantics describing how such an Abstraction Engine would interact with the rest of the system, and discussed a prototype BDI based Abstraction Engine and the issues this raises in terms of a suitable language for generating discrete abstractions from continuous data. We believe that this is the first work linking autonomous agents and control systems via a formal semantics.

7.1   Future Work

The work on hybrid agent systems with declarative abstractions for autonomous space software is only in its initial stages and considerable further work remains to be investigated.

Further Case Studies. We are keen to develop a repertoire of case studies, beyond the simple one presented here, which will provide us with benchmark examples upon which to examine issues such as more sophisticated reasoning tasks, multi-agent systems, forward planning, verification and language design.

In addition we aim, next, to investigate a case study involving multiple satellites attempting to maintain and change formation in low Earth orbit. This presents significant planning challenges.

Custom Language. At the moment the BDI language we are using for the Abstraction Engine is not as clear as we might like. In particular the functions of abstraction and reification are not so easy to "read off" from the code and are obscured somewhat by housekeeping tasks associated with maintaining consistent shared beliefs about which thrusters are in operation.

A further degree of declarativeness can be achieved within the Abstraction Engine by separation of abstraction evaluation and the control features. Due to the dynamic setting in which abstraction is performed "on-the-fly" reacting to incoming sensory data, it can be naturally seen as query processing for data streams [12; 13]. This viewpoint would provide a clean semantics for abstraction evaluation, based on the theory of stream queries [13] and would hopefully avoid the need to devote too much space to storing data logs. We also aim to investigate the extent to which techniques and programming languages developed for efficient data stream processing (from e.g., [2; 17]) can be re-used within the Abstraction Engine. It is possible that something similar might be used for the reification process as well, although this is more speculative.

We are interested in investigating programming languages for the Reasoning Engine – e.g., languages such as *Jason* [6] or 3APL [8] are similar to Gwendolen, but better developed and supported. Alternatively it might be necessary to use a language containing, for instance, the concept of a *maintain* goal. Much of a satellite's operation is most naturally expressed in terms of *maintaining* a state of affairs (such as a remaining on a particular path).

Planning and Model Checking. At present the `M-file` employed to create a new controller that will return the satellite to the desired orbit uses a technique based on hill-climbing search [19]. We are interested in investigating temporal logic and model-checking based approaches to this form of planning for hybrid automata based upon the work of Kloetzer and Belta [18].

Model checking techniques also exist [5] for the verification of BDI agent programs which could conceivably be applied to the Reasoning Engine. Abstraction techniques would then be required to provide appropriate models of the continuous and physical engines and it might be possible to generate these automatically from the abstraction and reification functions.

There is also a large body of work on the verification of hybrid systems [1; 14] which would allow us to push the boundaries of verification of such systems outside the limits of the Reasoning Engine alone.

Multi-Agent Systems. We are interested in extending our work to multi-agent systems and groups of satellites that need to collaborate in order to achieve some objective. In particular there are realistic scenarios in which one member of a group of satellites loses some particular functionality meaning that its role within the group needs to change. We believe this provides an interesting application for multi-agent work on groups, teams, roles and organisations [9; 15; 10; 20], together with the potential for formal verification in this area.

Since the individual agents in this system will be discrete physical objects and will be represented as such in any simulation we don't anticipate major challenges to the architecture itself from moving to a multi-agent scenario. However we anticipate interesting challenges from the point of view of coordination and communication between the agents.

References

[1] Alur, R., Courcoubetis, C., Halbwachs, N., Henzinger, T.A., Ho, P.-H., Nicollin, X., Olivero, A., Sifakis, J., Yovine, S.: The Algorithmic Analysis of Hybrid Systems. Theoretical Computer Science 138(1), 3–34 (1995)

[2] Arasu, A., Babu, S., Widom, J.: The cql continuous query language: semantic foundations and query execution. The VLDB Journal 15, 121–142 (2006)

[3] Clarke, A.C.: Extra-Terrestrial Relays: Can Rocket Stations Give World-wide Radio Coverage? Wireless World, 305–308 (1945)

[4] Bordini, R.H., Dastani, M., Dix, J., El Fallah Seghrouchni, A. (eds.): Multi-Agent Programming: Languages, Platforms and Applications. Springer, Heidelberg (2005)

[5] Bordini, R.H., Dennis, L.A., Farwer, B., Fisher, M.: Automated Verification of Multi-Agent Programs. In: Proceedings of the 23rd IEEE/ACM International Conference on Automated Software Engineering (ASE), L'Aquila, Italy, pp. 69–78 (September 2008)

[6] Bordini, R.H., Hübner, J.F., Vieira, R.: Jason and the Golden Fleece of Agent-Oriented Programming. In: Bordini, et al [4], ch. 1, pp. 3–37

[7] Branicky, M.S., Borkar, V.S., Mitter, S.K.: A Unified Framework for Hybrid Control: Model and Optimal Control Theory. IEEE Transactions on Automatic Control 43(1), 31–45 (1998)

[8] Dastani, M., van Riemsdijk, M.B., Meyer, J.-J.C.: Programming Multi-Agent Systems in 3APL. In: Bordini, et al [4], ch. 2, pp. 39–67

[9] Ferber, J., Gutknecht, O.: A Meta-model for the Analysis and Design of Organizations in Multi-agent Systems. In: Proceedings of the Third International Conference on Multi-Agent Systems (ICMAS), pp. 128–135. IEEE Computer Society, Los Alamitos (1998)

[10] Fisher, M., Ghidini, C., Hirsch, B.: Programming Groups of Rational Agents. In: Dix, J., Leite, J. (eds.) CLIMA IV 2004. LNCS (LNAI), vol. 3259, pp. 16–33. Springer, Heidelberg (2004)

[11] Goebel, R., Sanfelice, R., Teel, A.R.: Hybrid Dynamical Systems. IEEE Control Systems Magazine 29(2), 28–93 (2009)

[12] Grohe, M., Gurevich, Y., Leinders, D., Schweikardt, N., Tyszkiewicz, J., den Bussche, J.V.: Database Query Processing Using Finite Cursor Machines. Theory of Computing Systems 44, 533–560 (2009)

[13] Gurevich, Y., Leinders, D., Van den Bussche, J.: A Theory of Stream Queries. In: Arenas, M. (ed.) DBPL 2007. LNCS, vol. 4797, pp. 153–168. Springer, Heidelberg (2007)

[14] Henzinger, T.A., Ho, P.-H., Wong-Toi, H.: HyTech: A Model Checker for Hybrid Systems. International Journal on Software Tools for Technology Transfer 1(1-2), 110–122 (1997)

[15] Hübner, J.F., Sichman, J.S., Boissier, O.: A Model for the Structural, Functional, and Deontic Specification of Organizations in Multiagent Systems. In: Bittencourt, G., Ramalho, G.L. (eds.) SBIA 2002. LNCS (LNAI), vol. 2507, pp. 118–128. Springer, Heidelberg (2002)

[16] Ingrand, F.F., Georgeff, M.P., Rao, A.S.: An Architecture for Real-Time Reasoning and System Control. IEEE Expert: Intelligent Systems and Their Applications 7(6), 34–44 (1992)

[17] Jain, N., Mishra, S., Srinivasan, A., Gehrke, J., Widom, J., Balakrishnan, H., Çetintemal, U., Cherniack, M., Tibbetts, R., Zdonik, S.: Towards a Streaming SQL Standard. In: Proceedings of Very Large Databases, Auckland, New Zealand, pp. 1397–1390 (August 2008)

[18] Kloetzer, M., Belta, C.: A Fully Automated Framework for Control of Linear Systems From Temporal Logic Specifications. IEEE Transactions on Automatic Control 53(1), 287–297 (2008)

[19] Lincoln, N.K., Veres, S.M.: Components of a Vision Assisted Constrained Autonomous Satellite Formation Flying Control System. International Journal of Adaptive Control and Signal Processing 21(2-3), 237–264 (2006)

[20] Pynadath, D.V., Tambe, M., Chauvat, N., Cavedon, L.: Toward Team-Oriented Programming. In: Jennings, N.R. (ed.) ATAL 1999. LNCS, vol. 1757, pp. 233–247. Springer, Heidelberg (2000)

[21] Rao, A.S., Georgeff, M.P.: BDI agents: From theory to practice. In: Proceedings of the First International Conference on Multi-Agent Systems (ICMAS), San Francisco, USA, pp. 312–319 (June 1995)

[22] Veres, S.M.: Natural Language Programming of Agents and Robotic Devices: Publishing for Humans and Machines in sEnglish. SysBrain Ltd (2008)

[23] Tabuada, P.: Verification and Control of Hybrid Systems: A Symbolic Approach. Springer, Heidelberg (2009)

[24] Tiwari, A.: Abstractions for Hybrid Systems. Formal Methods in Systems Design 32, 57–83 (2008)

[25] Varaiya, P.: Design, Simulation, and Implementation of Hybrid Systems. In: Donatelli, S., Kleijn, J. (eds.) ICATPN 1999. LNCS, vol. 1639, pp. 1–5. Springer, Heidelberg (1999)

[26] Veres, S.M., Lincoln, N.K.: Sliding Mode Control of Autonomous Spacecraft — in sEnglish. In: Proceedings of Towards Autonomous Robotics Systems (TAROS), Edinborough, UK (2008)

[27] Veres, S.M., Molnar, L.: Publishing Documents on Physical Skills for Intelligent Agents in English. In: Proceedings of the Tenth IASTED International Conference on Artificial Intelligence and Applications (AIA), Innsbruck, Austria (2010)

[28] Watson, R.: An Application of Action Theory to the Space Shuttle. In: Gupta, G. (ed.) PADL 1999. LNCS, vol. 1551, pp. 290–304. Springer, Heidelberg (1999)

[29] Wooldridge, M., Jennings, N.R.: Intelligent Agents: Theory and Practice. The Knowledge Engineering Review 10(2), 115–152 (1995)

Executing Specifications of Social Reasoning Agents

Iain Wallace and Michael Rovatsos

School of Informatics, The University of Edinburgh,
Edinburgh EH8 9LE, UK
{Iain.Wallace,Michael.Rovatsos}@ed.ac.uk

Abstract. Social reasoning theories, whilst studied extensively in the area of multiagent systems, are hard to implement directly in agents. They often specify properties of beliefs or behaviours but not the way these should affect the computational reasoning mechanisms of a concrete agent design. The Expectation-Strategy-Behaviour (ESB) framework addresses this problem by separating and abstracting social reasoning from other practical reasoning, providing the computational machinery that is necessary to perform social reasoning in practice. We present an extension to previous work on ESB to an implemented reasoning system which enables the execution of concise and modular declarative social reasoning rules. We review the foundations of the abstract ESB framework and present the implementation of a reasoner based on CTL model checking. Our system allows for conditioning agent behaviours on complex preconditions and verification of properties to aid the agent designer. It also allows for easy integration with a BDI reasoning system. We exemplify the suitability of ESB for social reasoning constructs with a detailed example of Joint Intention theory in ESB and illustrate the generality with an overview of another implemented social reasoning scheme, and extensions to both.

1   Introduction

In many multiagent environments, achieving coordinated behaviour requires social reasoning on the part of individual agents. This includes reasoning about others and one's relationships with them, or about social objects such as norms and social laws, commitments and conventions, deontic notions such as obligations, permissions, and prohibitions, trust and reputation. While there exists a very rich literature on social reasoning theories, there is hardly any support for implementing the suggested frameworks in actual systems at the level of general-purpose tools to aid agent design and implementation. On the one hand, there exist formal languages for describing action and cooperation theories but these do not include a computational framework for processing such specifications, e.g. [1,2]. On the other hand, there exist implemented frameworks, but they are either specific to a *particular* social reasoning theory [3,4], or have only been implemented in a specific software application [5]. General approaches to

A. Omicini, S. Sardina, and W. Vasconcelos (Eds.): DALT 2010, LNAI 6619, pp. 112–129, 2011.

multiagent reasoning have a lot to offer the community, as shown by the success of BDI. Maintaining a high level of generality allows a method to be applied to many different existing ideas, for their comparison, implementation or to realise the benefits of their combination. A general method capturing key social reasoning abstractions would therefore be of benefit to research on MAS.

In [6], we proposed the Expectation-Strategy-Behaviour (ESB) architecture. ESB is an abstract framework designed to unify many social reasoning approaches, whilst providing the computational machinery to process declarative specifications of a given social reasoning framework. ESB is based on specifications of an agent's beliefs regarding hidden properties of a system (such as the internal attributes of others or the status of social objects) together with belief revision mechanisms that specify how these beliefs are updated. Such a general formalism is useful for capturing social reasoning theories from the agent's point of view, rather than at the system level. At its most general social reasoning requires some mechanism for modifying beliefs about social state and ESB provides a means to specify these mechanisms.

Treating social reasoning as a separate component has several benefits. Foremost, reasoning about interaction makes designing and implementing MAS complex and general abstractions specific to this task may ease it. Additionally a unifying declarative specification for social reasoning could allow for interesting agent interactions based on combinations of social reasoning techniques.

We also presented an abstract interpreter for ESB [6] specifications that constructs graph-based models of expectation sets, determines how these change over time, and allows for querying the expectation status at runtime. While this is a first step toward providing generic implementation support for varied social reasoning methods, the system presented previously does not specify a concrete reasoning engine that enables the whole cycle of ESB based reasoning and execution. What is required is a means of specification, algorithms for model generation, querying mechanisms, and integration with a practical reasoning system to combine social reasoning with other rational reasoning capabilities. In this paper, we present an ESB reasoning engine that provides this missing functionality and can be readily used to implement social reasoning frameworks in BDI agents. Our system allows for:

- defining declarative ESB specifications of social reasoning rules. These specify the properties of a social reasoner without worrying about procedural processing, and are easily extended in a modular way;
- automated model generation based on these specifications, model restriction to achieve boundedly rational reasoning, and querying of logical constraints via model checking;
- an interface to generic AgentSpeak(L) [7] specifications to integrate the ESB reasoning component with specifications of BDI agent designs in a loosely coupled way so as to maximise reusability.

With this functionality, our system ESB-RS (ESB Reasoning System) provides comprehensive design and implementation support for existing and new social reasoning frameworks, while maintaining a clear separation of social reasoning from other types of practical reasoning. As far as the authors are aware, no other related work provides an implementation of a general social reasoning engine separated from the practical reasoner.

We proceed as follows: in Section 2, we review the abstract ESB framework as presented in [6]. Section 3 presents the design of our overall ESB reasoning system, and its implementation with the NuSMV model checking system [8] and the Jason [9] implementation of AgentSpeak(L). In Section 4, we exemplify the suitability of the proposed ESB reasoning system by describing the well-known theory of Joint Intentions [10] in ESB and implementing it in our reasoning engine. This finishes with an overview of other work to capture social reasoning in ESB and then Section 5 concludes.

2   The ESB Framework

The ESB framework is an abstract model for practical social reasoning systems based on the concept of *expectations*, which are defined as follows:

> An *expectation* is a *conditional belief* regarding a statement whose truth status may be eventually *verified* by a *test* and updated according to specified *responses* to the test.

Expectations take the form of a belief Φ held by an agent A under condition C. When C holds, depending on the outcome of a test T, the agent will update its expectations if the expected belief was confirmed ρ^+ (positive response), and ρ^- if not (negative response).

Strategies constrain the style and scope of the agent's reasoning process, whilst behaviours form the link between the representation of social concepts in the expectations and the practical reasoning process.

In the general case, an expectation is represented as follows:

$$\mathbf{Exp}(N\ A\ C\ \Phi\ T^+\ T^-\ \rho^+\ \rho^-)$$

N is the *name* of the expectation, taken from a set of all expectation labels $\mathbf{EXP} = \{N, N', \ldots\}$.

A is the *agent* holding this expectation, from a set of agents $\{A, A', \ldots\}$.

C is the *condition* under which the expectation holds. Evaluated over the agent's beliefs like the guards on BDI plans.

Φ is the expected belief, i.e. an event or an expectation[1] that another agent is assumed to hold

---

[1] Nesting expectations allows modelling of other agent's mental states, and adaptive behaviour on the part of either agent.

T^+, T^- are the *tests* which confirm (T^+), or reject (T^-), the expectation of Φ. Tests are split for the purposes of the implementation described here. E.g. a test may succeed when another agent performs an expected task, or fail when a certain amount of time elapses.

ρ^+/ρ^- are the positive/negative *responses* to the tests. Each is specified in terms of two sets of expectations: those to remove, and those to add.

To illustrate ESB we shall re-use from [6] an example based on the Rummy [11] card game. It is only required to understand that players are trying to collect either runs of cards in a suit, or sets of the same value card. On their turn a player must pick up a card. They then create any sets they can and discard, play passes to the next player. In our example domain, an expectation could be that if opponent B picks up a $2\diamondsuit$ (C), then we expect (Φ) them to be collecting 2s. The test (T) is if they pickup or discard another 2. The corresponding positive response (ρ^+) is to remove expectations that they are collecting a run. The negative response (ρ^-) is to remove this expectation itself (leaving others suggesting they are collecting a run).

Strategies specify ways to process sets of expectations. Consider all possible sets of expectations that could arise from future observations of test outcomes - a strategy is a particular way of traversing the graph that results from mapping out all possible future expectation combinations. A strategy therefore controls how the agent reasons based on expected future outcomes. To continue our Rummy example, a strategy could consider only those future states where the opponent plays according to mini-max principles (with an evaluation function based on the utility of cards). Or more simply, when the game nears the end one could bound the depth of the graph considered to the likely number of hands.

Behaviours determine how the overall expectation base affects the agent's practical reasoning and actions. They are conditioned on statements about expectations, and the truth value will be established by applying the agent's strategy to the expectation base. This condition is tied to an action, which is not necessarily a direct physical action, but rather a modification of the agent's beliefs (at the practical reasoning level, rather than social). An example might be to only allow discards of $2\diamondsuit$ (action) if the opponent is not expected to be collecting 2s, or to be collecting them in the future (condition).

Expectations, together with *strategies* and *behaviours* provide us with a natural way for describing social reasoning methods and devising modular social reasoning designs from belief revision mechanisms regarding hidden properties in the system (such as the mental states of other agents). The notion of *expectation* captures all the elements that are necessary to link beliefs held about non-observable parts of the system with practical reasoning. It also allows us to express belief dynamics at a practical, procedural level while benefiting from declarative representations.

2.1   The Operation of an ESB Agent

The ESB theory proposes that there are advantages to separating social reasoning from practical reasoning about actions in the world. In this work, we assume the

ESB component to be combined with a BDI practical reasoner and the interface between the two reasoners to be the belief revision function of the BDI interpreter.

To demonstrate ESB, we adapt a simple set of expectations and their graph from [6] (Figure 1). For brevity, expectations are labelled with a number, and only the responses are shown in the table. States in the graph show the active set of expectations in that state. The responses define how the state changes according to the tests. The convention used is that an arc labelled "¬2" is the transition caused by the test for expectation 2 failing, or simply "2" for the success case. Where an arc bears more than one label, it represents parallel arcs grouped for clarity. To refer to components of these expectations we will use notation like "$\Phi(1)$" to specify the expected belief Φ of expectation 1. Correspondingly $T^+(1)$ would be the positive test condition for expectation 1 and so on.

Expectations and Responses

Name	ρ^+	ρ^-
1	add(3,4) remove(2,5)	remove(1)
2	add(5) remove(1,3,4)	add(3,4) remove(2,5)
3	-	add(2,5) remove(1,3)
4	-	add(2,5) remove(1,3)
5	add(2) remove(1,3,4)	add(1,3,4) remove(2,5)

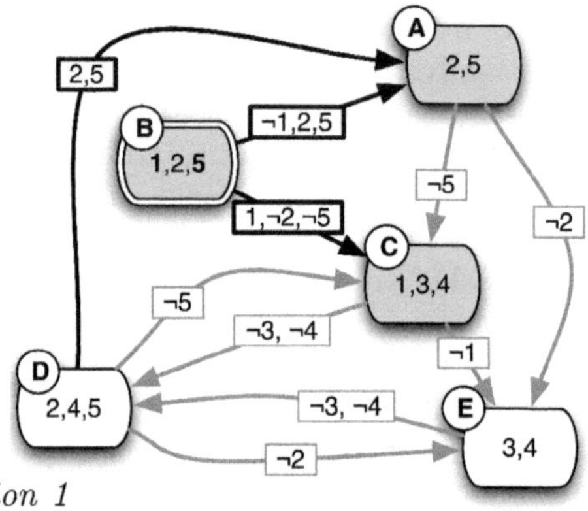

Behaviour Conditions: $B1.\ \mathbf{E}\Diamond(3) \triangleright Action\ 1$
$B2.\ \mathbf{A}\Box(\mathbf{A}\Diamond 2) \triangleright Action\ 2$

Fig. 1. A simple ESB example (adapted from [6])(Bold arcs indicate reduction according to strategy)

The language for the behaviour conditions follows Computation Tree Logic (CTL). It is a branching time logic specifying possible futures, and only knowledge of a few operators is required here. There are quantifiers over paths and specific to paths. **E** and **A** mean "there exists a path" and "for all paths". For paths, $\Box$ and $\Diamond$ can be read as "always" and "eventually", i.e. in all states or in some future state on the respective paths.

An agent is provided with a specification of all expectations **EXP** = $\{1, 2, 3, 4, 5\}$, and maintains the sets $EXP_A = \{1, 2, 5\}$ (active expectations, state B in the graph) and $EXP_C = \{1, 5\}$ (current expectations where C holds, shown in bold).

Other required inputs for the reasoning cycle are:

- The current belief base.
- The strategy in use.
- The set of behaviour rules.
- The practical reasoner ESB is combined with.

The output from the process is the updated expectation state, belief base and any actions performed by the practical reasoning component.

An ESB agent's reasoning cycle proceeds as follows:

1. Update EXP_C to contain those expectations from EXP_A where C holds. *State B is active in the example, and the agent holds 1 and 5 to be true.*
2. For $E \in EXP_C$ add $\Phi(E)$ to the agents beliefs (stored in the BDI reasoner). *We add $\Phi(1), \Phi(5)$.*
3. Apply the strategy to create the restricted strategy graph by considering only a subset of transitions from the current state. *Our example has an optimistic agent, that considers only ρ^+ responses, those where there is a positive transition in our graph (marked in bold). Applied to the active state B, this leaves the subgraph of the grey highlighted states as the strategy graph.*
4. For each behaviour, where the behaviour condition is *true*, add the specified belief (the corresponding *action*) to the belief base. *The example behaviours are written in a CTL style. B1 says "3 is possible", this is true in state C. B2 says "2 is always possible" and is false, as state A is in the strategy graph.*
5. Perform BDI plan selection and action execution as normal. This is before expectation responses are applied, in case actions are sensing actions that affect test outcomes.
6. For $E \in EXP_C$
   (a) If test $T^+(E)$ applies, update expectations as per the response $\rho^+(E)$
   (b) else if $T^-(E)$ applies, update expectations as per the response $\rho^-(E)$
   If we assume that $T^+(5)$ holds, then the expectations are updated to place the agent in state A.

The responses will update the set of expectations, so there may be some overlap where one expectation is added but another response causes its removal. In this case, the current system applies them all recursively, in the order specified by the designer (if they still apply given previous effects). This results in an expectation set consistent with the agent's observations, relative to its current expectations.

3 An ESB Reasoner

ESB only specifies a framwork for social reasoning, and so must be combined with a practical reasoning component. The main components of a complete ESB-RS agent are:

- A BDI reasoning engine, in this case Jason [9].
- A set of plans for practical reasoning, here they are specified in AgentS-peak(L) [7].
- An ESB engine, to maintain the expectations and interface with Jason.
- An ESB specification in terms of its expectations, strategy and behaviours.

Of these only the last has previously been presented in [6]. The contribution here is a description of the algorithms required for the ESB engine, and coupling

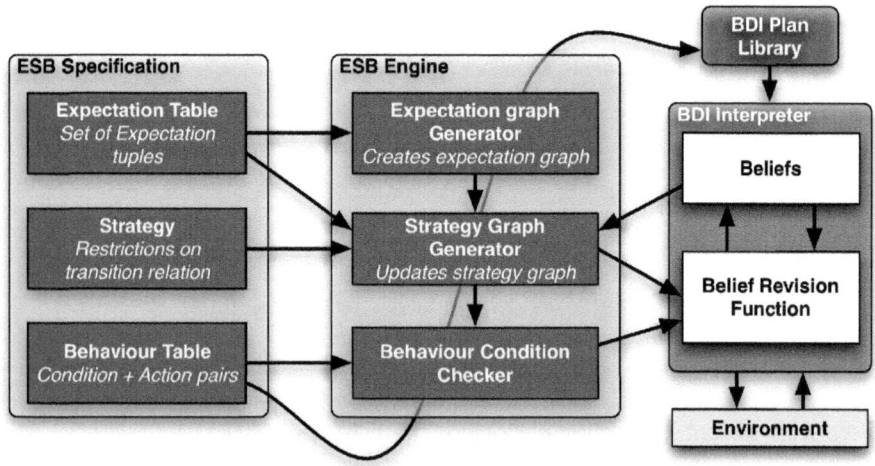

Fig. 2. Overview of an ESB-RS Agent

of this engine with the BDI interpreter. We present an evaluation based on the case studies of joint intentions [10] and the robosoccer example presented later.

The interactions between these components are illustrated in Figure 2. The principal interaction between the social and practical reasoning components is via the belief revision function (BRF). Expectations are updated based on the agent's perceptions and beliefs. The control of the agent's social interactions is also in terms of beliefs, as these can act as guards on plans which carry out actions.

The execution of ESB-RS can be roughly described as follows. The expectation graph is generated from the specifications. This is only done once, as after this initial step the agent can simply track its current state in the graph. Then, in each reasoning cycle, the beliefs from the BDI part, this expectation graph and the strategy specification are used to create the reduced strategy graph. This is then used by the behaviour condition checker to select the applicable behaviour actions, which are used to update the agent's beliefs accordingly. With the belief-based interface to the BDI practical reasoner, it is necessary for the designer to develop behaviour actions that work in tandem with relevant plans.

3.1   Expectations

The language of expectations is defined formally in [6]. The agent's current state is captured by three sets of expectations: current, active and inactive, updated according to the algorithm described in section 2.1.

In ESB-RS we transform the expectations into a finite state machine (FSM) at a lower level of abstraction than the expectation graph of previous work. Behaviour conditions are however defined in terms of the expectation graph. Accordingly we must transform a declarative expectation specification into a form suitable for efficient behaviour checking. The graph may be thought of as a FSM, where it is necessary to check if certain properties hold (the behaviour conditions) given an initial state (defined by EXP_C). This intuition naturally suggests the use of model checkers, which aim to solve a similar problem. To be able to apply a model checker for ESB reasoning requires algorithms to create the state descriptions and transition relation from our sets of expectations.

To specify an ESB agent's execution as an FSM, we do not have to consider all the combinations of expectations that form states in the expectation graph explicitly. This is one of the advantages brought by the model checker, as it implicitly considers these combinations. The FSM is defined in terms of individual expectation dynamics, which are specified more easily. Testing a condition on a particular expectation graph state, or setting the current state, is done by specifying the state of all individual expectations. This finer grained approach is possible as each state in an expectation graph can be considered not as one state, but as a high level abstraction of the set of states where only a subset of expectations are relevant. This concept, and the following algorithm to create an FSM with equivalent properties to the conceptual expectation graph model represent the key new development presented in this paper. It allows the use of the NuSMV [8] model checker, and ultimately makes it possible to easily implement the previous ESB theory.

Creating the FSM, we are concerned with only the parts of each expectation that describe the dynamics:

Condition $\in \{True, False, DC\}$ – Each expectation can be considered to be *True* or *False* (holds or does not), if it is in the active set EXP_A, or "don't care" (DC) if it is not. Expectations in EXP_C are of course *True*.

$\Phi \in \{True, False\}$ – This is as per **condition**, or *False* where condition is *DC*.

Test $\in \{Tp, Tm, NA\}$ – The test is either positive (Tp) or negative (Tm) or not-applicable (NA). It is not-applicable whenever the expectation is *DC*.

Responses ρ^+, ρ^- – The add- and remove-sets of expectations for each response are used to define the transition relation of the FSM.

The set of expectation graph states translate to the FSM as the set of all unique combinations of each expectation's condition (though of course many will be unreachable). From this it follows that it is only necessary to specify how each individual expectation changes to define the FSM transition relation and the complete graph is captured. Each expectation is specified in terms of its variables, and expressions for the next state in terms of the current state variables. This is done as follows:

INPUT: The set of all expectations **EXP**.
OUTPUT: An FSM, specified in terms of each expectation's dynamics.

Each expectation E ∈ **EXP** has components:
    E.Condition ∈ {True, False,DC}
    E.Test ∈ {Tp,Tm,NA}
The sets of expectations added and removed by responses:
    E.Tp.addSet,E.Tp.removeSet,E.Tm.addSet,E.Tm.removeSet

Next state for each E calculated as follows:
 FOR every other expectation O ∈ **EXP**
    IF (O.Test = Tp) & (E in O.Tp.addSet) **THEN**
      E.Condition ∈ {True,False}, **RETURN**
    ELSE IF (O.Test = Tm) & (E in O.Tm.addSet) **THEN**
      E.Condition ∈ {True,False}, **RETURN**
    ELSE IF (O.Test = Tp) & (E in O.Tp.removeSet) **THEN**
      E.Condition ∈ {DC}, **RETURN**
    ELSE IF (O.Test = Tm) & (E in O.Tm.removeSet) **THEN**
      E.Condition ∈ {DC}, **RETURN**
    END IF
 END FOR
 IF E.Condition ∈ {True,False} **THEN**
   E.Condition ∈ {True,False}, **RETURN**
 ELSE IF E.Condition = DC **THEN**
   E.Condition ∈ {DC}, **RETURN**
 END IF

When the condition is assigned and returns, assign the test:
 IF E.Condition ∈ {DC} **THEN**
   E.Test ∈ {NA}
 ELSE
   E.Test ∈ {Tp,Tm,NA}
 END IF

This algorithm does not represent actual implemented code, but captures how the specification of the FSM for the NuSMV model checker is procedurally specified. The problem of actually creating the FSM for the purposes of model checking from this description of its transition relation is handled by the model checker. This is a key benefit of this approach. As it is a simple operation to generate this specification and the complexity of the problem of building the FSM is handled by the model checker.

Each expectation is defined in terms of its component variables and how they change from state to state. The algorithm is tricky to understand, but easily described in a more natural manner. The for-loop says that if this expectation is in an add-set of another expectation where the relevant test applies, then it will become active (True or False – it may or may not be current). Similarly if it appears in a relevant remove-set then it will be set to DC. If neither case applies, each expectation's condition may at the next step change between False or True, however if it is DC then it stays as such. The test for an expectation is not applicable (NA) if the expectation is inactive, otherwise it may be the positive case (Tp), negative (Tm) , or neither (NA).

3.2 Strategies

Strategies are so called, as they influence the overall style of the agent's social reasoning rather than being concerned with the details. A simple example would be an optimistic agent, which considers only the positive response transitions - effectively assuming its assumptions about other agent's mental states are always correct. Alternatively it is possible for strategies to have a greater influence on an agent's behaviour. For example, the expectations could be restricted to those consistent with a particular opponent model.

Strategies are implemented as a set of constraints on the transition relation. Each constraint is a boolean expression which must be satisfied in all states. This means that the transitions from a given state are constrained to those where the next state meets all the strategy constraints. The atoms in the constraints are the components of each expectation. These can be combined using various operations defined by the model checker used to check behaviour constraints, NuSMV [8]. Operations can include logical propositions, case statements etc.

For example, the graph could be restricted to consider only those states reachable assuming tests, if they apply, always have a positive outcome Tp. The constraint to achieve this would be to limit the next state as follows:

$$next(E.Test : \{Tp, NA\})$$

This says that for any state, in the next state the test must have the positive outcome, if it applies at all. Specific expectations, or expectation graph states (conjunctive combinations of expectations) can also be excluded by name, for example:

$$next(Exp1.C : \{DC\}) \ \& \ next(Exp3.C : \{DC\})$$

This can allow for more complex strategies, which can be generated. An example would be removing states that do not meet some decision- or game-theoretic criteria as suggested in [6].

3.3 Behaviours

Behaviour conditions are checked by constructing a graph from a set of expectations, and checking conditions based on the current state and possible (or impossible) future states. This naturally suggests an approach based on model checking, as the problem is very similar. Model checking presents an attractive advantage - it is only necessary to describe the states each expectation may have, and the relatively simple relations between them, and the model checker will allow us to form relatively complex queries about expectation graph concepts.

NuSMV allows the checking of CTL logic formulae, allowing us to express possibilities and necessities. A simple example is the condition "If I might hold expectation 2 in the future" which is captured as $\mathbf{E}\Diamond(\Phi(2))$ (there exists a path where eventually $\Phi(2)$). Having described the implementation of the ESB-RS engine to execute declarative specifications, we now proceed to several examples illustrating its usefulness.

4   Evaluation

In this section we evaluate ESB's suitability for capturing social reasoning concerns by demonstrating that this key concept of Joint Intentions (JI [10]) can be easily expressed. This is explored with a detailed description of a JI implementation in ESB-RS, and a subsequent extension. We follow this with an overview of a normative reasoning system also captured in ESB-RS and a brief discussion.

4.1   Joint Intentions in ESB-RS

Kumar et al. [12] describe the Request Conversation Protocol (RCP) for establishing a joint persistent goal (JPG). The difference between a Joint Intention and a JPG is in the mutual belief throughout executing the action that it is done as a team. So given a pair of agents who believe that they are doing the action as a team, the request protocol brings about a state of joint intentions between the agents. ESB is ideally suited to capture Joint Intentions, as the JI centres around commitments the agent holds based on its beliefs about expected commitments of the other agent.

The RCP defined in terms of a set of communication acts, with associated semantics and mental states that two agents go through to form a JPG. Figure 3 shows the communication acts, and the states the agents go through. If agent X is requesting an action of Y, the intuition is simple. X firsts requests an action from Y, X now holds a persistent weak achievement goal (PWAG) toward Y. Y either agrees or refuses, in the "agree" case Y now also holds a PWAG toward X to achieve the goal. There is now a JI. X has a goal for Y to do some action, and Y has a goal to do this action relative to X's desire to do so.

To simplify the example, we omit the case where the requesting agent cancels the request.

There are several primitive components that the protocol is built upon: the individual commitments; persistent goal (PGOAL) and persistent weak achievement

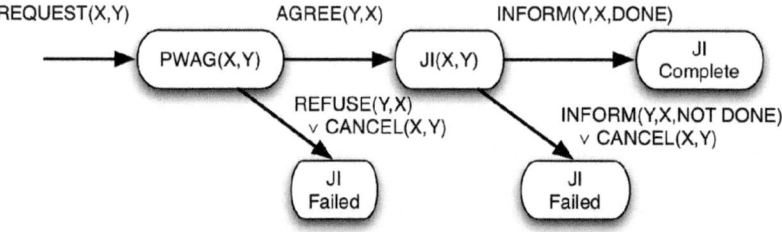

Fig. 3. The Request Conversation Protocol (adapted from [12])

goal (PWAG); and the speech acts REQUEST, AGREE, REFUSE and INFORM. The formal definitions can be found in [12], but a description of a PWAG is useful here. "PWAG(X,Y,A,Q)" says agent X has a persistent goal to achieve A, given relevancy condition Q, and will have a persistent goal to notify Y that A is achieved, or becomes impossible or irrelevant ($\neg$Q holds).

These primitives are all considered as actions the agent can perform, be they communicative or holding an individual commitment. They are not social reasoning, this will be separated out into the ESB side of the reasoner, and acts on top of these basic components. The primitives are therefore implemented in the BDI practical reasoner component, and not described here.

Only three expectations are needed to allow the agent to use the above primitives to form and act on a joint intention. The expectations used are shown in table 1. The agent holding each expectation is assumed to be "self", and the other either X or Y depending on the role played. The three expectations can be explained as follows:

1. When I have a PWAG, and expect Y also has the PWAG relative to my own goal, I expect a JI to do A exists. The positive test outcome is I believe A (the action was performed), not Q (is no longer relevant) or F (failed). The negative result is harder to express neatly. Loosely it is that A, not Q or F is believed and this is not communicated by the other agent - they have not upheld their part of the joint commitment. Even if they do not directly observe the completion event, they should reply to ensure mutual belief.
2. When I receive AGREE(A,Q,F) from Y, I expect Y holds PWAG(Y,X,A,[Q $\wedge$ PWAG(X,Y,A,Q)]). The relevancy condition for Y's PWAG also includes that X still has the commitment toward the goal. Intuitively, it makes no sense for an agent to perform a requested action if the requester is no longer committed to it. The positive test is that Y informs me of A, not Q or F, negative test is I observe A, not Q or F and Y does not inform me as per 1.
3. When I receive REQUEST(A,Q,F) from X expect X holds PWAG(X,Y,A,Q). The tests are as 2, only obviously I expect X to inform me.

Although these expectations follow logically from the semantics of the communication acts, they are still *assumptions* about another agent's mental state, and so are separated out as social reasoning, for the advantages described in [6].

Only a couple of responses are required. In the failure cases the belief that the other agent has agreed or requested an action is removed. The effect is to remove the expected PWAG from the belief base, and thus the expectation of a JI (if any). In addition, it may be desirable to add some response actions as a result of JI being upheld or not. An obvious case would be maintaining a list of other agents who have been proven willing to co-operate, to aid future decisions.

In this simple set of expectations, there is no real need to choose a strategy, as there are not significant numbers of transitions in the graph. Strategies are envisaged as becoming more useful to bound and direct reasoning in more complex situated examples.

Table 1. JI Expectations

Expectation	1. ExpJI	2. ExpAgree	3. ExpReq
Condition	pwag(self,Y,A,Q) ∧ pwag(Y,self,A, [Q ∧ pwag(self,Y,A,Q)])	agree(A,Q,F) [source(Y)]	request(A,Q,F) [source(X)]
Φ	ji(self,Y,A)	pwag(Y,self,A, [Q ∧ pwag(self,Y,A,Q)])	pwag(X,self,A,Q)
T+	A ∨ ¬Q ∨ F	(A ∨ ¬Q ∨ F) [source(Y)]	(A ∨ ¬Q ∨ F) [source(X)]
T−	A ∨ ¬Q ∨ F [source(¬Y)]	(A ∨ ¬Q ∨ F) [source(¬Y)]	(A ∨ ¬Q ∨ F) [source(¬X)]
ρ^+	-	-	-
ρ^-	-	remove agree(A,Q,F)	remove request(A,Q,F)

The behaviour (*condition* ▷ *action*) pairs represent the interface between the social and practical reasoner. Only one behaviour is required for an agent to act upon joint intentions, that is:

ji(self,Y,A) ▷ *add_belief*(haveJI(A))

This says when I expect I have a JI to do an action A, add the synthetic belief *haveJI(A)* to the belief base. This belief represents the JI and should act as a guard on all plans that require the JI to succeed. So it can be read simply as, "allow joint plans only when I have a joint intention". This seems very obvious and simple but this is the nature of Joint Intentions. It is the most basic building block on top of which more complex social reasoning and interaction can be built. Here it is specified explicitly, rather than designed into a system implicitly.

Although the above is all that is strictly necessary to express joint intentions, ESB provides an easy route to simply and generically answer the social reasoning questions of when to request a joint action, and when to agree to one. Both are necessary considerations for any implementation, and bridging the gap from theory to implementation is a key driver of our work.

The first consideration is when to request a JI. Specifically, when it is possible in the future to hold a JI toward A, and it is desired, then request:

$\mathbf{E}\lozenge$(ji(self,Y,A)) ∧ (**desire** A) ▷ *add_belief*(requestJI(A))

The condition is similar for agreeing to a request, the only difference being the requirement that a request has been received:

request(A,Q,F) ∧ $\mathbf{E}\lozenge$(ji(self,Y,A) ∧ (**desire** A) ▷
add_belief(agreeRequest(A))

In terms of expectation graphs, the condition says that if from the current state, a possible future expectation state includes one in which I hold a JI - then it is sensible to request (or agree) to one. The converse is that it is not rational to request or agree to a JI if an agent doesn't believe that its future reasoning (or the other agent's) can bring about this state.

4.2   Extended Example

To evaluate how ESB can be easily used in practice, and extended in a modular way, we present a robotic soccer example. The situation we consider here is an example of a team plan to score a goal - thus requiring joint commitment between agents, as presented above. The scenario we consider involves three team-mates, one with the ball. The agent in possession of the ball wishes one agent to go up either side of the pitch, one as a feint and the other to pass the ball to, then shoot.

If the agent with the ball is Andy, wanting to pass to Barney and have Cathy perform the feint, the intended operation is as follows. Andy must form a JI with Barney to move up the pitch receive a pass and shoot, and with Cathy to move up the pitch. But we can also assume that each agent also has practical reasoner plans to score goals a variety of ways, in different situations. To handle when to request and agree to joint actions in this example, we take the set of expectations presented previously, and add two expectations as follows:

ExpFree. When another agent doesn't have the ball, expect they are "free" (to accept requests). The test for this is if they accept or refuse a request. The positive response is to add ExpJI and ExpAgree from table 1 to the current set, and remove ExpTeam.

ExpTeam. When another agent has the ball, expect it to desire a joint intention for some team action to score. The test is if they request some joint action. The positive response is to add ExpJI and ExpReq from table 1 to the current set, and remove ExpFree.

This produces the expectation graph shown in Figure 4. The basic idea of these expectations is to demonstrate one of ESB's strengths - bounding reasoning. By only adding the expectations about joint intentions to the current set when they become applicable, it reduces the number of conditions and expectations that must be maintained. This also provides a very natural way to represent any scenario where an agent may act in different "scenes" performing different roles. Also simply by extending the above general JI expectations, in a modular fashion, we get this benefit. So it is easy to add and integrate reasoning rules together.

Fig. 4. Expectation Graph for the Robosoccer Agents. Edges are annotated with the responses defining the state transitions.

We now have enough of the example defined to demonstrate another advantage of ESB. It is possible to easily perform checks on sets of expectations to aid the designer. For example, in this case the intention is that an agent should only ever eventually either be in a state to expect to receive a request for a JI, or to try and form one. By exploiting the automatically generated FSM, we can query the model checker at design time, and check if the set of expectations meets our design. In this case we test to ensure it's always the case that both expectations do not hold together:

$$\mathbf{A}\square\neg(ExpAgree \wedge ExpReq)$$

If this test should fail,the model checker provides an error trace shows us exactly the states and transitions leading to the failure, and we can correct our design accordingly.

As well as implementation specific tests, it is also possible to describe general tests that the ESB formalism allows and that can be applied to any design. It is reasonable to expect that if there is an expectation which can never hold, then there is a problem with the design. We check the following condition for each expectation:

$$\mathbf{E}\lozenge(Expectation)$$

In our example, if it were to be broken by making the response of ExpTeam empty, then this test would fail for ExpReq. We could then either fix our design through manual inspection of the expectations, or by identifying more specifically when the behaviour is not as intended by checking a more complex property and inspecting the error trace.

Behaviours are as easily extended as the expectations. As before, we have the behaviour to add a belief noting when we have a joint intention, so that BDI plans can take advantage of this. When we expect that a JI is held, plans depending on it are allowed via a guard belief representing this. The behaviours presented above to dictate when we expect it is possible to form a JI can be included as before, or for convenience slightly extended as follows:

$$\mathbf{E}\lozenge(ji(self,Y,A)) \wedge free(Y) \triangleright add\_belief(requestJI(Y))$$

$$request(A,Q,F) \wedge \mathbf{E}\lozenge(ji(self,Y,A)) \wedge free(self) \triangleright$$
$$add\_belief(agreeRequest(A))$$

Here we add in the requirements on the expectations that relate to agents being free to accept JIs, and only agreeing to a JI if an agent is itself free. The intuition here is that if an agent has the ball, it will have better options for scoring itself and will not agree to a proposed joint action (though it may propose one itself). As the first behaviour uses the temporal operators, even although an agent initially is in a state where no expectations about JIs are current, the condition takes into account possible future reasoning, and so the behaviour holds.

The final component of the soccer agents is the set of BDI plans. In AgentS-peak(L) plans are of the form:

```
+!goal : guard
 -> actions or subgoals.
```

Plans are selected on a priority ordering from the set of relevant plans - those whose guard holds, and trigger meets the current goal. So, amongst other plans to achieve the goal score, the social reasoning agents have the following plans:

```
 +!score : haveBall & ji(self,Barney,Pass)
          & ji(self,Cathy,Feint)
    <- passTo(Barney).
+!score: request(Andy,Action) & agreeRequest(Action)
    <- .tell(Andy,agree(Action)).
+!score : ji(self,Andy,Action)
    <- do(Action).
+!score : haveBall & requestJI(Barney,Cathy)
    <- request(Barney,Pass);
       request(Cathy,Feint).
```

The beliefs **underlined** are synthetic ones added by behaviours, and represent the interface between the ESB social reasoner and BDI practical reasoner. Using beliefs added by the ESB reasoner as guards on plans helps bound the agent's reasoning in another important way - it is only necessary to consider plans consistent with the agent's current social reasoning.

4.3   Further Implementations

As well as the JI based implementations described in detail in this paper, several other implementations of social reasoning schemes have also been implemented for evaluation purposes and are described in [13].

In addition to the ESB-RS implementation of JI, a BDI-only implementation was created for comparison. The comparison is limited as there is not much of the JI process that can be considered as pure social reasoning, the bulk of the effort was in creating the communicative acts, rather than the selection of when to carry out the acts. The RCP protocol to establish a JI is fairly restrictive, so there is no great difficulty in encapsulating this purely in BDI. The main benefit seen by the ESB-RS version was easy extensibility. This is due to the modular nature of the ESB specification. The soccer extension shows how it is trivial to add additional expectations, without changing existing expectations, that reason about when to attempt to form a JI and accept requests. It is easy to see how this could be extended to combining social reasoning schemes. For example, agents could jointly commit to following certain norm specifications.

As a contrast to the agent centric JI reasoning process, an example of system level social reasoning was also implemented in the form of creating a norm autonomous agent. This implementation follows the design of the NoA Normative Agent architecture [14]. NoA describes a model and implementation for agents to account for norms in their practical reasoning. A transformation from a NoA norm specification to ESB is described in [13]. NoA describes norms in terms of activation and deactivation conditions, and allows them to specify either states or actions that are obligated, permitted or prohibited. In ESB-RS the scope of the norm can be captured using the conditions and tests and behaviour rules are used to ensure the corresponded states or actions are achieved (or not).

This implementation was evaluated using two examples described in [14]. A simple blocks-world example and a more complex three-agent Letter of Credit protocol. It was shown that the key properties of the NoA system were preserved in the transformation into an ESB-RS implementation.

The NoA system is quite different from the reasoning required for JI, and so illustrates the ability for ESB-RS to capture and execute diverse social reasoning schemes. The differences the different examples allowed us to draw some conclusions. It was possible to capture the social reasoning methods in ESB-RS, without implementing specific cases. The Letter of Credit and robosoccer extended examples showed how easy it was to extend the implementations due to the modular design inherent in ESB. However, there is some disadvantage to agent design. The very generality of ESB meant that there were several different ways each scheme could have been captured, and some care was needed to choose the best way.

5   Conclusion

This paper presents ESB-RS, a practical social reasoning system built upon ESB [6]. We have shown through the specification and implementation of Joint Intentions, that although general (indeed because of the generality) it is capable of representing social reasoning theories whilst removing the concern of managing the procedural processing. The extension of this example to a robosoccer agent allowed us to evaluate the modularity of the agent specification, showing how additional reasoning schemes can be combined, and how the agent's reasoning can be bounded. These points were reinforced with a normative agent ESB-RS implementation, also summarised here.

Additional benefits of ESB-RS to the agent designer have been demonstrated. The model checker based implementation allows a user to check the operation of the agent's reasoning matches their intent, and the ability to perform general tests on the sanity of an expectation set has been described.

An obvious question is "how general is ESB-RS?", and the related question of "what classes of reasoning system can be captured?" By showing that the most basic social requirement of Joint Commitment can be implemented with ESB-RS we have taken a first step toward answering this question. Further work will focus on evaluating not only this, but other ESB-RS implementations of social reasoning schemes, to explore its adequacy to represent a wide range of social methods. The description of the NoA implementation is a start to this work. A problem is the lack of classification of social reasoning techniques, their different levels of abstraction, and the lack of existing implementations for comparison.

Taking a broader view, we have shown that it is possible to create an implementation of the ESB framework, which itself forms the bridge necessary for us to implement varied examples of social reasoning for agents. This is the driver of our contribution, as ESB-RS now makes it possible to create agents using previously un-implemented social reasoning schemes, combinations of these, and eases the development of novel social agents. This is the direction we hope to take in future work. By implementing other social reasoning schemes we will refine the ESB-RS reasoner, and in the process hopefully gain a new understanding of practical agent social reasoning.

References

1. Allouche, M., Boissier, O., Sayettat, C.: Temporal social reasoning in dynamic multi-agent systems. In: Proceedings of the Fourth International Conference on MultiAgent Systems (ICMAS 2000), pp. 23–30. IEEE, Los Alamitos (2000)
2. Sauro, L., Gerbrandy, J., van der Hoek, W., Wooldridge, M.: Reasoning about action and cooperation. In: Proceedings of the Fifth International Joint Conference on Autonomous Agents and Multi-agent Systems (AAMAS 2006), pp. 185–192. ACM Press, New York (2006)
3. Broersen, J., Dastani, M., Hulstijn, J., Huang, Z., van der Torre, L.: The boid architecture - conflicts between beliefs, obligations, intentions and desires. In: Proceedings of the Fifth International Conference on Autonomous Agents, pp. 9–16. ACM Press, New York (2001)
4. Dignum, F., Kinny, D., Sonenberg, L.: From Desires, Obligations and Norms to Goals. Cognitive Science Quarterly 2(3-4), 407–430 (2002)
5. Sichman, J.S., Demazeau, Y.: On social reasoning in multi-agent systems. Revista Iberoamericana de Inteligencia Artificial 13, 68–84 (2001)
6. Wallace, I., Rovatsos, M.: Bounded Social Reasoning in the ESB Framework. In: Decker, S., Sichman, J., Sierra, C., Castelfranchi, C. (eds.) Proceedings of the Eighth International Joint Conference on Autonomous Agents and Multiagent Systems (AAMAS 2009), pp. 1097–1104 (2009)
7. Rao, A.: AgentSpeak(L): BDI agents speak out in a logical computable language. In: Perram, J., Van de Velde, W. (eds.) MAAMAW 1996. LNCS, vol. 1038, pp. 42–55. Springer, Heidelberg (1996)
8. Cimatti, A., Clarke, E., Giunchiglia, F., Roveri, M.: NuSMV: a new Symbolic Model Verifier. In: Halbwachs, N., Peled, D.A. (eds.) CAV 1999. LNCS, vol. 1633, pp. 495–499. Springer, Heidelberg (1999)
9. Bordini, R.H., Hübner, J.F., Wooldridge, M.: Programming Multi-Agent Systems in AgentSpeak using Jason. Wiley, Chichester (2007)
10. Cohen, P.R., Levesque, H.J.: Teamwork. Noûs 35, 487–512 (1991)
11. Rummy.com - The Rules of Rummy (2008), http://rummy.com/rummyrules.html
12. Kumar, S., Huber, M.J., Cohen, P.R., McGee, D.R.: Toward a formalism for conversation protocols using joint intention theory. Computational Intelligence 18(2), 174–228 (2002)
13. Wallace, I.: Social Reasoning in Multi-Agent Systems with the Expectation-Strategy-Behaviour Framework. PhD thesis, School of Informatics, University of Edinburgh (2010)
14. Kollingbaum, M.: Norm-governed Practical Reasoning Agent. PhD thesis, University of Aberdeen (2005)

Logic of Information Flow
on Communication Channels*

Yanjing Wang[1], Floor Sietsma[2], and Jan van Eijck[2]

[1] Department of Philosophy, Peking University, Beijing 100871, China
[2] Centrum Wiskunde en Informatica,
P.O. Box 94079, NL-1090 GB Amsterdam, The Netherlands

Abstract. In this paper, we develop an epistemic logic for specifying and reasoning about information flow on the underlying communication channels. By combining ideas from Dynamic Epistemic Logic (DEL) and Interpreted Systems (IS), our semantics offers a natural and neat way of modeling multi-agent communication scenarios with different assumptions about the observational power of agents. We relate our logic to the standard DEL and IS approaches and demonstrate its use by studying a telephone call communication scenario.

1 Introduction

The 1999 'National Science Quiz' of *The Netherlands Organisation for Scientific Research (NWO)*[1] had the following question:

> *Six friends each have one piece of gossip. They start making phone calls. In every call they exchange all pieces of gossip that they know at that point. How many calls at least are needed to ensure that everyone knows all six pieces of gossip?*

To reason about the information flow in such a scenario, we want to take into account the following issues: the messages that the agents possess (e.g. secrets), the knowledge of the agents, the dynamics of the system in terms of information passing (e.g. telephone calls) and the underlying communication channels (e.g. the network of landlines). To incorporate specific designs for such issues, we first need to make a choice between two mainstream logical frameworks for multi-agent systems: *Interpreted Systems* and *Dynamic Epistemic Logic*.

Interpreted Systems (ISs), introduced by [15] and [8] independently, are mathematical structures that combine history-based temporal components of a system with epistemic ones (defined in terms of *local states* of the agents). ISs are convenient to model knowledge development based on the given temporal development

---

* This paper is the full version of an extended abstract with the same title appeared in the proceedings of AAMAS'10.
[1] For a list of references about the problem c.f. [12].

A. Omicini, S. Sardina, and W. Vasconcelos (Eds.): DALT 2010, LNAI 6619, pp. 130–147, 2011.
© Springer-Verlag Berlin Heidelberg 2011

of a system. In ISs the epistemic structure is generated from the temporal structure in a uniform way. However, the generation of temporal structures is not specified in the framework.

A different perspective on the dynamics of multi-agent systems is provided by Dynamic Epistemic Logic (DEL) [9,2]. The main focus of DEL is not on the temporal structure of the system but on the epistemic impact of events as the agents perceive them. The development of a system through time is essentially generated by executing so-called *action models* on a static initial model, to generate an updated static model. The epistemic relations in the initial static model and in the action models are not generated uniformly as in IS. Instead, they are designed by hand.

In recent years, much has been said about the comparison of the two frameworks, based on the observation that certain temporal developments of the system in IS can be generated by sequences of DEL updates on static models (see, e.g., [22,11,10]). In this paper, we will demonstrate further benefits of combining the two approaches by presenting a framework where epistemic relations are generated by matching local states and a history of observations as in ISs, while keeping the flexibility of explicit actions as in DEL approaches.

The puzzle of the telephone calls was briefly discussed in [25, Ch. 6.6] within the original DEL framework. In [21] the author raised the research question whether the communication network can be made explicit in DEL. An early proposal to fill in this line of research can be found in [19]. Communication channels in an IS framework made their appearance in [16]. Recent work in [14,1] addresses the information passing on so-called *communication graphs* or *interaction structures*, where *"messages"* are either atomic propositions or Boolean combinations of atomic propositions. In [27] a PDL-style DEL language is developed that allows explicit specification of protocols. The present paper attempts to blend the DEL and IS approaches to model communication along channels. More specifically, the contributions of this paper are:

- Combining insights from DEL and IS, we propose a logic $\mathcal{L}^{I,M}$ to specify and reason about the information flow over underlying communication channels. Unlike the previous work [14,1,19], we can *specify* the communication protocols in our language and deal with information flow in terms of both *messages* and higher-order formulas.
- The semantics of $\mathcal{L}^{I,M}$ is given on single-state models with respect to different observational equivalence relations generated in IS-style, which are also studied and compared in this paper.
- The basic actions in $\mathcal{L}^{I,M}$ are given DEL-style internal structures by the semantics. This allows us to model various communicative actions such as message passing and group announcements. In particular we define an external informing action, which essentially announces the protocol that agents are supposed to follow, thus making it common knowledge. Therefore we can explicitly specify more details of epistemic protocols such as the ones

discussed in [13]. It turns out to make a crucial difference whether epistemic protocols are assumed to be common knowledge or not among the agents carrying out the protocol (see also [26,27] for detailed discussions).
- Based on our semantics, we also propose a generic method of epistemic modeling where the initial model is simply the *real world* and all the initial assumptions are specified explicitly by means of formulas of $\mathcal{L}^{I,M}$. This significantly simplifies the modeling procedure. According to our semantics, the relevant possible states can be automatically constructed while evaluating the formulas. In particular, there is no need to specify the complete state space at the beginning.
- As a case study, we model telephone communications among agents. We show that it is impossible to obtain new common knowledge by telephone calls or voice mails but that we can get arbitrarily close to common knowledge if we not only can send messages but also make statements like "I know j got message m".

The paper is organized as follows. We introduce our logic $\mathcal{L}^{I,M}$ in Section 2. Section 3 relates our logic to the standard DEL and IS approaches. Section 4 introduces a modeling method and illustrates this method by a study of variations on the puzzle that was mentioned above. The final section concludes and lists future work.

2   Logic $\mathcal{L}^{I,M}$

2.1   Language

Let I be a finite set of agents, M be a finite set of message terms, and A be a finite set of basic actions. A communication network *net* is represented as a hypergraph of agents in I, namely a set of subsets of I as in [1]. For example a hypergraph $net = \{\{1,2\},\{1,2,3\}\}$ denotes a network in which there is a private channel $\{1,2\}$ between agents 1 and 2 and there is a public channel used by all three agents.

The set $Prop_{I,A,M}$ of basic propositions is defined by

$$p ::= has_i m \mid com(G) \mid past(\bar{\alpha}) \mid future(\bar{\alpha})$$

with $i \in I$, $m \in M$, $G \subseteq I$ and $\bar{\alpha} = \alpha_0; \alpha_1; \ldots; \alpha_k \in A^*$.

$has_i m$ is intended to mean that i possesses the message m;[2] while $com(G)$ expresses that group G forms a channel in the network; $past(\bar{\alpha})$ says that the sequence of actions $\bar{\alpha}$ just happened and $future(\bar{\alpha})$ means that $\bar{\alpha}$ can be executed according to the current protocol. The formulas of $\mathcal{L}^{I,M}$ are built from the set $Prop_{I,A,M}$ as follows:

$$\phi ::= \top \mid p \mid \neg\phi \mid \phi_1 \wedge \phi_2 \mid \langle \pi \rangle \phi \mid C_G \phi$$
$$\pi ::= \alpha \mid \varepsilon \mid \delta \mid \pi_1; \pi_2 \mid \pi_1 \cup \pi_2 \mid \pi^*$$

---

[2] *Has* is a commonly used predicate in the logic of security protocols to model declarative knowledge about messages c.f., e.g., [18].

with $p \in Prop_{I,A,M}$, $G \subseteq I$, $\alpha \in A$ and ε, δ as constants for empty sequence and deadlock respectively.

The intended meaning of the formulas is mostly as usual as in dynamic epistemic logics: $C_G\phi$ expresses *"the agents in group G commonly know ϕ"*, $\langle \pi \rangle \phi$ expresses *"the protocol π can be executed, and at least one execution of π yields a state where ϕ holds"*.

As usual, we define $\perp$, $\phi \vee \psi$, $\phi \rightarrow \psi$, $\langle C_G \rangle \phi$ and $[\pi]\phi$ as the abbreviations of $\neg \top$, $\neg(\neg\phi \wedge \neg\psi)$, $\neg\phi \vee \psi$, $\neg C_G \neg \phi$ and $\neg\langle \pi \rangle \neg \phi$ respectively. Let Π be the set of all protocols π. We also use the following additional abbreviations:

$$
\begin{vmatrix}
K_j\phi := C_{\{j\}}\phi \\
has_i M' := \bigwedge_{m \in M'} has_i m \\
dhas_G M' := \bigwedge_{m \in M'} \bigvee_{j \in G} has_j m \\
com(net) := \bigwedge_{G \in net} com(G) \wedge \bigwedge_{G \notin net} \neg com(G) \\
\pi^n := \underbrace{\pi; \pi; \ldots; \pi}_{n} \\
\Sigma\Pi' := \bigcup_{\pi \in \Pi'} \pi \text{ where } \Pi' \subset \Pi \text{ is finite.}
\end{vmatrix}
$$

where $K_j\phi$ means that agent j knows ϕ; $dhas_G M'$ says the messages in M' are distributed among agents in G; $com(net)$ specifies the communication channels in the network.

By having both *has* and K operator in the language, we can make the distinction between knowing about a message and knowing about its content. $K_i has_j m \wedge \neg has_i m$ and $K_i has_j m \wedge has_i m$ can express the *de dicto* reading and *de re* reading of knowing a message m respectively. For example, let m be the hiding place of Bin Laden, then $K_{CIA} has_{Al-Qaeda} m \wedge \neg has_{CIA} m$ expresses that CIA knows that Al-Qaeda knows the hiding place, which is, however, a secret to CIA.

2.2   Semantics

First of all, we give interpretations to our action symbols α by defining their internal structures. Let $Form^{-\langle\pi\rangle}(\mathcal{L}^{I,M})$ be the set of all the $\mathcal{L}^{I,M}$ formulas without $\langle \pi \rangle$ modalities. Each $\alpha \in A$ can have an internal structure given by an *interpretation function* $\iota : A \rightarrow \mathcal{P}(I) \times Form^{-\langle\pi\rangle}(\mathcal{L}^{I,M}) \times (\mathcal{P}(M))^{|I|} \times (\Pi \cup \{\#\})$. Thus $\iota(\alpha)$ is a tuple:

$$\langle F, \phi, N_0 \ldots N_{|I|}, \rho \rangle$$

Here we define $Obs(\iota(\alpha)) = F$ as the set of agents that can observe α; $Pre(\iota(\alpha)) = \phi$ is the precondition that should hold in order for α to be executable[3]; $Pos(\iota(\alpha)) = \langle N_0 \ldots N_{|I|}, \rho \rangle$ (with $\rho \in \Pi \cup \{\#\}$) is the postcondition which lists the set of messages N_i that are delivered to i by action α for each i and the protocol ρ that the agents are going to follow after executing α. If $\rho = \#$, then the agents should keep

---

[3] It will become clear when we define the semantics of $\mathcal{L}^{I,M}$ formulas that the action symbols in $\langle\pi\rangle$-free formulas are treated without referring to their internal structures given by ι, thus avoiding the circularity in the definition of the semantics.

following the current protocol. If $\rho = \pi$ for some $\pi \in \Pi$ then they should change their protocol to π. In this paper we assume that the agents can always observe the actions that deliver messages to them: if $N_j \neq \emptyset$ in $\iota(\alpha)$ then $j \in Obs(\iota(\alpha))$. The converse does not hold since agents may observe actions that do not deliver any messages to them.

Note that by excluding the preconditions in the form of $\langle \pi \rangle \phi$, the interdependence of actions are limited but still useful, e.g., for action α, $future(\alpha)$ is allowed as a precondition meaning that α can be executed only when it was planned according to the current protocol.

In order to interpret basic propositions in $Prop_{I,A,M}$ we let the finer structure of the basic propositions correspond with a finer structure in the states, replacing the traditional valuation in Kripke structures used in the DEL-approaches:

Definition 1. *Let the state space* $S = \mathcal{P}(\mathcal{P}(I)) \times (\mathcal{P}(M))^{|I|} \times (A)^* \times (\mathcal{P}(M))^{|I|} \times \Pi$. *A state* $s \in S$ *for* $\mathcal{L}^{I,M}$ *is thus a tuple:*

$$\langle net, M_0, \ldots, M_{|I|}, \bar{\alpha}, M_0', \ldots, M_{|I|}', \pi \rangle$$

Here $IS(s, i) = M_i'$ is i's current set of messages (information set), $AM(s) = \bar{\alpha}$ is the action history, $CC(s) = net$ is the available communication network and $Prot(s) = \pi$ is the protocol that agents have to follow from this state. We let $AM_k(s) = \alpha_k$ in $\bar{\alpha}$ and $l(s) = |AM(s)|$ be the *length* of s. Note that each state also contains the information of the initial distribution of the messages: $M_0, \ldots, M_{|I|}$. From s we can recover the initial state of the system before any actions were executed:

$$Init(s) = \langle net, M_0, \ldots, M_{|I|}, \epsilon, M_0, \ldots, M_{|I|}, (\Sigma A)^* \rangle.$$

The action history in the initial state is empty, thus $AM(Init(s)) = \epsilon$. We also assume that all the actions are allowed initially, thus $Prot(Init(s)) = (\Sigma A)^*$.

Intuitively, each state represents a past temporal development of the system with its constraint for the future actions. Note that the past is linear ($AM(s)$ is a single sequence of actions), while the future can be branching ($Prot(s)$ may allow several possible sequences of actions).

$has_i m$, $com(G)$ and $past(\bar{\alpha})$ can be interpreted in a straightforward way at a state s according to $IS(s, i)$, $CC(s)$ and $AM(s)$ respectively. To give the semantics for $future(\bar{\alpha})$ at a state s, we need to check whether $\bar{\alpha}$ *complys* with the current protocol $Prot(s)$ and compute the remaining protocol after the execution of $\bar{\alpha}$ in order to know what the new protocol is. For this, we first recall the language of regular expressions $L(\pi)$:

$$L(\delta) = \emptyset \qquad L(\varepsilon) = \{\epsilon\} \qquad L(\alpha) = \{\alpha\}$$
$$L(\pi; \pi') = \{\bar{\alpha}; \bar{\beta} \mid \bar{\alpha} \in L(\pi), \bar{\beta} \in L(\pi')\}$$
$$L(\pi \cup \pi') = L(\pi) \cup L(\pi')$$
$$L(\pi^*) = \{\epsilon\} \cup \{\bar{\alpha}_1; \ldots; \bar{\alpha}_n \mid \bar{\alpha}_1, \ldots, \bar{\alpha}_n \in L(\pi)\}$$

The language of an *input derivative* $\pi \backslash \bar{\alpha}$ of $\pi \in \Pi$ w.r.t. a sequence of actions $\bar{\alpha}$ is defined as $L(\pi \backslash \bar{\alpha}) = \{\bar{\beta} \mid \bar{\alpha}; \bar{\beta} \in L(\pi)\}$(cf. [4]). Intuitively, $\pi \backslash \bar{\alpha}$ is the remaining protocol of π after executing $\bar{\alpha}$. The input derivatives can be computed efficiently e.g., we can derive $(\alpha \cup (\beta; \gamma))^* \backslash \beta = (\alpha \backslash \beta \cup (\beta; \gamma) \backslash \beta); (\alpha \cup \beta; \gamma)^* = (\delta \cup (\varepsilon; \gamma)); (\alpha \cup \beta; \gamma)^* = \gamma; (\alpha \cup (\beta; \gamma))^*$ (see [6] for an axiomatization of regular expression with input derivatives).

Similar to [5,1], we give the truth value of complex $\mathcal{L}^{I,M}$ formula on *single* states instead of *pointed Kripke models*. The semantics of epistemic formulas depends on the action interpretation ι and the relation $\sim_i^x$ to be defined later. For any state s we define:

$$
\begin{aligned}
s &\vDash_\iota has_i(m) \Leftrightarrow m \in IS(s, i) \\
s &\vDash_\iota com(G) \Leftrightarrow G \in CC(s) \\
s &\vDash_\iota past(\bar{\alpha}) \Leftrightarrow \bar{\alpha} \text{ is a suffix of } AM(s) \\
s &\vDash_\iota future(\bar{\alpha}) \Leftrightarrow Prot(s) \backslash \bar{\alpha} \neq \delta \\
s &\vDash_\iota \neg\phi \Leftrightarrow s \nvDash_\iota \phi \\
s &\vDash_\iota \phi \wedge \psi \Leftrightarrow s \vDash_\iota \phi \text{ and } s \vDash_\iota \psi \\
s &\vDash_\iota C_G\phi \Leftrightarrow \text{for all } v, \text{ if } s \sim_G^x t \text{ then } t \vDash_\iota \phi \\
s &\vDash_\iota \langle \pi \rangle \phi \Leftrightarrow \exists s' : s[\![\pi]\!]_\iota s' \text{ and } s' \vDash_\iota \phi
\end{aligned}
$$

where $\sim_G^x$ is the reflexive transitive closure of $\bigcup_{i \in G} \sim_i^x$. The protocols π function as *state changers* w.r.t. ι:

$$
\begin{aligned}
s[\![\varepsilon]\!]_\iota s' &\Leftrightarrow s = s' \\
s[\![\delta]\!]_\iota s' &\Leftrightarrow \text{ never} \\
s[\![\alpha]\!]_\iota s' &\Leftrightarrow s \vDash_\iota Pre(\iota(\alpha)) \text{ and } s' = s|_{Pos(\iota(\alpha))} \\
s[\![\pi_1; \pi_2]\!]_\iota s' &\Leftrightarrow s[\![\pi_1]\!]_\iota \circ [\![\pi_2]\!]_\iota s' \\
s[\![\pi_1 \cup \pi_2]\!]_\iota s' &\Leftrightarrow s[\![\pi_1]\!]_\iota \cup [\![\pi_2]\!]_\iota s' \\
s[\![(\pi_1)^*]\!]_\iota s' &\Leftrightarrow s[\![\pi_1]\!]_\iota^* s'
\end{aligned}
$$

where $\circ, \cup$ and $*$ at right-hand side express the usual composition, union and reflexive transitive closure on relations respectively. Given $Pos(\iota(\alpha)) = \langle N_0, \ldots, N_{|I|}, \rho \rangle$, $s|_{Pos(\iota(\alpha))}$ is the result of executing action α at s defined as:

$$
s|_{Pos(\iota(\alpha))} = \langle net, M_0, \ldots, M_{|I|}, \bar{\beta}; \alpha, M_0' \cup N_0, \ldots, M_{|I|}' \cup N_{|I|}, f(\rho) \rangle
$$

where $f(\rho) = \begin{cases} \pi \backslash \alpha \text{ if } \rho = \# \\ \pi' \quad \text{ if } \rho = \pi' \end{cases}$.

Now we define $\sim_i^x$, the epistemic relation of an agent i between states. A state s is said to be *consistent* if $Init(s)[\![AM(s)]\!]_\iota s$. It is easy to see that for any s, $Init(s)$ is always consistent[4].

We define that $t \sim_i^x t'$ iff the following conditions are met:

consistency. t and t' are consistent.
local initialization. $IS(Init(t), i) = IS(Init(t'), i)$
local history. $AM(t)|_i^x = AM(t')|_i^x$, where x is the *type of observational power* of agents.

---

[4] Note that we can actually omit the current information sets $IS(s, i)$ in the definition of a state, and compute it by applying the actions in $AM(s)$, thus only generate consistent states. We keep the current information sets there to simplify notations and make it more efficient to evaluate basic propositions according to the semantics.

The type of observational power of the agents, $AM(t)|_i^x$, defines the local history. Many definitions of $AM(t)|_i^x$ are possible, giving the agents different observational powers. Several reasonable definitions are:

1. $AM(t)|_i^{set} = \{\alpha \text{ appearing in } AM(t) \mid i \in Obs(\iota(\alpha))\}$ as in [1].
2. $AM(t)|_i^{1st}$ is the subsequence of $AM(t)$ which only keeps the first occurrence of each $\alpha \in AM(t)|_i^{set}$ as in [3].
3. $AM(t)|_i^{asyn}$ is the subsequence of $AM(t)$ which only keeps all the occurrences of each $\alpha \in AM(t)|_i^{set}$, as in *asynchronous* systems (cf., e.g., [20]).
4. $AM(t)|_i^{\tau}$ is the sequence obtained by replacing each occurrence of $\alpha \notin AM(t)|_i^{set}$ in $AM(t)$ by τ, as in *synchronous* systems with prefect recall (cf., e.g., [24]).

It is clear from the above definition that $\sim_i^x$ is an equivalence relation and the following holds:

Proposition 1. $\sim_i^{\tau} \subseteq \sim_i^{asyn} \subseteq \sim_i^{1st} \subseteq \sim_i^{set}$.

We then call the semantics defined by $\sim_i^x$ the *x-semantics*, and denote the corresponding satisfaction relation as $\models_{\iota}^x$. When ι is fixed and clear we also write $\models^x$ for the satisfaction relation. Recall that we require that the agents can always observe the actions that change his information set. Then we have:

Proposition 2. *For any consistent state* t, t': $t \sim_i^x t'$ *implies* $IS(t, i) = IS(t', i)$ *where* $x \in Sem = \{set, asyn, 1st, \tau\}$.

Proof. By Proposition 1, $t \sim_i^x t'$ implies $t \sim_i^{set} t'$ for all $x \in Sem$. Therefore we only need to prove the claim for $x = set$. Suppose $t \sim_i^{set} t'$ then by the definition of $\sim_i^{set}$, $IS(Init(t), i) = IS(Init(t'), i)$ and $AM(t)|_i^{set} = AM(t')|_i^{set}$. So at t and t' agent i initially had the same messages and has observed the same actions. Since agents can always observe the actions that change his information set then we know the same message passing actions relevant to i have happened for t and t'. Since the actions can only add messages to the information set and never delete messages from them, it doesn't matter how often or in which order those actions have been executed. Therefore the information sets of agent i in t and t' are identical. □

2.3   Communicative Actions

In this section, we will define some useful basic actions with their internal structures[5]. To simplify the presentation, we abuse the notation of action names to stand for their internal structures as well, when the context is clear. Thus we let $Obs(\beta) = Obs(\iota(\beta))$ and similar for $Pre(\beta)$ and $Pos(\beta)$. Recall that the internal structure of an action β is a tuple $\langle F, \phi, N_0, \ldots, N_{|I|}, \rho \rangle$ such that $N_j = \emptyset$ for $j \notin Obs(\beta)$. We now list some basic actions with their internal structures in Table 1.

---

[5] Namely, a specific mapping ι which gives certain action names the corresponding internal structures.

Table 1. Some important communicative actions

β (communication among the agents):	Obs :	Pre : common part is: $com(Obs(\beta)) \wedge future(\beta) \wedge$	Pos $(j \in Obs(\beta))$:
$send^i_G(M')$	$G \cup \{i\}$	$has_i M'$	$N_j = M', \rho = \#$
$share_G(M')$	G	$dhas_G M'$	$N_j = M', \rho = \#$
$sendall^i_G(M')$	$G \cup \{i\}$	$has_i M' \wedge \bigwedge_{m \notin M'} \neg has_i m$	$N_j = M', \rho = \#$
$shareall_G(M')$	G	$dhas_G M' \wedge \bigwedge_{m \notin M'} \neg dhas_i m$	$N_j = M', \rho = \#$
$inform^i_G(\phi)$	$G \cup \{i\}$	$K_i \phi$	$N_j = \emptyset, \rho = \#$
β (external actions):	Obs :	Pre :	Pos :
$exinfo(\phi)$	I	ϕ	$\rho = \#$
$exprot(\pi')$	I	$\top$	$\rho = \pi'$

The first group of actions are communicative actions that are done by the agents. These actions must abide by the communication channels and the protocol, which is enforced by having $com(Obs(\beta)) \wedge future(\beta)$ in the precondition. $send^i_G(M')$ is the action that i sends the set of messages M' to the group G. Apart from respecting the channel and the protocol, the precondition $has_i M'$ enforces that agent i should possess any messages he wants to send. The postcondition of $send^i_G(M')$ ensures that the messages in M' are added to the message sets of the agents in G. The action $share_G(M')$ shares the messages in M' within the group G. A precondition of $share_G(M')$ is that the messages from M' are already distributed knowledge in the group. $sendall^i_G(M')$ differs from $send^i_G(M')$ in the extra precondition that M' should contain *all* the messages that i has. Similarly for $shareall_G(M')$. $inform^i_G(\phi)$ is the group announcement of an arbitrary formula ϕ within $G \cup \{i\}$. A precondition of $inform^i_G(\phi)$ is that i should know ϕ is true before he can announce it.

The second group of actions are public announcements that do not respect the channels or the protocol. They model the external information that is given to the agents. $exinfo(\phi)$ models the public announcement of a formula ϕ. The only precondition of this announcement is that ϕ should hold. The postcondition is empty. Knowledge of ϕ among the agents is created by the fact that all agents can observe the action. Since all agents know the execution of this action would only be possible if ϕ would hold, all agents know that ϕ holds at the moment it is announced. $exprot(\pi')$ announces the protocol π' that the agents are supposed to follow in the future. Its postcondition changes the protocol to π' and knowledge of the protocol is created because all agents observe the announcement.

We can define more complex actions based on the above basic actions, as we will demonstrate in Section 4.

3   Comparison with IS and DEL

The results in this section relate our logic to IS and DEL approaches. Theorem 1 shows that by the semantics of $\mathcal{L}^{I,M}$, an interpreted system is generated implicitly from a single state. Together with Theorem 1, Proposition 3 demonstrates that compared to DEL, our approach is powerful and concise in modeling actions. Let us compare our approach to IS first. In the following we only consider consistent states.

Let the history of s w.r.t. a fixed ι be a sequence: $hist_\iota(s) = s_0 s_1 \ldots s_{l(s)}$ where $s_0 = Init(s)$, $s_{l(s)} = s$ and $s_k \llbracket \alpha_k \rrbracket_\iota s_{k+1}$ for any k such that $\alpha_k = AM_k(s)$. Clearly then $s_0 s_1 \ldots s_k = hist_\iota(s_k)$ for any $k \leq l(s)$. Let $ExpT_\iota^x$ be the Interpreted System with action labels with respect to x-semantics $\{H, \{\rightarrow_\alpha \mid \alpha \in A\}, \{R_i \mid i \in I\}, V\}$, where:

- $H = \{hist_\iota(s) \mid s \text{ is consistent.}\}$
- $\langle s_0 \ldots s_n \rangle \rightarrow_\alpha \langle s_0 \ldots s_n s_{n+1} \rangle \Leftrightarrow s_n \llbracket \alpha \rrbracket_\iota s_{n+1}$.
- $\langle s_0 \ldots s_n \rangle R_i \langle s_0' \ldots s_m' \rangle$ iff $s_n \sim_i^x s_m'$.
- $V(\langle s_0 \ldots s_n \rangle)(p) = \top \Leftrightarrow s_n \models_\iota^x p$ where $p \in Prop_{I,A,M}$.

The language of $\mathcal{L}^{I,M}$ can be seen as a fragment of *Propositional Dynamic Logic* (PDL): $\mathcal{L}_{pdl}^I$ with basic action set $A \cup I$. Here the common knowledge operator C_G can be seen as $[(\Sigma G)^*]$ in $\mathcal{L}_{pdl}^I$. Let $\Vdash_{PDL}$ denote the usual semantics of $\mathcal{L}_{pdl}^I$, then it is not hard to see:

Theorem 1. *For any formula $\phi \in \mathcal{L}^{I,M}$ and for each consistent $\mathcal{L}^{I,M}$-state s:*

$$s \models_\iota^x \phi \Leftrightarrow ExpT_\iota^x, hist_\iota(s) \Vdash_{PDL} \phi.$$

This result shows that if we abstract away the inner structure of basic propositions and actions, then our logic can be seen as a PDL language interpreted on ISs that are generated in a particular way w.r.t some constraints. Note that this result does not imply the decidability of $\mathcal{L}^{I,M}$ since although PDL is decidable on general Kripke structures, we do not know yet whether it is decidable on the restricted class of generated models $ExpT^x$.

Now consider the DEL language $\mathcal{L}_{del}^I$:

$$\phi ::= \top \mid p \mid \neg\phi \mid \phi_1 \wedge \phi_2 \mid \langle \mathbb{A}, e \rangle \phi \mid C_G \phi$$

where p is in a set of basic propositions $Prop$, $G \subseteq I$ and $\mathbb{A}$ is an *action model* with e as its designated action. Action models are tuples of the form $(E, \{\asymp_i\}_{i \in I}, Pre, Pos)$ where $\asymp_i$ models agents i's observational power on events in E (e.g. $e_1 \asymp_i e_2$ means i is not sure which one of e_1 and e_2 happened); the precondition function $Pre : E \rightarrow \mathcal{L}_{del}^I$ describes when an event can happen and the postcondition $Pos : E \rightarrow (Prop \rightarrow \mathcal{L}_{del}^I)$ models the factual changes caused by the event by changing the truth value of basic proposition p to the truth value of $Pos(e)(p)$ (cf. [2,23] for details of action models). The semantics for epistemic formulas is as usual and

$$\mathbb{M}, s \Vdash_{DEL} \langle \mathbb{A}, e \rangle \phi \Leftrightarrow \mathbb{M} \otimes \mathbb{A}, (s, e) \models \phi$$

Where, given a static Kripke model $\mathbb{M} = (W, \{R_i\}_{i \in I}, V)$ and an action model $\mathbb{A} = (E, \{\asymp_i\}_{i \in I}, Pre, Pos)$, the updated model is $\mathbb{M} \otimes \mathbb{A} = (W', \{R_i'\}_{i \in I}, V')$ with:

$$W' = \{\langle w, e \rangle \mid \mathbb{M}, w \Vdash Pre(e)\}$$
$$R'_i = \{(\langle w, e \rangle, \langle v, e' \rangle) \mid wR_i v \text{ and } e \asymp_i e'\}$$
$$V'(\langle w, e \rangle)(p) = \top \Leftrightarrow \mathbb{M}, w \Vdash Pos(e)(p)$$

To facilitate a comparison, let us consider $\mathcal{L}^{I,M,-*}$, the star-free fragment of $\mathcal{L}^{I,M}$. Let $ExpK^x(s)$ be the Kripke model $\{W, \{R_i \mid i \in I\}, V\}$ obtained by the *expansion* of the state s according to x−semantics, with:

- $W = \{s' \mid s \sim^x_I s'\}$ where $\sim^x_I$ is the reflexive transitive closure of $\{\sim^x_i \mid i \in I\}$.
- $R_i = \sim^x_i |_{W \times W}$.
- $V(s)(p) = \top \Leftrightarrow s \models^x p$ where $p \in Prop_{I,A,M}$.

Note that although I, A, M are assumed to be finite, W in $ExpK^x(s)$ can still be infinite due to the fact that we record the past explicitly in the states and there may be infinitely many possible histories.

Based on $ExpK^x(s)$ it seems plausible to obtain a similar correspondence result as Theorem 1 for $\mathcal{L}^{I,M,-*}$ and $\mathcal{L}^I_{del}$, since the basic actions in $\mathcal{L}^{I,M,-*}$ look like special cases of pointed action models in DEL. However, the result does not hold in general. To see this, we first recall a fact from [22]: If we see $\langle \mathbb{A}, e \rangle$ as a basic action modality when considering PDL semantics, then for any formula $\phi \in \mathcal{L}^I_{del}$:

$$\mathbb{M}, s \Vdash_{DEL} \phi \Leftrightarrow Forest(\mathbb{M}, \mathcal{A}), (s) \Vdash_{PDL} \phi \quad (\star)$$

where $\mathcal{A}$ is the set of action models and $Forest(\mathbb{M}, \mathcal{A})$ is the IS generated by executing all possible sequences of action models in $\mathcal{A}$ on $\mathbb{M}, s^6$. We now show that the effects of actions in $\mathcal{L}^{I,M}$ cannot be simulated by action models in general.

Proposition 3. *There exists some action interpretation ι such that there is no translation of action models $T : A \to \mathcal{A}$ satisfying:*

for all $\mathcal{L}^{I,M}$-states s: $T(ExpT^x_\iota), hist_\iota(s) \leftrightarrows Forest(ExpK^x(s), \mathcal{A}), (s)$

where $x \in \{set, 1st, asyn\}$ and $T(ExpT^x_\iota)$ is the IS obtained from $ExpT^x_\iota$ by replacing each label of $\alpha \in A$ by $T(\alpha) \in \mathcal{A}$ and $\leftrightarrows$ is the bisimulation w.r.t. transitions lablled by $I \cup \mathcal{A}$.

Proof. In [22] it is shown that $Forest(ExpK^x(s), \mathcal{A})$ must satisfy the property of *Perfect Recall* meaning that if the agents can not distinguish two sequences of action $\bar{\alpha}; \alpha$ and $\bar{\beta}; \beta$ then they can not distinguish $\bar{\alpha}$ and $\bar{\beta}$. However, $ExpT^x$ clearly does not satisfy this property for $x \in \{set, 1st, asyn\}$ in general. For example, $send^i_j(M); \gamma \sim^x_j \gamma; send^i_j(M)$ where $x \in \{set, 1st, asyn\}$ and γ is some action j cannot observe, but $send^i_j(M) \not\asymp^x_j \gamma$. □

If we consider τ−semantics, then a correspondence result can be obtained. Given an action interpretation ι, let $T^\iota_{DEL} : \mathcal{L}^{I,M,-*} \to \mathcal{L}^I_{del}$ be defined as follows:

---

^{6} Due to the limit of space, readers are referred to [22] for details.

$$
\begin{aligned}
T^{\iota}_{DEL}(\top) &= \top \\
T^{\iota}_{DEL}(p) &= p \\
T^{\iota}_{DEL}(\neg\phi) &= \neg T^{\iota}_{DEL}(\phi) \\
T^{\iota}_{DEL}(\phi_1 \wedge \phi_2) &= T^{\iota}_{DEL}(\phi_1) \wedge T^{\iota}_{DEL}(\phi_2) \\
T^{\iota}_{DEL}([\alpha]\phi) &= [ExpA^{\tau}_{\iota}(\alpha)]T^{\iota}_{DEL}(\phi) \\
T^{\iota}_{DEL}([\pi_1 \cup \pi_2]\phi) &= T^{\iota}_{DEL}([\pi_1]\phi) \wedge T^{\iota}_{DEL}([\pi_2]\phi) \\
T^{\iota}_{DEL}([\pi_1 ; \pi_2]\phi) &= T^{\iota}_{DEL}([\pi_1][\pi_2]\phi)
\end{aligned}
$$

where $ExpA^{\tau}_{\iota}(\alpha)$ is the pointed action model $\{E, \{R_i \mid i \in I\}, V, e_{\alpha}\}$ obtained by the *saturation* of the action α according to $\tau-$semantics:

- $E = \{e_{\beta} \mid \beta \in A\}$
- $e_{\beta} R_i e_{\beta'} \Leftrightarrow \iota(\beta) = \iota(\beta')$ or $i \notin Obs(\beta) \cup Obs(\beta')$.
- $Pre(e_{\beta}) = T^{\iota}_{DEL}(Pre(\beta))$.
- If $Pos(\beta) = \langle N_0, \ldots, N_{|I|}, \rho \rangle$ then:

$$
Pos(e_{\beta})(has_i m) = \begin{cases} \top & \text{if } m \in N_i \\ has_i m & \text{otherwise} \end{cases}
$$

$$
Pos(e_{\beta})(com(G)) = com(G)
$$

$$
Pos(e_{\beta})(past(\bar{\gamma};\gamma)) = \begin{cases} past(\bar{\gamma}) & \text{if } \gamma = \beta \\ \bot & \text{otherwise} \end{cases}
$$

$$
Pos(e_{\beta})(future(\bar{\gamma})) = \begin{cases} future(\beta;\bar{\gamma}) & \text{if } \rho \text{ in } Pos(\beta) \text{ is } \sharp \\ \top & \text{if } \rho \text{ in } Pos(\beta) \text{ is } \pi \text{ and } \pi\backslash\bar{\gamma} \neq \delta \\ \bot & \text{if } \rho \text{ in } Pos(\beta) \text{ is } \pi \text{ and } \pi\backslash\bar{\gamma} = \delta \end{cases}
$$

Based on the above translation, the star-free fragment of $\mathcal{L}^{I,M}$ can be seen as a version of DEL on generated models:

Theorem 2. *For any $\phi \in \mathcal{L}^{I,M,-*}$ and for any consistent $\mathcal{L}^{I,M}$-state s:*

$$
s \models^{\tau}_{\iota} \phi \Leftrightarrow ExpK^{\tau}_{\iota}(s), s \Vdash_{DEL} T_{DEL}(\phi).
$$

4   Applications

4.1   Common Knowledge

Our framework gives an interesting perspective on common knowledge. We first focus on asynchronous semantics. It may not be surprising that we cannot reach common knowledge without public communication. We might think that achieving common knowledge becomes easier if we can publicly agree on a common protocol before the communication is limited to non-public communication. However, in the case of asynchronous semantics we still can not reach common knowledge, even if we can publicly agree on a protocol. In this section we fix the action interpretation ι as in Section 2.3 thus omitting ι in $\models^x_{\iota}$ and $[\![\pi]\!]_{\iota}$. Recall that we say an action α *respects the communication channel* if $Pre(\alpha) \models com(Obs(\alpha))$.

Theorem 3. *For any state s with $I \notin CC(s)$, any protocol π containing only communications that respect the communication channels, any $\varphi \in \mathcal{L}^{I,M}$ and any sequence of actions $\bar{\alpha}$:*

$$
s \models^{asyn} \langle exprot(\pi) \rangle (\neg C_I \varphi \rightarrow \neg \langle \bar{\alpha} \rangle C_I \varphi)
$$

Proof. Let $s[\![exprot(\pi)]\!]t$ and suppose $t \models^{asyn} \neg C_I\phi$. Towards a contradiction, let $\bar{a}$ be the minimal sequence of actions such that $t \models^{asyn} \langle\bar{a}\rangle\phi$. Let $\bar{a} = \bar{\beta}; \alpha$, $t[\![\bar{\beta}]\!]u$ and $u[\![\alpha]\!]v$. Since $I \not\subseteq CC(s)$ and α respects the communication channel, $Obs(\alpha) \neq I$ so there exists $j \notin Obs(\alpha)$. Then $AM(u)|_j^{asyn} = AM(v)|_j^{asyn}$ so $u \sim_j^{asyn} v$. Since $\bar{a}$ was minimal, $u \not\models^{asyn} C_I\varphi$. But then $v \models^{asyn} \neg K_j C_I\varphi$, therefore $v \not\models^{asyn} C_I\varphi$. $\square$

Essentially, even if the agents agree on a protocol beforehand, the agents that cannot observe the final action of the protocol will never know whether this final action has been executed and thus common knowledge is never established. This is because in the asynchronous semantics, there is no sense of time. If we could add some kind of clock and the agents would agree to do an action on every "tick", the agents would be able to establish common knowledge. This is exactly what we try to achieve with our τ-semantics. Here every agent observes a "tick" the moment some action is executed. This way, they can agree on a protocol *and* know when it is finished. We will show examples of how this can result in common knowledge in the next section on the telephone call scenario.

Here we will first investigate what happens in τ-semantics if we *cannot* publicly agree on a protocol beforehand. We will show that in this case we cannot reach common knowledge of basic formulas. We start out with a lemma stating that actions preserve the agent's relations.

Lemma 1. *For any two states s and t and any action α, if $s \sim_i^\tau t$ and we have s', t' such that $s[\![\alpha]\!]s'$ and $t[\![\alpha]\!]t'$ then $s' \sim_i^\tau t'$.*

Proof. Suppose $s \sim_i^\tau t$. Then $AM(s)|_i^\tau = AM(t)|_i^\tau$. Suppose $i \in Obs(\alpha)$. Then $AM(s')|_i^\tau = (AM(s)|_i^\tau; \alpha) = (AM(t)|_i^\tau; \alpha) = AM(t')|_i^\tau$. Suppose $i \notin Obs(\alpha)$. Then $AM(s')|_i^\tau = (AM(s)|_i^\tau; \tau) = (AM(t)|_i^\tau; \tau) = AM(t')|_i^\tau$. So $s' \sim_i^\tau t'$. $\square$

This result may seem counter-intuitive, since for example a public announcement action may give the agents new information and thus destroy their epistemic relations. However, in our framework we model the new knowledge introduced by communicative actions by the fact that these actions would not be possible in states that do not satisfy the precondition of the action. In this lemma we assume that there are s', t' such that $s[\![\alpha]\!]s'$ and $t[\![\alpha]\!]t'$. This means that s and t both satisfy the preconditions of α, so essentially no knowledge that distinguishes s and t is introduced by α.

Now we define a fragment $\mathcal{L}_{bool}$ of our logic as follows:

$$\phi ::= has_i m \mid com(G) \mid \neg\phi \mid \phi_1 \wedge \phi_2$$

It is trivial to show that any action that does not change the agent's message sets or the protocol does not change the truth value of these basic formulas:

Lemma 2. *Let α be an action that can be executed on the state s but does not change the agent's message sets or the protocol. For any $\phi \in \mathcal{L}_{bool}$: $s \models \phi \leftrightarrow \langle\alpha\rangle\phi$.*

Combining the properties of the actions from the previous lemma, we call an action α_d^G to be a *dummy action* for a group of agents G if its internal structure has the precondition $com(G) \wedge future(\alpha_d^G)$, for it does not change the message sets of the agents or the protocol and $Obs(\alpha_d^G) = G$. An example of dummy action is $inform_G^i(\top)$. We could see it as "talking about irrelevant things".

Theorem 4. *Let A be a set of basic actions respecting the communication channels such that for any agent i there is a dummy action α_d^G such that $i \notin G$. Let s be a state such that $I \notin CC(s)$ and it is common knowledge at s that the protocol is $\pi = (\Sigma A)^*$ (any action in A is allowed). Then for any $\phi \in \mathcal{L}_{bool}$ and any sequence of actions $\bar{\alpha}$,*

$$s \vDash^\tau \neg C_I \phi \rightarrow \neg \langle \bar{\alpha} \rangle C_I \phi$$

Proof. Similar to the proof of theorem 3, we suppose towards a contradiction that $s \vDash^\tau \neg C_I \phi$ and there is a minimal sequence $\bar{\alpha} = \bar{\beta}; \alpha$ such that $s \vDash^\tau \langle \bar{\beta} \rangle (\neg C_I \phi \wedge \langle \alpha \rangle C_I \phi)$. Since $I \notin CC(s)$ and α respects the communication channel, there is $i \notin Obs(\alpha)$. Suppose $s[\![\bar{\beta}]\!]u$, then $u \vDash^\tau \neg C_I \phi$. Therefore there exists u' such that $u \sim_I u'$ and $u' \vDash^\tau \neg \phi$. Now consider the dummy action α_d^G such that $i \notin G$. Clearly α_d^G can be executed on each state along the $\sim_I$ path from u to u'. In particular there are v and v' such that $u[\![\alpha_d^G]\!]v$ and $u'[\![\alpha_d^G]\!]v'$. By lemma 1 it is not hard to see that $v \sim_I^\tau v'$. Since $\phi \in \mathcal{L}_{bool}$, by lemma 2 we have $v' \vDash^\tau \neg \phi$. Thus $v \nvDash^\tau C_I \phi$. Let $u[\![\alpha]\!]t$. Since $i \notin Obs(\alpha)$ and $i \notin Obs(\alpha_d^G)$, $AM(t)|_i^\tau = (AM(u)|_i^\tau; \tau) = AM(v)|_i^\tau$, thus $t \sim_i^\tau v$. Therefore $t \nvDash^\tau C_I \phi$, which contradicts our assumption. $\square$

4.2   Telephone Calls

Before going to the specific scenario of the telephone calls, we propose the following general modeling method:

1. Select a finite set of suitable actions A with internal structures to model the communications in the scenario.
2. Design a single state as the *real world* to model the initial setting, i.e., $s = \langle net, \bar{M}_i, \epsilon, \bar{M}_i, (\Sigma A)^* \rangle$ where net models the communication network and $\bar{M}_i$ models "*who has what information*".
3. Translate the informal assumptions of the scenario into formulas ϕ and protocols π in $\mathcal{L}^{I,M}$.
4. Use $exinfo(\phi)$ and $exprot(\pi)$ to make the assumptions and the protocol common knowledge.

We will demonstrate how we use this method to model the telephone call scenario. Let us first recall the scenario: in a group of people, each person has one secret. They can make private telephone calls among themselves in order to communicate these secrets. The original puzzle we mentioned in the introduction concerns the minimal number of telephone calls needed to ensure everyone gets to know all secrets. We start out by selecting a set of suitable actions A. We define:

$$call_j^i(M') := \bigcup\nolimits_{M'' \subseteq M'} shareall_{\{i,j\}}(M'')$$
$$mail_j^i(M') := \bigcup\nolimits_{M'' \subseteq M'} sendall_{\{j\}}^i(M'')$$

Here $call_j^i(M')$ is the call between agent i and j where they share all messages out of M' that they possess [7]. Later on we will also be interested in what happens if the agents can only leave *voicemail* messages instead of making two-way calls. For this purpose we use $mail_j^i(M')$, where agent i sends all messages out of M' he possesses to agent j. The third kind of communication we are interested in will be when the agents can call each other and communicate formulas instead of messages. This is modeled by $inform_j^i(\phi)$. Let $M_I = \{m_0, ..., m_{|I|}\}$ be the set of all secrets. For suitable finite sets of formulas Φ and protocols Π [8], we define

$$A = \bigcup_{\phi \in \Phi} exinfo(\phi) \cup \bigcup_{\pi \in \Pi} exprot(\pi) \cup \bigcup_{i,j \in I} call_j^i(M_I) \cup \bigcup_{i,j \in I} mail_j^i(M_I) \cup \bigcup_{i,j \in I, \phi \in \Phi} inform_j^i(\phi),$$

where we include $exinfo(\phi)$ and $exprot(\pi)$ because we need them to make the assumptions and the protocol of the scenario common knowledge.

Next, we define the communication network and the agent's message sets. Each agent has one secret so we define $M_i = \{m_i\}$. The agents can only communicate in pairs, so the communication network is $net_I^{tel} = \{\{i,j\} \mid i \neq j \in I\}$. Then the initial state is:

$$s_I^{tel} = \langle net_I^{tel}, \{m_0\} \ldots \{m_{|I|}\}, \epsilon, \{m_0\} \ldots \{m_{|I|}\}, (\Sigma A)^* \rangle$$

We are interested in situations with different communicative powers for the agents, which can be characterized by protocols that restrict the possible basic actions. We define $\pi_{call} := (\bigcup_{i,j \in I} call_j^i(M_I))^*$, $\pi_{mail} := (\bigcup_{i,j \in I} mail_j^i(M_I))^*$ as the protocols where the agents can only make telephone calls or send voicemails, respectively. We define $\pi_{\text{call, inform}} := (\bigcup_{i,j \in I} call_j^i(M_I) \cup \bigcup_{i,j \in I} mail_j^i(M_I))^*$.

As for the informal assumptions of the scenario, we assume it is common knowledge that every agent has one secret, and we assume the communication network is common knowledge. We use the following abbreviations:

$$\begin{aligned}
\texttt{OneSecEach}_I &:= \bigwedge_{i \in I} (has_i m_i \wedge \bigwedge_{j \neq i} \neg has_j m_i) \\
\texttt{TP} &:= exinfo(com(net_I^{tel}) \wedge \texttt{OneSecEach}_I) \\
\texttt{TP}_{act} &:= \texttt{TP}; exprot(\pi_{act}) \\
\texttt{HasAll}_I &:= \bigwedge_{i \in I} has_i M_I
\end{aligned}$$

$\texttt{OneSecEach}_I$ states that every agent has one secret known only to him. $\texttt{TP}_{act}$ is the action of announcing the assumptions of the scenario and protocol π_{act} where $act \subseteq \{call, inform\}$. $\texttt{HasAll}_I$ expresses that every agent knows every secret, which is the goal we want to reach.

In order to reason about the number of calls the agents need to make to reach their goal, we use the following abbreviations:

$$\begin{aligned}
\langle\rangle^{\leq n}\phi &:= \langle \bigcup_{k \leq n} (\Sigma A')^k \rangle \phi \\
\langle\rangle^{min(n)}\phi &:= \langle\rangle^{\leq n}\phi \wedge \neg \langle\rangle^{\leq n-1}\phi
\end{aligned}$$

where A' is the set of all actions in A that respect the channels, i.e., excluding *exprot*, *exinfo* and other external actions. $\langle\rangle^{\leq n}\phi$ expresses that we can reach a

---

[7] Here M' encodes the *relevant context* e.g. messages that are *"about work"*.

[8] For example, the sets of formulas/protocols up to the length of certain large number.

state where ϕ holds by sequentially executing at most n actions from A without external information or any changes in protocol. $\langle\rangle^{min(n)}\phi$ expresses that n is the minimal such number. The reason we exclude these actions is because we essentially want to know whether we can reach ϕ with the current protocol. The external actions do not abide by the protocol, so we should not consider them[9].

Then the following result states that we need exactly $2|I| - 4$ calls to make sure every agent knows all secrets:

Proposition 4. *For any $x \in Sem$:*

$$s_I^{tel} \models^x \langle TP_{call}\rangle\langle\rangle^{min(2|I|-4)} HasAll_I$$

A proof of this proposition is given in [12]. The protocol given there is the following: pick a group of four agents 1 ... 4 and let 4 be their *informant*. Let all other agents call agent 4, then let the four agents communicate all their secrets within their group and let all other agents call agent 4 again. In our framework we can express this as follows: $call_5^4(M_I); ...; call_{|I|}^4(M_I); call_2^1(M_I); call_4^3(M_I);$ $call_3^1(M_I); call_4^2(M_I); call_5^4(M_I); ...; call_{|I|}^4(M_I).$

Another interesting question arises when the agents cannot make direct telephone calls, but they can only leave voicemail messages. This means that any agent can tell the secrets he knows to another agent, but he cannot in the same call also learn the secrets the other agent knows. How many voicemail messages would we need in this case?

Proposition 5. *For any $x \in Sem$:*

$$s_I^{tel} \models^x \langle TP_{mail}\rangle\langle\rangle^{min(2|I|-2)} HasAll_I$$

Proof. Consider the following protocol: $mail_2^1(M_I); mail_3^2(M_I); ...; mail_{|I|}^{|I|-1}(M_I);$ $mail_1^{|I|}(M_I); mail_2^{|I|}(M_I); ...; mail_{|I|-1}^{|I|}(M_I)$. Clearly, this results in all agents knowing all secrets. The length of this protocol is $2|I|-2$. We claim this protocol is minimal. To see why this claim holds, first observe that there has to be one agent who is the first to learn all secrets. For this agent to exist all other agents will first have to make at least one call to reveal their secret to someone else. This is already $|I|-1$ calls. The moment that agent learns all secrets, since he is the first, all other agents do not know all secrets. So each of them has to receive at least one more call in order to learn all secrets. This also takes $|I|-1$ calls which brings the total number of calls to $2|I|-2$.   □

As we saw above, it is possible to make sure all agents know all secrets. However, in these results the secrets are not *common knowledge* yet, since the agents do not know that everyone knows all secrets. We will investigate whether we can establish common knowledge of $HasAll_I$. If there are only three agents, this is possible by making telephone calls:

---

[9] Note that $\langle\rangle^{\leq n}$ serves as a generalization of the *arbitrary announcement* that is added to DEL in [17].

Proposition 6. *If $|I| \leq 3$ then for some $n \in \mathbb{N}$:*

$$s_I \models^\tau \langle TP_{call} \rangle \langle \rangle^{\leq n} C_I HasAll_I$$

Proof. For $|I| < 3$ the proof is trivial. Suppose $|I| = 3$, say $I = \{1, 2, 3\}$. A protocol that results in the desired property is $call_2^1(M_I); call_3^2(M_I); call_1^2(M_I)$. After execution of this protocol all agents know all secrets. From the way they learned these secrets the agents can deduce what communications have happened. Since all agents can reason about each others knowledge it is common knowledge that all agents have all secrets. □

We do not extend this result for the case with more than three agents. If there are more than three agents, agents that are not participating in the phone call will never know which of the other agents are calling, which makes it much harder to establish common knowledge. A different interesting question is whether the agents will be able to reach common knowledge if they can tell each other arbitrary formulas of the language, using the *inform* action. This reduces the possibilities to reach common knowledge since the dummy action $inform_G^i(\top)$ is allowed. The agents have no clue whether any information is transferred when they observe a τ action so they can never reach common knowledge, not even in the case that $|I| = 3$. This directly follows from Theorem 4.

Proposition 7. *For any $n \in \mathbb{N}$, if $|I| > 2$ then:*

$$s_I \not\models^\tau \langle TP_{call,inform} \rangle \langle \rangle^{\leq n} C_I HasAll_I$$

Now imagine a situation where the agents are allowed to publicly announce beforehand a specific protocol they are going to follow which is more complex than just the set of actions they can choose from. Then, in our τ-semantics, it is possible to reach common knowledge:

Proposition 8. *There is a protocol π of call actions such that*

$$s_I \models^\tau \langle TP; exprot(\pi) \rangle \langle \rangle^{\leq n} C_I HasAll_I$$

Proof. Let π be the protocol given in the proof of proposition 4. Since each agent observes a τ at every communicative action, they can all count the number of communicative actions that have been executed and they all know when the protocol has been executed. So at that moment, it will be common knowledge that everyone has all secrets. □

This shows the use of the ability to communicate about the future protocol and not only about the past and present. There are many more situations where announcing the protocol is very important, for example in the puzzle of 100 prisoners and a light bulb [7] or many situations in distributed computing.

5 Conclusions and Future Work

We developed an expressive dynamic epistemic logic tailored for specifying and reasoning about the information flow over communication channels. We also proposed an intuitive lightweight modeling method for multi-agent communication scenarios. The logic and the modeling method were put to use in the telephone call example.

Our framework is very flexible in modeling different observational powers of agents and various communicative actions. For example, we can define the communicative action in [14] : "i gets j's information without j noticing that" as $\alpha = download_j^i(M)$ with $Obs(\iota(\alpha)) = i$, $Pre(\iota(\alpha)) = com(\{i,j\}) \wedge has_j M$ and a suitable postcondition adding messages to i's information set[10]. Therefore our framework can facilitate the comparison among different approaches with different assumptions. The table below summarizes the setting of our framework compared to others:

Reference	Actions	Information flow	Obs. Power
[19]	inform	propositions	$\equiv^\tau$
[14]	download	Boolean atomic propositions	$\equiv^\tau$
[1]	inform	positive atomic propositions	$\equiv^{set}$
Our work	by design	messages or formulas	by design

Among many others, we left the following issues for future work: the complexity analysis of the satisfiablity problem and model checking problem of $\mathcal{L}^{I,M}$; the more general communication channels e.g., asymmetric channels; actions that can change the communication channels (cf. [19]); other actions which are "partially observable" to agents, e.g., BCC in emailing; and announcements of protocols with tests (cf. [26] for further discussions).

References

1. Apt, K.R., Witzel, A., Zvesper, J.A.: Common knowledge in interaction structures. In: Heifetz, A. (ed.) Proceedings of TARK 2009, pp. 4–13 (2009)
2. Baltag, A., Moss, L.: Logics for epistemic programs. Synthese 139(2), 165–224 (2004)
3. Baskar, A., Ramanujam, R., Suresh, S.P.: Knowledge-based modelling of voting protocols. In: Samet, D. (ed.) Proceedings of TARK 2007, pp. 62–71 (2007)
4. Brzozowski, J.A.: Derivatives of regular expressions. Journal of the ACM 11(4), 481–494 (1964)
5. Cohen, M., Dam, M.: A complete axiomatization of knowledge and cryptography. In: Ong, L. (ed.) Proceedings of LICS 2007, pp. 77–88. IEEE Computer Society, Los Alamitos (2007)
6. Conway, J.H.: Regular Algebra and Finite Machines. Chapman and Hall, Boca Raton (1971)
7. Dehaye, P.O., Ford, D., Segerman, H.: One hundred prisoners and a light bulb. Mathematical Intelligencer 24(4), 53–61 (2003)
8. Fagin, R., Halpern, J.Y., Vardi, M.Y., Moses, Y.: Reasoning about Knowledge. MIT Press, Cambridge (1995)

---

[10] [14] phrases such download action with propositions instead of messages.

9. Gerbrandy, J., Groeneveld, W.: Reasoning about information change. Journal of Logic, Language and Information 6(2), 147–169 (1997)
10. Hoshi, T.: Epistemic Dynamics and Protocol Information. PhD thesis, Stanford University (2009)
11. Hoshi, T., Yap, A.: Dynamic epistemic logic with branching temporal structures. Synthese 169(2), 259–281 (2009)
12. Hurkens, C.A.J.: Spreading gossip efficiently. Nieuw Archief voor Wiskunde 5/1(2), 208–210 (2000)
13. Moses, Y., Dolev, D., Halpern, J.Y.: Cheating husbands and other stories: A case study of knowledge, action, and communication. Distributed Computing 1(3), 167–176 (1986)
14. Pacuit, E., Parikh, R.: Reasoning about communication graphs. In: van Benthem, J., Gabbay, D., Löwe, B. (eds.) Interactive Logic – Proceedings of the 7th Augustus de Morgan Workshop, Texts in Logic and Games, Amsterdam, pp. 135–157 (2007)
15. Parikh, R., Ramanujam, R.: Distributed processes and the logic of knowledge. In: Proceedings of the Conference on Logic of Programs, London, UK, pp. 256–268. Springer, Heidelberg (1985)
16. Parikh, R., Ramanujam, R.: A knowledge based semantics of messages. Journal of Logic, Language and Information 12(4), 453–467 (2003)
17. Ågotnes, T., Balbiani, P., van Ditmarsch, H., Seban, P.: Group announcement logic. Journal of Applied Logic 8(1), 62–81 (2009)
18. Ramanujam, R., Suresh, S.P.: Deciding knowledge properties of security protocols. In: Proceedings of TARK 2005, pp. 219–235. Morgan Kaufmann, San Francisco (2005)
19. Roelofsen, F.: Exploring logical perspectives on distributed information and its dynamics. Master's thesis, University of Amsterdam (2005)
20. Shilov, N.V., Garanina, N.O.: Model checking knowledge and fixpoints. In: Ésik, Z., Ingólfsdóttir, A., Ésik, Z., Ingólfsdóttir, A. (eds.) Proceedings of FICS 2002, vol. NS-02-2, pp. 25–39 (2002)
21. van Benthem, J.: 'One is a lonely number': on the logic of communication. In: Chatzidakis, Z., Koepke, P., Pohlers, W. (eds.) Proceedings of Logic Colloquium 2002, Wellesley MA, pp. 96–129. ASL & A.K. Peters (2002)
22. van Benthem, J., Gerbrandy, J., Hoshi, T., Pacuit, E.: Merging frameworks for interaction. Journal of Philosophical Logic 38(5), 491–526 (2009)
23. van Benthem, J., van Eijck, J., Kooi, B.: Logics of communication and change. Information and Computation 204(11), 1620–1662 (2006)
24. van der Meyden, R., Shilov, N.: Model checking knowledge and time in systems with perfect recall. In: Pandu Rangan, C., Raman, V., Sarukkai, S. (eds.) FST TCS 1999. LNCS, vol. 1738, pp. 432–445. Springer, Heidelberg (1999)
25. van Ditmarsch, H.: Knowledge Games. PhD thesis, University of Groningen (2000)
26. Wang, Y.: Epistemic Modelling and Protocol Dynamics. PhD thesis, University of Amsterdam (2010)
27. Wang, Y., Kuppusamy, L., van Eijck, J.: Verifying epistemic protocols under common knowledge. In: Heifetz, A. (ed.) Proceedings of TARK 2009, pp. 257–266 (2009)

Distributed Abductive Reasoning with Constraints*

Jiefei Ma, Krysia Broda, Alessandra Russo, and Emil Lupu

Department of Computing, Imperial College London
{j.ma,k.broda,a.russo,e.c.lupu}@imperial.ac.uk

Abstract. Abductive inference has many known applications in multi-agent systems including planning, scheduling, policy analysis and sensing data interpretation. However, most abductive frameworks rely on a centrally executed proof procedure whereas many of the application problems are distributed by nature. Confidentiality and communication overhead concerns often preclude agents' knowledge from being centralised. We present in this paper a distributed abductive reasoning framework with a flexible and extensible proof procedure that permits collaborative abductive reasoning between agents over decentralised knowledge. The proof procedure is sound and complete upon termination, and can perform concurrent computation. To the best of our knowledge, this is the first distributed abductive system that can compute non-ground conditional proofs and handle arithmetic constraints.

1 Introduction

Abductive reasoning is a powerful mechanism for reasoning with incomplete knowledge that generates *conditional* proofs, the conditions being *abduced* assumptions that, together with a given knowledge-base, imply the conclusion of the proof. Abduced assumptions can be viewed, within the context of a knowledge-base, as an *explanation* of the conclusion. Abductive Logic Programming (ALP) [10] is the combination of abductive reasoning and Logic Programming, in which the knowledge-base is a logic program paired with a set of integrity constraints – queries that must never succeed – used to define constrains upon the assumptions that can be abduced. ALP is a general *knowledge-based* problem solving method which has been used in a wide range of real world applications: in cognitive robotics [17], for abducing higher-level descriptions of the world from sense data, in planning [16], for abducing action events that would result in a desired state of the world, using a knowledge-base about effects of actions on features of the world, and in diagnostic analysis of system specifications [5], for abducing system traces that would lead to property violations.

---

* This research is continuing through participation in the International Technology Alliance sponsored by the U.S. Army Research Laboratory and the U.K. Ministry of Defence.

A. Omicini, S. Sardina, and W. Vasconcelos (Eds.): DALT 2010, LNAI 6619, pp. 148–166, 2011.

These application problems have a corresponding formulation in the multi-agent context. Several robots may collaboratively try to abduce an agreed higher-level description of the state of the world, from their separate sense data, that is consistent with their collective constraints on the abduced information. Similarly, parties of a coalition networks, supporting joint-rescue operations for an earthquake-hit zone, may collaboratively reason about the dependency of their policies to abduce circumstances of policy violations, which would obstruct the success of their rescue operation. In these *distributed knowledge-based* problem solving tasks each agent has an *incomplete knowledge* of the problem domain. A robot sense data provides only a partial description of the state of the world, and policies of a rescue party constitute only part of the knowledge involved in a collective rescue operation. Communication overheads and confidentiality concerns often prevent solutions for these tasks being engineered by centralizing the agents' knowledge into a single computation point and using existing ALP proof procedures [11,6,8,12,7].

Therefore, to address distributed knowledge-base problem solving tasks where knowledge and constraints are distributed across (the reasoning module of) agents, a generic distributed abductive reasoning algorithm is needed that allows agents to co-operatively construct collective conditional proofs, and guarantee that their abduced conditions satisfy the relevant integrity constraints of all the agents. In [14], we have proposed a first distributed abductive reasoning system (DARE). Whilst the main emphasis of DARE is the openness of its architecture, the algorithm is limited to the construction of *ground* proofs: agents cannot accept non-ground negative queries or abduce non-ground assumptions. For example, in a simple web service domain, in which an agent has the knowledge $can\_fly(Pilot, Day) \leftarrow free(Pilot), \neg storm(Day)$ and a second (weather forecast) agent has the information $storm(monday)$, and $free$ is an abducible assumption, the DARE system cannot compute the conditional answer $free(X), Y \neq monday$ for a non-ground query $can\_fly(X, Y)$, as this would require the first agent to abduce the non-ground assumption $free(X)$ and the second agent to construct a proof for the non-ground sub-query $\neg storm(Y)$. In addition, arithmetic constraints are not allowed in the agent knowledge, making DARE unsuitable for classes of problems where reasoning about numerical values (e.g., time, cost) is required during the collaborative proof.

The focus of this paper is to present a new distributed abductive reasoning system, called DAREC, that overcomes the limitations of DARE, thus supporting a wider class of distributed knowledge-based problem solving tasks. Specifically, DAREC addresses four key issues. Firstly, *how to guarantee consistency of abduced non-ground assumption with all agents' integrity constraints* during a collaborative proof. In DARE, since abduced assumptions can only be ground, their integrity constraints need to be checked by the agents only once. This is not longer sufficient for non-ground abduced assumptions. In DAREC, integrity constraints on abduced assumptions are collected dynamically, and are checked whenever a new asummption is abduced. Secondly, *how to handle negative non-ground queries correctly.* Variables in negative non-ground queries may be either existentially or universally quantified e.g., $\forall Day.\neg storm(Day)$ and $\exists Day.\neg storm(Day)$. DAREC treats such (non-ground) negative queries as collected *dynamic* integrity constraints. Thirdly, *how and when to solve the arithmetic constraints during the collaborative reasoning.* In principle, all relevant arithmetic constraints collected by the agents in their conditional answers during local reasoning could be solved at the end of a collective proof by a centralised (or distributed) constraint satisfaction solver. DAREC instead checks the satisfaction of collected arithmetic constrains incrementally (i.e., whenever a new one is collected), as this helps reducing the search space for abduced assumptions during the reasoning process. Finally, *how to minimise the communication between agents.* An "eager interaction" between agents, as it is the case in DARE, whereby sub-queries are sent between agents whenever an agent needs help or whenever a new assumption is abduced, to guarantee global consistency, may require many message exchanges. DAREC adopts flexible coordination strategies.

In summary, the DAREC system makes use of a flexible and customisable proof procedure that permits collaborative abductive reasoning among decentralised agents. The collaborative reasoning can be seen as a state rewriting process, with a set of *local inference* rules, and a set of *state transitional* rules that coordinates *synchronised backtracking* among agents. The reasoning state, initially containing just the query, is exchanged between the agents. Agents rewrite the state during their local inference by adding relevant (non-ground) assumptions and (dynamically generated) integrity constraints, and check consistency of assumptions and constraints collectively stored so far in the state. A (global) conditional answer can be extracted from the final state when the overall collaborative proof succeeds. Successful proofs include solutions for the arithmetic constraints and abduced assumptions consistent with the integrity constraints of all the agents. The algorithm allows different application-dependent coordination strategies, such as one that encourages each agent to delay interactions with other agents (e.g. for help or for global consistency check) as much as possible, thus reducing inter-agent communications during the reasoning process. Agents' concurrent computation between synchronised backtracking is also supported.

The paper is organised as follows. Section 2 describes the advantages of the DAREC with respect to other related systems. Section 3 summarises basic notations and terminologies. Sections 4 and 5 present, respectively, the distributed abductive framework and the proof procedure illustrating it with a running example. Section 6 gives soundness and completeness results of the algorithm. Various extensions to the system are then discussed in Section 7, followed by a brief description of the implementation and its preliminary benchmarking results in Section 8. Finally, Section 9 concludes the paper.

2   Related Work

Several well-known proof procedures for centralised abductive reasoning have been proposed in the literature, e.g. Kakas-Mancarella (KM) [11], SLDNFA [6], IFF [8], ACLP [12], CIFF [7] and the ASystem [15]. The KM and ACLP approaches rely on the interleaving of *abductive* and *consistency* derivations, which would make the co-operation strategy between agents less flexible. The IFF and CIFF, on the other hand, use a special IFF-theory as knowledge-base of an abductive logic framework – the program consists of if-and-only-if definitions (e.g. the completion of rules [4]). In a distributed setting, predicate definitions (i.e. rules) may be distributed across agents, it is therefore not possible to construct predicate completions in each agent's knowledge-base. The ASystem does not suffer from these limitations and the state rewriting feature of its proof procedure makes it a good basis for a general distributed abductive reasoning approach. Our DAREC builds its proof procedure upon the ASystem algorithm.

To our knowledge only two other distributed abductive reasoning systems have been proposed in the literature, the ALIAS [2] and the DARE [14] system. Although the SCIFF proof procedure [1] is an extension of the CIFF to multi-agent systems, for reasoning and verifying agents behaviour and compliance to protocols, the knowledge-base and the computation process itself are both centralised. It is therefore not directly related to our DAREC. Both ALIAS and DARE extend the KM proof procedure to the multi-agent context, and, because of the limiting features of the KM algorithm, they cannot handle non-ground queries, non-ground abducibles and arithmetic constraints. In ALIAS, the knowledge base of agents uses a special language called $LAILA$ [3] for specifying statically and a priori, the communications with other agents. Consistency of the abduced assumptions is only required locally. On the other hand, both in DARE and DAREC the collaboration among agents is dynamically defined, by means of the *yellow page* directory that allows an agent to dynamically identify other helper agents; the notion of consistency of the abduced assumptions is global with respect to the integrity constraints of all the agents. However, as discussed in Section 1, DAREC is significantly different from DARE. Its proof procedure is based on a state rewriting principle, which enables more flexible co-operation strategies than the rigid one imposed in DARE by the interleave feature of the KM procedure, and it can handle a much larger class of knowledge-based distributed problem solving problems (i.e. distributed abductive reasoning with non-ground queries and answers, and with arithmetic constraint support).

3   Preliminary

In logic programming, a term is a constant, a variable or a function $F(t_1, \ldots, t_n)$ where F is a n-ary function symbol (with $n \geq 1$) and t_i is a term. An *atomic formula* (or *atom* in brief) is a proposition or an n-ary predicate P followed by an n-tuple of terms, e.g., $P(t_1, \ldots, t_n)$ (or $P(\vec{t})$). An equality atom (resp. inequality) is $t_1 = t_2$ (resp. $t_1 \neq t_2$) where t_1 and t_2 are terms. A *finite domain constraint* atom (or *constraint in brief*) is an boolean expression in the CLP language [20], e.g. $X > Y \times 3$, $Z \in \{1, 2\}$. A *literal* is either an atom ϕ (called *positive literal*, or the negation of an atom, written as $\neg\phi$ (and called *negative literal*). A *clause* is either a *rule*, $\phi \leftarrow \phi_1, \ldots, \phi_n$ ($n \geq 0$), or a *denial* $\leftarrow \phi_1, \ldots, \phi_n$ ($n > 0$), where ϕ, called *head* literal, is an atom, and ϕ_i, called *body* literal, is a literal. A rule with empty body is called a *fact*. All free variables appearing in a clause are *universally quantified* with the scope of the whole clause.

In abductive logic programming (ALP), predicates different from equality and CLP atoms, can be divided into two sets – *abducible* and *non-abducible*. Only non-abducible atoms can be head literals, but both abducible and non-abducible atoms can be body literals. Therefore, non-abducible atoms represent the knowledge that can be defined as rules; whereas abducible atoms represent the assumptions that may be made while proving a non-abducible. For example, given the set of two rules, { *"shoes_wet ← grass_wet"* , *"grass_wet ← rain"*} where *rain* is an abducible atom, a conditional proof of *shoes_wet* can be constructed making the abduced assumption *rain*. Thus, ALP can be used to reason with incomplete knowledge. Formally, an *abductive logic framework* $\mathcal{F}$ is a tuple $\langle \Pi, \mathcal{AB}, \mathcal{I} \rangle$, where Π is a finite set of rules called the *background knowledge*, $\mathcal{AB}$ is a set of abducible predicates, and $\mathcal{I}$ is a set of denials called the *integrity constraints*. Occasionally we may abuse the notation and let $\mathcal{AB}$ denote the set of all abducible atoms. Every integrity constraint must contain at least one positive abducible literal (this allows the agents to perform integrity checks only when a relevant abducible is assumed). An *abductive query* (or *query* in brief) is a conjunctive formula written as $\phi_1, \ldots, \phi_n$ where each ϕ_i is a literal (called a *goal*) and all free variables appearing in the query are *existentially quantified* with the scope of the whole query. Given an abductive framework $\mathcal{F}$ and a query $\mathcal{Q}$, an *abductive answer* is $\langle \Delta, \theta \rangle$, where $\Delta \subseteq \mathcal{AB}$ and θ is a substitution, such that $\Pi \cup \Delta \models \mathcal{Q}\theta$ and $\Pi \cup \Delta \not\models \mathcal{I}$.

4   Distributed Abductive Framework

In this section we define the notion of a DAREC framework. We assume a given fixed set of agents, where each agent's knowledge is modelled as an abductive framework. In Section 7 we discuss how to extend the framework to cater for a *dynamically changing* set of agents.

Definition 1. *A distributed abductive framework is a tuple $\mathcal{F}^{dis} = \langle \Sigma, \widehat{\mathcal{F}} \rangle$ where*

- Σ *is the set of agents (identifiers);*
- *each agent* $i \in \Sigma$ *is an abductive framework* $\mathcal{F}_i = \langle \Pi_i, \mathcal{AB}_i, \mathcal{I}_i \rangle$
- $\widehat{\mathcal{F}} = \{\mathcal{F}_i \mid i \in \Sigma\}.$

Given a system query (also called *global query*), the agents collaboratively compute a conditional proof, using their respective knowledge and making assumptions in terms of abducibles. In this paper we assume that all the agents agree on the possible assumptions they can make. i.e. they share the same set of abducible predicates, i.e., $\mathcal{AB}_i = \mathcal{AB}_j$ for any $i, j \in \Sigma$.

Definition 2. *Let $\mathcal{F}^{dis} = \langle \Sigma, \widehat{\mathcal{F}} \rangle$, be a distributed abductive framework. A distributed abductive answer for a given query $\mathcal{Q}$ is a pair $\langle \Delta, \theta \rangle$ such that:*
(1) $\Delta \subseteq \bigcup_{i \in \Sigma} \mathcal{AB}_i$;   (2) $\bigcup_{i \in \Sigma} \Pi_i \cup \Delta \models \mathcal{Q}\theta$;   (3) $\bigcup_{i \in \Sigma} \Pi_i \cup \Delta \models \bigcup_{i \in \Sigma} \mathcal{I}_i.$

Condition (3) above requires the abduced assumptions (Δ) to be consistent with all the agents' integrity constraints. This is understood as *global consistency*.

4.1   Example

We illustrate in what follows an example application of our distributed abductive framework in the context of an ambient intelligent system for a sheltered home for elderly people, where mobile or embedded devices are used for monitoring in house security and aiding the daily life of the occupants.

Example 1. Ann and Bob live in the same care home, where a number of sensing devices are installed. For example, a corridor sensor (C) detects movements along the corridor, and a window monitor (W) can check which window(s) of the house are open/closed. There is also a home controller (H) that can respond to events taking place inside the house, such as setting off an alarm if an intruder is detected, or notifying a nurse when a resident is in difficulty. Bob has a mental condition. Unless taking regular medication, he tends to wander around the house instead of staying in bed. So Bob is always carrying a personal device (B) that logs his medication intakes. Ann is in good health and can leave the house when necessary, e.g. going to a dental appointment. Ann also carries a personal device (A) which keeps her calendar and appointments. All the sensing and personal devices (except the base sensors, like the corridor sensor, which merely generates detected event notifications to H) have reasoning capability.

At 12pm on Monday, C detects movement and informs H, which needs to work with various devices to explain the event and take an appropriate action.

This system is modelled as a distributed abductive framework since for efficiency reasons the real-time monitoring data cannot be centralised, and for confidentiality reasons Bob's and Ann's personal knowledge also cannot be centralised. The set of agents is given by all the reasoning devices (i.e. $\Sigma = \{A, B, W, H\}$), each represented as an abductive framework (containing its knowledge at 12pm).

Bob cannot walk in the corridor $(wlkC)$ if he has taken medicine (tkM) in the past 2 hours. His most recent intake is at 11am.

$$\left[\begin{array}{l} \Pi_B = \{\, tkM(11).\,\} \\ \mathcal{I}_B = \{\leftarrow wlkC(bob, T), tkM(T1), T - 2 \leq T1, T1 \leq T.\} \end{array}\right]$$

Ann has a dental appointment (apt) from 11am to 1pm.

$$\left[\begin{array}{l} \Pi_A = \left\{\begin{array}{l} out(ann, T) \leftarrow apt(T1, T2), T1 \leq T, T \leq T2. \\ apt(11, 13). \end{array}\right\} \\ \mathcal{I}_A = \emptyset \end{array}\right]$$

The **window monitor** has the status information of the windows on different floors (flr). An open window $(open(w))$ on 1st floor $(flr))$ is a possible point of entry $(pntEntry)$ for an intruder.

$$\left[\begin{array}{l} \Pi_W = \left\{\begin{array}{l} pntEntry(T) \leftarrow open(W), flr(W, 1). \\ flr(w1, 1). \\ flr(w2, 2). \\ open(w1). \end{array}\right\} \\ \mathcal{I}_W = \emptyset \end{array}\right]$$

The **home controller** has knowledge about possible causes to known events.

$$\left[\begin{array}{l} \Pi_H = \left\{ \begin{array}{l} mnt(cor, T) \leftarrow occupant(X), wlkC(X, T). \\ mnt(cor, T) \leftarrow pntEntry(T), wlkC(intrd, T). \\ occupant(X) \leftarrow X \in \{ann, bob\} \end{array} \right\} \\ \mathcal{I}_H = \{ \leftarrow wlkC(X, T), X \neq intrd, out(X, T). \} \end{array} \right]$$

To explain the notified event of movement in the corridor $(mnt(cor, 12))$, H needs to find out who could be walking in the corridor $(wlkC)$ at 12. It could be an occupant or an intruder $(intrd)$. If it is Bob, then a nurse needs to be notified (remotely). If it is an intruder, then the alarm needs to be set off. If it is Ann, no action needs to be taken. All agents have the abducible predicate $wlkC$.

5   Distributed Abductive Proof Procedure

Intuitively, our DAREC proof procedure can be seen as a *distributed state rewriting* process. A *reasoning state* is passed like a "token" among the agents, and only the agent holding the state token may modify it by means of a set of *inference rules*. There are two types of inference rules, *local* and *transitional*. The local inference rules, extended from a centralised abductive system (ASystem) [15], are used by an agent to locally reduce non-abducible goals to conditions – constraints and abducibles which can be collected as assumptions – or to non-abducible sub-goals that other agents can collaboratively prove. Transitional rules enable instead the collaboration among agents and the enforcement of global consistency check.

Our proof procedure assumes that agents (i) execute their proofs honestly when requested, and (ii) know who to ask for help when their proof reduce to non-abducible goals that they cannot solve. The first assumption ensures that the agents *are willing to cooperate* and do not sabotage the collaboration. The second assumption enables the agents to *know how to cooperate*, and can be abstracted as an agent selection function, which takes a state (containing the remaining goals) as input and returns a suitable state recipient agent. This function can be implemented in different ways and using application dependent heuristics. For example, it can be defined as a task-allocation protocol, such as *auction, contract net* or simple *matching making*. Without loss of generality, we assume it to be a publicly accessible *directory* that records the agent IDs and the associated set of non-abducible predicates that the agent knowledge defines (but not the definitions themselves). General heuristics could be used in this case, such as choosing, as state recipient, the agent who knows the highest number of unresolved non-abducible goals in the current state of a collaborative proof.

A state has two main components – the set of unresolved *goals* and the set of *stores* containing the currently accumulated assumptions and constraints for the original query. During collaboration, an agent can ask another agent for help in resolving a non-abducible goal by sending the state to it. This request for help may be postponed to a later time: the requesting agent may *delay* the non-abducible goal and continue instead with its local inference on other goals. In a given state, the set of unresolved goals is therefore partitioned into current goals, which can be solved locally, and delayed goals. Abducibles and denial constraints are dynamically accumulated during the local reasoning process and added to the appropriate store in the current state, so that they can be checked by the other agents when the state is passed around.

Definition 3. *Given a set Σ of agents, a state Θ is the pair $\langle \mathcal{G}, \mathcal{ST} \rangle_\Sigma$, where $\mathcal{G}$ is a set of goals, partitioned into two sub-sets $(\mathcal{G}C, \mathcal{G}D)$, such that:*

- *each goal in $\mathcal{G}C$ is either a literal, or a failure goal $\forall \overrightarrow{X}. \leftarrow \phi_1, \ldots, \phi_n (n > 0)$, where $\overrightarrow{X}$ is the set of universally quantified variables of the goal, and*
- *each goal in $\mathcal{G}D$ is a non-abducible (called delayed goal),*

and $\mathcal{ST}$ is a tuple of four stores $\langle \Delta, \Delta^*, \mathcal{E}, \mathcal{C} \rangle$ where:

- *Δ is a set of abducibles;*
- *Δ^* is a set of denials $\forall \overrightarrow{X}. \leftarrow \phi_1, \ldots, \phi_n (n > 0)$ where ϕ_1 is either an abducible or a non-abducible;*
- *$\mathcal{E}$ is a set of (in-)equalities and $\mathcal{C}$ is a set of constraints.*

All free variables in Θ are existentially quantified with the scope the whole state.

A denial in Δ^* whose first literal in the body is a non-abducible is called *denial on non-abducible*. It represents the requirement that such literal must not be solvable in conjunction with other body literals of the denial by any agent. We assume, also, that for each element in $\mathcal{G}$, Δ and Δ^*, the state maintains the information of which agent has *seen* it. We use $L^\mathcal{S}$ to denote the fact that an element L has been seen by the set $\mathcal{S}$ of agents. Informally, a goal (or abducible/denial) has been seen by an agent if it has been delayed (or checked) by that agent. The meaning of "seen" will become clearer with the description of the inference rules.

When an initial query is sent to the system, an *initial state* is created and sent to a *suitable* agent (e.g. the agent who knows most of the goals in the state). The initial state contains the query as the set of current goals, none of which has been seen by any agent, and all the stores are empty. The state can then be modified by the agents in turn. A DAREC derivation can be abstracted as a tree where each agent is a state and the root is the initial state. The children of each agent are either (a) all the states that can be constructed from that agent for a selected goal G using a local inference rule, or (b) the states that can be obtained after transitional rules are applied. The derivation stops when a *solved state* is obtained after a finite number of steps, or backtracks when no rule is applicable, in which case the last state is labelled as *failed*. A DAREC derivation for a query $\mathcal{Q}$ *fails* when all the leaf agents are labelled failed, and *succeeds* when it reaches at least one solved state.

Definition 4. *A solved state involving a set Σ of agents, is $\Theta_{sol} = \langle \mathcal{G}^\emptyset, \mathcal{ST} \rangle_\Sigma$, where $\mathcal{G}^\emptyset = (\emptyset, \emptyset)$, and*

- $\mathcal{ST}$ is consistent (i.e. $\Delta \cup \Delta^* \cup \mathcal{E} \cup \mathcal{C}$ is satisfiable);
- all abducibles in Δ and all denials on non-abducibles in Δ^* have been seen by all agents in Σ.

Definition 5. Let $\Theta_{sol} = \langle \mathcal{G}^\emptyset, \mathcal{ST} \rangle_\Sigma$ be a solved state for a query $\mathcal{Q}$, where $\mathcal{ST} = \langle \Delta, \Delta^*, \mathcal{E}, \mathcal{C} \rangle$. A DAREC answer is a pair $\langle \theta, \Delta \rangle$ extracted from Θ_{sol} where θ is the variable substitution for all free variables of $\mathcal{Q}$ and Δ induced by $\mathcal{ST}$.

The DAREC proof procedure includes three transitional rules. The TR rule is applied as soon as an agent receives a state; the TH and TC rules are applied when an agent requests for help or consistency check respectively. These rules will be described in detail in the next section. Figure 1 provides the pseudo-code of the proof procedure as it is executed by an agent in the system. Note that after a state is sent out by the current agent, if a *backtracking* signal is received (because of another solution is requested or a helper fails to help), the current agent resumes the computation from the latest *choice point* created by the non-deterministic "select" action.

```
PROC receive_state(Θ₀) BEGIN
  Θ₁ := apply_trans_rule(TR, Θ₀);
  process_state(Θ₁);
END PROC
PROC process_state(Θ₁) BEGIN
  IF Θ₁ is solved state THEN
      send Θ₁ to the global query issuser;
      BACKTRACK_WHEN_REQUESTED;
  ELSE
      IF TH or TC should be applied THEN // state passing
         NewAgent := select_recipient(Θ₁);
         Θ₂ := apply_trans_rule(TH/TC, Θ₁);
         send Θ₂ to NewAgent;
         BACKTRACK_WHEN_REQUESTED;
      ELSE // local inference
         G := select_safe_goal(Θ₁);
         LRule := applicable_local_rule(G);
         States := apply_local_rule(LRule, Θ₁);
         NON-DETERMINISTICALLY select Θ₃ from States;
         process_state(Θ₃);
      END IF
  END IF
END PROC
```

Fig. 1. Pseudo-code of the DAREC Proof Procedure

5.1   Inference Rules

In this section we define the inference rules of our DAREC proof procedure and we illustrate some of them with small examples.

Infer. Rule 1 (TR – Receive State). *Let* $\Theta_i = \langle (\mathcal{GC}, \emptyset), \mathcal{ST} \rangle_\Sigma$ *be a state received by an agent* $ag \in \Sigma$, *then the next state is* $\Theta_{i+1} = \langle (\mathcal{GC}_{i+1}, \emptyset), \mathcal{ST} \rangle_\Sigma$, *where* $\mathcal{GC}_{i+1}$ *is obtained from* $\mathcal{GC}_i$ *as follows:*

- *for every abducible* $a(\overrightarrow{u}) \in \Delta$ *not seen by* ag, *for every integrity constraint* "$\leftarrow \Phi$" $\in \mathcal{I}_{ag}$ *such that* $\Phi = \{a(\overrightarrow{v})\} \cup \Phi^-$ *and* $\overrightarrow{Y} = vars(\Phi)$, *their resolvent* "$\forall \overrightarrow{Y}. \leftarrow \overrightarrow{u} = \overrightarrow{v}^1, \Phi^-$" *is added to* $\mathcal{GC}_i$;
- *for every denial on non-abducible* "$\forall \overrightarrow{X}. \leftarrow p(\overrightarrow{u}), \Phi$" $\in \Delta^*$ *not seen by* ag, *for every rule* "$p(\overrightarrow{v}) \leftarrow \Phi'$" $\in \Pi_{ag}$ *such that* $\overrightarrow{Y} = vars(p(\overrightarrow{v})) \cup vars(\Phi')$, *their resolvent* "$\forall \overrightarrow{X} \overrightarrow{Y}. \leftarrow \overrightarrow{u} = \overrightarrow{v}, \Phi', \Phi$" *is added to* $\mathcal{GC}_i$;
- *and all such abducibles and denials become seen by* ag.

Example: agent β *applies TR*

$$\begin{vmatrix} given & \Sigma = \{\alpha, \beta\}, \Pi_\beta = \{\text{"}p(U,V) \leftarrow r(U), w(V)\text{"}\}, \mathcal{I}_\beta = \{\text{"} \leftarrow a(Z), \neg q(Z)\text{"}\} \\ if & \Theta_i = \langle (\mathcal{G}_i, \emptyset), \langle \{a(X)^{\{\alpha\}}\}, \{\text{"}\forall Y. \leftarrow p(X,Y)\text{"}^{\{\alpha\}}\}, \mathcal{E}_i, \mathcal{C}_i \rangle \rangle_\Sigma \\ then & \Theta_{i+1} = \langle (\{\text{"}\forall Z. \leftarrow X = Z, \neg q(X)\text{"}, \text{"}\forall YUV. \leftarrow X = U, Y = V, r(X), w(Y)\text{"}\} \\ & \cup \mathcal{G}_i, \emptyset), \langle \{a(X)^{\{\alpha, \beta\}}\}, \{\text{"}\forall Y. \leftarrow p(X,Y)\text{"}^{\{\alpha, \beta\}}\}, \mathcal{E}_i, \mathcal{C}_i \rangle \rangle_\Sigma \end{vmatrix}$$

TR must be applied by any agent that receives a state, before using any local inference rule. It enforces that the current agent (e.g., β in the example) checks all the new abducibles collected by other agents (e.g., $a(X)$) against its local integrity constraints, and "resumes" the *negation as failure* (NAF) [4] processes for the non-abducibles associated with the denials in Δ^*. The two operations may generate new failure goals (e.g., "$\forall Z. \leftarrow X = Z, \neg q(X)$" is generated after checking $a(X)$, and "$\forall YUV. \leftarrow X = U, Y = V, r(X), w(Y)$" is generated after processing the collected denial on non-abducible in the state). In addition, the new state *remembers* the agent has seen the checked abducibles and denials, so if a successor state is passed back to the agent, they will not be checked again.

Infer. Rule 2 (TC – Request Consistency Check). *Let* $\Theta_i = \langle (\mathcal{GC}_i, \mathcal{GD}_i), \mathcal{ST} \rangle \rangle_\Sigma$ *be the current state held by an agent* $ag \in \Sigma$. *If there exists an abducible in* Δ *or a denial on non-abducible in* Δ^* *not seen by some other agent* $ag' \in \Sigma$, *then* ag *passes a new state* $\Theta_{i+1} = \langle (\mathcal{GC}_i \cup \mathcal{GD}_i, \emptyset), \mathcal{ST} \rangle_\Sigma$ *to* ag', *where all the goals in* $\mathcal{GD}_i$ *become seen by* ag.

Infer. Rule 3 (TH – Request Help). *Let* $\Theta_i = \langle (\mathcal{GC}_i, \mathcal{GD}_i), \mathcal{ST} \rangle_\Sigma$ *be the current state held by an agent* $ag \in \Sigma$. *If* $\mathcal{GD}_i \neq \emptyset$, *then* $\Theta_{i+1} = \langle (\mathcal{GC}_i \cup \mathcal{GD}_i, \emptyset), \mathcal{ST} \rangle_\Sigma$ *is a new state where all the goals in* $\mathcal{GD}_i$ *become seen by* ag, *and* ag *passes* Θ_{i+1} *to another agent* $ag' \in \Sigma$ *chosen by the agent selection strategy.*

TC is necessary to ensure that the collected abducibles are consistent with all the agents' integrity constraints, and that all the NAF processes can finish (and succeed) amongst all the agents. In contrast, TH is necessary to allow agents to ask for help to resolve a goal. Note that it is unnecessary for ag to ask for

---

^{1} $\overrightarrow{u} = \overrightarrow{v}$ denotes the set of equalities constructed from the two lists of arguments $\overrightarrow{u}$ and $\overrightarrow{v}$.

"help" on assumed abducible, (in)equality and constraint goals, and failure goals must be solved by ag locally. Therefore, only non-abducible goals can be delayed. When these two rules are applied, delayed goals in $\mathcal{G}D$ are moved back to $\mathcal{G}C$, and marked as seen by ag. No agent can delay the same goal twice, so avoiding loops among a set of agents asking for the same help between themselves.

Sometimes given a state, several inference rules may be applicable. For example, given a state where $\mathcal{G}C$ and $\mathcal{G}D$ are non-empty and where some abducibles in Δ have not been seen by all agents, the state holder ag may either apply TC to ask others to check the abducibles, or apply TH to ask for help for the delayed goals, or apply some local inference rules to solve the current goals. An *inference rule selection strategy* (or *agent interaction strategy*) decides whether to apply a transitional rule or a local inference rule given a state, and it can affect how often the agents interact and the overall performance of the agent collaboration (see Section 8). For example, an *eager* strategy may force agents to choose TH or TC whenever it is possible, whereas a *lazy* strategy may force the agents to choose local inference rule whenever there are non-dalyed goals, i.e., each agent computes as much as it can before passing out the state. The general DAREC proof procedure allows different application dependent agent interaction strategy to be adopted.

The DAREC proof procedure includes ten local inference rules for an agent to resolve a selected goal from the state it holds. Let $\Theta_i = \langle (\mathcal{G}C_i, \mathcal{G}D_i), \langle \Delta_i, \Delta_i^*, \mathcal{E}_i, \mathcal{C}_i \rangle \rangle_\Sigma$ be the current state held by an agent $ag \in \Sigma$, and $\mathcal{G}C_i \neq \emptyset$. A goal $\phi \in \mathcal{G}C_i$ is selected *non-deterministically*, making $\mathcal{G}C_i^- = \mathcal{G}C_i - \{\phi\}$. The next state Θ_{i+1} is generated after one of the following local inference rules is applied by ag. In the description of local rules, only changes to the state components are reported, and OR denotes a *non-deterministic* change to the state.

Infer. Rule 4 (LD1 – Resolve Non-abducible). *If* $\phi = p(\overrightarrow{u})$ *is a non-abducible, one of the following changes is made (non-deterministically):*

- *let* "$p(\overrightarrow{v}) \leftarrow \Phi$" $\in \Pi_{ag}$, *then* $\mathcal{G}C_{i+1} = \{\overrightarrow{u} = \overrightarrow{v}\} \cup \Phi_1 \cup \mathcal{G}C_i^-$ OR
- $\mathcal{G}C_{i+1} = \mathcal{G}C_i^-$ *and* $\mathcal{G}D_{i+1} = \mathcal{G}D_i \cup \{\phi\}$, *if* ϕ *has not been seen by* ag *before.*

This rule allows ag to resolve a non-abducible goal with a rule in its background knowledge Π_{ag}, or to ask another agent to resolve it (later).

Infer. Rule 5 (LA1 – Resolve Abducible). *If* $\phi = a(\overrightarrow{u})$ *is an abducible, let* $a(\overrightarrow{v}_j)$ $(j = 1, \ldots, n)$ *be* n *abducibles in* Δ_i, *then one of the following changes is made (non-deterministically):*

- $Gc_{i+1} = \{\overrightarrow{u} = \overrightarrow{v}_j\} \cup \mathcal{G}C_i^-$ OR
- $\Delta_{i+1} = \{\phi\} \cup \Delta_i$ *and* $\mathcal{G}C_{i+1} = \mathcal{G}C_i^- \cup R_\Delta \cup R_{\Delta^*} \cup R_{IC}$, *where* $R_\Delta = \{$"$\leftarrow \overrightarrow{u} = \overrightarrow{v}_j$" $\mid j = 1, \ldots, n\}$, $R_{\Delta^*} = \{$"$\forall \overrightarrow{X}. \leftarrow \overrightarrow{u} = \overrightarrow{w}, \Phi$" $\mid$ "$\forall \overrightarrow{X}. \leftarrow a(\overrightarrow{w}), \Phi$" $\in \Delta_i^*\}$, $R_{IC} = \{$"$\forall \overrightarrow{X}. \leftarrow \overrightarrow{u} = \overrightarrow{w}, \Phi^-$" $\mid$ "$\leftarrow \Phi$" $\in \mathcal{I}_{ag}$ *and* $\Phi = \{a(\overrightarrow{w})\} \cup \Phi^-\}$, *and* $\phi \in \Delta_{i+1}$ *becomes has been seen by* ag.

Example: agent α applies LA1

$$
\begin{array}{|ll|}
given & \Sigma = \{\alpha, \beta\}, \mathcal{I}_\alpha = \{\text{``} \leftarrow a(V), w(V)\text{''}\} \\
if & \Theta_i = \langle(\{a(X)\} \cup \mathcal{G}_i, \emptyset), \langle\{a(Z)^{\{\alpha,\beta\}}\}, \{\text{``}\forall Y. \leftarrow a(Y), r(Y)\text{''}\}, \mathcal{E}_i, \mathcal{C}_i\rangle\rangle_\Sigma \\
then & \Theta_{i+1} = \langle(\mathcal{G}_i, \emptyset), \langle\{a(Z)^{\{\alpha,\beta\}}\}, \{\text{``}\forall Y. \leftarrow a(Y), r(Y)\text{''}\}, \{X = Z\} \cup \mathcal{E}_i, \mathcal{C}_i\rangle\rangle_\Sigma \\
or & \Theta'_{i+1} = \langle((\{X \neq Z, \text{``}\forall V. \leftarrow X = V, w(V)\text{''}, \text{``}\forall Y. \leftarrow X = Y, r(Y)\text{''}\} \cup \mathcal{G}_i, \emptyset), \\
& \langle\{a(X)^{\{\alpha\}}, a(Z)^{\{\alpha,\beta\}}\}, \{\text{``}\forall Y. \leftarrow a(Y), r(Y)\text{''}\}, \mathcal{E}_i, \mathcal{C}_i\rangle\rangle_\Sigma
\end{array}
$$

LA1 allows reusing an abducible already assumed or assuming new abducible (e.g., in the example Θ_{i+1} and Θ'_{i+1} are the resulting state respectively). In the case a new abducible is assumed, three sets of new failure goals are added: R_Δ ensures that the new abducible is different from any existing abducible in Δ_i (e.g., $X \neq Z$ in Θ'_{i+1}), R_{Δ^*} ensures that it is consistent with the dynamically collected constraints in Δ_i^* (e.g., "$\forall Y. \leftarrow X = Y, r(Y)$" in Θ'_{i+1}), and R_{IC} ensures that it is consistent with ag's local integrity constraints $\mathcal{I}_{ag}$ (e.g., "$\forall V. \leftarrow X = V, w(V)$" in Θ'_{i+1}).

Infer. Rule 6 (LN1 – Resolve Negation). *If $\phi = \neg p(\overrightarrow{u})$, then $\mathcal{G}C_{i+1} = \mathcal{G}C_i^- \cup \{\leftarrow p(\overrightarrow{u})\}$.*

Infer. Rule 7 (LC1 – Resolve Constraint). *If ϕ is a constraint, then $\mathcal{G}C_{i+1} = \mathcal{G}C_i^-$ and $\mathcal{C}_{i+1} = \mathcal{C}_i \cup \{\phi\}$, if $\mathcal{C}_{i+1}$ is consistent.*

Infer. Rule 8 (LE1 – Resolve (In-)Equality). *If ϕ is an (in-)equality, then $\mathcal{G}C_{i+1} = \mathcal{G}C_i^-$ and $\mathcal{E}_{i+1} = \mathcal{E}_i \cup \{\phi\}$, if $\mathcal{E}_{i+1}$ is consistent.*

The rules LC1 and LE1 add a constraint or a (in)equality to the stores, and their application succeeds only if the new stores are *consistent*. LN1 simply "converts" a negative goal to a failure goal, so that later it can be processed by one of the following local rules:

If ϕ is a failure goal of $\forall \overrightarrow{X}. \leftarrow \Gamma$, where Γ is not empty, a *safe* sub-goal φ is non-deterministically selected from Γ and let $\Gamma^- = \Gamma - \{\varphi\}$. Unsafe sub-goals refer to those that can cause *floundering* in the reasoning process, and will be described explicitly in the relevant rules. If the only sub-goal that can be selected is unsafe, then the whole computation aborts and reports error[2].

Infer. Rule 9 (LD2 – Fail Non-abducible). *If $\varphi = p(\overrightarrow{u})$ is a non-abducible, let $F = \text{``}\forall \overrightarrow{X}. \leftarrow p(\overrightarrow{u}), \Gamma^-\text{''}$, then $\mathcal{G}C_{i+1} = \mathcal{G}C_i^- \cup \{\text{``}\forall \overrightarrow{X}\overrightarrow{Y}. \leftarrow \overrightarrow{u}=\overrightarrow{v}, \Phi, \Gamma^-\text{''} \mid \text{``}p(\overrightarrow{v}) \leftarrow \Phi\text{''} \in \Pi_{ag} \text{ and } \overrightarrow{Y} = vars(\overrightarrow{v}) \cup vars(\Phi)\}$ and $\Delta_{i+1}^* = \Delta_i^* \cup \{F\}$, and $F \in \Delta_{i+1}^*$ becomes seen by ag.*

Example: agent α applies LD2

$$
\begin{array}{|ll|}
given & \Sigma = \{\alpha, \beta\}, \Pi_\alpha = \{\text{``}p(U) \leftarrow r(U)\text{''}, \text{``}p(V) \leftarrow w(V)\text{''}\} \\
if & \Theta_i = \langle(\{\text{``} \leftarrow p(X), q(X)\text{''}\} \cup \mathcal{G}_i, \emptyset), \langle\Delta_i, \Delta_i^*, \mathcal{E}_i, \mathcal{C}_i\rangle\rangle_\Sigma \\
then & \Theta_{i+1} = \langle(\{\text{``}\forall U. \leftarrow X = U, r(U), q(X)\text{''}, \text{``}\forall V. \leftarrow X = V, w(V), q(X)\text{''}\} \cup \mathcal{G}_i, \emptyset), \\
& \langle\Delta_i, \{\text{``} \leftarrow p(X), q(X)\text{''}^{\{\alpha\}}\} \cup \Delta_i^*, \mathcal{C}_i\rangle\rangle_\Sigma
\end{array}
$$

---

[2] This is usually caused by a bug in the background knowledge specification.

This rule mimics the NAF process by the current agent (α in the example) locally, which is a part of the global NAF process among all the agents in Σ. Therefore, the denial on non-abducible (e.g., " $\leftarrow p(X), q(X)$ ") needs to be added to Δ_{i+1}^* during the reasoning. If the current agent is not the only agent in Σ, then TC must be applied before a solved state can be obtained, which implies that TR will be eventually applied by all other agents. The successful NAF processes performed by all the agents constitute a successful global NAF process for the non-abducible.

Infer. Rule 10 (LA2 – Fail Abducible). *If $\varphi = a(\overrightarrow{u})$ is an abducible, let* $F = "\forall \overrightarrow{X}. \leftarrow a(\overrightarrow{u}), \Gamma^{-}"$, *then* $\mathcal{G}C_{i+1} = \mathcal{G}C_i^- \cup \{"\forall X. \leftarrow \overrightarrow{u}=\overrightarrow{v}" \mid a(\overrightarrow{v}) \in \Delta_i\}$ *and* $\Delta_{i+1}^* = \Delta_i^* \cup \{F\}$.

Example: agent α applies LA2

$$
\begin{vmatrix}
given & \Sigma = \{\alpha, \beta\} \\
if & \Theta_i = \langle(\{"\forall X. \leftarrow a(X), p(X)"\} \cup \mathcal{G}_i, \emptyset), \langle\{a(Y)^{\{\alpha\}}, a(Z)^{\{\alpha\}}\}, \Delta_i^*, \mathcal{E}_i, \mathcal{C}_i\rangle\rangle_\Sigma \\
then & \Theta_{i+1} = \langle(\{"\forall X1. \leftarrow X1 = Z, p(X1)", "\forall X2. \leftarrow X2 = Y, p(X2)"\} \cup \mathcal{G}_i, \emptyset), \\
& \langle\{a(Y)^{\{\alpha\}}, a(Z)^{\{\alpha\}}\}, \{"\forall X. \leftarrow a(X), p(X)"\} \cup \Delta_i^*, \mathcal{E}_i, \mathcal{C}_i\rangle\rangle_\Sigma
\end{vmatrix}
$$

In order to succeed the whole failure goal (e.g., "$\forall X. \leftarrow a(X), p(X)$" in the example), we need to succeed all of its instances that contains a matching collected abducible (e.g. $a(Y)$ or $a(Z)$). This rule generates the instances as additional failure goals (e.g, "$\forall X1. \leftarrow X1 = Z, p(X1)$" and "$\forall X2. \leftarrow X2 = Y, p(X2)$"). However, new matching abducibles (such as $a(V)$) may be assumed in the later computation, and the original failure goal must still be satisfied. Therefore, the failure goal needs to be added to Δ_{i+1}^* and is checked whenever a new abducible is assumed, i.e. it is a *dynamic integrity constraint*.

Infer. Rule 11 (LN2 – Fail Negation). *If $\varphi = \neg p(\overrightarrow{u})$ is a negative literal and $vars(\overrightarrow{u}) \cap \overrightarrow{X} = \emptyset$, then $(\mathcal{G}C_{i+1} = \mathcal{G}C_i^- \cup \{p(\overrightarrow{u})\})$ OR $(\mathcal{G}C_{i+1} = \mathcal{G}C_i^- \cup \{"\forall\overrightarrow{X}. \leftarrow \Gamma^{-}"\} \cup \{\leftarrow p(\overrightarrow{u})\})$.*

A negative literal (sub-goal) inside a failure goal is *unsafe* if any of its variables is universally quantified with the scope of the whole failure goal (e.g. a member of $\overrightarrow{X}$ of ϕ). In order to succeed the failure goal ϕ, we can either fail φ by showing its positive form (i.e. the first possible new state), or fail any of the remaining literals Γ^- (i.e. the second state). Adding also a goal $\leftarrow p(\overrightarrow{u})$ in the second case is to avoid overlapping solutions to be derived from the two possible new states.

Infer. Rule 12 (LC2 – Fail Constraint). *If φ is a constraint where $vars(\varphi) \cap \overrightarrow{X} = \emptyset$, let $\overline{\varphi}$ be the negated expression of φ, then $(\mathcal{G}C_{i+1} = \mathcal{G}C_i^-$ and $\mathcal{C}_{i+1} = \mathcal{C}_i \cup \{\overline{\varphi}\}$, if $\mathcal{C}_{i+1}$ is consistent) OR $(\mathcal{G}C_{i+1} = \mathcal{G}C_i^- \cup \{"\forall\overrightarrow{X}. \leftarrow \Gamma^{-}"\}$ and $\Delta_{i+1} = \Delta_i \cup \{\varphi\}$ if Δ_{i+1} is consistent).*

A constraint sub-goal is unsafe if it contains any universally quantified variables. LC2 is similar to LN2, since it either tries to succeed the negation of sub-goal or tries to fail any of the remaining sub-goals.

Infer. Rule 13 (LE2 – Fail Equality). *If φ is an equality of the form $t = s$,*

1. *if $t = p(\overrightarrow{u})$ and $s = p(\overrightarrow{v})$, then: $\mathcal{G}C_{i+1} = \mathcal{G}C_i^- \cup \{\text{"}\forall \overrightarrow{X}. \leftarrow \overrightarrow{u} = \overrightarrow{v}, \Gamma^-\text{"}\}$;*
2. *if $t = p(\overrightarrow{u})$ and $s = q(\overrightarrow{v})$, then: $\mathcal{G}C_{i+1} = \mathcal{G}C_i^-$;*
3. *if $t \in vars(s)$ or $s \in vars(t)$, then: $\mathcal{G}C_{i+1} = \mathcal{G}C_i^-$;*
4. *if $t \in \overrightarrow{X}$, let $\theta = \{t/s\}$, then: $\mathcal{G}C_{i+1} = \mathcal{G}C_i^- \cup \{\text{"}\forall \overrightarrow{X}. \leftarrow \Gamma^-\text{"}/\theta\}$;*
5. *if t is an existential variable (i.e. $t \notin \overrightarrow{X}$) and $vars(s) \cap \overrightarrow{X} = \emptyset$, let $\theta = \{t/s\}$, then: $\mathcal{G}C_{i+1} = \mathcal{G}C_i^-$ and $\mathcal{E}_{i+1} = \mathcal{E}_i \cup \{t \neq s\}$, if $\mathcal{E}_{i+1}$ is consistent OR $\mathcal{G}C_{i+1} = \mathcal{G}C_i^- \cup \{\text{"}\forall \overrightarrow{X}. \leftarrow \Gamma^-\text{"}/\theta\}$ and $\mathcal{E}_{i+1} = \mathcal{E}_i/\theta$ and $\mathcal{C}_{i+1} = \mathcal{C}_i/\theta$, if $\mathcal{E}_{i+1}$ and $\mathcal{C}_{i+1}$ are consistent;*

and (4) and (5) also hold for the symmetric case of $s = t$.

In LE2, cases (1)-(4) implement the standard unification algorithm. Case (5) is similar to LN2 or LC2, and it generates two possible new states. LE2 doesn't handle inequality such as $t \neq s$ because such a sub-goal can be seen as $\neg(t = s)$ and can be handled by LN2, as long as it is safe.

5.2   Example Trace

Here is a (simplified) reasoning trace for Example 1. Let $\mathcal{Q}=mnt(cor, 12)$ be a global query initiated by H, and assume a left-to-right goal selection strategy and a lazy agent interaction strategy are adopted. We only outline the key steps:

1. **H**: created a state containing $mnt(cor, 12)$ as the goal;
2. Local inference by **H**: it abduced $wlkC(X, 12)$ with $X \in \{ann, bob\}$ using the first rule in Π_H; it then resolved the abducible with its only integrity constraint, and collected the denial " $\leftarrow out(X, 12)$";
3. **H** passed the state to **B**, which started a local inference: it resolved the abducible with its integrity constraint to obtain $X = bob$ and the failure goal "$\forall T1. \leftarrow tkM(T1), 12 - 2 \leq T1 \leq 12$";
4. **B** could not satisfy the failure goal (Bob took medicine at 11 so the constraints $12 - 2 \leq 11 \leq 12$ could not be falsified). Hence, **B** backtracked and added the constraint $X \neq bob$ instead;
5. **B** passed the state to **A**, which started a local inference: it had no integrity constraint for the abducible, but it had to check " $\leftarrow out(X, 12)$". It resumed the NAF process of $out(X, 12)$ using the first rule in Π_A, and obtained a failure goal "$\forall T1, T2. \leftarrow X = ann, apt(T1, T2), T1 \leq 12, 12 \leq T2$". However, this goal could not be satisfied with $X = ann$ as Ann had an appointment between 11 and 13.
6. **A** backtracked but could not add $X \neq ann$ instead, as it would be inconsistent with $X \in \{ann, bob\}, X \neq bob$. **A** sent a backtracking signal to **B**, who then sent the signal to **H**.
7. **H** then backtracked to use the second rule in Π_H. It collected a delayed goal $pntEntry(12)$ and abduced $wlkC(intrd, 12)$.
8. **H** passed the state to **W**, which started a local inference: it could successfully resolve the only goal $pntEntry(12)$. Therefore, a final answer $wlkC(intrd, 12)$ was returned to **H**.

6   Soundness and Completeness

The DAREC proof procedure is *sound* and *complete* only with respect to a three-valued semantics [18] for which, given a global query $\mathcal{Q}$ and a DAREC answer $\langle \theta, \Delta \rangle$, the interpretation (completion) of all abducibles (i.e. $\mathcal{AB}$) is defined as $I_{\Delta\theta} = \{A^{\mathbf{t}} \mid A \in \Delta\theta \wedge A \in \mathcal{AB}\} \cup \{A^{\mathbf{f}} \mid A \notin \Delta\theta \wedge A \in \mathcal{AB}\}$. Due to lack of space, only the main aspects of the soundness and completeness proofs are briefly outlined here.

Theorem 1 (Soundness of DAREC). *Given a distributed abductive framework $\mathcal{F}^{dis} = \langle \Sigma, \widehat{\mathcal{F}} \rangle$ and a global query $\mathcal{Q}$, if there is a successful DAREC derivation for $\mathcal{Q}$ with answer $\langle \theta, \Delta \rangle$, then*

$$1.\ \bigcup_{i \in \Sigma} \Pi_i \cup I_{\Delta\theta} \models_3 \mathcal{Q}\theta; \qquad 2.\ \bigcup_{i \in \Sigma} \Pi \cup I_{\Delta\theta} \models_3 \bigcup_{i \in \Sigma} \mathcal{I}_i;$$

where $\models_3$ is the logical entailment under the three-valued semantics for abductive logic programs [18].

Theorem 2 (Completeness of DAREC). *Let $\mathcal{F}^{dis} = \langle \Sigma, \widehat{\mathcal{F}} \rangle$ be a distributed abductive framework and $\mathcal{Q}$ a global query, suppose there is a finite DAREC derivation tree T for $\mathcal{Q}$. If $\bigcup_{i \in \Sigma} \Pi_i \cup \bigcup_{i \in \Sigma} \mathcal{I}_i \cup \exists \mathcal{Q}$ is satisfiable under the three-valued semantics, then T contains a successful branch.*

The above proofs build upon the ASystem's soundness and completeness results, and use the notion of *meaning of a state* – a first-order logic formula denoted as $\mathcal{M}(State)$ and representing the conjunction of all the components in a state.

Let us consider first the soundness proof and let us assume $S_0, \ldots, S_N$ to be a successful derivation where S_0 and S_N are the initial and the solved state respectively. The proof uses the following two intermediate lemmas: (i) the correctness of each inference rule, i.e., given two consecutive states S_j and S_{j+1} in a derivation $(0 \leq j < N)$, $\bigcup_{i \in \Sigma} \Pi_i \models_3 \mathcal{M}(S_{j+1}) \Rightarrow \mathcal{M}(S_j)$ where $\Rightarrow$ is the logical *implication*; and the properties (ii) $\models_3 S_0 \Rightarrow \mathcal{Q}$ and $\bigcup_{i \in \Sigma} \Pi_i \models_3 I_{\Delta\theta} \Rightarrow \mathcal{M}(S_N)$, which hold by reflexivity. Statement (1) in Theorem 1 is then shown using (i) and (ii) through chain of implications. Similarly for Statement (2) in Theorem 1, but showing also that for any integrity constraint $IC \in \bigcup_{i \in \Sigma} \mathcal{I}_i$ containing an abducible atom $A \in \Delta\theta$, it holds that $\bigcup_{i \in \Sigma} \Pi_i \models_3 I_{\Delta\theta} \Rightarrow IC$.

As for the DAREC completeness proof, the idea is to show that any DAREC derivation tree can be "reduced"' to an equivalent A-System derivation and use the ASystem's completeness theorem. We first define a special inference rule selection strategy (Ξ_f), for which the TH rule is applied as soon as a goal is delayed, and the TC rule is applied (by all agents in turn) as soon as an abducible or denial on non-abducible is collected; and assume an arbitrary goal selection strategy Υ_a. The proof has the following steps. Given a query $\mathcal{Q}$, we show, first, that any finite DAREC derivation tree T^D obtained with Ξ_f and Υ_a is equivalent to a finite ASystem derivation tree T^A obtained with Υ_a. Secondly, we show that a finite DAREC derivation tree $T^{D'}$ obtained with any arbitrary inference rule selection strategy Ξ_a and a fair goal selection strategy Υ_a is equivalent to the finite DAREC derivation tree T^D obtained using Ξ_f and a more restricted fair goal selection strategy Υ_r based on Υ_a, i.e., $T^{D'}_{\Xi_a+\Upsilon_a} \equiv T^D_{\Xi_f+\Upsilon_r} \equiv T^A_{\Upsilon_r}$. By the ASystem's completeness theorem (which holds with any fair goal selection strategy), if $\bigcup_{i\in\Sigma}\Pi_i \cup \bigcup_{i\in\Sigma}\mathcal{I}_i \cup \exists\mathcal{Q}$ is satisfiable, T^A must contain a successful branch, and, hence, $T^{D'}$ must also have a successful branch.

That three-valued completion semantics, chosen for the theorems instead of other stronger semantics, such as the stable model semantics [9], is due to the fact that top-down inference procedures, like abduction, may suffer from looping. In practice, looping can be avoided either by implementing a depth-bounded search strategy or by ensuring that the overall logic program satisfies certain properties (e.g., abductive non-recursive [19]).

7   Discussions

The DAREC proof procedure described so far can be extended in several ways in order to support applications where confidentiality or efficiency are main concerns. We briefly describe here these extensions.

Global and Local Predicates. In the definition of the DAREC framework, given in Section 4, non-abducible predicates are considered *global*, which implies that Negation as Failure for a non-abducible must be performed by all the agents. Moreover, as stated in Section 5, we have so far assumed that agents must expose to others all the non-abducibles they know. In some application domains, e.g., decentralised policy analysis, it is however desirable to distinguish between *global* versus *local* non-abducible predicates. A non-abducible is local to an agent if and only if it is known by the agent only and it does not appear in any other agent's program or integrity constraints. Allowing local non-abducibles has the benefits of improving the computational efficiency of the system and supporting confidentiality. In the former case whenever an agent needs to fail a local non-abducible (i.e. by LD2), its denial does no longer need to be added to the store Δ^* of the state and checked by all the other agents. In the latter case, agents can express private knowledge in terms of local non-abducible predicates which will not be shared with other agents. However, to ensure during the proof that no local predicates appear in a state that is passed from one agent to another, particular goal selection strategies must be adopted which would give priority to local goals versus global goals.

Concurrent Computation. The DAREC proof procedure described in Figure 1 enforces synchronised (global) backtracking among the agents, namely whenever an agent sends out a state, it backtracks only when it is requested; and, at any time, only one agent (that is holding the state) can perform reasoning (by rewriting the state). There is room, however, for concurrent computation allowing agents to backtrack immediately after it sends out a state. Solved states found during backtracking could be sent back to the query issuer straightaway, and any state, suitable for the application of TH or TC rule, constructed during backtracking can be "buffered". In this way, as soon as a global backtracking request is received, a buffered state can be sent out immediately, if there is any.

Open Networks. Although the DAREC framework presented in this paper is for *closed* networks (i.e. a fixed set of agents), it is very easy to extend it to *open* networks, where agents may join or leave during collaborative reasoning. This can be easily achieved in the following way. First, we *assume* that whenever an agent joins or leaves the system, all other agents are notified. Secondly, we extend the state to be $\langle \mathcal{G}, \mathcal{ST}, S \rangle$, where S is a *set* of agent IDs. Before a state is passed from an agent ag_1 to another agent ag_2, ag_1 adds ag_2's ID to S if S does not contain it (i.e. extension to the TH and TC rules). For example, let $A \rightsquigarrow_1 B \rightsquigarrow_2 C \rightsquigarrow_3 D \rightsquigarrow_4 B \rightsquigarrow_5 C \rightsquigarrow_6 A$ be a sequence of state passing between four agents, then at the end $S = \{A, B, C, D\}$:

- when a new agent joins, nothing is changed as the TC rule ensures that the agent will check Δ and Δ^* for consistency before a solved state is obtained;
- when an agent ag leaves, (1) all the remaining agents will *discard* its computations (including choice points) for the states whose S contains ag; (2) the agent who added ag's ID to S will try to send the state to another suitable helper (if any), or backtrack from that point. In the example, assuming that C leaves, then D, B and A will discard the computations they have done after $\rightsquigarrow_3$, and B will backtrack from $\rightsquigarrow_2$.

Any agent that has not received the state can leave without affecting the reasoning process. Open networks suffer, however, of some drawbacks. The completeness of the proof procedure may be affected: an agent may join the system "too late" in the reasoning process and miss the opportunity to help others (it was not there when an agent asked for help for a non-abducible that it knows). The proof procedure may not terminate: an agent keeps cycling between joining the system, modifying the state, and then leaving the system. Special restriction in the implementation could be imposed that forbid *buggy* agents from joining and leaving too many times would be needed in order to avoid such problems.

8   Implementation

A proof of concept DAREC prototype system has been implemented in YAP-Prolog [3], which provides TCP communication API and constraint satisfaction solver libraries. The prototype incorporates the extensions discussed in Section 7. In order to benchmark the system, we have also developed a test case generator, which takes a series of adjustable input parameters, such as the total number of agents and the average size of each agent's logic program, and then randomly generates a set of logic programs. Each of the logic programs can then be imported by an agent, and arbitrarily selected queries can be submitted to the agents. During benchmarking, we recorded the number of messages exchanged between agents and the time taken for computing the queries. Empirical results (e.g. 5 agents in total, each of which has about 250 rules, and the average number of conditions in each rule is 10, where on average 3 of them are global/shared

---

[3] http://www.dcc.fc.up.pt/~vsc/Yap/

predicates) showed that for two third of the tested queries, the distributed abductive algorithm (with *delay-interaction* strategy) computes the answers about 26%∼517% faster than a centralised computation (i.e. single agent abductive reasoning with the merged logic programs). This was expected as concurrent computation was performed during distributed reasoning. We also ran the distributed algorithm with and without the delay-interaction strategy. The experiments showed that the former computes the answers about 130%∼2996% faster and has about 114%∼2871% less exchanged messages than the latter (note that execution without interaction delays is like that of the DARE algorithm [14]).

9   Conclusion and Future Work

In this paper we have presented DAREC, the first distributed abductive reasoning system with arithmetic constraints support. DAREC allows application-dependent agent interaction strategies to be adopted for reducing inter-agent communications, and facilitates concurrent computation to be performed during collaborative reasoning. The system (with simple extensions) is suitable for a large class of knowledge-based distributed problem solving problems, including ambient intelligent systems here briefly described. As future work, we will perform more benchmarking to investigate how different goal selection strategies, agent selection strategies and agent interaction strategies may impact the system performance in different applications. The current version of the DAREC system does not deal with communication failures, as it simply assumes that communication channel and agents are reliable. However, in practice such assumption may not always be applicable. We have also developed a *speculative abductive reasoning* framework, which has an answer revision mechanism for coping with communication breakdowns during a distributed reasoning task [13]. As future work we will incorporate the speculative extension into the DAREC system, and perform benchmarking.

References

1. Alberti, M., Gavanelli, M., Lamma, E., Mello, P., Torroni, P.: The SCIFF abductive proof-procedure. In: Bandini, S., Manzoni, S. (eds.) AI*IA 2005. LNCS (LNAI), vol. 3673, pp. 135–147. Springer, Heidelberg (2005)
2. Ciampolini, A., Lamma, E., Mello, P., Toni, F., Torroni, P.: Cooperation and competition in ALIAS: A logic framework for agents that negotiate. Annals of Mathematics and Artificial Intelligence 37(1-2), 65–91 (2003)
3. Ciampolini, A., Lamma, E., Mello, P., Torroni, P.: LAILA: A language for coordinating abductive reasoning among logic agents. Computer Language 27(4), 137–161 (2001)
4. Clark, K.L.: Negation as failure. In: Logic and Data Bases, pp. 293–322 (1977)
5. Craven, R., Lobo, J., Ma, J., Russo, A., Lupu, E.C., Bandara, A.K.: Expressive policy analysis with enhanced system dynamicity. In: Proceedings of the ACM Symposium on Information, Computer & Communication Security, pp. 239–250 (2009)

6. Denecker, M., De Schreye, D.: SLDNFA: An abductive procedure for abductive logic programs. Journal of Logic Programming 34(2), 111–167 (1998)
7. Endriss, U., Mancarella, P., Sadri, F., Terreni, G., Toni, F.: The CIFF proof procedure for abductive logic programming with constraints. In: Alferes, J.J., Leite, J. (eds.) JELIA 2004. LNCS (LNAI), vol. 3229, pp. 31–43. Springer, Heidelberg (2004)
8. Fung, T.H., Kowalski, R.A.: The IFF proof procedure for abductive logic programming. Journal of Logic Programming 33(2), 151–165 (1997)
9. Kakas, A., Mancarella, P.: Generalised stable models: A semantics for abduction. In: Aiello, L.C. (ed.) Proceedings of the European Conference on Artificial Intelligence, ECAI 1990, Stockholm, Sweden, pp. 385–391. Pitman Publishing (1990)
10. Kakas, A.C., Kowalski, R.A., Toni, F.: Abductive logic programming. Journal of Logic and Computation 2(6), 719–770 (1992)
11. Kakas, A.C., Mancarella, P.: Abductive logic programming. In: Proceedings of the Workshop Logic Programming and Non-Monotonic Logic, pp. 49–61 (1990)
12. Kakas, A.C., Michael, A., Mourlas, C.: ACLP: Abductive constraint logic programming. Journal of Logic Programming 44(1-3), 129–177 (2000)
13. Ma, J., Broda, K., Goebel, R., Hosobe, H., Russo, A., Satoh, K.: Speculative abductive reasoning for hierarchical agent systems. In: Dix, J., Leite, J., Governatori, G., Jamroga, W. (eds.) CLIMA XI. LNCS, vol. 6245, pp. 49–64. Springer, Heidelberg (2010)
14. Ma, J., Russo, A., Broda, K., Clark, K.: DARE: a system for distributed abductive reasoning. Autonomous Agents and Multi-Agent Systems 16(3), 271–297 (2008)
15. Van Nuffelen, B.: Abductive Constraint Logic Programming: Implementation and Applications. PhD thesis, Department of Computer Science, K.U.Leuven (2004)
16. Shanahan, M.: An abductive event calculus planner. Journal of Logic Programming 44(1-3), 207–240 (2000)
17. Shanahan, M.: Perception as abduction: Turning sensor data into meaningful representation. Cognitive Science 29(1), 103–134 (2005)
18. Teusink, F.: Three-valued completion for abductive logic programs. Theoretical Computer Science 165(1), 171–200 (1996)
19. Verbaeten, S.: Termination analysis for abductive general logic programs. In: Proceedings of the International Conference on Logic Programming, pp. 365–379 (1999)
20. Wallace, M.: Constraint logic programming. In: Kakas, A.C., Sadri, F. (eds.) Computational Logic: Logic Programming and Beyond. LNCS (LNAI), vol. 2407, pp. 512–532. Springer, Heidelberg (2002)

Understanding Permissions through Graphical Norms

Nir Oren[1], Madalina Croitoru[2], Simon Miles[3], and Michael Luck[3]

[1] Department of Computing Science, University of Aberdeen, Scotland
n.oren@abdn.ac.uk
[2] LIRMM, University Montpellier II, France
croitoru@lirmm.fr
[3] Department of Informatics, King's College London, United Kingdom
{simon.miles,michael.luck}@kcl.ac.uk

Abstract. Norm-aware agents are able to reason about the obligations, permissions and prohibitions that affect their operation. While much work has focused on the creation of such norm-aware agents, less effort has been placed on enabling system designers and users to understand the *interactions between* norms. Providing designers with such an understanding can aid in eliminating redundant norms and errors in norm specifications, while enhancing user understanding can increase the trust placed in a system. In this paper we make use of conceptual graph based semantics to provide a graphical representation that is designed to enhance the understanding of the interactions between different types of norms. More specifically, permissions derogate obligations and prohibitions, and the latter two norm types interact by conflicting with each other. Tracking these interactions in standard symbolic norm representations is difficult given a large set of norms, yet our work allows for the easy understanding of whether a permission causes obligation or prohibition derogation.

1 Introduction

Understanding and controlling the behaviour of agents in open multi-agent systems is, as has often been asserted, a particularly hard problem. The natural autonomy of the agents, and the unpredictability derived from allowing agents from different sources to be included in an open system, suggests that there must be some means to encourage beneficial outcomes from such systems. *Norms* have been proposed as a mechanism by which agents can have some expectations of the behaviour of others while still retaining autonomy of action. Specifically, norms, in the form of obligations, prohibitions and permissions, state what is to be expected from agents without the assumption that those expectations will always be met — norms can be violated.

However, even where norms are effectively enforced, and individually well understood, this does not mean that a system as a whole will have predictable behaviour. In part, this is because multiple norms can interact, collectively placing complex expectations on agents. In addition, individual norms are often applicable only in given circumstances, rather than over the course of the system lifetime, so examining norms in isolation from a running system may not help to understand the actual exhibited behaviour. Combining these two points, we may observe an agent apparently violating an

A. Omicini, S. Sardina, and W. Vasconcelos (Eds.): DALT 2010, LNAI 6619, pp. 167–184, 2011.

obligation, but actually being exempted from that obligation by a *permission* that applies in those particular circumstances. In consequence, we require a means to interpret the effect of multiple interacting norms on an agent during system execution.

The final, and possibly largest, obstacle to interpreting how a multi-agent system is being affected by multiple norms is the form of the norms themselves. In order to correctly reason about and act on norms, such norms must be encoded in some unambiguous form. To this end, most approaches consider norms as logical statements or abstract data structures using encoded domain-based knowledge. However, from the perspective of a user, particularly a non-technical user, attempting to understand how a system is being affected by interacting norms, this is an entirely unhelpful format for explanation.

In order to overcome these obstacles, we propose a graph-based representation of norms that must satisfy a number of requirements, including being easily understandable by non-experts. Visual representations can aid designers in simplifying a complex set of norms, and can help users interpret the status of a normative system; our focus in this paper lies in supporting these aspects relating to aid for designers and users. Critically, therefore, our representation must be *semantics preserving* in that there must be a sound and complete translation between the textual and graphical norm representations. In this sense, operations on norms should also be applicable to their graphical representation. By assigning a tree structure to norms, we can perform norm interpretation through tree path traversal, and the problem of reasoning about the status of a norm (that is, whether it is violated or complied with) becomes one of detecting homomorphisms in our graph structures. More generally, this work enables both the structure of a norm and its underlying representation to be illustrated graphically, so that norm reasoning translates directly into operations on the graphical representation, making our representation suitable for all stages of knowledge representation and reasoning.

In this paper, we describe an approach to aiding users in understanding how interacting norms affect the behaviour of agents in a running system. With regard to norm interaction, we focus on a particular issue: *derogation* [13], whereby permissions interact with obligations to exempt agents from some of their obliged behaviour under particular circumstances. For example, consider an obligation on a mechanic to repair a car by some specific date. If the car is not repaired by that date, then the mechanic has violated the obligation. However, if a permission has been given to the mechanic to repair the car by some later date, then the mechanic is able to ignore (i.e. not comply with) the original obligation without being considered in violation of it. The permission has thus *derogated*, or temporarily cancelled, the obligation. However, if the permission is removed, then the mechanic is viewed as having violated the original obligation.

To allow derogation to be detected and understood within a running system, we build on several pieces of work. First, we use a norm model that makes explicit the circumstances under which norms apply [10], in such a way that we can detect at runtime which norms may interact. Second, we encode this norm model in a graph based representation (a tree) in which nodes at each level map to one part of the corresponding condition for that level in the norm. Last, we employ *conceptual graphs* [11] as a means of representing norm conditions graphically, and provide a mapping from the norm model to this representation. Conceptual graphs have a formal semantics, and their graph based representation makes them well suited to depicting information that has structure and interconnections. Moreover, labelled graph homomorphism between two conceptual graphs has been shown to be sound and complete with respect to set theoretic semantics for a subset of First Order Logic. This ensures the semantic foundations of our graph based reasoning and, by colouring the graphs, we can also show how the norms' effects and interactions change as the system runs. In earlier work [3], we described how individual obligations can be represented graphically, and how the status of these obligations can be determined. Here, we extend this basic work to take into account the possibility of permissive norms, and show how interactions between norms (namely a permission derogating an obligation) can be detected and visualised.

The remainder of this paper is structured as follows. In the next section, we provide an overview of our normative model, after which we provide a brief introduction to conceptual graphs. We then demonstrate how the normative model can be encoded with conceptual graphs. The problem of permission derogation is tackled in Section 4.2, after which we discuss related and future work.

2   Permissions and the Normative Model

Norms make different kinds of specification on a target agent's behaviour. For example, some norms specify what an agent should do (*obligations*), some what it should not do (*prohibitions*), and some what it may do (*permissions*); our model focuses on *obligations* and *permissions*. While obligations are well understood, permissions have been defined very differently by different approaches in the past, and it is worth highlighting what we intend by them. One distinction made is between weak and strong permissions [1]. Here, *weak permissions* are those that exist, in effect, by default (that is, they are what one is free to do anyway), and are typically not considered to be norms. Conversely, *strong permissions* are those issued by some authority that may not be overridden by a lower level authority (in an institutional sense). Alternatively, a permission may also be expressed as an explicit exception to an obligation [1]; by taking advantage of a such a permission, what is otherwise considered a violation of an obligation is no longer considered a violation. It is this latter view of permissions that we adopt here.

Understanding whether permissions have derogated obligations requires an unambiguous model in which we can evaluate whether each such norm applies in a given system state. A complete formal description of our normative model is available elsewhere [10]; in this paper, we outline the model, illustrating it with an example (adopted from [3], but extended for this paper), in order that we can show how it is subsequently used for computing permissions.

Consider the situation in which an agent *Alice* takes her car to a repair shop. The repair shop provides a guarantee to its customers that any car will be repaired within seven days of arriving at the shop. Clearly, the repair shop has an obligation upon it, whenever a car arrives, to repair it within seven days. Furthermore, once this obligation is fulfilled, the specific instance of this obligation is lifted, and the repair shop no longer needs to repair the car. However, if a car is not yet repaired, the obligation remains on the repair shop as long as the car is not repaired (even after seven days have passed). Now, if a power failure occurs, the repair shop need not honour its original guarantee, but will instead have an extra week to repair the car. Here, there is a second norm, which provides a permission allowing the repair shop to temporarily ignore its obligation in a specific situation.

From this example, we can associate a number of attributes with a norm. First, norms have a *type*. In our example, we refer to an *obligation* and a *permission*, but norms can also impose prohibitions. Norms also have an *activation condition*, identifying the situation in which an obligation, permission or prohibition is imposed. In our example, the obligation's activation condition triggers when a car arrives at the repair shop, while the permission triggers when a power failure occurs. Clearly, obligations and prohibitions also impose some constraint on the entity affected by the norm. We refer to this attribute as the *normative condition*. In our example, the obligation's normative condition is the requirement that the car be repaired within seven days. For a *permission*, the normative condition identifies the state of affairs that can hold without an obligation or permission being considered *violated*. In the example, this allows the car not to be repaired. Now, at some point in time, an obligation (or permission) ceases to affect its target. In the example, once the car is repaired, the shop is no longer obliged to repair it (in the case of the permission, once 14 days have passed, the permission is no longer in force). Norms thus impose an *expiration condition*. Finally, norms affect specific entities within a system. Thus, *Alice* is not obliged to repair her car within seven days, but the repair shop is obliged to do so. A norm must thus identify a set of *norm targets* that are affected by it. Both the obligation and permission within the example have the repair shop as their target.

It is important to distinguish between the guarantee that the repair shop makes to repair a car within seven days of its arrival, and the obligation imposed upon it to repair a specific car (for example, the car belonging to *Alice*) once it arrives. We refer to the former as an *abstract norm* which, under a specific set of circumstances (such as the arrival of a car at the repair shop) becomes an *instantiated norm*. This then obliges, permits, or prohibits its target from *seeing to it that* some state of affairs holds. Clearly, an abstract norm can be instantiated multiple times (perhaps simultaneously). For example, multiple cars may arrive at the repair shop in one day. If a power failure occurs during that day, the permission to repair the cars later applies to all of these cars, but not to cars arriving later. Thus, instantiated norms are handled individually. In the case of an obligation, one norm may be violated (if the associated car is not repaired in time), while another may be discharged (if the associated car is repaired).

More formally, permissions and obligations refer to states and events in an environment, in turn represented by some logical predicate language $\mathcal{L}$, such as first order logic. We represent a norm as a tuple of the form:

$$\langle NormType,$$
$$NormActivation,$$
$$NormCondition,$$
$$NormExpiration,$$
$$NormTarget \rangle$$

where (*i*) $NormType \in \{obligation, permission\}$; and (*ii*) $NormActivation$, $NormCondition$, $NormExpiration$ and $NormTarget$ are all well formed formulae (*wff*) in $\mathcal{L}$. Thus, the following abstract norm represents the requirement that a repair shop must repair a car within seven days of its arrival at the shop[1]:

$$\begin{aligned}
\mathbf{repair} : \quad &\langle obligation, \\
&arrivesAtRepairShop(X, Car, T_1), \\
repaired(Car) \vee (currentTime(CurrentTime) &\wedge before(CurrentTime, T_1 + 7days)), \\
&repaired(Car), \\
&repairShop(X)\rangle
\end{aligned}$$

Similarly, the permission to delay the repair of a car can be written as follows:

$$\begin{aligned}
\mathbf{delay} : \quad &\langle permission, \\
&powerFailure(X, T_1), \\
&\neg repaired(C), \\
currentTime(CurrentTime) \wedge before(&CurrentTime, T_1 + 14days), \\
&repairShop(X)\rangle
\end{aligned}$$

For simplicity of presentation (and with some abuse of notation), we mix events and states within norms. A more complex underlying language, such as the Event Calculus [6], would allow us to disambiguate these concepts.

An instantiated norm is created from an abstract norm when the latter's activation condition evaluates to true (subject to further constraints as discussed in [10]). This involves copying the abstract norm and binding the new norm's variables to the values that caused the activation condition to be true [10], which offers a logical semantics for instantiation and processing of norms.

Now, if we assume that Alice's car (represented by the constant c_1) arrives at Bob's repair shop at time 12, the predicate $arrivesAtRepairShop(bob, c_1, 12)$ evaluates to true. This predicate is the abstract **repair** norm's activation condition, and when instantiated, we obtain the following instantiated norm:

$$\begin{aligned}
\mathbf{repair'} : \quad &\langle obligation, \\
&arrivesAtRepairShop(bob, c_1, 12), \\
repaired(c_1) \vee (currentTime(CurrentTime) &\wedge before(CurrentTime, 19)), \\
&repaired(c_1), \\
&repairShop(bob)\rangle
\end{aligned}$$

It should be noted that an instantiated norm can still contain variables (for example, $CurrentTime$ in **repair'**). These variables are bound, as appropriate, to identify whether the norm's expiration or normative conditions have been met. For example, the $CurrentTime$ variable is bound, whenever the norm is evaluated, to the system's current time. However, an instantiated norm's activation condition is always ground.

A norm's status (instantiated or abstract, violated, expired, etc.) is monitored by a *normative environment*, and can be referred to by other norms. (Further details can be found in [8], though space constraints limit further elaboration here.) For example,

---

[1] Unless otherwise stated, we make use of Prolog notation within our formulae: variables begin with an uppercase letter, and constants with a lowercase letter.

a norm stating that "If the car has not been repaired after seven days, the client is permitted to request a free repair", could be written as:

$$\langle permission,$$
$$violated(\textbf{repair}),$$
$$request(client(C), repairShop(X), repairCost(Car, 0)),$$
$$false,$$
$$client(C)\rangle$$

Here, the *violated* predicate refers to the norm's status, evaluating to true only if there is an instantiated **repair** norm whose normative condition is false, *and* there is no *permission* that allows this normative condition to be false. The *request function* represents a primitive communicative action, from the customer C to the repair shop, asking for a free repair.

In this way, permissions interact with obligations by allowing the obligation's normative condition to be false without the obligation being deemed to be violated. Importantly, when there is a large number of norms, the interactions between them can make it extremely difficult for humans to determine those situations in which there are such permissions. Our aim in this paper is to show how we may use conceptual graphs to enhance human understanding of executing normative systems.

3   Representing Norms as Conceptual Graphs

3.1   Conceptual Graphs

Conceptual graphs were introduced by Sowa (cf. [12]) as a diagrammatic system of logic with the purpose "to express meaning in a form that is logically precise, humanly readable and computationally tractable" [12]. In this paper, we use the term "conceptual graphs" to denote the family of formalisms rooted in Sowa's work, and enriched and extended with a graph-based approach (as in [2]).

A conceptual graph (CG) encodes knowledge within two graph-based representations. First is the basic ontology or vocabulary utilised by the CG, known as its *support*, and composed of hierarchies of concepts and relations. The support is visualised via Hasse diagrams, for drawing a partial order, representing a specialisation relation, $t' \leq t$, stating that t' is a specialisation of t. Figure 1 illustrates the concept hierarchy used in the car repair example, and Figure 2 illustrates the relation hierarchy. As can be seen within Figure 2, relations are organised by arity.

Second, we encode all other knowledge in a graph labelled with nodes corresponding to concepts and relations. Edges link concept nodes to relation nodes, labelled by types of the support (also called the vocabulary). Concept nodes are drawn as rectangles and relation nodes as ovals. An order is imposed on the edges, corresponding to the *k-ary* relation captured by the relation node, by numbering the edges from 1 to k. Figure 3 shows this type of *basic graph* (BG), expressing the fact that a car arrived at the repair shop at a certain time. The $*$ character represents a generic variable.

CGs have an associated set theoretic first order logic semantics, defined by a mapping Φ [12]. CGs are equivalent to the positive, conjunctive and existential fragment of first

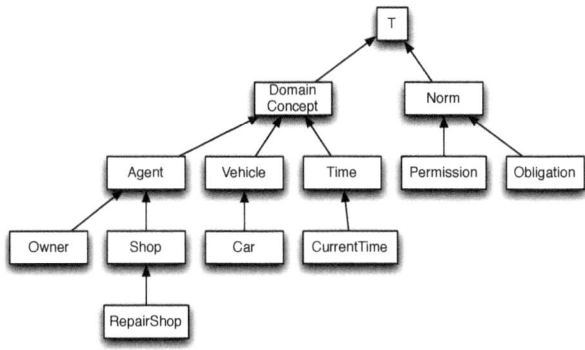

Fig. 1. Conceptual graph support: the concept hierarchy

order logic. More recent work has extended the basic CG formalism; for example, [9] introduces some types of negation to CGs.

The fundamental theorem of conceptual graphs allows us to translate between first order logic and conceptual graphs. More specifically, the fundamental theorem states that, given two basic graphs G and H, there is a homomorphism from G to H if and only if $\Phi(G)$ is a *semantic consequence* of $\Phi(H)$ and $\Phi(V)$ where V is the vocabulary. This result demonstrates the soundness and completeness of BG homomorphism with respect to entailment in the subset of first order logic mentioned above. The consequence of this theorem is that a homomorphism between two graphs is, in effect, an explanation as to why logical subsumption takes place. Since such homomorphisms can be represented graphically, this allows for visual representations of logical subsumption. Such a graphical representation of an explanation is a unique feature of CGs, and an alternative logic-based graphical representation language would have to include a separate explanation layer in addition to the representation layer itself.

3.2 From Norms to Conceptual Graphs

By encoding structured knowledge graphically, CGs can provide a way to depict and interpret the states that norms go through; that is, whether they have been activated, violated, fulfilled, or expired. Then, by connecting depictions of permissions and obligations, we can understand whether an obligation has truly been violated, or whether a permission derogates this under current circumstances.

In modelling norms with CGs, one complexity we face is that norms can sometimes be fulfilled by multiple different actions, events or states. Intuitively, if these conditions are separated by disjunctions they can be evaluated using a tree-like structure by the norm environment reasoner. We thus define a structure, referred to as a *norm tree*, with every level of the tree corresponding to one type of condition in the norm. Moreover, at every level, we break the condition into a disjunction of positive first order logic conjunctions. This representation ensures that the normative reasoning is sound and complete with respect to a particular kind of path finding in the norm tree (finding at least one satisfied level node). In what follows, we assume that a norm's *target* is a

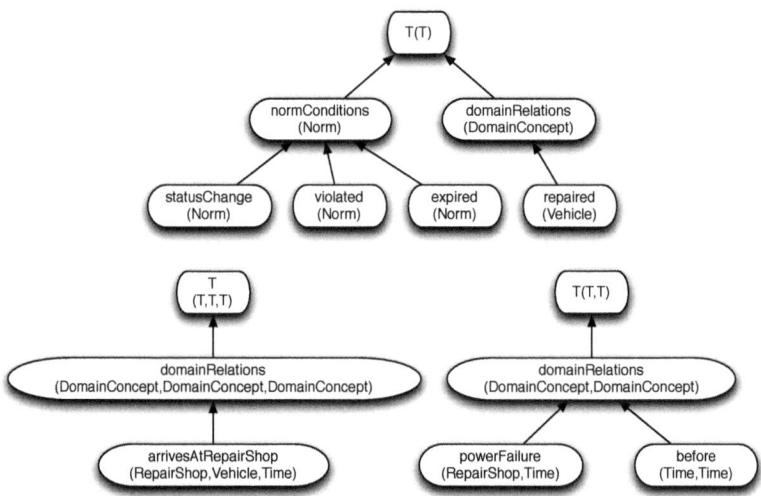

Fig. 2. Conceptual graph support: the relation hierarchy

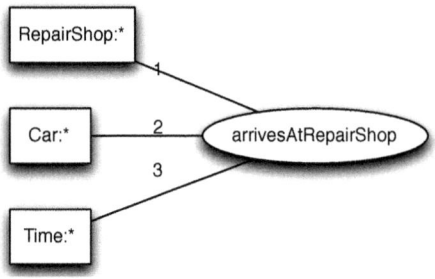

Fig. 3. A generic basic conceptual graph fact

conjunctive formula (and can thus be represented as a CG). Now, when instantiated, a norm's activation condition becomes fixed, and its normative and expiration conditions are used to determine its status. We now proceed to define the norm tree in more detail.

A norm tree represents both abstract and instantiated norms. Its root is associated with the entire norm (more specifically, its *type* and *target*), while the remaining levels represent different portions of the norm. Nodes in the second level are associated with the activation condition, nodes in the third level are associated with the normative condition, and nodes in the fourth level with the expiration condition. Each of the nodes within the tree has an associated CG representation of its content, as illustrated in Figure 4.

Given this, different branches of the norm tree can be used to represent disjunctive conditions within a specific norm attribute. Thus, for example, a norm with a normative condition of the form $a \vee b$ would have two branches at the norm tree's third level. As indicated above, we assume that the norm target parameter consists of a conjunctive

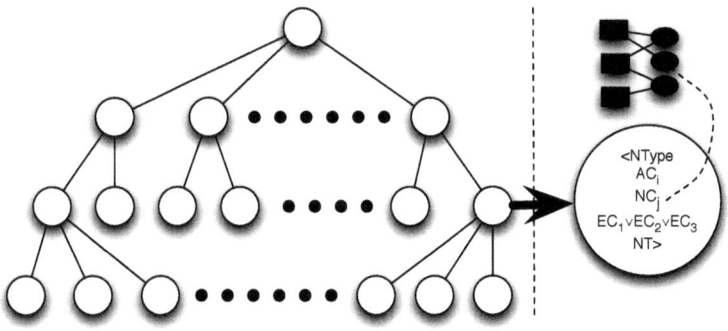

Fig. 4. A conceptual representation of a norm tree

combination of predicates (in other words, a norm is associated with a specific group of individuals rather than applying to some subgroup *or* another), and that all other parameters (except for norm type), may contain disjunctions. In this way, in order to represent the norm as a norm tree, we transform all its attributes into disjunctive normal form, to get a norm represented as follows:

$$\langle Type, \bigvee_{i=1,a} AC_i, \bigvee_{j=1,c} NC_j, \bigvee_{k=1,e} EC_k, NT \rangle \tag{1}$$

where AC_i, NC_j, EC_k and NT are all conjunctive first order formulae so that, for example, $AC = \bigvee_{i=1,a} AC_i$. Furthermore, by assuming negation as failure we can ensure that all of these formulae are positive (by introducing an explicit predicate for negation), and can therefore represent each as a conceptual graph, defined on some given support (i.e. the domain ontology).

Given a norm N in disjunctive normal form as in (1) above, we define its norm tree as a tree for which each node contains a norm and is labelled by a CG as follows:

1. The root node of the tree contains norm N and is labelled by a CG identifying the norm's type and targets (i.e. $Type$ and NT).
2. The root node has a child nodes (i.e. nodes at level one), where, for $i = 1 \ldots a$, child node i is labelled with the CG representing AC_i and contains a norm N^i of the form:

$$\langle Type, AC_i, \bigvee_{j=1,c} NC_j, \bigvee_{k=1,e} EC_k, NT \rangle$$

3. Each node at level two, which is a child of N^i, and is labelled with a CG representing NC_j, contains a norm N^{ij} for $j = 1 \ldots c$ of the form:

$$\langle Type, AC_i, NC_j, \bigvee_{k=1,e} EC_k, NT \rangle$$

4. Each node at level three, which is a child of N^{ij}, and is labelled with a CG representing EC_k, contains a norm N^{ijk} for $k = 1 \ldots e$ of the form:

$$\langle Type, AC_i, NC_j, EC_k, NT \rangle$$

3.3   Example

Consider the norm utilised in our car repair example, which obliges the repair shop to repair a car within seven days of its arrival. The left hand side of Figure 5 illustrates the norm tree that is associated with this norm. For simplicity, we have ignored the norm target parameter, assuming that it is present in the root node. The dotted line between the nodes and the CGs identify which nodes are labelled with which CGs. It should be noted that the *function* relation, found in the right hand normative condition node, is used to compute whether the current time is greater than 7 days from the time the car arrived for repair. This is used to simplify the CG shown in the figure; within a complete system, this CG would make use of an arithmetic function to add 7 days to the car's arrival time, and then make use of the an additional function or predicate to compare the current time to the deadline and determine whether the car has been repaired in time.

The right hand side of Figure 5 illustrates the norm tree for the permission found in our example. Since no disjunctions exist within the activation, expiration and normative conditions, this norm tree has no branches.

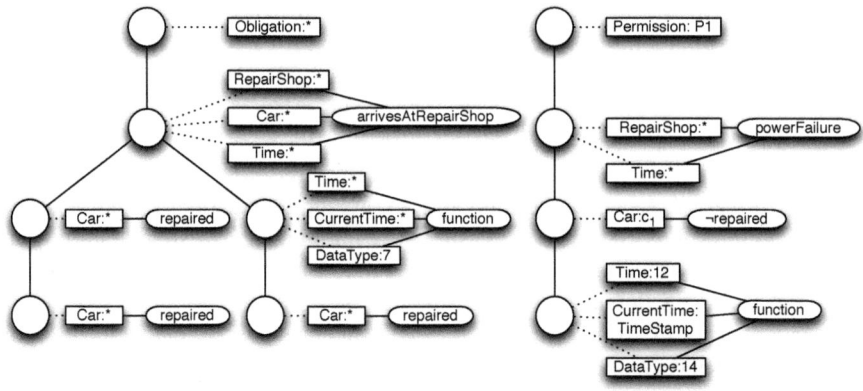

Fig. 5. The norm tree for the abstract obligation norm (left) and abstract permission norm (right) found in the repairshop example

4   Permissions in Conceptual Graph Norms

Having described how norms can be represented as norm trees, we now turn our attention to computing the status of a norm. In [10], we defined a number of different kinds of norm status, such as identifying whether a norm is instantiated, being complied with, expiring, etc. Many of these can be computed by checking for the existence of projections between the facts in the environment and the conceptual graph annotations of the norm tree. However, determining whether some obligation or prohibition n is violated requires examining not only the norm tree for n, but also any permissions that allow for this situation to occur. In this section, we describe how a norm is instantiated and how norms can be evaluated by examining only its norm tree, and then we turn our attention to norm violation and the interactions between obligations, prohibitions and permissions.

4.1 Projections on CG Norms

So far we have described only how abstract norms can be represented as norm trees, but we can illustrate how norms are instantiated by examining what occurs in our car repair example when there is a power failure at the repair shop. In such a situation, the new fact $powerFailure(bob, 12)$ is added to the knowledge base, stating that there is a power failure at Bob's repair shop at time 12, which delays the repair by 7 days (extending from 7 to 14).

The new fact projects onto the norm's activation condition CG annotation. This mapping thus instantiates some of the generic nodes in the various CGs, obtaining the instantiated norm illustrated in Figure 6. For clarity, we colour CG nodes grey within instantiated norms and white within abstract norms. Note that the norm's type now refers to a specific instance of norm N, namely $P1$. Note, too, that multiple instantiated versions of the same abstract norm can exist in the system simultaneously. However, each of these will have a different set of variable bindings, and thus a different CG associated with the norm tree.

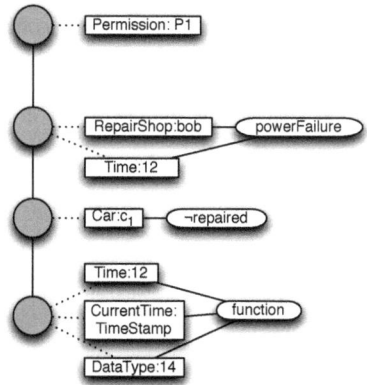

Fig. 6. The norm tree for an instantiated norm found in the repairshop example

Similarly, we can evaluate norms in relation to their satisfaction or expiration, for example. Consider the norm tree shown in Figure 7, containing a mixture of black and grey nodes, the latter of which correspond to nodes that have been satisfied or, in other words, to nodes for which there is a projection between the environment (on the right of Figure 7) and the corresponding CG annotation. Black nodes are those that are not satisfied[2]. Thus, for example, there is no projection between the node representing the expiration condition (which states that car c_1 is repaired) and the CG on the right of the

---

[2] It should be noted that the example of Figure 7 is very simple, and was selected for its ease of understanding. It does not demonstrate the inferential power of CGs.

figure, which represents the facts in the knowledge base. If, at some later point, the car is repaired, these black nodes will instead become grey. From the colour, we can infer that the norm is instantiated, its norm condition is satisfied (as there is at least one node at the norm condition level that is not black), and it has not expired.

4.2   Computing Violation with Permissions

One critical norm aspect which cannot be computed directly form the norm's norm tree is whether the norm is violated or not. This is because of the way in which we treat permissions.

In [1], the authors point out that permissions can be viewed as exceptions to obligations and prohibitions, and this is how permissions are handled by our model. Thus, for example, given an obligation on the repair shop to repair a car within 7 days, a permission to instead repair the car within 14 days *derogates* the obligation. While the obligation may not be complied with (because the car may not be repaired within 7 days), the repair shop will not be in violation of the obligation unless 14 days have expired.

Permissions thus do not exist in isolation, but instead act as exceptions to other types of norms. This means that in evaluating whether an obligation or prohibition is violated, one must consider not only the possibly violated norm itself, but also the permissions present in the system. Given a large normative system, identifying the appropriate permission that may cause a violation not to occur can be challenging. Our visual approach can help overcome the cognitive load imposed by this problem by highlighting the appropriate permission(s) preventing a norm from being violated.

If a power failure occurred at time 14, then the (instantiated) permission allowing Bob to repair car c_1 within 14 days (i.e. by day 28) is written as follows:

$$\langle permission,$$
$$powerFailure(bob, 14),$$
$$\neg repaired(c_1),$$
$$currentTime(CurrentTime) \wedge before(CurrentTime, 28days),$$
$$repairShop(bob)\rangle$$

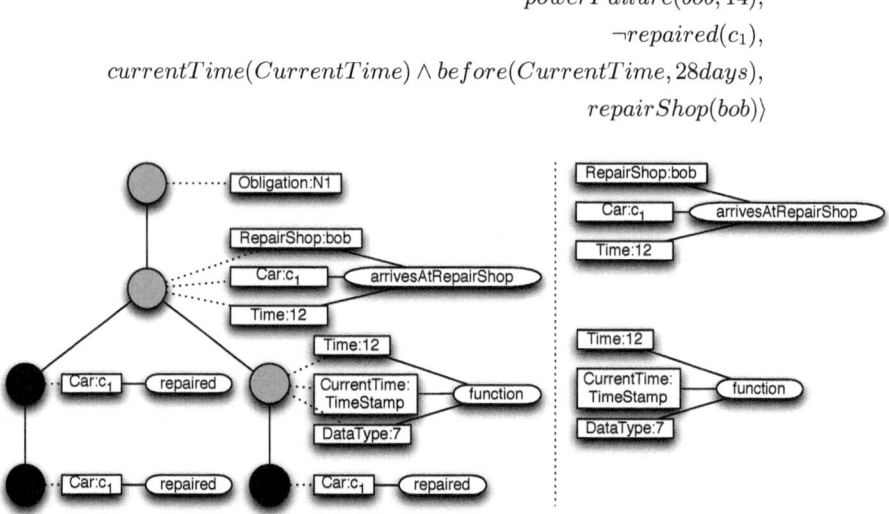

Fig. 7. A norm tree evaluated according to the knowledge base shown on the right

Conceptually, in order to determine whether an instantiated and un-expired permission derogates an obligation or prohibition, we must check whether the permission's norm condition is *consistent* with the obligation. If it is not consistent, in the sense that the permission allows the negation of the obligation, then derogation takes place, otherwise the permission does not affect the obligation. In our example, $\neg repaired(c_1)$ is inconsistent when evaluated against $repaired(c_1)$, and the permission thus derogates the obligation. This check for consistency thus lies at the heart of our work. Clearly, such a consistency check requires the ability to represent and reason about the negation of a relation. However, the standard CG formalism is unable to represent such negated relations, and we make use of an extension to CGs first proposed by Mugnier and Leclère to show how the consistency check can be performed from within the CG formalism. Their approach computes the *completed* form of a conceptual graph G (essentially, adding in explicitly negated relations that were previously implicitly negated by omission); that is, the CG that "defined over a support S, is the unique CG obtained from G by adding all possible negative relations" [9, Definition 9]. Thus if we don't know that a car has been repaired, we now explicitly state that it has not been repaired. Due to space constraints, rather than provide full details of this approach, we refer the reader to the original work by Mugnier and Leclère.

Given this completed CG, if the permission's normative condition cannot be projected into the CG (because the car has in fact been repaired, for example), the permission derogates the obligation (or rather, that node in the norm tree for which the CG projection is unsuccessful, which will not be coloured black). The permission, and relevant concepts and relations that derogate the permission can then be displayed to the user to explain why the norm is not in violation. If, on the other hand, the permission is not relevant to the obligation, then a violation occurs, and the violated norm can again be highlighted in order to show the user its status. Given a norm tree for an (instantiated, unexpired) obligation N, the norm it represents is thus violated if and only if all of its nodes at the normative condition level are coloured black.

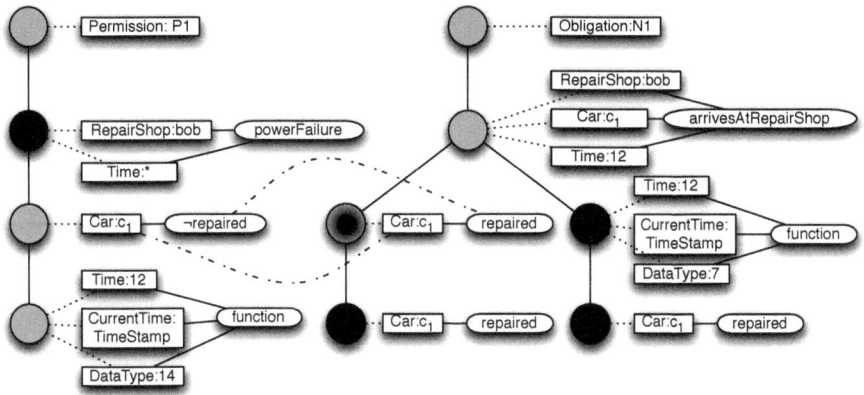

Fig. 8. A norm tree for a permission (left), and obligation (right) evaluated according to some knowledge, showing how the permission derogates the obligation

Figure 8 illustrates the derogation of an obligation by a permission. Dashed lines indicate links between the concepts and relations found in the two nodes, and the normative condition node marked with a grey node with a black centre in the obligation indicates that the node, while evaluating to false, is derogated by a permission. From the figure, it is clear that the obligation is not violated. Note that the permission's activation condition node is black. We assume that while a power failure occurred in the past (instantiating the permission), there is currently no power failure.

4.3   Case Study

To illustrate the overall framework, we consider an additional scenario in which rapid response medical units must perform some duties when an emergency situation occurs. These units have the following obligation:

> "If a state of emergency has been declared, a rescue unit is obliged to travel to a casualty, and then pick them up, or provide them with medicine until they have no more space and are out of medicines".

Formally, this obligation is represented as follows:

$$\langle obligation,$$
$$stateOfEmergency() \wedge casualty(C),$$
$$travel(U,C) \wedge (collect(U,C) \vee medicate(U,C)),$$
$$noSpace(U) \wedge noMedicine(U),$$
$$rescueUnit(U)\rangle$$

The disjunctive normal form of the obligation's normative condition is:

$$(travel(U,C) \wedge collect(U,C)) \vee (travel(U,C) \wedge medicate(U,C))$$

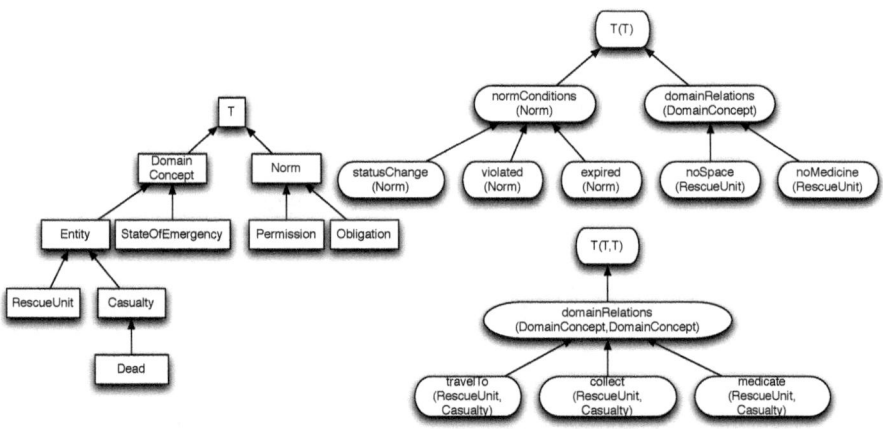

Fig. 9. The CG support composed of the concept hierarchy (left) and relation hierarchies (right)

Given this, we assume a very simple permission representing casualty triage: "If the casualty is dead, there is no need to medicate them". Formally, this is as follows:

$$\langle permission, dead(C), \neg medicate(U, C), false, rescueUnit(U) \rangle$$

In order to construct the norm tree, we begin by identifying the concepts and relations found in this scenario, where the concepts include $StateOfEmergency$, $Casualty$, $RescueUnit$, $Dead$, and the relations include $travel$, $collect$, $medicate$, $noSpace$ and $noMedicine$. These concepts and relations yield the support displayed in Figure 9, and the abstract norms illustrated in Figure 10.

Now assume that a state of emergency exists, and that a dead casualty $c1$ has been detected by a rescue unit $r1$. Furthermore, $r1$ has space and medicine available. Given that the rescue unit has not travelled to the casualty, collected it, or provided medicine, is it in violation of its obligation?

In order to determine this, we must compute the complete CG of the instantiated obligation's normative condition. Figure 11 shows the completed form of the graph for both the left and right hand branches of the instantiated *obligation* norm tree's normative condition nodes. The dotted lines within Figure 11 illustrate that the *permission*'s normative condition projects into the obligation's right hand branch normative condition. However, no such projection is possible into the left hand branch. Therefore, the

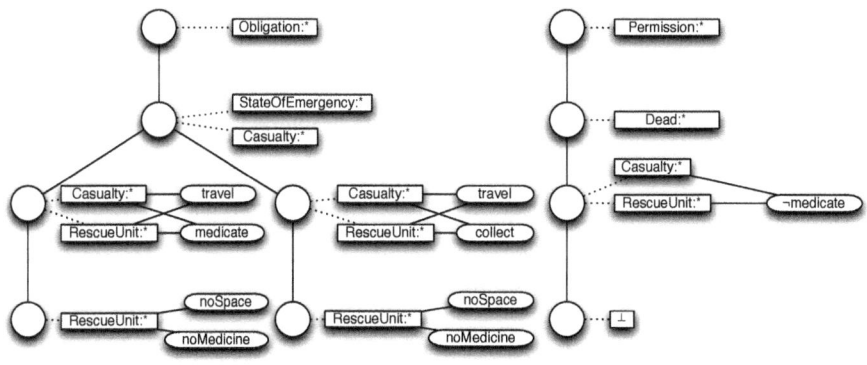

Fig. 10. The abstract norm trees

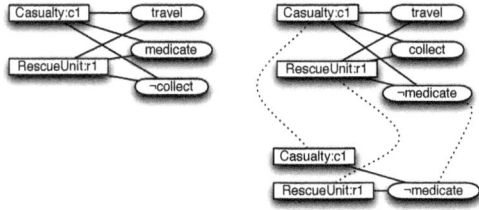

Fig. 11. The completed form of the obligation's normative condition (top left and top right), with the projection of the permission's normative condition

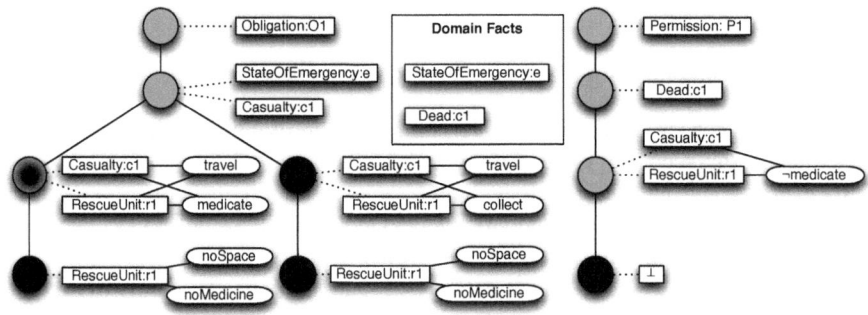

Fig. 12. Norm instantiation according to the domain facts

permission derogates the left hand branch of the obligation's norm condition, and the norm is not violated. This is shown in Figure 12.

5   Conclusions

Our approach to aiding understanding of the effects of norms in a multi-agent system brings together several ideas. First, norms do not apply equally through a system's lifetime, but start and cease to place expectations on agents, possibly multiple times through the system lifetime. Second, understanding the effects of an individual norm is inadequate in cases in which multiple norms may interact. Third, a representation of norms adequate for those norms to be reasoned over or monitored by software is not necessarily ideal for explanation to users. While there is already work applicable to each of these three issues, cosnidering all three together is necessary to provide effective explanation of real system behaviour.

With regard to the applicability of norms over time, we note that the focus of much research on norms lies in identifying the properties of a norm or normative system at some specific point in time so that, while the conditional nature of norms has long been recognised, properties such as the ability of a norm to expire have been ignored. An exception to this is work by Governatori et al. [4], who propose a defeasible logic based approach to norm representation, allowing a norm to expire by having it be defeated once some deadline is reached. However, such an approach makes it harder for a norm to be instantiated again if needed (a defeater to the defeater must be introduced).

The problem of detecting interactions between norms has been explored from different perspectives (derogation, contrary-to-duty norms, overriding obligations, etc.), and it is clear that the problem of identifying interactions with a large set of norms is challenging. This problem is exacerbated by considering the first issue above: norms apply in particular circumstances and so their interaction depends on the current situation. Detecting how norms *could* interact to affect agents' behaviour is often not as helpful as understanding how they actually *do* affect that behaviour.

Little existing work deals with norm explanation, instead assuming that the system is fully and correctly automated (thus requiring no explanation), or that the user has sufficient technical knowledge to be able to understand the norm's representation and interactions. Even in the latter case, a more intuitive, graphical explanation may be advantageous when trying to reason about complex interactions between large groups of norms. One notable exception to the dearth of work regarding norm explanation lies in [7], where the authors explain the causes of norm violation by making use of a causal graph. This explanation is then fed into a policy engine that attempts to determine whether there are some mitigating circumstances for the violation. If these are present, penalties against the violator can be ignored or reduced. However, the work does not deal with the underlying semantics of norms, and thus cannot aid the user in determining whether a violation actually took place.

In this paper, we have combined a rich norm model with a graphical model of norms using concept graphs to explore how derogation of obligations through *permissions* can be visually depicted for users as a system executes. In [3], a number of possible directions for further work were proposed, which are also relevant here. First, and most critical, this involves undertaking user studies of our system in order to determine whether the visual representation can enhance system understanding, as suggested by [2]. Second, the formal semantics of conceptual graphs allows for inference over CGs using projection; in principle, this could be extended to allow a user to detect and understand normative *conflict*. Projection can also act as a *similarity* measure, and can thus be applied to determining the trustworthiness of contracts (as encoded by groups of norms) along the lines suggested by Groth et al. [5]. Finally, we have focused on the status of norms at a single point in time; we plan to investigate how our approach can aid in explaining interactions not only between simultaneously active norms, but also how they can be used to identify and explain temporally distributed normative interactions.

References

1. Boella, G., van der Torre, L.: Permissions and obligations in hierarchical normative systems. In: Proceedings of the 9th International Conference on Artificial Intelligence and Law, pp. 109–118 (2003)
2. Chein, M., Mugnier, M.-L.: Graph-based Knowledge Representation: Computational Foundations of Conceptual Graphs. Springer, London (2008)
3. Croitoru, M., Oren, N., Miles, S., Luck, M.: Graph-based norm explanation. In: Research and Development in Intelligent Systems XXVII, Proceedings of AI 2010: The Thirtieth SGAI International Conference on Innovative Techniques and Applications of Artificial Intelligence, pp. 35–48. Springer, Heidelberg (2010)
4. Governatori, G., Hulstijn, J., Riveret, R., Rotolo, A.: Characterising deadlines in temporal modal defeasible logic. In: Orgun, M.A., Thornton, J. (eds.) AI 2007. LNCS (LNAI), vol. 4830, pp. 486–496. Springer, Heidelberg (2007)
5. Groth, P., Miles, S., Modgil, S., Oren, N., Luck, M., Gil, Y.: Determining the trustworthiness of new electronic contracts. In: Aldewereld, H., Dignum, V., Picard, G. (eds.) ESAW 2009. LNCS, vol. 5881, pp. 132–147. Springer, Heidelberg (2009)
6. Kowalski, R.A., Sergot, M.J.: A logic-based calculus of events. New Generation Computing 4(1), 67–95 (1986)
7. Miles, S., Groth, P., Luck, M.: Handling mitigating circumstances for electronic contracts. In: Proceedings of the AISB 2008 Symposium on Behaviour Regulation in Multi-agent Systems, pp. 37–42. The Society for the Study of Artificial Intelligence and Simulation of Behaviour (April 2008)

8. Modgil, S., Faci, N., Meneguzzi, F., Oren, N., Miles, S., Luck, M.: A framework for monitoring agent-based normative systems. In: Proceedings of The 8th International Conference on Autonomous Agents and Multiagent Systems, vol. 1, pp. 153–160 (2009)
9. Mugnier, M.-L., Leclère, M.: On querying simple conceptual graphs with negation. Data Knowledge Engineering 60, 468–493 (2007)
10. Oren, N., Panagiotidi, S., Vázquez-Salceda, J., Modgil, S., Luck, M., Miles, S.: Towards a formalisation of electronic contracting environments. In: Hübner, J.F., Matson, E.T., Boissier, O., Dignum, V. (eds.) COIN@AAMAS 2008. LNCS, vol. 5428, pp. 156–171. Springer, Heidelberg (2009)
11. Sowa, J.F.: Conceptual Graphs. IBM Journal of Research and Development 20(4), 336–375 (1976)
12. Sowa, J.F.: Conceptual Structures: Information Processing in Mind and Machine. Addison-Wesley, Reading (1984)
13. Stolpe, A.: Relevance, derogation and permission: a case for a normal form for codes of norms. In: Governatori, G., Sartor, G. (eds.) DEON 2010. LNCS, vol. 6181, pp. 98–115. Springer, Heidelberg (2010)

Symbolic Model Checking Commitment Protocols Using Reduction

Mohamed El-Menshawy[1], Jamal Bentahar[1], and Rachida Dssouli[2]

[1] Concordia University, Faculty of Engineering and Computer Science, Canada
[2] Concordia University, Canada and UAE University, Faculty of Inf. Tech., UAE
m_elme@encs.concordia.ca, bentahar@ciise.concordia.ca,
dssouli@ciise.concordia.ca

Abstract. Using model checking to verify that interaction protocols have given properties is widely recognized as an important issue in multi-agent systems where autonomous and heterogeneous agents need to successfully regulate and coordinate their interactions. In this paper, we investigate the use of symbolic model checkers to verify the compliance of a special kind of interaction protocols called commitment protocols with some properties such as liveness and safety. These properties are expressed as formulae in a new temporal logic, called CTLC, which extends the temporal logic CTL with modality for social commitments. Our approach shows that the problem of model checking CTLC can be reduced to the problem of model checking either CTLK or ARCTL, which are extensions of CTL. We finally present an implementation and report on the experimental results of verifying the Contract Net Protocol modeled in terms of commitments and associated actions using the symbolic model checkers MCMAS and extended NuSMV.

Keywords: Multi-Agent Systems, Commitment Protocols, Symbolic Model Checking, Protocol Properties.

1 Introduction

Over the last two decades, the researchers on Multi-Agent Systems (MASs) have been focused both on defining a clear and standard semantics for Agent Communication Languages (ACLs), such as FIPA-ACL[1], and developing multi-agent interaction protocols. The developers of FIPA-ACL have addressed the challenge of incorporating ACL and protocols by proposing a set of multi-agent interaction protocols, called FIPA-ACL protocols[2]. These protocols can be viewed as specific ACLs designed for particular purposes such as *Request Interaction Protocol (RIP)*, *English Auction Interaction Protocol (EAIP)* and *Contract Net Protocol (CNP)*. In

---

[1] This term stands for the Foundation for Intelligent Physical Agents' Agent Communication Language–see for examples, FIPA-ACL specifications (1997, 1999, 2001, 2002),
http://www.fipa.org/repository/aclspecs.php3

[2] See for examples, FIPA-ACL Interaction Protocols (2001, 2002),
http://www.fipa.org/repository/ips.php3

A. Omicini, S. Sardina, and W. Vasconcelos (Eds.): DALT 2010, LNAI 6619, pp. 185–203, 2011.

particular, CNP is designed from online business point of view to reach agreements among interacting agents. FIPA-ACL protocols have succeed in specifying the rules governing interactions and coordinating dialogues among agents by: 1) restricting the range of allowed follow-up communicative acts at any stage during a dialogue; and 2) describing the sequence of messages that FIPA compliant agents can exchange for particular applications. However, these protocols are quite rigid to be used by autonomous agents (that do what is best for themselves) as they are specified so that agents must execute them without possibility of handling exceptions that appear at run time, which restricts the protocols' flexibility.

Recently, social approaches have been proposed to overcome FIPA-ACL protocols' shortcomings. In particular, social approaches advocate declarative representations of protocols and give semantics to protocol messages in terms of social concepts. Bentahar et al. [2] have proposed a framework capable of specifying effective multi-agent interaction protocols using a combination of argumentation theory and social commitments. Fornara and Colombetti [12] have based the semantics of agent communication protocols on social commitments such that the meanings of exchanged messages are denoted by social commitments and their associated actions. Yolum and Singh [29] have developed an approach to flexibly specify multi-agent interaction protocols wherein protocols capture the dynamic behaviors of the agents in terms of creation and manipulation of commitments to one another. All these protocols have the characteristic of being commitment-based and are called commitment protocols. Furthermore, Chopra, Yolum and Singh have developed a formalism to represent and reason about commitment protocols called *commitment machines* based on either *event calculus* or *non-monotonic theory* of actions in terms of causal logic [28,6]. This formalism can represent flexible protocols that enable agents to exercise their autonomy by dealing with exceptions and making choices. In the same line of research, Singh [24] has generalized the formalism of commitment machines to include natural non-terminal protocols (or protocols that have cycles) analogous to those in real-life business applications.

In addition to providing flexibility during run time, these approaches make it possible to provide a meaningful basis for compliance of agents with a given protocol. This is because commitments can be stored publicly (or observed by all participating agents) and agents that do not satisfy their commitments at the end of the protocol can be identified as non-compliant [25,7,26]. In order for these approaches to make use of all these advantages, they should integrate rigorous design and automatic verification of interaction protocols within the same framework. For instance, Venkatraman et al. [25] have presented an approach for locally testing whether or not the behavior of an agent in open systems complies with a given commitment protocol specified in Computational Tree Logic (CTL). Cheng [5] and Desai et al. [10] have used OWL-P to specify commitment protocols and their compositions. To verify their protocols against some properties expressed in Linear Temporal Logic (LTL), they translate them into PROMELA code, which is the input language of the automata-based model checker SPIN. Yolum [27] has defined three "generic properties" taken from distributed systems that can be incorporated in a design tool to "semi-automate" the specification of commitment protocols at design time.

Motivation. In this paper, we aim to introduce CTLC, a CTL-like logic for social commitments. We present a fully-automatic verification technique of commitment protocols specified on the basis of this logic using symbolic model checking. This is done by introducing a mechanism to reduce the problem of model checking CTLC to the problem of model checking either CTLK [21], to directly use the MCMAS symbolic model checker [17], or ARCTL [20] to use the extended version of the NuSMV symbolic model checker introduced in [16]. The present paper inspires by the methodology introduced in [16] to perform the reduction. Finally, we present experimental results for the verification of the Contract Net Protocol, taken from e-business domain as a motivating example and specified in the proposed logic, against some desirable properties using MCMAS and the extended version of NuSMV.

Overview of Paper. The remainder of this paper is organized as follows. We begin in Section 2 by presenting the definition of social commitments and briefly summarizing the formalism of the interpreted systems used as the model of our CTLC logic. We then discuss generally the problem of model checking using MCMAS and NuSMV. In Section 3, we present CTLK and ARCTL and how the problem of model checking CTLC can be reduced to the problem of model checking either CTLK or ARCTL. Thereafter, we proceed to introduce commitment protocols and their translation along with expressing some properties in Section 4. The experimental results of verifying the Contract Net Protocol using MCMAS and the extended version of NuSMV is discussed in Section 5. In Section 6, we discuss relevant literature. We conclude the paper in Section 7.

2   Preliminaries

2.1   Commitments and Associated Actions

Social commitments have been recently gained attentions in MASs community. This is because they are formal and concise methods for describing how autonomous and heterogeneous agents communicate with one another. In particular, a social commitment is an engagement in the form of business contract between two agents: a creditor who commits to a course of action and a debtor on behalf of whom the action is done. In this paper, we distinguish between two types of commitments: unconditional commitment and conditional commitment that we need to represent commitment protocols.

Notation 1. *Unconditional commitments are denoted by $C(i, j, \varphi)$, where i is the debtor, j is the creditor and φ is a well-formed formula (wff) in the proposed CTLC logic representing the commitment content. $C(i, j, \varphi)$ means i socially (i.e., publicly) commits to j that φ holds.*

Notation 2. *Conditional commitments are denoted by $\psi \rightarrow C(i, j, \varphi)$, where "$\rightarrow$" is the logical implication, i, j and φ have the above meanings and ψ is a wff in the proposed CTLC logic representing the commitment condition.*

We will use $CC(i, j, \psi, \varphi)$ as an abbreviation of $\psi \to C(i, j, \varphi)$. In order to manipulate social commitments during the progress of protocols, we introduce a set of associated actions (or operations), called commitment actions. These actions are used to capture dynamic behavior of participating agents. Defined in [23], these actions can be classified into two party actions and three party actions. The former ones need only two agents to be performed: *Create*, *Withdraw*, *Fulfill*, *Violate* and *Release*. The latter ones need an intermediate agent to be completed: *Delegate*. In the following, we present the declarative representation of these actions where i, j and k denote agent names.

- $Create(i, j, C(i, j, \varphi))$ to establish a new commitment.
- $Withdraw(i, j, C(i, j, \varphi))$ to cancel an existing commitment.
- $Fulfill(i, j, C(i, j, \varphi))$ to satisfy the commitment content.
- $Violate(i, j, C(i, j, \varphi))$ to reflect there is no way to satisfy the commitment content.
- $Release(j, i, C(i, j, \varphi))$ to free a debtor from carrying out his commitment.
- $Delegate(i, k, C(i, j, \varphi))$ to delegate an existing commitment to another debtor to satisfy it on his behalf.

2.2   Interpreted Systems and CTLC Logic

An interpreted system as introduced by Fagin et al. [11] is a formalism that models the temporal evolution of a system of agents to reason about knowledge and temporal properties. We start with assuming that a MAS is composed of n agents $\mathcal{A} = \{1, \ldots, n\}$. Each agent i is characterized by a set of local states L_i and a set of local actions Act_i. In this paper, these actions include the commitment actions and a special action ϵ_i denoting the "null" action for agent i. Thus, when an agent performs the null action, the local state of this agent remains the same. Moreover, for each agent $i \in \mathcal{A}$, I_i defines an initial state and a local protocol $\mathcal{P}_i : L_i \to 2^{Act_i}$, which is a function that maps the current state of the agent i with the set of enabled actions for that state. The agents act within an "environment" (e), which can be also modeled with a set of local states L_e, a set of local actions Act_e and a local protocol $\mathcal{P}_e$. This can be seen as a special agent that can capture any information that may not pertain to a specific agent.

Definition 1 ([11]). *A set G of global states in a MAS is: $G \subseteq L_i \times \ldots \times L_n \times L_e$, where a state $g = (l_1, \ldots, l_n, l_e) \in G$ can be seen as a "snapshot" of all agents in the MAS at a given time and $l_i(g)$ represents the local state of agent i in the global state g.*

The evolution function that determines the transitions for an individual agent between its local states is defined as follows: $t_i : L_i \times L_e \times ACT \to L_i$, where $ACT = Act_1 \times \ldots \times Act_n \times Act_e$ and each component $a \in ACT$ is a "joint action", which is a tuple of actions (one for each agent). The global evolution function $t : G \times ACT \to G$ is defined as follows: $t(g, act_1, \ldots, act_n, act_e) = g'$ iff there exists $a \in ACT$ such that (i) for each agent i that is able to perform

a, we have $t_i(l_i, l_e, a) = l'_i$; and (ii) for each agent j that is unable to perform a, we have $t_j(l_j, l_e, \epsilon_j) = l_j$. Notice that we use a special class of interpreted systems in which at each moment only one agent can perform an action in a global evolution function and I denotes a set of initial states. Finally, given a set Φ_p of atomic propositions and the valuation function V for those propositions $V : G \rightarrow 2^{\Phi_p}$, an interpreted system is a tuple:

$$\mathcal{IS} = \Big\langle (L_i, Act_i, \mathcal{P}_i, t_i)_{i \in \mathcal{A}}, (L_e, Act_e, \mathcal{P}_e, t_e), I, V \Big\rangle$$

Computation tree logic of social commitments CTLC is an extension of CTL [9,11] with the commitment modality $\mathsf{C}(i, j, \varphi)$. In particular, the syntax of CTLC is given by the following BNF grammar, where $p \in \Phi_p$ is an atomic proposition:

$$\varphi ::= p \mid \neg \varphi \mid \varphi \vee \varphi \mid \mathbf{EX}\varphi \mid \mathbf{EG}\varphi \mid \mathbf{E}(\varphi \mathsf{U} \varphi) \mid \mathsf{C}(i, j, \varphi)$$

where the CTLC temporal modalities have the standard meaning as in CTL—for example, $\mathbf{EX}\varphi$ means that "there is a path where φ holds at the next state in the path". $\mathsf{C}(i, j, \varphi)$ is read as "agent i commits towards agent j to bring about φ". Other derived operators are defined in a standard way, see for example [9,11]. In order to interpret CTLC formulae, a Kripke model $M = (W, I, R_t, R_{sc}, V)$ is associated to a given interpreted system $\mathcal{IS}$ as follows:

- W is the set G of global states,
- $I \subseteq W$ is the set of initial states, which are defined in $\mathcal{IS}$,
- the temporal transition relation $R_t \subseteq W \times W$ is defined using the global evolution function t,
- the relation $R_{sc} : W \times \mathcal{A} \times \mathcal{A} \rightarrow 2^W$ is the social accessibility relation for social commitments. It is defined by $w' \in R_{sc}(w, i, j)$ iff $\exists \overline{w} : l_i(w) = l_i(\overline{w})$ and $l_j(\overline{w}) = l_j(w')$,
- V is the valuation function as defined in $\mathcal{IS}$.

Excluding the commitment modality, the semantics of CTLC formulae is defined in the model M as usual (semantics of CTL), see for example [9,11]. The notation $M, \langle w \rangle \models \varphi$ means the model M satisfies φ at a state w where $\models$ is the standard satisfaction relation. The commitment modality $\mathsf{C}(i, j, \varphi)$ is satisfied in the model M at a state w iff the content φ is true in every accessible state from this state using $R_{sc}(w, i, j)$. Formally:

$$M, \langle w \rangle \models \mathsf{C}(i, j, \varphi) \text{ iff for all } w' \in W, \text{ if } w' \in R_{sc}(w, i, j) \text{ then } M, \langle w' \rangle \models \varphi$$

2.3 Model Checking Using MCMAS and NuSMV

Model checking is a method of formal verification used to verify if a system satisfies given properties. In a nutshell, the problem of model checking is: given a Kripke model M and property φ (expressed as a wff), does the model satisfy that property? If an error is located (i.e., $M \nvDash \varphi$), the process will return a "counter-example" showing the steps in which the error state was reached. Otherwise, it will return true (i.e., $M \models \varphi$). Recently, model checking has been used to verify MASs [17]. Verifying these systems is becoming more and more necessary because they are increasingly used in several applications such as web-based applications [25], business processes [5,10] and artificial institutions [26].

This paper focuses both on the symbolic model checkers MCMAS [17] and the extended version of NuSMV [16], which are built on Ordered Binary Decision Diagrams (OBDDs) that alleviate to overcome the "state-explosion" problem. In particular, MCMAS is a tool used to solve the problem of model checking MASs. MCMAS also has the following features: 1) it can check a variety of properties specified as CTL formulae, epistemic, and cooperation modalities; 2) it supports variables of the following types: Boolean, enumeration and bounded integer where arithmetic operations can be performed on bounded integers; 3) it supports counter-example/witness generation for efficient display of traces falsifying/satisfying properties; and 4) it supports fairness constraints, which are useful in eliminating bad or unwanted agents' behaviors. MCMAS uses Interpreted System Programming Language (ISPL) as an input language. A system of agents is encoded in ISPL using the interpreted system components. ISPL allows user to define atomic propositions over global states of the system. The logic formulae to be checked by MCMAS are defined over these atomic propositions.

On the other hand, the NuSMV symbolic model checker [8] is written in ANSI C. It is a reimplementation and extension of SMV, the first model checker based on OBDDs. NuSMV is able to process files written in an extension of the SMV language. In this language, it is possible to describe finite state machines by means of declaration and instantiation mechanisms and processes and to express a set of requirements in CTL and LTL. In addition to the above features, NuSMV has the same features of MCMAS as MCMAS is technically an extended version of NuSMV. NuSMV can also check Real-Time CTL specifications, which specifies discrete timing constraints. However it does not model interpreted systems as it is not specially designed for MASs but can overcome this limit by indirectly checking interpreted system properties, which are encoded into its variables.

3   Model Checking CTLC

In this section, we briefly review CTLK (a logic of time and knowledge). We then show how the problem of model checking CTLC can be reduced to the problem of model checking either CTLK or ARCTL.

3.1   CTLK Logic

CTLK [21] is an epistemic logic on branching time; it allows for the expression of properties that contain a notion of knowledge. In particular, given a set of atomic propositions Φ_p, the syntax of CTLK is given by BNF grammar as follows:

$$\varphi ::= p \mid \neg\varphi \mid \varphi \vee \varphi \mid \mathbf{EX}\varphi \mid \mathbf{EG}\varphi \mid \mathbf{E}(\varphi\mathbf{U}\varphi) \mid \mathbf{K}_i\varphi$$

where the epistemic modality $\mathbf{K}_i\varphi$ is used to represent "knows" that is agent i knowing φ. As in CTL, other temporal operators can be defined in a standard way, see for example [9,11]. To define the semantic of CTLK formulae, a Kripke model of the form $M = (S, S_0, T, \sim_i, \ldots, \sim_n, V)$ is associated to a given interpreted system $\mathcal{IS}$, where: S is a set of global states; $S_0 \subseteq S$ is a set of initial global states; $T \subseteq S \times S$ is a transition relation; $\sim_i \subseteq S \times S$ are the epistemic relations defined for all $i \in \mathcal{A}$ where $s \sim_i s'$ iff $l_i(s) = l_i(s')$; and V is the valuation function as defined in $\mathcal{IS}$.

Intuitively, the epistemic relation $s \sim_i s'$ means that the local state of the agent i in the current global state s is indistinguishable from the local state of this agent in the accessible state s'. The semantics of $K_i\varphi$ is defined as follows:

$M, \langle s \rangle \models K_i\varphi$ iff for all $s' \in S$ if $s \sim_i s'$ then $M, \langle s' \rangle \models \varphi$

Hereafter, we use $\widehat{K}_i\varphi$ as an abbreviation of $\neg K_i \neg \varphi$. Its semantics is as follows:

$M, \langle s \rangle \models \widehat{K}_i\varphi$ iff for some $s' \in S$ if $s \sim_i s'$ then $M, \langle s' \rangle \models \varphi$

3.2 Reducing CTLC to CTLK

In this section, we show how the problem of model checking CTLC (see Sect.2.2) can be reduced to the problem of model checking CTLK. This reduction enables us to directly use MCMAS. The problem is as follows: given a CTLC model M_{sc} and a CTLC formula φ_{sc}, we have to define a CTLK model $M = \mathcal{F}(M_{sc})$ and a CTLK formula $\mathcal{F}(\varphi_{sc})$ such that $M_{sc} \models \varphi_{sc}$ iff $\mathcal{F}(M_{sc}) \models \mathcal{F}(\varphi_{sc})$. Let $\mathcal{A} = \{1, \ldots, n\}$ be a set of agents, and $M_{sc} = (W, I, R_t, R_{sc}, V)$ be a model for CTLC associated to the interpreted system $\mathcal{IS} = \Big\langle (L_i, Act_i, \mathcal{P}_i, t_i)_{i \in \mathcal{A}}, (L_e, Act_e, \mathcal{P}_e, t_e),$
$I, V \Big\rangle$. The model $\mathcal{F}(M_{sc})$ is a CTLK model $M = (S, S_0, T, \{\sim_i\}_{i \in \mathcal{A}}, V)$ defined as follows:

- $S = W \cup \overline{S}$ where $\overline{S}$ is constructed as follows: for all states w and w' such that $w' \in R_{sc}(w, i, j)$ add a state $\overline{s}$ in $\overline{S}$ such that $V(\overline{s}) = V(w')$ and $l_i(\overline{s}) = l_j(w')$.
- $S_0 = I$.
- the transition relation $T = R_t \cup \overline{R}_t$ where $\overline{R}_t$ is constructed as follows: for all states w and w' such that $w' \in R_{sc}(w, i, j)$ add a transition in $\overline{R}_t$ between s ($s \in S$ and $s = w$) and the added $\overline{s}$.
- the epistemic relations $\{\sim_i\}_{i \in \mathcal{A}}$ are obtained as follows: for all w and w' such that $w' \in R_{sc}(w, i, j)$, we have $s \sim_i \overline{s}$ and $\overline{s} \sim_j s'$ where $w = s$, $w' = s'$ and $\overline{s}$ is the added state ($s, \overline{s}, s' \in S$).

Figure 1 illustrates an example of the reduction process from CTLC to CTLK. The reduction of a CTLC formula into a CTLK formula is recursively defined as follows:

- $\mathcal{F}(p) = p$, if p is an atomic proposition.
- $\mathcal{F}(\neg\varphi) = \neg\mathcal{F}(\varphi)$ and $\mathcal{F}(\varphi \vee \psi) = \mathcal{F}(\varphi) \vee \mathcal{F}(\psi)$.
- $\mathcal{F}(EX\varphi) = EX\mathcal{F}(\varphi)$ and $\mathcal{F}(E(\varphi U\psi)) = E(\mathcal{F}(\varphi)U\mathcal{F}(\psi))$.
- $\mathcal{F}(EG\varphi) = EG\mathcal{F}(\varphi)$ and $\mathcal{F}(C(i, j, \varphi)) = \widehat{K}_i\mathcal{F}(\varphi) \wedge EX\,\widehat{K}_j\mathcal{F}(\varphi)$

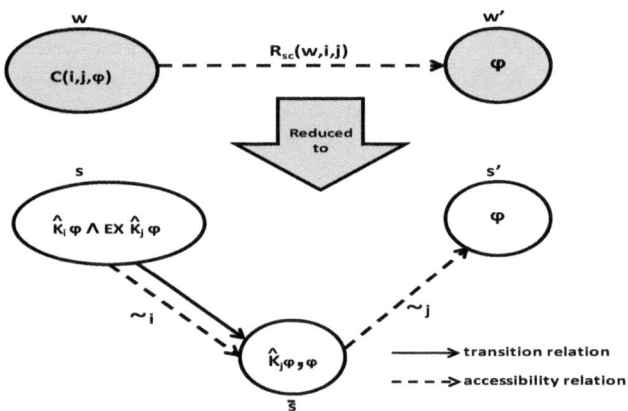

Fig. 1. An example of the reduction process from CTLC to CTLK

Thus, this reduction allows us to model check CTLC formulae by model checking their reductions in CTLK using the MCMAS tool. The most important case in this reduction is the one about commitments (see Fig.1). The following theorem proves the correctness of our reduction from CTLC to CTLK.

Theorem 1 (Correctness). *Let M_{sc} and φ_{sc} be respectively a CTLC model and formula and let $\mathscr{F}(M_{sc})$ and $\mathscr{F}(\varphi_{sc})$ be the corresponding model and formula in CTLK. We have $M_{sc} \models \varphi_{sc}$ iff $\mathscr{F}(M_{sc}) \models \mathscr{F}(\varphi_{sc})$.*

Proof. We prove this theorem by induction on the structure of the formula φ_{sc}:

- If φ_{sc} is a pure CTL formula, the correctness is straightforward from the fact that CTLK is also an extension of CTL.
- If φ_{sc} is not a pure CTL formula, by induction over the structure of φ_{sc}, all the cases are straightforward once the case where $\varphi_{sc} = \mathrm{C}(i,j,\psi)$ is analyzed. In this case we have: $M_{sc}, \langle w \rangle \models \mathrm{C}(i,j,\psi)$ iff for all $w' \in R_{sc}(w,i,j)$ we have $M_{sc}, \langle w' \rangle \models \psi$.
  According to the definition of R_{sc}, we obtain: $M_{sc}, \langle w \rangle \models \mathrm{C}(i,j,\psi)$ iff for all w' such that there exists $\overline{w}$ and $l_i(w) = l_i(\overline{w})$ and $l_j(\overline{w}) = l_j(w')$ we have $M_{sc}, \langle w' \rangle \models \psi$.
  Since $l_j(\overline{s}) = l_j(w')$ and $V(\overline{s}) = V(w')$, we obtain: $\mathscr{F}(M_{sc}), \langle \overline{s} \rangle \models \mathscr{F}(\psi)$ and $\mathscr{F}(M_{sc}), \langle s' \rangle \models \mathscr{F}(\psi)$ and since $s \sim_i \overline{s}$ and $\overline{s} \sim_j s'$, so according to the semantics of $\widehat{\mathrm{K}}_i \mathscr{F}(\psi)$ and $\widehat{\mathrm{K}}_j \mathscr{F}(\psi)$, we get: $\mathscr{F}(M_{sc}), \langle \overline{s} \rangle \models \widehat{\mathrm{K}}_j \mathscr{F}(\psi)$ and $\mathscr{F}(M_{sc}), \langle s \rangle \models \widehat{\mathrm{K}}_i \mathscr{F}(\psi)$.
  So since $(s, \overline{s}) \in T$, we obtain $\mathscr{F}(M_{sc}), \langle s \rangle \models \widehat{\mathrm{K}}_i \mathscr{F}(\psi) \wedge \mathrm{EX} \, \widehat{\mathrm{K}}_j \mathscr{F}(\psi)$. ∎

3.3 Reducing CTLC to ARCTL

Lomuscio et al. [16] have proven that the problem of model checking CTLK can be automatically reduced to the problem of model checking ARCTL. ARCTL is an extension of CTL with action formulae, so it mixes among state formulae and action formulae. However, it restricts path formulae into paths whose actions satisfy a given action formula. Instead of directly reducing CTLC to ARCTL, we simply use the reduction from CTLK to ARCTL since we already reduced CTLC to CTLK. The reduction from CTLC to ARCTL is then obtained by transitivity (see dash arrow in Fig.2).

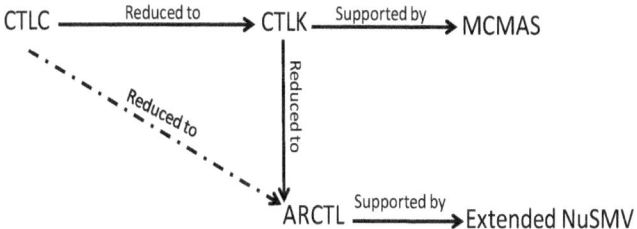

Fig. 2. The reduction processes of CTLC into CTLK and ARCTL

Before we introduce Lomuscio et al.'s reduction technique, we define the syntax of ARCTL using the following BNF grammar [20]:

$$\varphi ::= p \mid \neg\varphi \mid \varphi \vee \varphi \mid \mathrm{E}_\alpha \mathrm{X}\varphi \mid \mathrm{A}_\alpha \mathrm{X}\varphi \mid \mathrm{E}_\alpha(\varphi \mathrm{U}\varphi) \mid \mathrm{A}_\alpha(\varphi \mathrm{U}\varphi)$$
$$\alpha ::= b \mid \neg\alpha \mid \alpha \vee \alpha$$

where φ is state formula, α is action formula, $p \in \Phi_p$ (a set of atomic propositions) and $b \in \Phi_\alpha$ (a set of atomic actions). To define the semantics of ARCTL formulae, the model M is defined as follows: $M = \langle Z, Z_0, A, TR, V_P, V_A \rangle$, where: Z is a set of states; $Z_0 \subseteq Z$ is a set of initial states; A is a set of actions; $TR \subseteq Z \times A \times Z$ is a labeled transition relation; $V_p : Z \rightarrow 2^{\Phi_P}$ is a function that assigns to each state a set of atomic propositions to interpret this state; and $V_A : A \rightarrow 2^{\Phi_\alpha}$ is a function that assigns to each action a set of atomic actions to interpret this action.

The complete semantics of ARCTL is introduced in [20]. The reduction from a CTLK model $M = (S, S_0, T, \{\sim_i\}_{i \in \mathcal{A}}, V)$ to an ARCTL model $M = \langle Z, Z_0, A, TR, V_P, V_A \rangle$ is as follows:

- $Z = S$ and $Z_0 = S_0$.
- reconfiguring the set Φ_α such that $\Phi_\alpha = \{Run, Gt_i, \ldots, Gt_n\}$, where Run is an atomic proposition used to label temporal transitions defined by T and n propositions Gt_i (one for each agent) to label epistemics relations.
- the labeled transition relation TR combines both the temporal transition T and the epistemic relations $\{\sim_i\}_{i \in \mathcal{A}}$ under the following two conditions: for states $s, s' \in S$, (i) $(s, \{Run\}, s') \in TR$ iff $(s, s') \in T$; (ii) $(s, \{Gt_i\}, s') \in TR$ iff $s \sim_i s'$.

The reduction of a CTLK formula into an ARCTL formula is defined as follows [16,20]:

- $\mathscr{F}(p) = p$, if p is an atomic proposition.
- $\mathscr{F}(\neg\varphi) = \neg\mathscr{F}(\varphi)$ and $\mathscr{F}(\varphi \vee \psi) = \mathscr{F}(\varphi) \vee \mathscr{F}(\psi)$.
- $\mathscr{F}(\text{EX}\varphi) = \text{E}_{Run}\text{X}.\mathscr{F}(\varphi)$ and $\mathscr{F}(\text{E}(\varphi\text{U}\psi)) = \text{E}_{Run}(\mathscr{F}(\varphi)\text{U}\mathscr{F}(\psi))$.
- $\mathscr{F}(\text{EG}\varphi) = \text{E}_{Run}\text{G}.\mathscr{F}(\varphi)$ and $\mathscr{F}(\text{K}_i\varphi) = \text{A}_{Gt_i}\text{X}.\mathscr{F}(\varphi)$

Using the reduction from CTLK to ARCTL and our reduction from CTLC to CTLK, we obtain the reduction from CTLC to ARCTL (see Fig.2). However, we can also directly reduce CTLC to ARCTL. The reduction of all CTL formulae is straightforward. The reduction of the commitment formula is as follows: $\mathscr{F}(\text{C}(i,j,\varphi)) = \text{A}_{Gt_i}\text{X}.\mathscr{F}(\varphi) \wedge \text{E}_{Run}\text{XA}_{Gt_j}.\mathscr{F}(\varphi)$. The correctness of this reduction follows from Theorem 1 and the correctness of the reduction of CTLK to ARCTL.

4   Commitment Protocols

After reducing CTLC to CTLK and ARCTL, let us apply this reduction to a case study by verifying a commitment protocol. In this section, we define commitment protocols as a set of actions on commitments with respect to the given interpreted system $\mathcal{IS}$. These commitments are defined in our logic CTLC to capture the business interactions among agent roles. In addition to what messages can be exchanged and when, our protocol specifies the meaning of messages in terms of their effects on the commitments. The participating autonomous agents can communicate by exchanging messages in terms of creation and manipulation of commitments such that this exchanging is reliable, meaning that messages do not get lost and the communication channel is order-preserving.

Example 1. We consider the Contract Net Protocol (CNP)[3], as a motivating example to illustrate our representation of commitment protocols. The protocol starts with a manager requesting proposals for a particular task. Each participant either sends a proposal or a reject message. The manager accepts only one proposal among the received proposals and explicitly rejects the rest proposals. The participant with the accepted proposal informs the manager with the proposal result or the failure of the proposal.

Figure 3 depicts our representation of the CNP commitment protocol using commitments and associated actions. It begins with sending a call-for-proposals at state w_0, which means the manager M creates a conditional commitment: $Create(M, P, \text{CC}(M, P, proposal, reply))$ such that if a participant P sends a proposal, the manager will decide and reply with the result of the call-for-proposals (*proposal* and *reply* are *wff* in CTLC). Then, the participant at state w_1 could either accept this call-for-proposal, which means creating a conditional commitment such that if the manager accepts the proposal, the participant will deliver the result of the proposal or reject this call-for-proposal, which means releasing the received commitment and the protocol will achieve the failure state w_3 as a final state. After receiving the participant's proposal, the manager can accept this proposal or reject it.

---

[3] FIPA Contract Net Interaction Protocol Specification (2002),
   http://www.fipa.org/specs/fipa00029/index.html

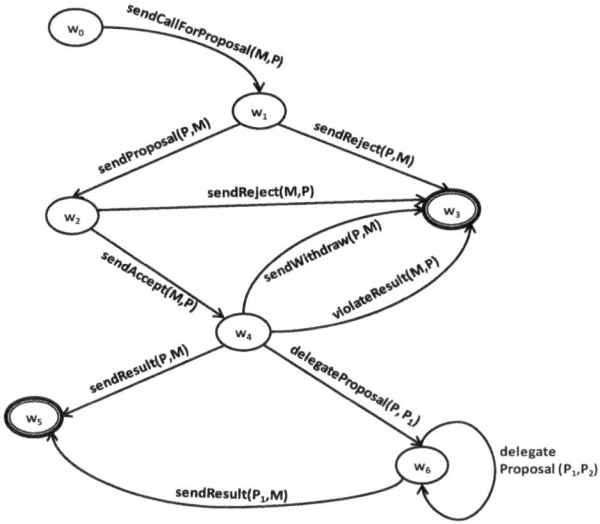

Fig. 3. Contract Net Protocol transitions

By sending the accept message to the participant, the conditional commitment will be transformed to an unconditional commitment at state w_4. At this state, the participant has four possibilities: 1) to withdraw his commitment and then move to the failure state w_3; 2) to delegate it to another participant (say P_1) to deliver the result to the manager on his behalf: $Delegate(P, P_1, \mathsf{C}(P, M, result))$; 3) to violate his commitment and then move to the failure state w_3; or 4) to directly send the result of the proposal to the manager and the protocol will achieve the successful state w_5 as a final state.

As in [28], the participant P_1 can delegate this commitment to another participant (say P_2), which delegates the commitment back to the participant P_1. The participants (P_1 and P_2) delegate the commitment back and forth infinitely often and this is presented by a transition loop at w_6. In a sound protocol, this behavior should be avoided (in Sect.4.2, we will show how to verify this issue). Finally, the participant P_1 can fulfill the delegated commitment by sending the result of the proposal to the manager and then moves to the successful state w_5.

Table 1 depicts the possible actions in the enhanced version of CNP and the corresponding commitment actions.

4.1 Translating Commitment Protocols

The main step in the verification of commitment protocols is translating them into ISPL (the MCMAS's input language) and SMV (the NuSMV's input language). An ISPL program reflects the structure of the interpreted system $\mathcal{IS}$ defined in the following four sections [22]:

Table 1. Actions in the CNP and the corresponding commitment actions

$sendCallForProposal(M, P)$	$Create(M, P, \mathtt{CC}(M, P, proposal, reply))$
$sendProposal(P, M)$	$Create(P, M, \mathtt{CC}(P, M, accept, result))$
$sendReject(P, M)$	$Release(P, M, \mathtt{CC}(M, P, proposal, reply))$
$sendAccept(M, P)$	$Fulfill(M, P, \mathtt{C}(M, P, reply))$
$sendWithdraw(P, M)$	$Withdraw(P, M, \mathtt{C}(P, M, result))$
$violateResult(P, M)$	$Violate(P, M, \mathtt{C}(P, M, result))$
$sendResult(P, M)$	$Fulfill(P, M, \mathtt{C}(P, M, result))$
$delegateProposal(P, P_1)$	$Delegate(P, P_1, \mathtt{C}(P, M, result))$
$delegateProposal(P_1, P_2)$	$Delegate(P_1, P_2, \mathtt{C}(P_1, P, result))$
$sendResult(P_1, M)$	$Fulfill(P_1, M, \mathtt{C}(P_1, M, result))$

1. Agents' declarations to define a list of ISPL agents with four sub-sections according to the following syntax: `Agent <agentID> <agent_body> end Agent` where `<agentID>` is an ISPL identifier and `<agent_body>` contains: 1) local states; 2) local actions; 3) local protocol; and 4) evolution function.
2. Evaluation function is defined as follows:
   `Evaluation <proposition> if <condition_on_states> end Evaluation` where `<proposition>` is an ISPL proposition and `<condition_on_states>` is a truth condition that defines a set of global states for atomic proposition.
3. Initial states to define the set of initial state conditions as follows:
   `InitStates <condition_on_states> end InitStates`
4. List of formulae needed to be verified is defined using the following syntax:
   `Formulae <formulae_list> end Formulae`

Our translation process begins by extracting the set of interacting agents: M, P, P_1 and P_2 in our protocol. For each agent, we define the possible commitment states as knowledge states using state variables in the `Vars` sub-section. These variables are of enumeration type, which also include the successful, and failure states. The local actions on commitments are directly defined using the `Actions` sub-section. Using these states and actions, we define the evolution function in the `Evolution` sub-section that captures the transition relations among states. The translation is completed by declaring a set of enabled actions at each state in the `Protocol` sub-section, a set of initial states in the `InitStates` section, and the list of formulae needed to be verified in the `Formulae` section.

As mentioned, we use the extended version of NuSMV introduced in [16], which also uses the extended version of SMV program to verify the translated ARCTL formulae. In the extended version of SMV, the set of interacting agents (M, P, P_1 and P_2 in our protocol) is defined in isolated modules `MODULE Agent<name>`. Figure 4 shows an example of a typical translation of interacting agents in our protocol into extended SMV modules. These modules are instantiated in the main module with the definition of initial conditions using the `TINIT` statement and the keyword `SPEC` to specify the formulae that need to be

```
MODULE main
      VAR M : Manager(args1,args2);
          P : Participant(args1,agrs2);
      TINIT(...);
      SPEC <formulae_list>;

MODULE Manager(args1,agrs2)
      VAR state: {...};
      IVAR action: {...};
      TINIT(...);
      TRANS(next(action)= case ... esac);
      TTRANS(next(state)= case ... esac);
```

Fig. 4. Example of agent translation into extended SMV module

checked. For each agent, we associate the SMV variables `<v1>`, ..., `<vn>` using the `VAR` statement to define the agents commitment states plus the successful and failure states. The actions of each agent are represented as input variables in `IVAR` statement. The protocol of each agent is defined as a relation among its local state and action variables in the `TRANS` statement. The labeled transitions between commitment states are encoded using the `TTRANS` statement and an initial condition using the `TINIT` statement. Internally, `TTRANS` statements expand to standard `TRANS` statements conditioned on $\{Run\}$ with the **next** and **Case** expressions that represent agent's choices in a sequential manner.

4.2   Protocol Properties

To achieve the flexibility that gives each agent a great freedom and compliance within the same framework, we need to verify the commitment protocols against some properties that capture important requirements in MASs. Specifically, Guerin et al. [14] have proposed three types of verification of multi-agent interaction protocols depending on whether the verification process is done at either design time or run time: 1) verify that an agent will always comply; 2) verify compliance by observation; and 3) verify protocol properties. We adopt the third type of verification for three reasons:

1. The desirable properties play an important role in verifying multi-agent interaction protocols [1,19], which reduces the cost of development process at design time and restricts agents' behaviors by removing bad behaviors without loosing the flexibility.
2. Verifying the compliance of multi-agent interaction protocols with specifications requires adding planner mechanisms equipped with reasoning rules in the code of each agent to reason about its actions to select appropriate ones that satisfy its goals at run time, which can be expensive and may increase the code of the agents [28,24].
3. Protocol properties have a classification in both reactive and distributed systems to guide protocol designers to check protocol specifications.

Some proposals have been put forward to formally express commitment protocol properties [5,10,26]. However, these proposals do not use a specific methodology to classify protocol properties. Hereafter, we use the classification introduced in [15] to classify temporal properties into: *Safety* and *Liveness*. Manna and Pnueli, in their seminal book [18] have extended the liveness property into: *Guarantee, Obligation, Response, Persistence* and *Reactivity*. In the following, the reachability, deadlock freedom, safety, liveness, and fairness constraint properties are temporal CTLC formulae that we use to check the CNP commitment protocol. Notice that the reachability property do the same function as guarantee property, fairness constraint property captures response and reactivity properties, and obligation property can be defined as a conjunction of safety and reachability properties. Moreover, we omit persistence property as it is mainly related to concurrent behaviors. Consequently, our temporal protocol properties include the properties introduced in [5,10,19] and satisfy the same functionalities of the properties presented in [27].

Reachability property. Given a particular state, is there a valid computation sequences to reach that state from an initial state. For example, in all paths in the future $(F)^4$, there is a possibility for the participant P to deliver the result of the proposal to the manager:

$$\varphi_1 = AFEF \; \text{CC}(M, P, proposal, reply)$$

Deadlock property. It is the negation of the reachability property, which is supposed to be false:

$$\varphi_2 = \neg AFEF \; \text{CC}(M, P, proposal, reply)$$

Fairness constraint property. The motivation behind this property is to rule out unwanted behaviors of agents and remove any infinite loop in our protocol. For example, if we define the formula:

$$\varphi_3 = AGAF \; \neg\text{C}(P_1, P_2, result)$$

as an unconditional fairness constraint, then a path is fair iff in all paths and in each state of these paths, in all emerging paths P_1 eventually does not delegate commitments. This constraint will enable us to avoid situations such as the participants delegate the commitment back and forth infinitely many times.

Safety property. This property means "something bad never happens". For example, in our protocol a bad situation is: the manager sends accept message, but the participant never delivers the result of the proposal:

$$\varphi_4 = AG(\neg\text{C}(M, P, reply) \; \wedge \; AG \; \neg\text{C}(P, M, result))$$

Liveness: means that "something good will eventually happen". For example, in all paths globally if the manager sends call-for-proposal, then there is a path in the future the participant will send proposal to the manager:

$$\varphi_5 = AG(\text{CC}(M, P, proposal, reply) \rightarrow EF \; \text{CC}(P, M, accept, result))$$

The above formulae are only some examples in our language.

---

[4] **EF**p is the abbreviation of **E**($true$ **U** p).

5   Experimental Results

We implemented the reduction tools on top of the two model checkers (MCMAS and extended NuSMV) and provided a thorough assessment of this reduction on two experiments. In the first experiment, we only consider two party actions on commitments. In the second one, we add more commitments' states by including three party actions on commitments. These experiments were meant to check the effectiveness of our reductions using MCMAS and extended NuSMV in terms of memory in use. They are performed on a laptop with running Windows XP SP2 and equipped with 2.20 GHz AMD Dual Core and 896MB of RAM.

Table 2. Verification results for CNP protocol

	First Experiment		Second Experiment	
	Extended NuSMV	MCMAS	Extended NuSMV	MCMAS
Model Size $|M|$	$\approx 10^{12}$	$\approx 10^{16}$	$\approx 10^{14}$	$\approx 10^{26}$
Memory in MB	≈ 4.77	≈ 6.37	≈ 4.77	≈ 6.53
# OBDD variables	21	27	23	44
# OBDD nodes	$1,241$	$2,905$	$1,494$	$11,885$
# agents	2	2	4	4

Table 2 depicts that there is no big difference in the results of extended NuSMV in the two experiments, but by adding three party actions, the number of OBDD variables and nodes in MCMAS are increased. Moreover, the number of OBDD variables and memory size increase by augmenting the number of agents from 2 to 4. The performance of model checker tools also depend on the size of the model M which we define as $|M| = |W| + |R_t|$, where $|W|$ is the number of possible combinations of the states and actions and $|R_t|$ is the temporal relation. In the first experiment, the number of OBDD variables with extended NuSMV (resp. MCMAS) is 21 (resp. 27), then the total state space $|W|$ is $2^{21} \approx 10^6$ (resp. $2^{27} \approx 10^8$). Whereas, in the second experiment, the total state space $|W|$ is $2^{23} \approx 10^7$ in extended NuSMV and $2^{44} \approx 10^{13}$ in MCMAS. We approximate $|R_t|$ as $|W|^2$, hence $|M| = |W| + |R_t| \approx |W|^2$ (see Table 2).

6   Related Work

Several proposals on using existing model checkers (e.g., SPIN and CWB-NC) by translating some agent specification languages (e.g., AgentSpeak(F)) into the languages used by these model checkers [4,5,10,1] have been put forward. In particular, Bordini et al. [4] have introduced the language AgentSpeak(F) and shown how the verification of this language can be translated to the verification of PROMELA code (the input language of the model checker SPIN). Bentahar et al. [1] have introduced the translation of ACTL* formulae into a variant of alternating tree automata called alternating Büchi tableau automata. Our approach follows the same line of research but it is based on symbolic model checking and not on automata-based model checking like SPIN. Consequently, our approach does not suffer from the state explosion problem, which is a common problem in the automata-based technique. Other researchers have proposed new algorithms for verifying temporal and epistemic properties, see for example [21]. In particular, Lomuscio et al. [17] have proposed MCMAS model checker to verify multi-agent systems based on binary encoding in terms of OBDD representations where properties are specified by means of epistemic modalities such as knowledge modality. This paper shows how high level interactions represented by social commitments can be translated to agents' knowledge without loosing social or public features that characterize commitments.

Recently, Viganò and Colombetti [26] have used symbolic model checking to verify institutions formally modeled with FIEVeL language in terms of the notion of "status function" where properties are specified in an ordered many-sorted first-order temporal logic (OMSFOTL). Their automatic verification process is mainly concerned with satisfying certain properties to guarantee the soundness of institutions without considering any standard temporal properties classification. They regulate interactions between agents in terms of deontic norms (e.g., obligations) that are captured with respect to institution structures. Thus, this model is less flexible than ours as, for example, they do not have possibilities to withdraw or delegate obligations. Gerard and Singh [13] have used CTL and MCMAS to verify protocol refinement that are defined in terms of social commitments without checking the conformance of protocols themselves before the refinement and without considering transition loop within protocol specifications. In terms of commitment protocol properties, Yolum [27] has presented the main generic properties that are required to develop commitment protocols at design time. These properties are categorized into three classes: *effectiveness,* *consistency* and *robustness.* Our properties meet the same functionalities, for example the reachability and deadlock-freedom can be used to satisfy the same objective of the effectiveness property.

7   Conclusion and Future Work

In this paper, we presented a new language CTLC to represent and reason about social commitments. We used this language to specify commitment protocols and their temporal properties in electronic business domains. We showed how to reduce the problem of model checking CTLC to the problem of model checking either CTLK or ARCTL. Thus, it is the first step towards achieving the following features within the same framework that formalizes commitment protocols: 1) formal (based on our logic); 2) meaningful (in terms of social commitments); 3) declarative (which focuses on what the message means not how the message is exchanged); 4) verifiable (using efficient and available symbolic model checking); and 5) property-based (in terms of formally defined properties). To clarify our approach, we have modeled the Contract Net Protocol (CNP) using commitments and associated actions. In our implementation, we conducted two experiments, which revealed promising results for multi-agent systems where interaction protocols are involved. There are many directions for future work. We plan to expand the formalization of commitment protocols with metacommitments. We also plan to investigate other reductions, particularly from CTL^{*c} (an extension of CTL^* with commitment modality) to $GCTL^*$ (generalized CTL^*) [3], so that we can use the CWB-NC model checker.

Acknowledgements

We would like to thank the reviewers for their valuable comments and suggestions. Jamal Bentahar and Rachida Dssouli would like to thank Natural Sciences and Engineering Research Council of Canada (NSERC) and Fond Québecois de la recherche sur la société et la culture (FQRSC) for their financial support.

References

1. Bentahar, J., Meyer, J.J.C., Wan, W.: Model Checking Agent Communication. In: Dastani, M., Hindriks, K.V., Meyer, J.J.C. (eds.) Specification and Verification of Multi-Agent Systems, 1st edn., pp. 67–102. Springer, Heidelberg (2010)
2. Bentahar, J., Moulin, B., Chaib-draa, B.: Specifying and Implementing a Persuasion Dialogue Game using Commitment and Argument Network. In: Rahwan, I., Moraïtis, P., Reed, C. (eds.) ArgMAS 2004. LNCS (LNAI), vol. 3366, pp. 130–148. Springer, Heidelberg (2005)
3. Bhat, G., Cleaveland, R., Groce, A.: Efficient Model Checking via Büchi Tableau Automata. In: Berry, G., Comon, H., Finkel, A. (eds.) CAV 2001. LNCS, vol. 2102, pp. 38–52. Springer, Heidelberg (2001)
4. Bordini, R.H., Fisher, M., Pardavila, C., Wooldridge, M.: Model Checking Agentspeak. In: Proceedings of the 2nd International Joint Conference on Autonomous Agents and Multiagent Systems, pp. 409–416. ACM, Melbourne (2003)
5. Cheng, Z.: Verifying Commitment based Business Protocols and their Compositions: Model Checking using Promela and Spin. Ph.D. thesis, North Carolina State University (2006)
6. Chopra, A.K., Singh, M.P.: Nonmonotonic Commitment Machines. In: Dignum, F. (ed.) ACL 2003. LNCS (LNAI), vol. 2922, pp. 183–200. Springer, Heidelberg (2004)
7. Chopra, A.K., Singh, M.P.: Producing Compliant Interactions: Conformance, Coverage and Interoperability. In: Baldoni, M., Endriss, U. (eds.) DALT IV 2006. LNCS (LNAI), vol. 4327, pp. 1–15. Springer, Heidelberg (2006)
8. Cimatti, A., Clarke, E., Giunchiglia, E., Giunchiglia, F., Pistore, M., Roveri, M., Sebastiani, R., Tacchella, A.: Nusmv 2: An Open Source Tool for Symbolic Model Checking. In: Brinksma, E., Larsen, K.G. (eds.) CAV 2002. LNCS, vol. 2404, pp. 359–364. Springer, Heidelberg (2002)

9. Clarke, E.M., Grumberg, O., Peled, D.A.: Model Checking. The MIT Press, Cambridge (1999)
10. Desai, N., Cheng, Z., Chopra, A.K., Singh, M.P.: Toward Verification of Commitment Protocols and their Compositions. In: Proceedings of the 6th International Joint Conference on Autonomous Agents and Multiagent Systems, pp. 144–146. ACM, Honolulu (2007)
11. Fagin, R., Halpern, J.Y., Moses, Y., Vardi, M.Y.: Reasoning About Knowledge. The MIT Press, Cambridge (1995)
12. Fornara, N., Colombetti, M.: Operational Specification of a Commitment-based Agent Communication Language. In: Proceedings of the 1st International Joint Conference on Autonomous Agents and Multiagent Systems, pp. 535–542. ACM, Bologna (2002)
13. Gerard, S.N., Singh, M.P.: Protocol Refinement: Formalization and Verification. In: Artikis, A., Bentahar, J., Chopra, A.K., Dignum, F. (eds.) AAMAS Workshop on Agent Communication (AC), Toronto, Canada, pp. 19–36 (2010)
14. Guerin, F., Pitt, J.: Guaranteeing Properties for E-Commerce Systems. In: Padget, J.A., Shehory, O., Parkes, D.C., Sadeh, N.M., Walsh, W.E. (eds.) AMEC IV 2002. LNCS (LNAI), vol. 2531, pp. 253–272. Springer, Heidelberg (2002)
15. Lamport, L.: Proving the Correctness of Multiprocess Programs. IEEE Transactions on Software Engineering 3(2), 125–143 (1977)
16. Lomuscio, A., Pecheur, C., Raimondi, F.: Automatic Verification of Knowledge and Time with Nusmv. In: Proceedings of the 20th International Joint Conference on Artificial Intelligence, pp. 1384–1389. Morgan Kaufmann Publishers Inc., Hyderabad (2007)
17. Lomuscio, A., Qu, H., Raimondi, F.: MCMAS: A Model Checker for the Verification of Multi-Agent Systems. In: Bouajjani, A., Maler, O. (eds.) CAV 2009. LNCS, vol. 5643, pp. 682–688. Springer, Heidelberg (2009)
18. Manna, Z., Pnueli, A.: The Temporal Logic of Rreactive and Concurrent Systems: Specification, 1st edn. Springer, Inc., New York (1991)
19. Medellin, R., Atkinson, K., McBurney, P.: Model Checking Command Dialogues. In: Proceedings of 2009 AAAI Fall Symposium on The Uses of Computational Argumentation, pp. 58–63. AAAI Press, Arlington (2009)
20. Pecheur, C., Raimondi, F.: Symbolic model checking of logics with actions. In: Edelkamp, S., Lomuscio, A. (eds.) MoChArt IV. LNCS (LNAI), vol. 4428, pp. 113–128. Springer, Heidelberg (2007)
21. Penczek, W., Lomuscio, A.: Verifying Epistemic Properties of Multi-Agent Systems via Bounded Model Checking. Fundamenta Informaticae 55(2), 167–185 (2003)
22. Raimondi, F.: Model Checking Multi-Agent Systems. Ph.D. thesis, University College London (2006)
23. Singh, M.P.: An Ontology for Commitments in Multiagent Systems: Toward a Unification of Normative Concepts. Artificial Intelligent and Law 7(1), 97–113 (1999)
24. Singh, M.P.: Formalizing Communication Protocols for Multiagent Systems. In: Proceedings of the 20th International Joint Conference on Artificial Intelligence, pp. 1519–1524. Morgan Kaufmann Publishers, Inc., Hyderabad (2007)
25. Venkatraman, M., Singh, M.P.: Verifying Compliance with Commitment Protocols: Enabling Open Web-based Multiagent Systems. Autonomous Agents and Multi-Agent Systems 2(3), 217–236 (1999)

26. Viganò, F., Colombetti, M.: Symbolic Model Checking of Institutions. In: Proceedings of the 9th International Conference on Electronic Commerce, pp. 35–44. ACM Press, Minneapolis (2007)
27. Yolum, P.: Design Time Analysis of Multi-Agent Protocols. Data and Knowladge Engineering 63(1), 137–1154 (2007)
28. Yolum, P., Singh, M.P.: Commitment machines. In: Meyer, J.J.C., Tambe, M. (eds.) ATAL 2001. LNCS (LNAI), vol. 2333, pp. 235–247. Springer, Heidelberg (2002)
29. Yolum, P., Singh, M.P.: Reasoning about Commitments in the Event Calculus: An Approach for Sepcifying and Executing Protocols. Annals of Mathematics and Artificial Intelligence 42(1-3), 227–253 (2004)

Author Index